FISHING
ATLANTIC SALMON

FISHING
ATLANTIC SALMON
The Flies and the Patterns

JOSEPH D. BATES, JR.
and
PAMELA BATES RICHARDS

edited by Bob Warren
forewords by Keith Fulsher and Bill Taylor
fly photography by Michael D. Radencich
paintings and pencil sketches by John Swan

STACKPOLE
BOOKS

Published by
STACKPOLE BOOKS
5067 Ritter Road
Mechanicsburg, PA 17055

Printed in Hong Kong

10 9 8 7 6 5 4 3 2 1

First edition

Additional photography by:
R. Valentine Atkinson
Bob O'Shaughnessy
Lewis C. Stone
Jack Swedberg
Gilbert Van Ryckevorsel
Belarmino Martinez

Line drawings by Dave Hall

Library of Congress Cataloging-in-Publication Data

Bates, Joseph D., 1903–
     Fishing atlantic salmon : the flies and the patterns /
Joseph D. Bates, Jr., with Pamela Bates Richards : photographs
by Michael D. Radencich.
          p.   cm.
     Includes index.
     ISBN 0-8117-0636-2 (hardcover)
     1. Atlantic salmon fishing.   2. Flies, Artificial.
I. Richards, Pamela Bates.   II. Title.
SH685.B395 1996
799.1'755—dc20   95-49549
                                                            CIP

Contents

Foreword

*J*oe Bates and I had become good friends as a result of our meeting and corresponding while he was researching material for *Streamer Fly Tying and Fishing.* After publication of that book in 1966 we continued to meet periodically in White Plains, New York, to discuss fly fishing. It was at one of those meetings in early March that I suggested to Joe that he write a book on hairwing Atlantic salmon flies.

Nothing of any substance on the subject was then in print, yet this style of fly had become extremely popular. I explained to Joe that I had thought of writing a book on the subject but my time requirements as a commercial banker prevented it. Anyway, he was much better qualified and more familiar with research channels. Joe was interested and soon began his usual thorough research. In December 1968, Joe wrote to tell me that Stackpole Books had given him the go-ahead.

Atlantic Salmon Flies and Fishing was published in 1970. The format followed Joe's streamer book but content covered far more than hairwing flies. An in-depth treatment of the Atlantic salmon and of fly styles and patterns, equipment, and fishing methods gave the book an international appeal. It was considered to be Joe's finest work and received great reviews. Both the limited and regular editions subsequently became valuable collector's items in the out-of-print market. In 1995, Joe's daughter, Pamela Bates Richards, and Stackpole reissued both books, making them both available to a new generation of anglers.

But Joe didn't rest on his laurels after *Atlantic Salmon Flies and Fishing* was published. Like most authors, he felt there was room for improvement and subsequently he worked on a revision that included much new material, supported by many more years of salmon fishing experience. That revision, however, was put aside during the early 1980s while he authored a beautiful book on the history of the salmon fly, *The Art of the Atlantic Salmon Fly,* drawing on his large collection of patterns for the twenty-three color plates of flies.

Joe died in 1988 at age eighty-five before he could further update and complete his revision of *Atlantic Salmon Flies and Fishing.* Luckily for those of us inter-

ested in good books on Atlantic salmon fishing, Pam saw the importance of Joe's revised manuscript and made arrangements with Stackpole to publish *Fishing Atlantic Salmon: The Flies and the Patterns*. During the review of Joe's work, Pam made some important discoveries of her own and has properly augmented the text where necessary. Significant in this regard is new information on the Rat and Cosseboom series of flies, which top the list of important North American patterns. When Pam and I discussed my reservations about the first edition's story about the origin of the Rat patterns—a story that Joe heard from Herb Howard during a dinner at my home in June 1969—she was inspired to do further research. That effort succeeded in uncovering the true origin of the *Rusty Rat* as well as new information on the original *Cosseboom* pattern. It was obvious from notes left by Joe that his main focus with the book had shifted to the flies and the patterns. The addition of Pam's discoveries and of a number of additional historical and practical patterns greatly increases the value of this book. But the text is only as Joe could research and write it and as he lived it. The beautiful color plates by Michael Radencich pay homage to Joe's vast salmon fly collection and to tiers, both past and contemporary, who produced these exquisite examples of the fly tier's art.

Joe would be proud of this book. He would also be pleased with the current efforts of North American fly tiers, whom he prodded in the original edition as not willing to take the time to learn how to dress the old classics as they were done in Britain. Today some of the most accomplished dressers of classic salmon flies are North Americans, and credit must go to internationally respected author of fishing books Colonel Joseph D. Bates, Jr. This book is a fitting climax to his work, and I hope you, too, enjoy it.

KEITH FULSHER
Eastchester, New York

*T*he Atlantic salmon is regarded by anglers throughout the world as the King of Fish, and similarly the flies anglers use to entice the majestic Atlantic salmon are considered the pinnacle of the art of fly tying. The rise of an Atlantic salmon to a well-cast fly is an experience matched by few others in fly fishing. Few people knew the sport of Atlantic salmon angling as did Colonel Joseph D. Bates. Like the Atlantic salmon and the beautiful flies used to catch them, he was at the top of his field.

Colonel Bates completed the text for *Fishing Atlantic Salmon: The Flies and the Patterns* in the early 1980s and was revising the manuscript at the time of his death in 1988. It is his seventeenth angling book, and surely his best. Sadly, he didn't live to see this work published, but thanks to the determined efforts of his daughter, Pamela Bates Richards, we have the chance to learn once more from the master.

I was a young teen when Bates's *Atlantic Salmon Flies and Fishing* was published, in 1970. The following year my parents gave me a copy as a birthday present, a gift I have treasured to this day. That book was a bible to me as I made the transition from trout fishing to the "sport of kings." I spent countless evenings at my vise, Bates book in hand, studying and learning to tie the flies of my Miramichi heroes, Bert Miner and Wally Doak, when my parents thought I was doing my homework. Colonel Bates was the acknowledged expert on the subject of Atlantic salmon flies, their history and dressing, and the men and women who originated and tied these most elaborate of fishing flies. *Fishing Atlantic Salmon,* along with *Atlantic Salmon Flies and Fishing* and *The Art of the Atlantic Salmon Fly,* are landmark contributions to the literature on the sport that reaffirm Bates's position alongside such legends as George Mortimer Kelson, T. E. Pryce-Tannatt, George LaBranche, and Edward Hewitt.

Besides being an expert on the subject of Atlantic salmon flies, Colonel Bates was a dedicated salmon conservationist. Throughout this book he points out the obvious injustices the Atlantic salmon faces in its struggle for survival and tells us what we must do to save it from extinction. With a lifetime of experience as an angler throughout North America and abroad, he witnessed firsthand the management regimes of most salmon-producing countries. Bates, who didn't mince words, points to many foolish management practices that led to the salmon's demise in New England and to its serious decline in Canada and overseas in a straight-from-the-hip style that is as refreshing as it is effective. The text for this book was written in the early 1980s, and as sad as it may seem, much of the poor and misguided management, habitat destruction, and overfishing that Colonel Bates admonishes remains today. Likewise, many of the recommendations he makes for addressing these problems remain prudent.

Colonel Bates was a strong supporter of the Atlantic Salmon Federation, and his writing appeared regularly in our quarterly magazine, the *Atlantic Salmon Journal*. In 1975 he edited the classic *Atlantic Salmon Treasury,* which celebrates the finest writing from the first twenty-five years of the *Atlantic Salmon Journal.* Until his death, Colonel Bates was a staunch defender of the King of Fish. He knew that the Atlantic salmon needed the cooperation of international governments to protect the species during its feeding migration throughout the North Atlantic. I believe Bates would have been pleased by the growing effectiveness of the North Atlantic Conservation Organization (NASCO) to regulate and control the destructive high-seas harvest of salmon. Like Lee Wulff, he believed that the best way to secure the salmon's future was for governments to classify it as a game fish and ban all commercial netting of the species. Had he lived a few more years, he would have witnessed the virtual end of Canada's commercial fishery as well as the suspension of the Greenland and Farose commercial fisheries.

Throughout this book there is a clear and eloquent plea for the conservation and wise management of this magnificent fish. In a few cases we have heeded the message and taken steps to control and even repair the damage we have done. The Atlantic salmon has finally been recognized, at least in North America, as a valuable and sustainable resource that can contribute much to rural economies. Recreational fishing has finally been accepted by bureaucrats and decision-makers as the wisest and best use of this resource. Colonel Bates, I am sure, would be pleased to know that commercial fishing in Canada, which recently harvested 350,000 salmon annually, has been all but eliminated. Privately funded buy outs of the Greenland commercial fishery by the Atlantic Salmon Federation and our partners, the North Atlantic Salmon Fund (NASF) and the National Fish and Wildlife Foundation (NFWF) have spared tens of thousands of large salmon. We continue to work vigorously to eliminate the fishery permanently by buying out licenses and providing alternative employment for fishermen. Catch-and-release angling is now an accepted practice, if not a regulation, on most North American salmon streams and with each passing season gains in popularity on the rivers of Scotland and Ireland. Poaching is no longer tolerated, enforcement activities have been stepped up, and our courts have increased penalties so that repeat offenders in some Canadian provinces are hit with fines of $10,000 and, in some cases, jail sentences. The time of poachers being hailed as folk heroes, which so infuriated Colonel Bates, is a thing of the past. Although we are making steady progress in our efforts to protect the mighty Atlantic salmon and the wild rivers that sustain them, there is so much more that remains to be done.

While suspensions and buy outs of commercial fishermen certainly spare thousands of salmon, and poaching is not as rampant as it once was, there are factors at play over which man has little control. Reports abound of more Atlantic salmon than ever dying in the ocean. Some authorities believe foreign vessels are harvesting enormous quantities of salmon beyond international boundaries. Others blame a host of environmental influences, including decreasing ocean temperatures and a shrinkage in salmon forage. What is certain is that despite valiant efforts to protect the species, salmon populations have not responded as expected.

We have reached a critical stage in the fight to save the Atlantic salmon. In the United States, the Fish and Wildlife Service and National Marine Fisheries Service have decided that stocks are so low that they require protection under the Endangered Species Act. In southwestern Nova Scotia, acid rain has wiped out the runs of thirteen once-productive rivers. It has been proven time and time again that hydroelectric dams and salmon don't mix, yet each year governments approve new hydro proposals for salmon rivers. The threats to the salmon's survival are many, and stocks on both sides of the North Atlantic teeter on the brink of levels needed to sustain healthy populations.

While I believe that Colonel Bates would be pleased with the progress we've made, I also believe that he would be quick to point out that much more remains to be done if we hope to ensure a bright future for the Atlantic salmon. Even though the salmon has become a symbol of nature's balance, it is still neglected by governments, power companies, and the forest industry in their rush to dam another river or clear-cut another forest. The Atlantic salmon is a precious sustainable resource that, when managed wisely, can bring joy to thousands of people and generate significant employment and revenue in regions where these commodities have traditionally been in short supply. Colonel Bates knew this and has stated it passionately and emphatically throughout this book. It is my sincere hope that all those who shared Colonel Bates's love of wild rivers, wild salmon, and the fine sport of angling hear his plea and join the Atlantic Salmon Federation's worldwide effort to save this noble species for this generation and for those who will follow us.

BILL TAYLOR
president
Atlantic Salmon Federation
St. Andrews, New Brunswick

Preface

$\mathcal{F}$rom 1946 to 1988 the muffled rhythms of a vintage typewriter could be heard coming from the study of Joseph D. Bates, Jr. Seventeen books and countless articles rolled across the carriage of the old machine, and although several were designated "the last," Joe never seemed to be quite finished. In 1980, one such last book was a revised edition of *Atlantic Salmon Flies and Fishing,* first published in 1970. In his introduction to the revision my father wrote, "As a result and as time passed I looked upon the original work with increasing distaste. It seemed that I had written it with insufficient experience and study. Since these are cumulative, my opinion may be similar about this one another decade hence, if I am still around to patch my waders."

The waders remained unpatched, just as I know his opinion would remain unchanged. Although the manuscript was complete, Joe, as his own severest critic, was never satisfied. It sat on the shelf while yet another book was written, and during that time, the nuances of the salmon fly became the focus of his obsession. The publication of *The Art of the Atlantic Salmon Fly* in 1987 left Joe without a project for at least a few days, and frequent requests for a new edition of *Atlantic Salmon Flies and Fishing* inspired him to dust off the abandoned manuscript.

With the encouragement and assistance of his first editor and lifelong friend, Angus Cameron, the project was under way, and one more Bates book was in the works. This one, however, could not be completed by its author; on September 30, 1988, Joe Bates died, quickly and quietly, leaving behind a desk that was testimony to his active and dedicated life. Surrounded by the familiar aromas of camphor, Hoppe's oil, Mixture No. 79, and leather books, Angus and I sat in the old study a few days later, exchanging Joe stories and sharing a little of his bourbon.

Angus pointed to the manuscript that sat where Joe had left it and explained the reservations of both author and editor. Later I would realize that Angus's words echoed Joe's, written eight years before in the introduction to the proposed book. Although, in 1980, an additional decade of experience in angling and its related subjects had added depth to the revision, by 1988 the work seemed dated to its author, who with his ever-expanding criteria was, as ever, unsatisfied.

Joe Bates was relentless in his research to document the patterns of the flies that so fascinated him. Understanding the history of the flies gave fishing them another dimension, and, during his ninth decade, he allowed the distraction of the flies to take the place of wading the rivers. His correspondence and notes from the last few years of his life are indications of the changes he was anticipating making in the manuscript.

The advent of hairwing patterns took place during the middle years of Joe's angling experience, and he was impressed with the practicality of the material and its motion in the water. He delighted in the fact that featherwing patterns could be converted to successful hairwing equivalents. His reverence for the classics remained, however, and his monumental collection of salmon flies grew accordingly. His admiration of the classic patterns tempted him to fish them, but, if they were of "exhibition quality," he clearly felt they should be preserved.

In the months, and now years, following my father's death, changes in angling have added to the voids Joe might have perceived in his own work. His deeply felt concern for the environment and the future of the salmon are now underscored by yet another decline in the New England fishery. New waters in which to find large fish have become available with the opening of Russia's rivers. Regulations to protect the salmon have changed, buy outs of the Greenland commercial fishery have further protected the species, and technological advances have altered tackle and fly-tying materials. Perhaps most astounding are the growing numbers of capable tiers pursuing the art of the salmon fly.

As my own fascination with the flies developed, I began to recognize the encyclopedic strength of the Bates collection and appreciate the interest others had in it. At the same time I became interested in the surviving manuscript, and I was frequently asked what would become of each. Respected members of the angling community encouraged the publication of the revision, while I wondered how to best document and share the collection. Combining the two seemed the ideal solution, and a plan took form.

As the editorial process began, one of our first decisions was to keep the text of the manuscript within the technical scope of the author's lifetime and not include in any detail changes that have occurred since it was written. With the goal of honoring Joe's collection and showing as many of the flies as possible, we did elect to expand on the classics as well as add a few patterns that are more contemporary than the text. Numerous notes from my father's files were added where it seemed appropriate. In the rare cases where the origins of patterns could be more clearly defined, we felt obligated to do so.

Through the talents of photographer Michael Radencich, we now have the opportunity to view and compare the contributions of several generations of tiers, from the very simple but effective patterns to the most complicated and elaborate. At times I allow myself the pleasure of thinking that Dad might be quite thrilled to see so many exquisite examples of the fine art of the salmon fly exhibited in one place.

Along with Michael's extraordinary photographic presentation is the artwork of John Swan. Having grown up fishing the Rangeley Lakes with his grandfather, John brings an understanding and empathy to both the subject and the project. His remarkable talent captures the mood and spirit of the angling experience like no other. No doubt this is due, in part, to the fact that John was weaned fishing original patterns. If there is a dearth of Bill Edson flies in the collector's market, it is because John has set them free in the branches and logs of Kennebago.

Less obvious aesthetically, but no less important to the work are the indisputable contributions of two others: Bob Warren and Helen Bates. As mentor and friend, Bob has given generously to a variety of Bates projects, and his profound dedication has allowed the completion of this one. And again, Helen Bates is the petite pillar behind her husband's, and now her daughter's, work. Although this book is dedicated to my father, in the most heartfelt sense it belongs to Helen Ellis Bates, who, for fifty years, has gracefully allowed her own wish list to be usurped by promises of "when the book is finished."

Although my father and I did not fish together often enough, we always found time to share a love of the outdoors and an appreciation for pastimes associated with it. Growing up I invariably knew that a walk in the woods could preempt Sunday school; Dad thought of them as the same. This sensitivity to things unspoken will remain my greatest debt to him. One can only guess what his choices might have been in completing this work, but if my father's delight in celebrating his collection and his research could be a fraction of my own, I am satisfied. As this project comes to an end, the cadence of the seasoned Underwood lingers.

PAMELA BATES RICHARDS
Newburyport, Massachuetts

Acknowledgments

*P*ersonally and on behalf of my father, I would like to express my most sincere appreciation to the following individuals and organizations. Their contributions and assistance have been invaluable to the completion of this work.

The American Museum of Fly Fishing, the Atlantic Salmon Federation, The North Atlantic Fly Tier's Guild, Stanley Bogden, Larry Borders, Megan Boyd, John Berger, Angus Cameron, Peter Castagnetti, Peter Deane, Pedro Dieppa, Jerry Doak, Dorothy Douglass, Warren Duncan, Gayland Hachey, Joe Hubert, Bill Hunter, Art Lee, Nick Lyons, Belarmino Martinez, Carolyn Capstick Meehan, Ted Niemeyer, Paul Schmookler, Andrew Stout, Bill Taylor, Bob Veverka, Orri Vigfusson, Rod Yerger, Jimmy Younger, Bill Wilbur, and Joan Wulff, and to Judith Schnell and Mark Allison for their editorial assistance.

Very special thanks go to Keith Fulsher and Mark Waslick for their generosity and dedication to the project and to Linda and Dan Warren for their unequivocal support.

And grateful and loving thanks to my brother, Bruce, to my daughters, Jameson and Ashley, and to my husband, Bill, for patience beyond logical limits.

—P. B. R.

Introduction

When my earlier book *Atlantic Salmon Flies and Fishing* was published in 1970, and during the ten years it remained in print, readers referred to it with satisfying kindness. Since its publication I have fished for salmon nearly all around the Atlantic and devoted countless out-of-season hours to researching the allied subjects of fly fishing and fishing flies wherever information could be found.

But as time passed, I looked upon the original work with increasing distaste. It seemed that I had written it with insufficient experience and study. Since these are cumulative, my opinion of this manuscript may be similar another decade hence if I am still around to patch my waders.

Having studied the literature on Atlantic salmon flies and fishing, I thought that important information could be culled and brought up to date in a single book which could also include contemporary experiences such as ways to hook uncooperative salmon. The permissible length of the book precludes reminiscences and other such trivia; information seems more valuable than reflection.

On thing stands clear. Most of us must dig deep into the piggy bank to afford time on good salmon rivers. There, with silvered salmon showing, we frequently fret because they ignore our flies and methods of presentation. Although there are no sure solutions to the varied situations encountered on the water, there are guidelines that can improve fishing success. It is better to learn them before going astream than to forfeit valuable fishing time and fun doing so. Learning from the written experiences of others can be both helpful and enjoyable, and I hope those who read this work will profit by it.

Included here are chapters on tactics and types of fishing, such as tips on locating salmon, fishing the floating line, sunk line, and dry fly; other chapters take us to salmon rivers around the Atlantic and discuss the flies used to fish them. Chapters 4 and 5 deal with the historic transformation of the salmon fly, featherwings from the plain to the complicated, and finally to the simply dressed hairwings, now deemed by most anglers as to be far more productive. If we think the fashions in salmon flies jumped from classics such as the *Jock Scott, Green Highlander,* and *Blue Doctor* straight to current favorites like the *Rusty Rat, Cosseboom,* and *Black Bear,* or one of its many variations, we miss a historic North American link between the fancy featherwings and the modern flies winged with hair. These chapters offer new reasons for fly selections under changing conditions and explain why. There is much more to it than merely picking a pattern because it was the one that did well yesterday.

While styles in salmon flies have become greatly simplified from the ornate extravagance of Victorian times, we look back with admiration to those olden days, when artisans created the most beautiful flies ever conceived. We may prefer a *Rusty Rat* to a *Jock Scott,* a *Gray Rat* rather than a *Silver Grey,* or a *Cosseboom* instead of a *Green Highlander* when fishing, but we must note a resurgence of interest in the gorgeous Victorian classics as supreme challenges to the fly-dressers' art.

We take great satisfaction in swimming flies we have tied ourselves, and the more attractive the better—perhaps one of the almost-forgotten classics which failed inspection for display and became a candidate to be discarded. Why not offer it to the salmon? When they are on the take, they may strike it avidly. When they aren't, experimentation is often the key to success. One of these ancient patterns may be just the ticket to hooking a big one. If the fly isn't of exhibition grade, the salmon could care less.

Anglers devoted to Atlantic salmon fishing worry about declining stocks. It is to our advantage to know why this is happening and to join together to help reverse the trends. For this reason this book digresses here and there from its subject of flies and fishing to explain what is going on in the salmon fisheries around the Atlantic. Knowing what is happening suggests what can be done about it. The Atlantic salmon is too noble a species to be treated as commonly as a cod and, ideally, should be regarded as a cherished game fish. The remarkable Atlantic salmon has been given, in most countries all around the Atlantic, a very hard time which it is the last of all fish to deserve. We see some rays of hope for its restoration.

So let's cooperate in conservation of the Atlantic salmon while we enjoy fishing them. May this book aid the beautiful and challenging silver leapers and those who seek them with rod and fly.

JOSEPH D. BATES, JR.
Longmeadow, Massachusetts

The Challenges of the Rivers

"Rapids"

A wild river framed by sky and forest, edged by rocks and ledges, tumbling and gliding toward the sea is an aisle in Nature's great cathedral. Present here is the King of Fishes—with a challenge to the angler inherent in its name. There is something special about fishing Atlantic salmon. It gladdens the heart and nourishes the soul and offers a way of life too seldom enjoyed by those of us who like to pit our wits, knowledge, and skill against the gleaming silver leaper.

Gazing upon a salmon river, I often wonder why it raises the hackles of excitement as no other rivers do. Surely, in part, it is the assurance that great and lusty fish lurk there, challenging temptation of the drifting fly wielded by tackle more appropriate for smaller and less combative species such as trout in quieter flows.

Perhaps it is the realization that this delicate tackle is the culmination of ages-old experimentation with such materials as horsehair, silkworm gut, and greenheart. To this was attached gaudy confections of unusual furs and rare feathers tied to hooks shaped from needles, cast by tweedy gentlemen upon historic rivers threading vales shadowed by rocky pinnacles topped by ancient castles. History hovers over the waters of famous salmon rivers like gathering mist.

Modern anglers probably are responding to the challenge of how to properly select and present a tiny fly with the hope that a great fish will rise up and take it and then attempt to rectify the error. Dominion of salmon over angler or angler over salmon is then determined by streaking runs into fast water punctuated by high vaulting jumps repeated in diminishing degree until the silver quarry either breaks away or is landed.

Whatever it is, it is a mania incurable, an infection that never heals, a way of life too seldom realized that beckons anglers to salmon rivers as often as they can arrange it.

Salmon rivers are ever-changing, to the fascination, elation, and frustration of the addicted anglers who fish them. In spate in the spring they may run deep, dark, and turbulent, often overflowing their banks to necessitate farms and fishing camps being built on high ground. In summer and fall they may sleep, warm and shallow, with barely a trickle shimmering over the riffles, thus imprisoning the salmon in the pools until the rains come.

Between these extremes come the rains, the rising water that brings schools of salmon up from the estuaries and frees the fish in the pools so that all may surge forward, joyfully leaping and sturdily swimming upward and onward to their spawning grounds.

When the rains afford moderate flow, the rivers are "right" for the salmon to rest or to move on, as they choose. These are the days the angler dreams of—the hours of the smashing strike, the spectacular leap, the powerful run, and the victory when the prize can be led to the net.

The real challenge comes at other times, when the fish are landlocked, lethargic and moodily suspicious of even the most artfully crafted and carefully presented confection of fur and feathers. The angler's problem then is how to select and how to present the fly in a manner that will tempt the fish to take it. When the water is low and clear, large salmon often can be seen and selected to fish over. This is the time for knowledge, skill, and patience. Often cast after cast will not produce as much as a flicker of a fin. Then, suddenly, an unusual presentation or the offering of a different pattern may result in a reaction—as subtle as the enhanced quivering of fins and tail or as dramatic as a majestic rise to inspect the new temptation more closely.

It is at these times that the angler must rely on "tackle" he cannot purchase—his innate wit and wisdom to triumph over his prey. There are many more ways to make reluctant salmon "take" than anglers of limited experience might suppose, which is partly what this book is about. The challenge and the thrill of fly fishing for salmon are greatest under adverse conditions. When the fish are in a taking mood, almost anyone can do it.

Canada's rocky Matapedia and wide, smoothly flowing Restigouche, meeting the salt at the Bay of Chaleur, are favorites of mine. I like to think of how they used to be—a way of life that passed away soon after the turn of the century, eliminated forever by motors and macadam.

In the little town of Matapedia, near the confluence of the two rivers, a major event for those not out fishing was to watch the shining black steam train of the Inter-Colonial Railway chuff into the little station to discharge numbers of tweedy gentlemen with their abundant supply of duffel bags and rod cases. These individuals were disposed to either the very British Hotel Restigouche (since torn

The author fishing in Iceland

down to make way for a motel) or the Restigouche Salmon Club, located in a meadow near the estuary. Many of these anglers were renowned as captains of industry. Some were taken to upriver camps by small boats, but others, often for weeks at a time, made their itinerant headquarters on a horse yacht that would ferry them to various salmon pools.

Unique to the Restigouche, horse yachts were a historic highlight of North American angling. Crude in construction, they were flat-bottomed conveyances about 10 feet wide and 50 feet long and drawing only 8 inches of water. Most of the platform was covered by a cabin with straight sides and a peaked roof. Inside were cooking, dining, and sleeping facilities, as well as space for crew and provisions. A huge wooden rudder curved over the stern, so arranged that the helmsman could operate it from the roof. Transportation was usually provided by three horses harnessed abreast to a yoked hawser fastened to the yacht. The driver rode the middle horse. Loaded and ready, he urged his horses into the stream to the clatters and splashes of hooves and the scraping of the hull over rocks.

When afloat, progress was placid, at a speed of about 3 miles an hour. While the cook in the galley prepared the evening meal, the anglers reclined comfortably on the little deck, watching farms and woodlands slowly pass and calling attention from time to time to big salmon porpoising as they traveled upstream.

The Restigouche, 200 yards wide in many places and without waterfalls, was an ideal river for horse yachts. Stops were made at favorite pools for as long as the anglers wished. They fished from canoes with long rods and big classic flies and were poled or paddled to casting positions by the guides. Occasionally other stops were made to visit friends in fishing lodges along the way, to purchase provisions from farms, and to rendezvous with other horse yachts going up- or downriver. The horses were brought on deck for the return trip and, for the most part, enjoyed a free ride while the conveyance was being guided down rapids and through pools by the boatman at the immense tiller.

Following closely at the end of this period, two very important angling discoveries were made in the Restigouche area. Just before World War I, the method of taking salmon on dry flies was perfected by Col. Ambrose Monell, George M. L. LaBranche, and Edward R. Hewitt, as described in LaBranche's book *The Salmon and the Dry Fly,* in Hewitt's book *Secrets of the Salmon,* and in chapter 9 of this one. In 1928, on the Upsalquitch tributary of the Restigouche, Col. Lewis S. Thompson added another trick to the angler's bag by discovering a way to drift a hairwing fly on a loose line to tempt reluctant salmon. He called it the Thompson Patent, now more familiarly known as the Patent.

But those days are now gone. In the late 1970s, for example, I fished the Matapedia in early June, guided from the Restigouche Motel by the noted Henry Lyons. Henry was waiting by my car, and we drove to a spot about ten miles upriver, where a beat had been engaged for the day. Henry's boat and motor were pulled up on the gravel, hidden from the road by a small patch of woods. I carried an 8 1/2-foot graphite rod with floating line and sinking tip, to which a 9-foot leader tapered to 8 pounds was attached. The fly was a #6 *Rusty Rat.* Also aboard was a 9-foot graphite rod with a floating line and a hard-to-sink floating fly of clipped deer hair called a *Bomber.* On these rivers, some anglers traditionally use classic rods of split bamboo, but the lightness and action of graphite are far more practical and make all-day casting much easier.

Henry regaled me with conversation that rarely stopped, mainly about his exploits and tribulations as a prisoner of Japan during World War II. I didn't remind him that he had told me the same stories before. He lowered the anchor and stopped the motor at a spot a moderate cast above a whitewater chute between some rocks. I false-cast the *Rusty Rat* and dropped it so that it would swing the short distance between the rocks just above the chute.

"River Tea"

The little fly hadn't swung more than a foot when a large boil erupted by it.

Nothing happened. Henry groaned. I put the fly in the same spot again; there was another boil. Nothing happened except that Henry groaned louder.

"That was a big fish. What happened?" he asked, probably full well knowing the answer.

I turned and looked at him ashamed.

"Henry, you know damn well what happened; I tightened before I felt the fish," I replied, "Leave me ashore or dump me overboard. You put me on a good fish and I ruined the chance."

Henry put on his kindest expression. "No, I don't think so," he said. "The salmon just rolled at the fly but didn't take it. Change to a smaller one while we rest the spot a bit, and then we'll try again."

We tried various tactics for half an hour but couldn't raise the fish, so we moved downstream.

Tightening too soon is a common reflex with people who are accustomed to fishing for trout. Under such conditions (with the exception of dry-fly fishing), never—repeat, *never*—tighten on a salmon until you feel it. The famous angler A. H. E. Wood recommended dropping the rod tip and releasing some line to provide slack. As the salmon turns with the fly with no tension on it, the fly is pulled by the dragging line into the hinge of the jaw, the best spot for secure hooking. Some anglers agree with Wood; others don't. In general, however, do not tighten on a salmon until you feel it (although there are exceptions to this, which will be discussed later). In the case described above, I am sure I tightened before I felt the fish and thus took the fly away. When a salmon strikes viciously, it will have the fly no matter what the angler does, but this isn't always the case. Salmon fishing is quite different from fishing for trout!

An hour or so before returning home for lunch, Henry and I arrived at John's Rock Pool. Henry used his pole to snub the canoe beside a midstream boulder where a reasonable cast would earn a good drift for the fly. The day had turned cloudless and the sun was bright—poor conditions. Several tactics proved fruitless.

I laid down the rod with the wet fly and picked up the one with the dry. "Now, Henry," I announced, "we are going to hook a salmon!"

Henry shrugged slightly. "What's that thing you've got on there?" he asked.

"It's a *Bomber*," I replied. "Just the ticket to float down this little run." Actually, my confidence was more verbal than sincere, but the *Bomber* is a good change-of-pace fly and sometimes produces surprising results. Also, salmon often will come to a dry fly when they won't look at a wet one.

The *Bomber* hadn't drifted more than a foot or so when a grilse rose and took it. Henry netted the small fish, twisted out the fly, and tossed the fly overboard.

I cast again. A big salmon came up and took the fly solidly. The fish made a long run downstream, and the fly pulled out.

"Let me see that fly," Henry said, picking up the leader. "That fish was hooked solidly in its jaw hinge."

Henry examined the fly and rather sheepishly handed it to me. The point and barb had been bent upward so much in taking the fly from the grilse that they were useless. After hooking a fish, you should always inspect the fly, even if only to touch up the point with a whetstone or file. You also should check the leader for damage and for wind knots, which can rob it of more than half its strength.

Perhaps an angling author shouldn't admit to a chain of errors that caused two big fish to be lost because of carelessness, but we learn by our mistakes.

We were back on the river again before four o'clock. The sun still shone from a cloudless sky, and nothing we tried brought results. Toward evening a strong wind began to gust upriver. At quarter of eight Henry glanced at his watch, and I knew we would stop fishing shortly.

On the last long cast of the drop, before we pulled anchor and dropped down to a new position, a gust caught the extending line and blew it far off course; the fly settled down into a tiny cove in front of a great rock partially hidden among bushes. My reflex was to pick it up and cast again, but before I could do so, there was a tremendous splashing boil in front of the rock, and a big salmon had the fly solidly.

The salmon streaked across and downriver, taking me quickly deep into the backing. Then it leaped while I lowered the rod tip to provide slack, tightening again as it reentered the water. I was able to reel it close in before it made another run, this one indicating that we could keep it in the pool. While I fought the fish, Henry slowly poled the canoe to a small beach where I could step ashore. Henry laid the bag of the net on the stream's bottom, and I guided the tired fish over it as he raised the net. In less than half an hour after being hooked, the beautifully silvered salmon was ours. It was a fresh female weighing just under 25 pounds.

"That was the most exciting strike I ever saw," I said as I lighted my pipe with shaking fingers. "Did you see the commotion that fish made as it took the fly? The salmon had it the instant it touched the water!"

Henry gripped my hand. "The instant it touched the water, you say? That salmon came up and had the fly *before* it touched the water!"

Milt Weiler

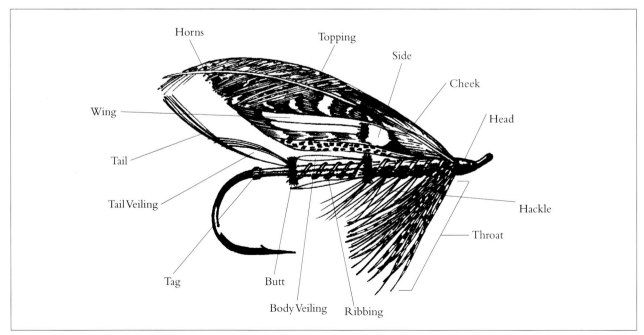

Figure 1. Parts of a salmon fly.

PLATE 1
ORIGINAL AND CONTEMPORARY MUDDLERS

Muddler
originated and dressed by Don Gapen

White Muddler
originated and dressed by Don Gapen

Muddler Variation
dressed by Ellis Hatch

Black Marabou Muddler
dressed by Ellis Hatch

Green Muddler
dressed by Ellis Hatch

If there is anything to learn from this, it is to look for salmon in shady spots while the sun is bright. Anyway, it indicates that we can count on Lady Luck's being on our side at least part of the time!

The lovely, diminutive Ste. Anne is quite different from the two bigger rivers I just described—a wild, turbulent, heavily forested stream so small that one could throw a stone from bank to bank at most places.

The Ste. Anne begins in the Gaspe Park wilderness midway on the peninsula and flows north into the St. Lawrence River. The government provides excellent accommodations in the park and books all-day downriver canoe trips for anglers. Only one or two trips are allowed per day in order to provide unspoiled fishing. While wading is permitted along the lower stretches, the canoe excur-

Muddler Minnow

Tail	Two narrow sections of natural (light mottled) turkey wing quill, of moderate length
Body	Flat gold tinsel; tied in about a quarter-inch behind hook eye; wound to tail, and back to starting point
Head	Black

Rest of dressing:

1. Apply a small bunch of gray squirrel hairs as a wing, tied on about a quarter-inch behind hook eye, extending two-thirds length of hook-shank.

2. On each side of the hair, tie in a section of dark mottled turkey wing about a quarter-inch wide, extending to tail (sections from a right and a left quill feather).

3. Apply over this a bunch of deer body hairs (as much as half the thickness of a lead pencil), leaving about a quarter-inch of the hair in front of the thread. Take three or four turns to secure and pull tight until hairs start to flare out and spread slightly around the bend of the hook.

4. Cut another bunch of deer hair and, after securing as above, cut off rear part so about a quarter-inch is in front and in back of the thread. Pull tight to make the hair flare out, as in step 3.

5. Clip the flared short hair to desired shape, usually in cone-shape toward eye of hook. Also clip off and trim to the desired shape about half of the bunch of hairs applied in step 3, leaving enough to complete the desired dressing of the wing (the remainder of clipped hair adding to the dressing of the collar). In doing this, more time will be spent trimming around the head than tying the rest of the fly. Enough cement should be used to ensure that the winging and collar will not slip.

This popular pattern, originated on the Nipigon River in northern Ontario, by Don Gapen, of Anoka, Minnesota, is intended to represent the Cockatush minnow, sometimes called *Muddlers*. While it was originated for bass and other freshwater species, it has been found to be an excellent salmon fly. It can be dressed either on standard or on light-wire hooks and, by sparse or heavier dressing and trimming, can be made to float (and be used as a skittering fly), made to float and then be pulled under, or be made for fishing deep on a sinking line. Considered one of the most successful flies of modern times, this versatile pattern can be dressed in many sizes and color combinations. One, also recommended for salmon, is the *White Muddler* (or *Missoulian Spook*). This is tied with white or grayish-white materials, with a silver ribbed body of white wool. White calf hair usually is used in this dressing.

sion is the main attraction and of course must be arranged far in advance.

My companion there on a warm midsummer day was Milton Weiler, friend and famous angling artist who contributed many of the drawings that grace my earlier books. With our guides and canoe, we climbed aboard an aged flatbed truck and set off for the stream where the canoe was launched. The truck departed to meet us downriver at dusk. I sat ahead of Milt, on the bottom of the fragile craft, while a French Canadian stood at either end to guide it downstream with long poles. The little river flowed fast, with whitewater curling around numerous rocks.

It soon became apparent that the guides had a trick up their sleeves for the entertainment of their sports. The guide in the bow, long pole poised, turned to joke with the one in the rear. We didn't understand much of the French, but ribald laughter prevailed while the speeding canoe made a beeline toward a large midstream rock. I presume the idea was for the passengers to shriek in alarm. But with split-second timing, the bowman turned from his conversation and set his pole to guide the canoe around the rock. Obviously, the guides were experts.

The fast little stream was so heavily forested with spruce and hardwood that it was difficult to see the sky in some places. Here and there a trout showed, but there were no signs of salmon. After half a mile or so of this, the canoe entered a quiet pool. The guides snubbed the craft against a shore and lighted their pipes. It was too deep to wade.

"Let's alternate ten casts apiece," I said to Milt. "You start." I thought I had seen a salmon show beside a midstream rock at the end of the small pool, but it was an obvious holding position; Milt knew his business, and I resisted giving advice.

He picked up his favorite ancient Leonard rod, with one of Dan Gapen's original *Muddlers* on the tippet, and made a roll cast to the far shore. The trees gave no room for backcasts. He fished the *Muddler* dry, and we watched it bob downstream while he mended his line.

A 10-inch trout came up and took the fly. Milt carefully released it.

"Damn things!" he said.

"You wouldn't say that about brook trout if you were fishing the Willowemoc," I replied with a chuckle.

"No, I wouldn't, but this is a different ballgame." He sent the fly out again. His ten casts produced the trout and a tiny parr, but no sign of a salmon.

"You could have reached that midstream rock," I remarked. "I think there's a salmon there."

"I saw it show," he answered. "It's your fish." Milt was like that.

Lee Wulff's *Royal Wulff* is an excellent floater and an occasional favorite of mine. I had tied it to an

8-pound tippet. A sidecast under the trees put it out far enough, and I shook out enough line for it to pass the rock. Just as it had used all the line I could give it, a salmon rose and sipped it in. When the fish took the fly, I came back on the rod, and it was hooked solidly. Not leaving the pool, it put on a very good show and was in the canoe in ten minutes. It weighed 11 pounds.

One of the guides pointed at his watch, and I nodded. We had a schedule to keep and several more pools to fish. On the fast ride down to the next one, the bowman didn't turn around in an attempt to alarm his passengers, but the banter between the guides increased. A salmon was in the boat, and they were happy.

The next two pools were small ones, and nothing showed. Apparently few salmon were in the river at the time. The fourth pool was a wide one, with the clearing of an abandoned farm on one side. I fished the upper part by wading, with no results. The lower part fanned out with a good gravel base before it riffled over the lip. Milt saw me looking at it.

"It's the hot spot, if there is one," he said.

"It's all yours," I answered.

He waded out and let his *Muddler* swing across the current, just under the surface. He lengthened his cast and tried again. A salmon took the fly savagely. The bright fish raced around the pool, jumping and shaking. Its acrobatics were so violent I thought it was foul-hooked, but when Milt finally landed it, the hook was solidly embedded in the tongue.

The guides were having lunch and hadn't bothered to build a fire, so we enjoyed sandwiches, apples, chocolate, and coffee. I produced a bottle of Wild Turkey bourbon, Milt's favorite, and we toasted the pretty river and our two salmon.

Later, Milt said, "Before we leave, try the tail of the pool. There's another salmon there."

I put on a size 8 *Blue Charm*. The salmon took the fly on the first swing. I brought it to beach as quickly as possible so that we could release it.

The second part of the trip produced two more salmon, which we also released, making a total of two kept and three put back to do what they came upstream to do.

As the canoe slipped downstream and the afternoon wore on, the wooded shoreline turned gradu-

The author with his wife, Helen Ellis Bates

ally to unkempt fields, with a few uninhabited farm buildings in poor repair. Finally, on the right shore, we saw the old truck and its driver awaiting us. Milt and I sat on a small dock while the canoe was being put aboard.

"They named this river after a lady saint," he remarked. "Very proper. She must have been a pretty one, because this is such a lovely river. How different salmon rivers are from each other: different rivers, different conditions, different challenges—something new all the time. Is that why it's so much fun?"

I nodded and opened my musette bag. "What's that sticking out?" Milt said, recognizing the neck of the bottle.

While we offered a final toast to the river, I looked at Milt's rod propped nearby. "You didn't change your fly even once," I said.

"No need to," he replied. "If there's a universal fly, it's the *Muddler*. You can fish it dry or work it wet. You can skitter it, grease-line it, or use it fishing

Scotland's Spey River bridge

BOB O'SHAUGHNESSY

PLATE 2
THE PURPLE KING

dressed by Syd Glasso

dressed by T. E. Pryce-Tannatt

dressed by Preston Jennings

Purple King

Body	Purple Berlin wool
Ribbing	Flat gold tinsel, lilac floss, and gold thread
Hackle	A bronze-black Spey-cock's hackle
Throat	Teal
Wing	Short brown mallard strips

Kelson (whose pattern appears above) thought the *Purple King*, originated by C. Grant in the early nineteenth century, was the best of the *King* series of Spey flies. He recommended that its body be tied with a mixture of blue and red Berlin wool in order to achieve the purple shade, later in the season using more red than purple in the dressing. Francis Francis presents a relative of this pattern, simply called the *Purple Fly* or *Purpie*.

the Patent. For most conditions, it's neither too dark nor too bright. You've got five boxes of salmon flies in your kit. I wouldn't trade a properly dressed *Muddler* for any one of them."

I wouldn't have made the trade either, because my fly boxes always carry *Muddlers*. There now are many variations, but for salmon fishing, the original version is hard to improve.

The driver and the guides were lounging beside the loaded truck. We climbed aboard for the ride back to the hotel. Next morning we enjoyed the beautiful forested drive along the lordly Grand Cascapedia to the Bonaventure, where we had arranged for a day of fishing.

Leaving North American waters, some of the greatest salmon angling in the world takes place on the rivers of Scotland, steeped in history and tradition. My wife, daughter, and I arrived in Grantown-on-Spey on a glowering June day for a week of salmon fishing with Arthur and Grace Oglesby, who conduct a fishing school in Grantown during part of each season.

While most salmon fishing in the British Isles is private, arrangements can be made for good water. The titled set controls only part of it, and visitors can put up at fishing hotels where use of the water is included. Since runs of salmon vary from river to river, it is important to make bookings for the most productive times. This seems to be a fair and sensible arrangement, because the owners, clubs, hotels, or associations safeguard their parts of the rivers.

During our week there, the weather was highly uncooperative, with rain, snow, sleet, and wind. A maxim of good fishing is that the air should be warmer than the water, which didn't happen. We hooked a few fish the hard way, with sinking lines in the deeper parts, using prawn imitations such as Esmond Drury's *General Practitioner* and Peter Deane's *Black-Eyed Prawn*. Valuable as "change-of-pace-flies," these also are aces in the hole when conditions are bad.

The gillies (sometimes incorrectly spelled ghillie, this term is used for a guide, especially in the British Isles and Norway, and is from the ancient Gaelic for "boy") were as fascinated by American tackle, flies, and methods as we were by theirs, even though they had seen similar equipment before. Gillies come in many ages, shapes, and sizes. The best ones usually are local men who make this their profession, rather than the part-timers. Our gillies were dedicated professionals and a joy to talk and fish with.

The gillies and some of the local anglers looked with tolerant amusement on our rods, none of which exceeded 9 feet, while theirs were between 12 1/2 and 14 feet, or even longer. I maintained that using their stout rods was less fun because they overpowered the fish, and remarked that we often used much lighter ones as short as 7 feet, or sometimes even shorter. They, however, were convinced that on windy days or for very long casts, theirs were superior; even if long casts could be accomplished with the shorter sticks, it was too much work.

Each side had a point or two in its favor. On calm days, the lighter rods surely were more fun to use and could bring a salmon to beach as quickly. But a windy day on a big pool, called "the best on the river," collapsed my casts as quickly as I could make them. Arthur, with his 14-footer and line to match, effortlessly put the fly way out where he wanted it with a minimum of difficulty. This usually was done by the Spey cast, which is made with sort of a reversed S casting motion, as described in Kelson's classic *The Salmon Fly.* The apparent ease with which he could accurately put a big fly far out into the wind was amazing. It isn't quite as simple as it looks.

The fabled Spey is a river of moderate size and intensity reminiscent of Canada's Matapedia except that one fishes in sight of ancient churches and homes, including a castle or two, in water so pure that it is used to make whiskey in the many distilleries scattered along its feeding streams. Being a

PLATE 3
THE SALSCRAGGIE, THE BRORA, AND THE HELMSDALE
DRESSED BY MEGAN BOYD

Megan Boyd at work in her bungalow, which overlooks the sea

LARRY BORDERS

heretic as far as Scotland's famous Highland Dew is concerned, and finding that the hotel's bar didn't stock American bourbon, I asked first off for a dry martini. The atmosphere and the company made up for the fact that it was made without ice, and the quantities of gin and vermouth were transposed.

One evening when Arthur Oglesby and Donald Overfield and I were discussing fashions in flies at a sturdy oak table in the bar, I compromised on something with rum in it. Arthur held his glass of (Scotch) whiskey up to the light and gazed at it lovingly.

"I can't understand why you don't enjoy this," he said to me.

"Sometimes I wonder if the only reason you like it is because a salmon once swam through it."

"I never thought of it quite that way," he replied, "but now you've made it taste even better."

Styles in flies used on the Spey have changed with the times. Traditional Victorian-era Spey patterns were noted, in part, for their long, flowing hackles, usually of gray or black heron, or from the lateral tail feather of a special breed of fowl known as the Spey cock. These flies were dressed with short wings usually of brown or gray mallard strips, dressed horizontally and laid close to the body, not extending beyond the bend. Bodies also were short, of crewels or Berlin wools of various and varying colors, and had no tags, tail, or butts. The tinsel rib-

bing was broad and accompanied by thread and twist. The method of application was contrary to the general rule, the hackle being tied in base-first so that the longest fibers were at the tail of the fly. The rear of the hackles extended considerably beyond the bend of the hook. A wigeon or teal feather, doubled, was used for the throat.

Spey flies were uniquely designed for a fast river, and even today they are popular and effective on many others. Wide latitudes are taken in their dressings, which makes some difficult to identify.

PLATE 4
THE BALMORAL
DRESSED BY BOB VEVERKA

Tag	Silver twist
Tail	Golden pheasant crest and tippet strands
Butt	Black ostrich herl
Body	Green and dark blue seal's fur, equally divided
Ribbing	Silver lace and silver tinsel
Hackle	Black heron from green seal's fur
Throat	Wigeon
Wings	Two strips of plain cinnamon turkey
Sides	Jungle cock (short and drooping)
Head	Black

(Kelson)

Examples are the three *Kings* (*Black, Green,* and *Purple*), *Carron, Grey Heron,* and *Lady Caroline.*

While these classics still are used to a declining extent, the popular modern patterns on the River Spey are largely hairwings, as well as various tube-fly configurations. Tradition, it seems, has given way to adaptations using hair and tubes rather than feathersand wool, and these are becoming standard on British rivers.

The warm sun reappeared as we left Grantown to visit a few of the famous rivers in northwestern Scotland. Many of these are small, rocky, and rapid, reminiscent of Iceland's pure and treeless tumbling streams. All offer differing challenges to anglers. Part of their charm is to reflect on what these streams were like a hundred years ago, and what types of anglers fished them with their long, stiff rods, lines of horsehair, and crude flies tied on irons hand-

forged from needles, to which eyes of twisted silkworm gut were affixed.

The ancient lore of angling is ever present on the challenging salmon streams of Scotland. The part of it that has to do with classic flies has been kept alive for the better part of this century by Megan Boyd, of Brora. Although retired, she is rightfully considered by many to be the reigning queen of the ancient art of salmon fly dressing. Prior to my visit to her in 1973, Megan and I had been pen pals for years. It was a thrilling privilege to watch her dress a perfect *Jock Scott* from memory, using all the proper feathers. She did it in exactly half an hour and gave it to me for a souvenir.

The sun shone brightly through cottony cumulus while we drove to Inverness. This ancient city is supported, in part, by the legend of the Loch Ness Monster. Canny Scotsmen can be vague with the

PLATE 5
THE WHITE-WINGED AKROYD, ORIGINATED AND DRESSED BY CHARLES AKROYD

PLATE 6
THE GORDON, DRESSED BY BILL HUNTER

Tag	Silver twist and yellow silk
Tail	Golden pheasant crest and tippet strands
Butt	Black ostrich herl
Body	First third: dark yellow silk. Remaining two-thirds: claret silk
Ribbing	Silver lace and flat silver tinsel
Hackle	Claret hackle, from dark yellow silk
Throat	Blue hackle
Wing	Two light red-claret hackles, back to back and veiled with peacock herl, light gray mottled turkey, dark mottled turkey, golden pheasant tail, bustard, swan dyed yellow and blue, and light mottled turkey dyed claret
Topping	Golden pheasant crest
Sides	Jungle cock
Horns	Blue macaw
Head	Black wool

The *Gordon* was originated in the 1890s by Cosmo Gordon, a fly dresser and angler who lived at Maryculter Lodge near Aberdeen on the Dee River. During the Victorian era, the *Gordon* was lionized, and variations that were either toned down or brightened up developed, causing Kelson to comment, "No two dressers of today make the fly alike."

Kelson's two patterns differ from Gordon's; Gordon often preferred using two hackles, jay at the throat and tippet in strands, rather than the whole feather. This pattern is Kelson's second dressing given.

truth when they have a good thing going, but inspired by a dram or two of their favorite brew, they admit they become hilarious over the fact that such a hoax could have been perpetrated on so many for so long. We returned the rented car there to its owner, who often deals with anglers fishing the Spey. He said, "Sorr, you were here a week too early. With the nice weather we've just been having, everyone has been hooking salmon."

Another fabled and favorite river is the Dee, which flows through Aberdeenshire, meeting the sea and a sister stream, the Don, at the city of Aberdeen. Our guide there was Alex Simpson, well known to fly dressers as a historian of Atlantic salmon flies. From a fishing standpoint, I wanted to meet Bessie Brown and to see the river Dee at Cairnton, where Arthur H. E. Wood perfected his famous technique of hooking salmon by a method he called "greased-line fishing," so named back in the 1920s when lines had to be greased to make them float.

The road up the Dee passes several castles, one of which is Balmoral, for which a fly is named. About 20 miles from Aberdeen is the famous Bridge of Feugh overlooking the falls of the same name, where salmon are seen leaping in season. Nearby is the town of Banchory, home of Bessie Brown. The daughter of the head gillie on an estate on the Dee, she was born into the world of salmon flies. Reputed to be one of Scotland's greatest salmon fly dressers in the old tradition, Bessie is also considered one of its best bagpipers.

Alex and I were welcomed most cordially with a pot of tea and some cakes in a small room where a table in the corner was piled with furs, feathers, silks, tinsels, and other bits and pieces necessary to her trade. Her pipes lay on another small table, and I hoped she would assemble them and play for us, but she preferred to discuss the people she knew who enjoyed fishing for salmon.

The Dee is called a big river, but it seemed to me rather moderate in size. It flows purposefully through wooded patches and farmlands in a seemingly endless progression of pools and rapids ideal for the resting and migration of salmon. We inspected as many pools as we could reach in the time allowed but saw few fish, probably because of the lateness of the season for this particular river. We didn't put a fly in it, lacking both time and permission. The Dee is

PLATE 7
TURN-OF-THE-CENTURY
CLASSICS OF SCOTLAND

Gardener (Dee)

Glen Grant (Spey)

Grey Eagle

only one among the great salmon rivers, and its distinction lies in the famous people who have fished it and the ages-old traditions tied to its heritage.

Distinctive to the renowned Aberdeenshire Dee are the Dee strip-wing patterns, one of the oldest styles still surviving. In early season, these flies were lightly dressed on large, long-shanked irons to make them sink deeper in the rough waters. Their very mobile hackles and wings give the Dee flies a distinct action as they work in the water. Characteristic features are slimness, economy of dressing, and the unusual set of the wings.

Most Dee patterns have bodies of seal's fur, bound tightly by ribbing, and picked out to show a slim core. The wings are composed of simple strips from the tail feathers of certain breeds of turkeys and are applied slightly splayed on the upper part of the hook to lie almost flat along the body of the fly. Hackles are long and flowing, usually of black or gray heron, but sometimes of cock or eagle (marabou), with one side stripped. Examples include the *Akroyd, Tricolour,* and *Eagles.* The *Eagles* are distinguished by long, fluffy hackles from the golden eagle; today marabou is substituted for the eagle feathers, with the usual Dee turkey wing.

Of these flies, the *Akroyd,* originated in 1878, is my favorite.

Akroyd	
Tag	Silver tinsel
Tail	Golden pheasant crest and tippets in strands
Body	First half: light orange seal's fur. Second half: black floss
Ribbing	Oval silver tinsel over the orange seal's fur; flat silver tinsel and twist over the black floss
Hackle	A lemon hackle over the orange seal's fur; a black heron hackle over the black floss
Throat	Teal
Wing	A pair of cinnamon turkey tail strips set flat and slightly splayed
Cheeks	Jungle cock, drooping
Head	Black

White turkey tail is often used, and the pattern is then called the *White-winged Akroyd*. The fly shown in Plate 5 was given to me by Megan Boyd. She says of it: "This fly, given to my father by Charles Akroyd, has black heron [throat] only, but I have seen many old gut-looped *Akroyds* with teal or guinea fowl throats. Charles Akroyd made the *White-winged Akroyd* too, and I think he made some with guinea fowl and some without. I do know that he nicknamed the fly 'the poor man's *Jock Scott,*' for the body is half yellow and half black."

Famous for patterns other than the type that bears its name, the Dee was also the home of Cosmo Gordon, who originated the fly aptly called the *Gordon* in the 1890s. This pattern is dressed with many slight variations, inspiring Kelson to comment, "No two dressers of today make the fly alike." Another pattern of the Victorian era, which originated on the Upper Mar section of the Dee, is the *Mar Lodge*. It too is often varied, especially the black center section of its body, and these variations are known by different names.

Following these developments, around the turn of the century, Dee patterns became smaller and simpler; many of these later patterns remain favorites today.

The Lives of the Salmon

"There is a lesser and greater reward in the catching of salmon; one relates to the mastery of skill, but the greater lies in cherishing the fish and knowing humility in the face of its saga."

—Orri Vigfusson

"Leaping Salmon"

$\mathcal{D}$eep down in the gravel of salmon river tributaries, there occurs each year an age-old ritual. In the fall, instincts guide the salmon through the laying of eggs in scattered beds more than 6 inches deep. To defend them from the depredations of insect larvae and hungry fish and birds, instincts also warn the salmon to separate and carefully cover her selected nests until her job is completed and, exhausted, she returns to the rehabilitating vigor of the sea.

Later, when the warming water of early spring trickles through chinks in the gravel, the eggs, soft, orange-pink, and little larger than buckshot, quiver with life. Fishlike heads and tails soon emerge, leaving suspended from the belly the yolk sac that will nourish the tiny salmon until it can wriggle freely and feed on microscopic life in the water. No more than half an inch long, these baby salmon are called *alevins*.

Salmon, in their several stages of development, are given various names. When the alevin has absorbed its yolk sac, it is called a *fry*. Longer than an inch but still less than fingersize, it is known as a *fingerling*. Exceeding finger length, it develops a dark back and lighter belly, with vertical bars called *parr marks* along its sides; in this stage, it is termed a *parr* and closely resembles a small brook trout, except primarily for its deeply forked tail.

The life of the parr in the river is a precarious one. Over the period they stay in the river, their chances of survival are less than one in a thousand. As they subsist and grow, devouring nymphs, insects, and later-born alevins, their numbers are constantly depleted by larger fish and diving birds. Depending on environmental factors, the little parr remain in the river for two to six years before they go to sea.

The avidity of the parr for insects is well known to anglers who go fly fishing for salmon. Very often a hungry parr catches its little mouth around the hook and gives the line a slight tap. Then the angler must carefully draw in the baby fish, lift it by the

Reflection, Dartmouth River

GILBERT VAN RYCKEVORSEL

Salmon parr GILBERT VAN RYCKEVORSEL

hook, turn the barb over, and let the parr wriggle off—usually with an invitation for it to return when it grows up!

As the parr reaches the river's estuary, it gradually takes on a silvery color, which hides the parr marks and indicates that it is almost ready to go to sea. In this stage, the brightly shining fish is called a *smolt*. Its age at this point is generally three years, occasionally more or less, depending again on environmental conditions. In Labrador, for example, they are five or six years of age at the time of this transition. Never free from the dangers of nature and man, the smolts that survive school together, often in tremendous numbers, awaiting by instinct the tide that is to take them to sea.

During the springtime change from parr to smolt, the vertical bars and troutlike spots are obscured by a deposit of silvery guanine in the skin.

This camouflage coat is created by an excretory substance and indicates internal physiological changes that are taking place to enable the baby salmon to transfer from its freshwater environment to the marine one in which it will grow. As the smolt journeys downstream, its memory is miraculously imprinted with the atmosphere of the native river that will guide its return to its birthplace to spawn. On its return, its silvered "armor" is spectacularly brilliant, but it gradually fades in fresh water—hence, one can distinguish fish that have recently returned from the sea from those that have been in the river some time.

Where the salmon go while they grow to adulthood in the sea is somewhat of a mystery. Research tells us that large numbers of salmon from both sides of the Atlantic migrate to waters off southwestern Greenland, while others travel to lesser-known feed-

The strength and determination of salmon running upriver is a sight to behold   MITCHELL CAMPBELL

ing grounds. There they mature rapidly, dining on the bounty the sea offers—unless they become the bounty. After one or more years in the salt water, the surviving salmon return to their rivers. That they almost all return to the rivers of their birth (as learned from the tagging of smolts and other research), and even to the very tributary wherein they were born, is astonishing: The return of the Atlantic salmon to their native river may span thousands of miles of open ocean, not unlike the unerring migrations of butterflies and birds.

When the salmon return to the region of their rivers and travel up or down the coast to identify the rivers of their birth, they must survive a new set of dangers. Their strength and swiftness may enable them to avoid predators such as seals, porpoises, and lampreys, but they are no match for the maze of nets and weirs that block many estuaries. Then, for the salmon that make it past the hazards of the estuarial and tidewater nets, there are dams to leap, fishways to negotiate, and, too often, the nets of poachers.

Scientists have concluded that when instinct brings the salmon back to its native territory, memory of the characteristics of the river of its birth guides the fish into it. The presumption is that every river has an identifying combination of chemical composition, odor, water pressure, taste, and perhaps temperature, and that salmon remember these characteristics and can follow them home.

Salmon may spend one, two, three, or even four years in the sea, growing bigger year by year. A salmon returning after its first year at sea is called a *grilse* and normally weighs between 2 and 8 pounds; a salmon that spends two or more winters at sea is called a *multi-sea-winter salmon (MSW)*. Those that have been at sea two winters usually weigh 8 to 15 pounds, and three-winter salmon and repeat spawners can weigh 20 to 30 pounds or more.

When the salmon first arrive in the river, they are in their prime—bright, fat, and strong—and a joy to observe or pursue. But as they do not feed to any appreciable extent after entering the river, their beauty and strength gradually diminish. As their appearance wanes, certain internal systems degenerate in favor of the development of their reproductive systems. During this time, the males' body cavities

fill with sperm, or *milt,* and the females' with eggs, or *roe.* The male salmon also develop a hook in the lower jaw, called a *kype.* Their minds are no longer on feeding, although, fortunately for anglers, they will by instinct take insects occasionally, and sometimes other things. They are totally occupied with their primal quest and are determined to reach their nuptial gravel beds as quickly as possible.

Whether or not salmon feed in fresh water and, if so, how much are questions debated over many decades. These questions are of particular interest to anglers because of the connection with what fly (or other lure) to use, what size, when, and why. Feeding is not the mere swallowing of material; it is the digestion, absorption, and use of the material by the body. The studies on this subject generally conclude that salmon will ingest a great variety of food, but they will not metabolize it.

Among others, the writings of Malloch, Chaytor, LaBranche, McFarland, Waddington, and Jones

A grilse

GILBERT VAN RYCKEVORSEL

The life cycle of the salmon: eggs, aelvin, parr, smolt, returning adult.

report that salmon will often readily take insects or flies floating in the water very much in the manner of trout—that, although what the salmon has ingested is often found in its mouth and gullet, it is not found in the stomach. Waddington, in 1948, reported, "The average salmon may 'swallow food' in the river but it can derive no nourishment from it. He does not take it because he is hungry; he is not, in fact, feeding." Collectively, these studies can be summed up by saying that, of a combined total of nearly five thousand salmon whose stomachs were studied, food remains were found in only nine.

Then why do salmon take flies? Once again, instinct seems to be the common denominator. Baby salmon in the parr stage of growth not only look like tiny brook trout, but feed like them, too. Except in the coldest climates, they thrive principally on insects, which are represented by artificial flies, or on much smaller fish, which may be represented by sparse wet flies. If, after one or more years at sea, a salmon can return from its wanderings and remember its own river, why can't it remember what it used to eat there? The returning salmon isn't hungry, but its mind may be imprinted with what it used to do in the river as a parr—that is, to sip in flies.

Lee Wulff, as a result of his vast experience, said, "I believe the main reason an Atlantic salmon takes a fly is due to its long stream life as a parr. As with young trout in the streams, the parr's food is mainly underwater insect forms. A salmon parr has a long (three years and over) river life and a long feeding period to remember. . . . In spite of the wide variety of flies that may work, I still think the basic urge to rise comes from a salmon's insect-feeding memories as a parr." It would follow, then, that this same instinct would extend to larger bait for larger and older fish, such as minnows and elvers.

Second, most creatures are curious and selective. Babies and puppies frequently mouth and reject items that capture their interest, or try to drive away objects that irritate them. The strike of an angry salmon is quite different from the casual rise and sipping caused by remembered behavior or curiosity. It is a savage attack that makes both the water and the blood of the angler boil. Thus, when a salmon sees a fly floating down on the surface or drifting or swinging in the current, it may rise because of resid-

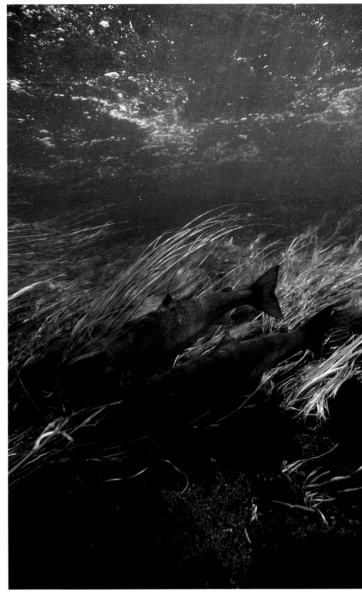

Strawberry Run, St. Mary's River GILBERT VAN RYCKEVORSEL

ual memory, curiosity, or anger—all of which are elements of instinct.

If salmon will take such diverse items as bugs, insects, berries, sweets, worms, and even cigarette butts, why should we be so fussy about offering them carefully dressed artificial flies in particular colors, shapes and sizes selected to suit the conditions of the water, temperature, and so on? There are simply no pat answers—the variables are too numerous and the species too unpredictable. This is fortunate, because conclusive answers about fly selection

"Steinfossen Pool"

and presentation methods would diminish the fun of fishing. The best one can do is to try to deal with varying conditions and likely responses, and enjoy the challenge of discovery. Years of personal experience and reading the extensive angling literature can provide valuable insight.

Salmon may enter their rivers at any time of the year, although there are peak periods. Their runs upriver in spring, summer, and fall vary from river to river and depend on the conditions of the rivers. Thus, by their peak periods, rivers may be known as spring, summer, or autumn rivers. By knowing when the runs of fish should occur, anglers can visit one river after another and expect good fishing throughout the season.

Grilse habitually ascend different rivers at different times. If you fish the Matapedia in early July, for example, you will almost always take salmon. But if you go there later in the season, you will take a larger proportion of grilse. People who have observed a few salmon and many more grilse in a pool say that the grilse will nearly always go for the fly first. Whether you are allowed (or expected) to release the fish or not varies from river to river; however, there is a two-fish limit on many Canadian rivers, and it can be disappointing to hook and land two grilse and have to stop fishing for the day, particularly when you have traveled far, at considerable expense, in the expectation of catching large salmon.

Often the size of the salmon is proportionate to the size of the river, but not always. Thirty-pounders occasionally are caught on the Miramichi, but they are fairly common on the Matapedia, a river of about the same size. Forty-pounders, or even larger, are taken on bigger rivers, such as the Restigouche and the Grand Cascapedia. In his excellent book *The Atlantic Salmon,* Anthony Netboy says, "No generalizations are possible about the size of adult salmon, although some countries like Norway and Scotland seem to breed heavier fish than others. Salmon weighing up to 70 pounds and more have been taken in these lands."

It is also believed that salmon, just like people, exist within different cultures. Simply put, all salmon do not behave the same way, and all rivers do not fish in the same way. Salmon indigenous to specific rivers have certain characteristics in common. These characteristics include the general appearance of the fish as well as behavior patterns, such as when they rest and when they move.

The strength and determination of salmon running upriver is quite a sight, especially when large numbers of them are negotiating an obstacle such as a waterfall or a dam. In his book *The Salmon,* Dr. J. W. Jones describes a salmon leaping 11 feet, 4 inches over a perpendicular waterfall at a vertical speed of 20 miles per hour. The fish will try again and again until the leap is accomplished. In one place, where the current of a small stream swept downward over a rocky chute caused by an inclined ledge, the salmon were smart enough not to try to swim the chute. Instead, they selected the thin, slower water at the edge of the ledge, and slithered upward over it easily in water insufficient to float them.

For one reason or another, salmon move mostly during the night or during the hours approaching night or daylight. During the day, or when the flow is insufficient for travel, they rest in pools. A pool devoid of salmon one day or even one hour may be full of them the next.

The trip up the river to the nesting areas in the tributary streams may take several weeks, delayed perhaps by low water or possibly because the fish do not want to reach their destinations until they are almost ready to spawn. The males and females spend considerable time resting in the pools at either end of the spawning bed, though the dominant male will frequently prod a female with his snout, push against her, or bully other males. The next stage is the movement of a female out of the pool and over the gravel. There she will select and cut her nests, called *redds,* in the riverbed by using strong thrusts

Leaping salmon

JACK SWEDBERG

of her tail to make saucerlike depressions about 6 inches deep.

In most spawnings, the eggs are ejected into the cracks between the stones at the bottom of the bed, where they are difficult to see and reasonably well sheltered from the shower of gravel the female sends down after the eggs are fertilized by the milt of the male. The "covering up" is usually continued at the beginning of the next spawning sequence. As many as eight such sequences, each farther upstream than the previous one, may be carried out before the female has deposited all her eggs.

A female salmon will lay about eight hundred eggs per pound of body weight, and repeat spawners may produce up to 50 percent more eggs than maiden fish. Interestingly, a male salmon may fertilize the eggs of several females. The reproductive functions of living things are wonderful in many ways. In the case of salmon, for example, nature has ensured that when a ripe female and a spent or nearly spent male are together, the female's eggs may be successfully fertilized even if insufficient milt remains in the male. Instances are recorded of male parr—weighing only fractions of an ounce—invading the beds of giant salmon while the male salmon is too occupied to drive them away (or perhaps he doesn't notice that one or two of the neighborhood boys are getting into the act!). The little parr, with their tiny vents close to the big one of the large female, instinctively deposit their milt over the eggs at the proper time.

This disparity in sizes, somewhat like a dinghy next to an ocean liner, may seem ludicrous, but scientific experiments in observation tanks prove otherwise: Small parr, sharing a tank with sterilized adult male salmon, can effectively fertilize the eggs of the female.

After spawning in the late fall or early winter, the salmon, exhausted by their efforts and lack of food, are emaciated and are called *kelts* (or "spent fish" or "black salmon"). Some die of disease; others (unlike the Pacific salmon, which die after a single spawning) drift downriver to the sea, where they can feed and regenerate and perhaps return, as beautiful as before and larger than ever, to spawn again or perhaps to provide superlative sport to the angler with his fly rod and fly.

An integral part of fishing for salmon is understanding their remarkable lives—lives that are predicated on instinct and heredity. Understanding the various periods in their development, and knowing something about their habitats and why they are in rivers at some times and not others, will enable you to fish more successfully. Then, when one of this noble species suddenly boils up to slam at your fly, the thrill of the fishing will be greater than it could have been before!

Catch and Release

Another of the many satisfactions in salmon fishing can be the safe release of the catch. The practice of catch and release is a relatively recent advance among conservation-minded anglers. Heated debate has long raged as to whether salmon caught by anglers should be released. Many government officials and anglers look unfavorably upon it—some anglers even comment that "one should not play with one's food." Others argue strongly in its favor for conservation reasons, especially releasing the larger females, unless the fish has been bleeding or is otherwise injured. The Atlantic Salmon Federation, in cooperation with

Catch and release

Dr. Bruce Tufts of Queens University and the New Brunswick and Canadian governments, spent several years researching the effects of catch and release on Atlantic salmon, and they determined that virtually every salmon carefully played, handled, and released will survive to spawn successfully.

One authority who recommends releasing seemingly healthy fish is Dr. Wilfred M. Carter, president emeritus of the Atlantic Salmon Federation, who provided the following instructions: "Keeping the net in the water, grasp the fish firmly just ahead of the tail, exerting a circular pressure. Usually the salmon will then lie quietly, allowing you to com-

plete the release. Remove the hook with small pointed pliers [or forceps], or use your thumb and forefinger to shake it loose. [The use of barbless hooks employed by many conscientious anglers makes this job easier.] Now remove the salmon from the net, continuing to support it in an upright position [keeping it in the water and taking great care not to touch the gill area] while you face it into the current for a minute or two to circulate water through the gills until it regains enough strength to swim away."

Then let it go and rejoice in the time you had together in the river.

Notes on Salmon Tackle

"Breakfast Fire"

About a century ago, during the Victorian Era, the properly equipped British angler usually was nattily attired in classic tweeds from bowler hat to stocking-foot waders. He carried a two-handed rod made of ferruled or spliced strips split from greenheart logs or built-cane, which was over 17 feet long and weighed between 2 and 3 pounds. To this was attached a "winch" at least 4 inches in diameter and weighing about 18 ounces that held about 150 yards of bulky line made of plaited and impregnated silk, terminating with a strong leader of silkworm gut. Attached to this was a fly, selected from hundreds of patterns, which could be between 4 and 5 inches long and composed of a dozen or two fancy ingredients, including the rarest of feathers.

Armed with this equipment, then thought proper for combating the King of Fishes, the angler sauntered from his castle or estate to streamside. He was attended by a gillie, whose job was to make the fishing pleasanter by gaffing the fish, changing flies, providing food and drink to the fisher, and keeping him out of trouble such as by lending strong arm support in fast water.

Fishing these big flies was accomplished by "waving" the cumbersome rod by casts known as "Spey," "roll," "underhand," "overhand," "switch," "flip," and "wind." The long rods were thought necessary to push the big flies out into the gusts, a rationale that made sense to an extent. The big flies were thought necessary for fishing deep in fast currents of big rivers, a theory long since exploded.

Modern anglers still use long rods with smaller flies on big rivers in such places as the British Isles, Norway, and to a lesser extent, Canada. These rods have been shortened to about 14 feet and are fashioned from fiberglass or graphite. They still make sense for casting into the wind and for handling very big fish in the fast, deep currents of big rivers. They can serve needed purposes, but, by American standards at least, they are less fun and less challenging than the lighter tackle more extensively used today.

What can you use currently? With proper accessories and in a suitable size, you can use your trouting rod. This little rod, usually employed in placid pools to hook trout weighing ounces, in fast currents will handle leaping silver giants weighing pounds. The sensation may be similar to trying to hold a bull by the tail. The result is safer and is a supreme thrill in angling excitement.

The fun of using light tackle on salmon was pioneered principally by Lee Wulff, a legend in his own time. Lee often uses the lightest rods he can

Victorian tackle

PLATE 8
SELECTED CONTEMPORARY TACKLE FOR SALMON
Photographed by Jack Swedberg

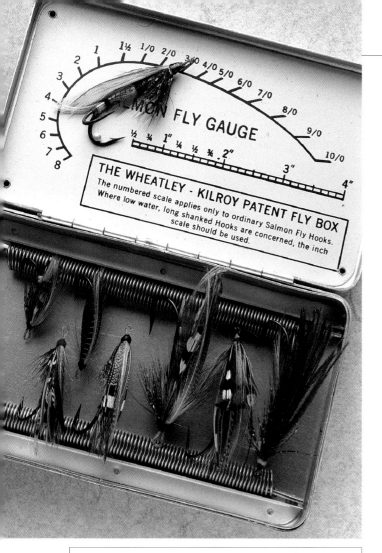

PLATE 9
A WHEATLEY BOX WITH
ANTIQUE DOUBLES

find, frequently in the neighborhood of 2 or 3 ounces. Of course, there are tricks of this trade, which will be covered later. Inspired by Lee and by Tony Ruiz Ochoa, an internationally famous light tackle expert I met on a river in Iceland, I tried this with my 2-ounce Orvis. It resulted in great success and greater excitement, but don't try it unless you have plenty of time on a river teeming with salmon.

Between these heavy and light tackle extremes, there is a middle ground that usually makes more sense, so let's explore it.

Rods

To put it in a nutshell, I think most anglers would agree that a single-handed rod between about 8 and 10 feet long accommodating a line weight from 7 to 10 in one of the forward tapers would be most generally useful. The choice between these extremes would depend more on the size of the rivers to be encountered than on the average weight of salmon expected in them.

For years, my favorites were fiberglass sticks for line weights 8, 9, and 10. These are still among my favorites for salmon, but I have come to prefer graphite, an opinion others may argue. The two rods I most use are an 8-foot, 4-inch (for a 7-weight line) and an 8 1/2-foot (for a 7- or 8-weight line). The latter weighs 3 15/16 ounces. I also use a 9-foot (for 9-weight line) and prefer it for deep wading or for use on windy days. Each of these three has taken salmon in the 25-pound range in fast or average water. I usually take two of the three along at a time. Each of these rods can handle one line weight larger than the manufacturer's rating. The dependable power and strength of rods properly built of these synthetic materials have made the long, heavy sticks, so popular in the past, much less necessary.

Although discriminating anglers in large numbers still seek and cherish handcrafted rods of split bamboo, the revolutionary improvements made in synthetics have converted many traditionalists to graphite. Today a preference for split bamboo is due primarily to pride of possession and aesthetics rather than to superior efficiency.

Made from cane strips of varying strengths, no two split-bamboo rods are exactly alike. Selecting one with "perfect action" is largely a matter of personal preference and is usually determined by such scientific testing as wiggling and woggling until the "right" rod is found. In spite of its superior aesthetics, split bamboo is heavier than its synthetic counterpart, a characteristic that can have a telling effect after a long day of constant casting.

Because of modern technology, all synthetic rods made by the same manufacturer in the same model number are identical. The action of rods can vary among manufacturers, however; those of one will be quite different from those of another, even if they appear similar. As a rule, manufacturers plan their rods so that they will handle with maximum efficiency the lines that fit them. Usually these are general-purpose rods with medium action, which is just what we want for use with most types of salmon flies.

A word of warning is appropriate here. There are ways of cost cutting in rod manufacture that may not be obvious in the finished product, but that will become very apparent in use. You can buy rods made by the leading quality manufacturers with confidence, but beware of bargains.

Discerning anglers often are not content with a general-purpose rod and may want to shop around to find one with faster action for dry-fly work, or slower action for heavier flies or streamers. In salmon fishing, however, dry flies usually are rather bulky for the best flotation, and big streamers also can be handled very well with a medium-action rod, so this type should prove excellent for all purposes.

PLATE 10
MINIATURE WORKING REELS
HAND-MACHINED BY
ROBERT HASKELL, NAPLES, MAINE

Green Rat
dressed by Bob Warren

Campbell
dressed by Bob Veverka

Black Dog
dressed by Mark Waslick

Ausable Wulff
originated and
dressed by Fran Betters

Flies of all types most commonly used on average-size rivers are in sizes 4, 6, and 8, which can be handled excellently with a #8 or #9 rod size, the most popular being about 9 feet long. Larger flies might cast better with a more powerful rod, and smaller flies with a less powerful one, but the nature of the water being fished should be the first consideration in determining the power of the rod. Rods longer than 10 feet are tiresome to cast with one hand, but two-handed rods present difficulty in handling the line. Rod length is primarily dictated by the distance of the cast needed, although you may want a longer one for deep wading and a shorter one for shore and boat fishing. Detachable butts, formerly common on the larger rods, are not as prevalent as they used to be and have largely been replaced by smaller fixed butt extensions.

Rods of the sizes described are usually fitted with locking reel seats. Be certain that the reel can be locked on tightly, because any wobble in the connection is dangerous and bothersome. If, when the connection is tightened, the reel does wobble a little, this can be adjusted by building up the reel seat with adhesive tape and/or by cutting a thin sheet of rubber to fit between reel foot and reel seat.

Lines

Since rod makers recommend the proper line size for each rod and line makers label the sizes of their lines quite accurately, anglers should have no trouble in matching them. This is very important, because mismatched tackle won't cast properly.

Atlantic salmon fishermen generally are concerned only with sizes 7 to 10. Size 9, for example, is the designation of a medium-powerful rod suitable for average rivers where a size 9 line usually is appropriate. Having selected a rod and knowing the line size most suitable for it, you now must decide on the type of line and its color.

Modern fly lines consist of a level core of braided nylon or Dacron coated with a heat-cured plastic finish, which is rigidly controlled for diameter and weight. This coating is accurately tapered to suit whatever type of line is being made, and its specific gravity also is precisely controlled to ensure that the line will float or will sink slowly or rapidly, as desired.

Fly lines are colored by the manufacturer to identify type, many floaters being white. Each type of line is identified by a series of letters and numbers. The prefix denotes the type, such as WF for "weight forward," and the suffix tells whether the line is made to float or to sink, such as F for "floating." Between these is given the size of the line. Thus, WF-9-F means a size 9 floating line with a weight-forward taper. Manufacturers may vary slightly in designating line size, so it is possible that, for example, a WF-10-F line may handle better on a size 9 rod than a WF-9-F.

The designations of L for "level" and DT for "double taper" have minor application to salmon fishing, although a few anglers like them. We are mainly concerned with weight forward lines, particularly when using big or bulky flies, especially in the winds so often encountered on salmon rivers. Weight-forward lines are available in various types of tapers other than regular, such as "bass bug," or "salt water," but you need not be bothered by these, at least at first. We are very much concerned, however, with weight-forward lines that float, sink, or float with a sinking tip. The last, in size 9 for example, is designated as WF-9-F/S. Sinking lines are available with various degrees of sinking ability—regular, or slow sinking, and faster-sinking high-density lines, some of which are made to sink faster than others. My general rule is to stay with the regular, or slow-sinking, type, unless there is reason to the contrary.

At one time I considered the most useful line to be the weight-forward one with a slow-sinking tip. It is excellent for swinging the sunk fly at midwater depth. If it is all you have astream, you can drift a dry fly with it even though the floating type, made for that purpose, is better. The sinking tip soon will pull the fly under, but it may float long enough to hook a salmon seen rising, or to be drifted over one you are trying to make rise.

When using this line as an expedient for dry-fly fishing, select a hard-to-sink type of fly like one of the Wulff patterns, or a *Bomber* or a *Muddler.* Any of these will drift several feet before sinking. The cast then can be completed by fishing wet, a method that often produces strikes. False-casting will dry the fly enough to repeat the operation. This line is excellent when salmon are not rising readily in streams of shallow or average depth.

The floating line without the sinking tip, though made for surface fishing, is also superior for the wet fly when you want to fish it in or just under

the surface film, which is often where the salmon take best. It is the ideal line for the greased-line method and for fishing the Patent. Easiest to pick up, the floating line also indicates the fly's position and makes action quicker to detect.

Sinking lines rarely are necessary for salmon fishing except in unusually deep rivers or pools. I never used to carry one, but now do because of situations like the following:

We were fishing a famous river in Iceland at a time when the river was too low and the air too cold. One beat was far upriver and contained an immense, very deep and crystal-clear pool. Where the entering fast water slacked off, we could see dozens of salmon slowly milling around in a compact circle known as a *circus,* the only one I ever have seen. The fish were deep and refused to rise for anything. Our buoyant lines couldn't sink our flies to them.

When we were assigned the same beat again, we brought reel spools containing sinking lines. One of us had a slow sinker, another a high-density fast sinker, and the third a high-density shooting head attached to 20-pound running line. Our guide, the son of the river manager, squatted on a high bluff overlooking the pool so that he could direct our efforts. As I recall, the flies used were #2 and #4 doubles in patterns such as *Silver Rat, General Practitioner,* and *Black-Eyed Prawn.*

Casts had to be long and into the incoming current to get the flies deep when they swung close to the school of salmon. The slow-sinking line didn't go deep enough before the current took it beyond the compact circle of fish. After a few tries with the higher-density lines, we were able to get the flies down to fish level and, going by the guide's sign language, could work them deep enough in the proper place at the right time of drift.

I would like to report that many salmon were hooked as the result of this experiment, but such was not the case. While most of the salmon remained uninterested, one now and then moved to a fly, thus indicating languid interest. It took many casts to get a strike, but when a fly managed to pass the right fish at the right time, the fish would take it

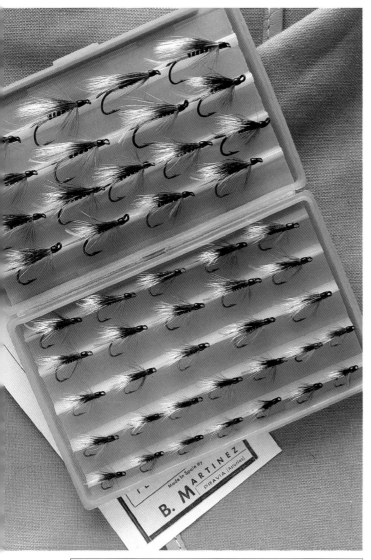

PLATE 12
ONE OF THE AUTHOR'S
FISHING BOXES CONTAINING
THE IRISH HAIRY MARY

dressed by Belarmino Martinez

three: a reel spool with a floater, one with a floater with a sinking tip, and a high-density sinker, even if the third is rarely needed. Some anglers carry two rods whenever convenient—one rigged for dry fly, and one for wet. Others carry only one rod, but with a reel that has extra spools holding the different types of lines. My usual habit is to take one rigged rod and to carry other lines on extra reel spools. These, along with fly boxes, rain gear, and so forth, are in a shoulder-strapped canvas bag, which can be dropped nearby while fishing. This kit also contains a plastic garbage bag to keep the canvas bag dry in wet weather, as well as a roll of plastic sleeving: Tie a knot in one end, cut off enough to hold a salmon or two, knot the other end, and the fish are kept clean and are easy to carry.

If a line made to float doesn't do so properly, that's because it is dirty. A good rubdown with fly line cleaner and a cleaning pad soon remedies this. A small cloth dipped in mild soap and tepid water is a substitute.

In salmon fishing, you need at least 100 yards of backing. Information that comes with the reel usually specifies the amount of backing that can be accommodated with various sizes of lines. If it doesn't, a solution is to put the line on first and then to reel on backing until the spool is comfortably (but not overly) full. Then reel off the backing and line (without twisting), reel on the backing tightly, and splice the rear end of the fly line to it.

One way to join backing and line is to splice a small loop in the line and make a loop in the backing that is large enough to pass over the reel or reel spool. Put the backing loop through the line loop, then over the spool, and pull the connection tight. The backing loop seems neatest when made with a perfection loop knot, which is sufficiently strong for this purpose.

A better way, in my opinion, is to join backing and line with a nail knot. This provides a smooth connection that passes freely through the rod's tip-top and can't slip, cut, or pull out when tied properly. Although called a nail knot, a 1-inch or so piece of plastic tubing is better than a nail or anything else in helping to tie this knot.

Another knot used for connecting two lines of dissimilar materials or diameters is the Albright knot. It is quick and easy to tie but is not as smooth as the nail knot.

leisurely and turn with it, thus hooking itself. We estimated that we each made over two hundred casts for a total of four salmon. The point is that when salmon won't rise to the fly, the fly must get down to the salmon.

Thus, sinking lines are necessary where and when they are needed, but they are not ordinarily needed on most rivers.

So what lines should a properly equipped angler usually carry? In my opinion, he should take all

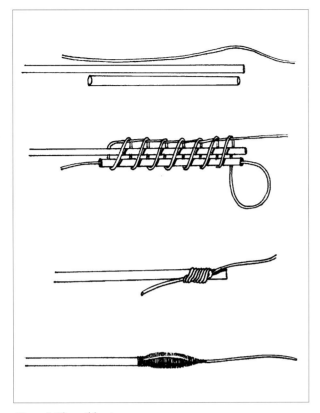

Figure 2. The nail knot.

Occasionally an angler may wish to use a favorite reel for salmon fishing, but its spool is too small to hold an adequate amount of line and backing. A remedy for this is to see how far you can cast comfortably with the line, then pull out about 5 feet more and cut the line at this point (which probably will be about 45 or 50 feet, or about half of the line). Put on backing as previously described, and join the end of the cut line to the backing. Backing usually is of braided Dacron of about 15 or 20 pounds test. Since this is much finer in diameter than the line, a large amount of backing can be put on a medium-size fly reel if the useless part of the line is eliminated.

The tippet strength of the leader seldom exceeds 15 pounds. It is most often less, and consequently there is no need to use braided backing that is much stronger than the tippet. Since the strength of braided backing may have deteriorated slightly, and since you will feel safer with backing you know is strong enough, a strength testing 5 or 10 pounds more than the strongest tippet you will use should be adequate. To avoid error, the backing on all reels should be of the same strength. I standardize this at

20 pounds, which should be sufficient for all North American rivers. If you plan to fish in Norway or other regions having extralarge salmon in extraturbulent rivers, the strength of your tackle should be determined by local custom.

Tapered lines sometimes come with an extra length of level line at the tip end so that you can cut off as much as you wish to balance your tackle properly. Since this level tip section has no appreciable casting weight, most of it should be clipped off. By doubling the line, you can see where the taper starts, and you should cut off all but a foot or two of the level section. Failure to do this may mean that the cast will not roll out as it should.

Fly lines are now available in a plethora of colors (including those with no color at all), with nearly as many opinions to accompany them. I prefer white floating lines because I can see them better, but it had never occurred to me that white would be less visible than other colors to fish.

Col. Esmond Drury, the renowned English angling authority, proved that white lines *are* less visible to fish. During a blitz in Malta in 1941, he shared a trench with a commando who was a frogman specializing in underwater demolition. The commando happened to mention that the most difficult target to locate underwater is a ship with a white hull. Some years later, Drury applied this information to angling and experimented with the visibility of various colored lines underwater. After considerable effort, he determined that white was, indeed, the least visible.

Drury wrote: "On the manufacturing side, Mil-

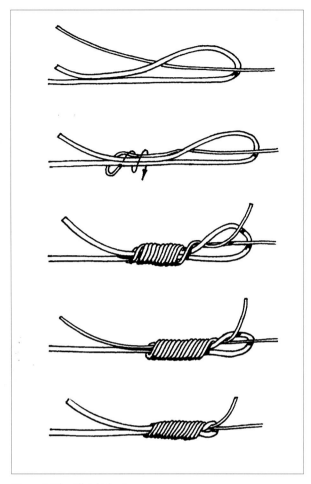

Figure 3. The Albright knot.

To tie the Albright knot, first make a loop in the end of the fly line and hold the ends between your left thumb and forefinger, with the loop extending to the right. Insert the backing line up through the loop, allowing an end of 8 to 10 inches. Pinch the backing line end between your left thumb and forefinger, along with the ends of the fly line loop. Next, make a series of about ten close, even wraps around all three lines with the backing line, covering each with your thumb and forefinger and maintaining even pressure. Insert the end of the backing line through the fly line loop in the same direction it entered. While holding the wraps between the thumb and forefinger, gently pull on the backing line while sliding the wraps toward the loop. Taking care not to let the wraps overlap one another, slowly push them with your thumb and forefinger while pulling on the backing line until the knot is tight. Pull both ends to make sure the knot is secure. The Albright knot is also an expedient way to connect the butt end of a leader to the fly line. The important thing to remember is to always make the loop in the heavier material.

wards was most helpful and produced the first white fly line to be made. British anglers are conservative people, and the white fly line didn't take on, but the Americans got hold of the idea and today most (floating) fly lines are white ones."

Those who wish to debate this point might consider Darwin's theory of the survival of the fittest. Over the ages, water birds with bellies other than white ceased to exist. Could this be because they were more conspicuous to predators looking upward from beneath the surface? The same applies to most gamefish, too.

Shooting Heads

The accepted fly-fishing method regardless of reel capacity is using only the easily castable weight-forward tapered part of the fly line. This section of the line is called a *shooting head,* and such lines can be purchased in all sizes and weights, thus making the cutting of expensive fly lines unnecessary. Shooting heads have long been popular with those who desire to cast to greater distances for competition or to reach distant fish in wide streams, as well as with those who want maximum backing on the reel.

The nail knot makes a good semipermanent connection if the rear end of the shooting head is not looped. Since several shooting heads usually are carried for surface fishing or fishing at various depths, it is handy to have the ends looped so that one head can be exchanged quickly for another on the running line. This attachment can be made with the five-turn clinch knot (not the improved clinch knot) in the same manner that the clinch knot is used to tie a hook to a leader. Several shooting heads, each properly labeled and in its plastic envelope, take little room in a pocket and make it possible to use a number of different types of lines on a single reel and spool.

As is often the case, shooting heads have both advantages and disadvantages: They allow a maximum amount of running line and backing on the reel, they make casting possible to longer distances with less false casting and fuss, and the narrower diameter of the running line gives less water resistance and thus less chance for hook pullout. If a salmon runs around rocks, the line is easier to lift off the water so that it can be passed over the obstacle. In the same vein, it is argued that a fly can be more readily "let down" the stream to a greater distance without imparting unnatural motion to it.

Regardless of these arguments, there are Atlantic salmon anglers who think that unnecessarily long casts are usually more detrimental than helpful. Too many anglers overfish salmon lies even with conventional equipment. Opponents think that the shooting head involves too much fuss and that it is awkward to handle the many coils of flimsy material that must be shot out for long casts.

If, in spite of the disadvantages, you do want to use a shooting head, you should, in fairness to the method, take enough time to learn how to use it efficiently.

Reels

This sporting tool can cost the Atlantic salmon angler tens, hundreds, and even thousands of dollars, and its requirements are largely obvious, or at least logical. First, it must be large enough to hold fly line and 100 or more yards of backing. In addition to adequate reel capacity, quite obviously you need a reel with a smooth drag that can be adjusted efficiently, thus avoiding snapped leaders and pulled-out

hooks. Since a salmon will exhaust itself by running and jumping, a fairly light drag is sensible under average conditions. The drag should be tested by pulling out line while someone holds the rod up. Often you will find that the adjusted drag is a bit too tight. In dry-fly fishing, where the leader tippet may be only 6 pounds or so, a very light drag is necessary.

Some of the newer reels are made with an outside flange on the spool. This allows you to "feather" the spool—that is, to provide extra braking power by pressure of the fingertips or palm while the spool is revolving. I consider this outside flange so important in supplying temporary extra braking power in controlling salmon that all of my salmon reels are equipped with it. Some anglers don't share this opinion and use reels without the outside flange.

Most fly reels for salmon are single-action—that is, they retrieve one turn of line with each turn of the handle. There are others of the multiplying type that take in more than one turn, usually 2 or 2 1/2. Because of their gearing, these reels are heavier and bulkier than their single-action counterparts, but

"Canoes on the Restigouche"

they do offer an advantage in retrieving line after salmon make long runs. With a single-action reel, you have to reel furiously when a lot of your backing is off the reel, because you must crank in many more turns than when the spool is nearly full.

When you are taken down into your backing, the drag of the reel increases as more line is taken out. Unless the drag has been set fairly lightly, it may be prudent to lighten it a little and then tighten it when all the backing has been regained. I prefer to use a lighter drag in the first place, because it seems dangerous to fool with it while battling a salmon. This, of course, is a matter of preference.

A third type of fly reel is the automatic. This reel has no place in Atlantic salmon fishing for many reasons, including the fact that it won't operate properly on long runs of fish.

Since extra spools are easier to carry than extra reels, you might wish to get one or two reel spools for different line types. When purchasing a reel, take care to select one that permits quick, easy changing of spools. Label each spool with the size and type of line it holds; it is very easy to forget!

In trout fishing, the reel's function is primarily to store line; with salmon, however, the long runs habitual to the fish make it advisable to own the finest reels you can afford. In selecting them, it is fun to see what new models are being offered in the best tackle shops or in mail-order catalogs illustrating high-quality equipment.

In freshwater fishing, reel maintenance is a minor problem. If even a grain or two of sand gets into the reel, remove the spool immediately, wash the parts, and wipe them dry. Reels should be taken apart for cleaning and light greasing of the moving parts before each trip. Little things often make a big difference in success with salmon!

Leaders

Long ago and after many years of fishing, I concluded that the most neglected part of a fly fisherman's tackle is the leader. Being casual in selecting or tying your own leaders may result in some frustration. Incorrectly sized leaders invariably end up dropping on the water in coils, having wind knots cast into them too often, wrapping themselves around the angler's neck, or breaking at the tippet when a big one hits. Frustrated fishermen notice

other casters who also lay out a good line but whose leaders roll over beautifully and without collapsing, thus delivering the fly properly for maximum effectiveness. They wonder how these casters do it. The successful casters understand the simple facts about tying or buying correctly tapered leaders.

Tying your own leaders is a simple matter, and all fly fishermen should be encouraged to do it. Indeed, it is part of the process of preparation in the cherished ritual of "getting ready." The alternative is to accept whatever can be found in stores—leaders that invariably are too small in the butt section. When the butt section is too light or too short, the heavy line and the too-light leader act as a hinge rather than a harmonious continuation of the line, and the whole thing collapses.

For tying correct leaders, follow the "two-thirds rule" or the "60 percent rule." If you are somewhere between the two, you can't go wrong.

The first part of the rule is that the butt section of the leader should be about two-thirds or about 60 percent of the diameter of the line. Let's say that the end of a size 8 line measures .039 with the micrometer. Two-thirds of this is .026, and 60 percent is .0234. Putting the micrometer on 30-pound monofilament, you find it measures .024 (brands vary somewhat). So here the butt section should begin with 30-pound-test monofilament.

The second part of the rule is that the heavy section should be about two-thirds or 60 percent of the length of the leader. The rest of it consists of a few short graduations down to a longer tippet. For example, let's say you want a 9-foot leader, which is a favorite length in wet-fly salmon fishing, and that you want to graduate it down to a 10-pound-test tippet, a favorite strength for flies in the size 4, 6, and 8 category.

Plan the leader on paper so that it will graduate down in size according to the rule:

3 feet of 30-pound-test	
2 feet of 25-pound-test	60 percent
1 foot of 20-pound-test	
8 inches of 17-pound-test	
8 inches of 15-pound-test	Graduations
8 inches of 12-pound-test	
12 inches of 10-pound-test	Tippet

You could make this leader a little longer and still stay within the rule by adding another 6 inches or so both to the butt section and to the tippet, giving you a 10-foot leader and allowing a little extra length in the tippet for changing flies.

Leaders can be planned to any length and tippet size and need only to come fairly close to the rule. As an experiment, a friend of mine who is a leading fly-rod expert made one 40 feet long, and he said it handled just as well as the tapered line. When properly tapered, the length of the leader has little bearing on performance.

Monofilament can be stiff or limp. If both are available, the stiff material can be used for the butt sections and the limp for the final graduations and the tippet. If leaders made according to this formula don't cast well, it is because the monofilament used is exceptionally limp. In that case, you will need to make each section one size larger and add another graduation to reach the same tippet size.

This rule is, of necessity, somewhat general because there are variations in diameter per pound-test and in the degree of suppleness of various brands of monofilament. In almost all cases, it will work very well. If it doesn't, adjustments can be made.

Some anglers disagree with this stiff butt and limp tip theory, maintaining that with the many types of monofilaments offered, the reverse can be true. They think that limp butt sections perform better and that stiff tips help the leader roll out better and turn the fly over better. Those who make their own leaders will find brands of monofilament to suit, regardless of which theory they accept. An easy solution is to make the entire leader of medium stiff monofilament.

To make your own leaders, it is necessary to learn only two knots: the perfection loop knot and the blood knot or the triple surgeon's knot. *Practical Fishing Knots,* by famous anglers Lefty Kreh and Mark Sosin, is heartily recommended.

The Perfection Loop Knot

This leader loop is used to make the loop at the butt end of the leader and is needed when a loop is spliced into the end of the fly line. Put the leader loop over the fly-line loop and pull the leader through the fly-line loop, making sure the two loops join in a figure-eight manner rather than allowing the leader loop to noose itself around the fly-line loop.

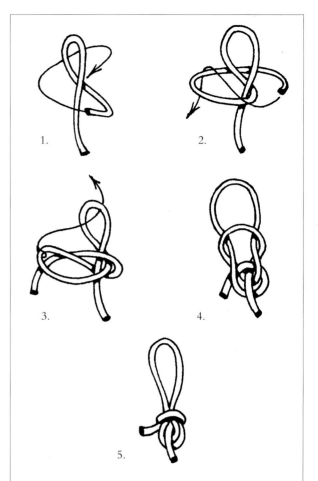

To tie the perfection loop knot, hold the piece of monofilament between left thumb and forefinger so that 6 inches or so of it extend and point upward. Holding the end with right thumb and forefinger, throw a small loop to the left so that it crosses behind the standing end. Holding this loop, bring the end toward you and pass it around the loop, clockwise, also grasping this between left thumb and forefinger. You now are holding two loops, the second one in front of the first.

Now take the short extending end of the monofilament and pass it between the two loops, also holding it between left thumb and forefinger. Grasp the front loop and work it through the rear loop, at the same time pulling it out a little. Still holding this tightly so that the knot won't slip, pull on the lower extension of the monofilament, thus closing the smaller loop. If the remaining loop starts to twist, hold it firmly to keep it from twisting, and pull downward on the lower extension and upward on the remaining loop until the knot is tight.

The knot can now be released from the fingers. Put a pencil or something similar through the loop and pull the loop as tight as possible. The short end of the monofilament will now extend to the left at a right angle from the loop, and it can be clipped off closely. By making the loops as small as desired, the perfection loop can be made in any size.

Figure 4. The perfection loop knot.

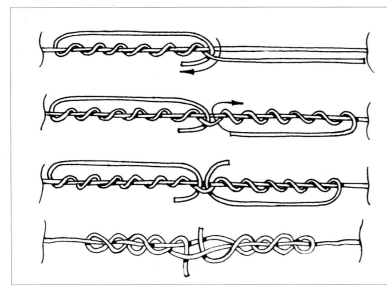

To tie the blood knot, lap the two ends to be joined (held between right thumb and forefinger), with 4 or 5 inches of each extending. Twist one end around the other strand five times, and place the end between the strands, holding it there as other end, but in the opposite direction from it. The knot can be released. Now pull on both strands of monofilament, being sure while doing so that the ends don't pull out. The knot will gather. (If the ends are too long they can be pushed back into the knot, if desired, to conserve monofilament.) Now pull the knot as tight as possible to test. Clip the ends close to the knot.

Figure 5. The blood knot.

The Blood Knot

The various graduations in the leader are made with blood knots. This easy knot sometimes frustrates anglers because one end or the other pulls out in closing it. Keep the ends long enough so that this won't happen, pushing them back into the knot after it has been partially closed. When partially closed, moisten before pulling it tight, then pull extremely tight, being careful that the turns seat properly. Avoid clipping the ends too closely unless there is foreign matter in the water that could catch on them. Otherwise, when strong tension is put on a big fish, one of the ends may pull out and loosen the knot.

The Triple Surgeon's Knot

Those who have trouble with the blood knot may prefer the easier triple surgeon's knot, although I don't like it as well, mainly because it can waste leader material.

Since this knot will waste a few inches of material, be sure to allow for this. Experiment with some spare material to learn to make the knot correctly. It's so easy that it can be done properly on the first attempt.

In my estimation, the double surgeon's knot, which is tied the same way but without the third pass, is about as efficient and saves passing the doubled ends through the loop the third time.

You can learn both of these knots in a few minutes, and a bit of practice will make them very simple

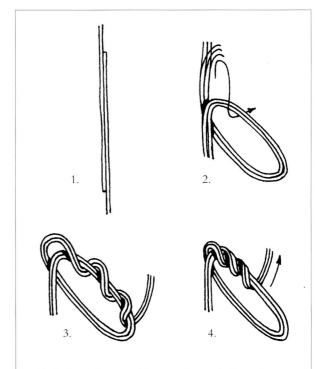

To tie the triple surgeon's knot, lay the two leader sections to be joined so that they overlap each other by about 6 inches. Keeping them parallel with each other (not twisted), bend them into a loop as shown. Take one of the doubled ends and pass it through the loop three times. Then pull each pair of doubled ends to close the knot, first moistening the coils in your mouth to reduce friction. When the knot is pulled tight, test the knot by pulling on each of the four sections. Then trim the tag ends. That's all there is to it!

Figure 6. The triple surgeon's knot.

to tie. Leader material in all necessary sizes is available on small spools at low cost. With this, it is fun to tie your own leaders wherever you may be, and it is a very handy trick of the trade when you want a special leader or when you are far away from stores.

There are also knotless tapered leaders; there is nothing wrong with them, but many anglers prefer to tie their own. Occasionally you'll have to tie in a heavier butt section because the knotless one is too light. And if the tippet size was right in the first place, you'll have to tie in a new tippet after changing flies several times.

Joining Leader and Line

I know of only three really satisfactory ways to join leader and line. One is to splice a small, smooth loop in the end of the line, put it through the leader loop, string the leader through it by its tip, and pull the connection tight, being sure the joining gathers in a figure-eight manner. The other options are to use the thirty-second nail knot or the needle knot.

The Thirty-Second Nail Knot. The nail knot, described earlier in this chapter, can be so simplified when used to join a leader to a line that it can be done properly in a matter of seconds. Lefty Kreh, one of the foremost fly-rod experts of these times, showed me how to do it. It must be done with a knotless leader, but a knotted leader can be tied to the monofilament butt after the knot has been completed.

This simplified knot is much quicker and easier to tie than to describe. It puts the former method of tying the nail knot out of business except for joining line and backing.

If you are using a knotted, tapered leader, the piece of monofilament you have just tied to the line acts as its butt section, and this butt section should be a little smaller in diameter than the line end and a little larger in diameter than the rest of the leader that will be tied to it. If the leader that is to be tied to it has a loop on the butt end, this loop is snipped off and the leader is tied to the (semi) permanent connection with a blood knot.

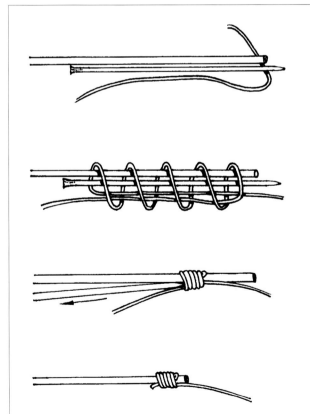

To tie the thirty-second nail knot, you need a fairly large common pin, a small nail, or a blunt needle of moderate size. Even a strong toothpick will do, because it only serves to provide stiffness when tying this knot.

As indicated in the illustration, hold the line end between left thumb and forefinger so that it extends about an inch. Also hold the leader butt (leader extending to the right) so that about an inch of it is behind thumb and forefinger, and hold the nail or needle with its point beside the line end. Take hold of the forward end of the leader and put it between left thumb and forefinger as well, holding its tip so that it points to the right and lies beside the line end and the nail. The rest of the leader hangs in a loop below the fingers. You now have four items grasped between left thumb and forefinger: the line end, the nail, the leader butt, and the leader tip.

Grasp the part of the leader butt extending from thumb and forefinger, and wind it clockwise to the left around the above four items, making five tight, close coils just in front of the thumbnail. Holding these coils in place between the left thumb and forefinger, take hold of the leader tip with the right thumb and forefinger and pull it to the right so that all of the leader is pulled between the coils as far as it will go. (At this point, be sure all five coils lie closely together.) Now you can let go of the knot, pull out the nail, and grasp the rearward protruding end of the leader butt with a pair of pliers. Also hold the leader that extends from the knot and pull in both directions; the coils will bite into the line to form a rigid connection. Snip off the excess butt end of the leader and the excess tip end of the line, and test the connection to be sure it has been pulled tight.

The rest is optional. You can coat the connection with Pliobond cement or varnish to make it smooth. You can leave about ¹/₄ inch of leader butt and line end and whip them and the knot with thread for added smoothness, also coating the whipped knot with cement or varnish.

Figure 7. The thirty-second nail knot.

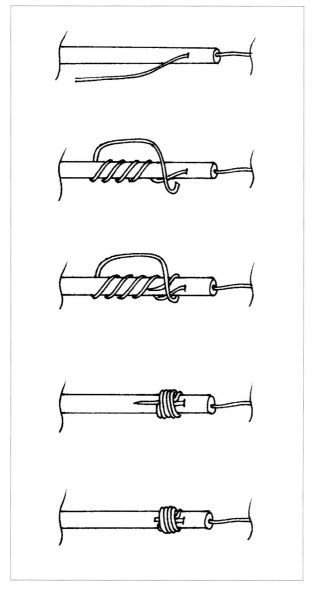

Figure 8. The needle knot.

To tie the needle knot, use a needle or pin to push a hole into the center of the fly line, making the instrument come out at least 1/8 inch from the line's end. When you withdraw the needle, the hole may close up enough to prevent your inserting the leader butt. One remedy is to insert a larger pin or needle, but not so large that it will rupture the line. Another method is to thread the needle with the leader and pull it through. To do this, you must taper the end of the leader to a point with a razor blade. After pulling it through the line, cut off the part of the leader that has been sliced and pull a few inches of leader through the hole as shown. Make four or five turns of the leader butt an inch or more from the end of the fly line, and double the leader butt back along the fly line's end as shown, ensuring that the two parts of the leader lie together. Now rewind the turns over the point where the leader emerges from the line, thus covering the base of the end of the leader butt and ending the winding as shown. Pull on the leader end with pliers and on the emerging leader by hand to tighten the coils and make them bite into the line. Clip off the excess leader end, and apply Pliobond or other lacquer to the connection. If you follow the drawings, this knot can be made easily.

In dry-fly fishing, the tippet can be much longer than in wet-fly fishing, even 2 or 3 feet long, to provide a longer float to the fly. Some anglers prefer very long tippets; others don't like the way they cast.

Nearly all salmon flies have eyes that are turned either up or down, usually up. The improved clinch knot, although stronger and quicker to tie, does not give a straight connection, so the turle knot is usually preferred. But the turle knot has been known to pull out. This can be prevented by tying an overhand knot in the end of the tippet and cutting off the excess after stringing on the fly. Then tie the turle knot and work the overhand knot up to it before looping it over the eye. This little precaution is a favorite of mine, and I never have known it to fail.

The size of the fly roughly dictates the size or strength of the tippet, which should be light enough to enable the fly to fish normally. Since salmon are not very leader-shy, you can use tippets between 10 and 15 pounds-test with reasonably large flies, but if conditions permit, you should use proportionately lighter tippets with smaller flies, and set the reel drag lighter to conform to the strength of the tippet. When water is low and clear, tippets in the lighter range are preferable. Strange as it may seem, 10-pound *soft* monofilament will fish a number 8 or 10 fly properly. Using this as a yardstick, you can determine the proper size of monofilament for larger or smaller flies.

Perhaps the only objection to rigging line and leader with this knot is that when stored on the reel, the leader will be in coils. Before use, stretching the leader will remove these coils. Test the strength of the leader frequently by this means or by pulling it to be sure all knots are joined properly and that there are no nicks to cause weakness.

The Needle Knot. Most anglers prefer to use a needle knot to join line to leader, because the leader butt comes out of the center of the fly line, making it easier to go through the rod's tip-top. There are similar knots also called the pin knot or needle knot, but this one seems easiest and best.

Most anglers who own efficient tackle and know how to use it prefer tapered leaders and usually are rather fussy about how they are made up. These men may be smirked at by fishermen who favor elementary methods and who therefore think level leaders or more simply tapered ones are just as good. The latter maintain that shorter leaders work as well as longer ones and that the weight of the fly will straighten them out and overcome the lack of tapering. Those who follow this line of thought believe that there has been too much trout-fishing leader theory applied to salmon angling. Using level or too simply tapered leaders seems to be a lazy expedient, however, because it is quite obvious that properly tapered ones have greater advantages in fly presentation.

When rigging a rod, don't start by threading the leader through the guides. This is the hard way, and if you let go, the whole thing will slip back. Instead, double the line near its end and thread the doubled line through the guides, with the leader following along. When a foot or two of the doubled line has been pulled through the tip-top, just shake the rod to pop out the leader. This prevents the line from falling back through the guides, whether or not there is a leader on it. I learned this useful tip from two old friends, Stu Apte and Lefty Kreh, both of whom are at the very top of the big league in fly fishing and were pioneers in saltwater fly fishing decades ago.

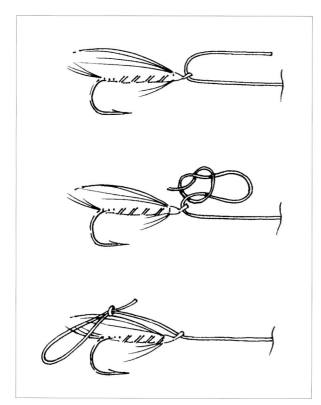

Figure 9. The turle knot.

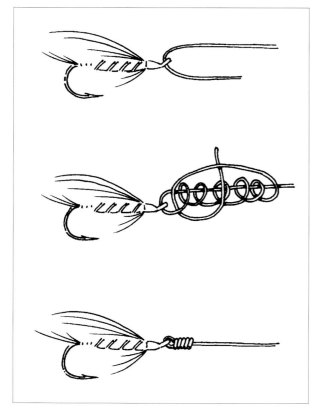

Figure 10. The improved clinch knot.

To tie the turle knot, thread the leader up (down on down-eyed hooks) through the eye of the hook and allow the fly to slide out of the way. Tie in an overhand knot at the very end of the leader. Make a slip noose in the end of the leader, and work the noose and the overhand knot together. Pass the noose over the fly and pull it tightly into position between the fly head and hook eye. Trim the end of the leader. The strength of this knot is about 80 percent that of the leader; to make the knot a bit stronger, use a double turn when forming the noose.

When a turle knot will not seat itself properly between the head of the fly and the eye of the hook, you'll have to use the improved clinch knot. It is tied by threading the leader through the eye of the hook and leaving about 6 inches at the end. Wrap the leader end around the standing leader five to eight turns, and push the end through the small loop at the eye of the hook. Then pass the leader end through the loop where the last wrap was made, and tighten the knot by pulling on both the hook and the standing end of leader. Moistening the knot before tightening it is sometimes helpful.

PLATE 13
A REPRESENTATIVE SELECTION OF ANTIQUE AND CONTEMPORARY HOOKS

#8/0 Dee Hook

#7/0 Round Bend Harrison Bartleet

#1 1/2 Harrison Celebrated Dublin Limerick   *#5/0 Blind Eye Au Lion D'Or*

#10 Harrison's Double Fly Hook

#2/0 Willis   *#6 Allcock Low-water Double*   *#6 Drury Treble*

#4 Sealey Low-water   *#1/0 Allcock Low-water*

#10/0 Mustad

#4 Wilson Dry Fly   *Partridge Single Salmon Sizes 12 to 5/0*

Hooks

Fish hooks have been vital food furnishers for centuries. Hooks were first mentioned in angling literature during the late fifteenth century, when they were made of needles, nails, or awls, depending on the size required. During the next century, two hooks were fastened together to create what we think of today as a "double." It is generally accepted that modern hooks were introduced about 1560 in Redditch, England, an important needle-manufacturing region.

Until just before the turn of the nineteenth century, hooks with metal eyes had not been perfected, and the salmon flies of that era were tied with eyes of twisted silkworm gut. Those that remain today are too weak in the eye to fish with and have become cherished collector's items that should be carefully preserved.

Traditional salmon hooks have a half-round parabolic bend and an upturned eye. These are referred to as hooks of the Limerick shape and are designed for superior strength. The best ones have a japanned black finish and are made with a returned eye rather than with the cheaper round eyes. One of the hooks used in modern salmon fishing is the bronzed Model Perfect trout fly hook, which has become equally popular, if not more so, in some regions, such as New Brunswick. This hook has a perfectly round bend, considered by many to be superior because it helps to prevent enlarging the hole of penetration when the salmon is fighting the fly.

These hooks sometimes are "kirbed" or offset in a reverse bend, or double-offset (offset both to the right and to the left), on the proven theory that these offsetting methods tend to pull the hook into a fish's jaw better than nonoffset designs do.

Kirbed and double-offset point hooks can be purchased that way or can be offset from straight bends with pliers. The August 1971 issue of *Trout and Salmon* reported on results of landing two hundred fish on each type of hook, for a total of six hundred salmon. The proportion of takes to landings was as follows:

Offset-point single hooks	78 percent
Double hooks	69 percent
Orthodox single hooks	62 percent

The penetration advantage of the offset point versus the orthodox one is obvious when one tries to pull each through something like the pages of a telephone book. Salmon anglers can get rather set in their ways and dislike changing from traditional hooks. Maybe we are missing something!

The maker's integrity is the best recommendation of quality in buying hooks. Because there are many fine points in hook manufacture, obtain the highest quality available. Some indications of quality such as modern heat-treating methods are not obvious even to experts. Improper heat treating will make hooks too brittle or too soft, causing them to either snap or straighten. Since japanned hooks are

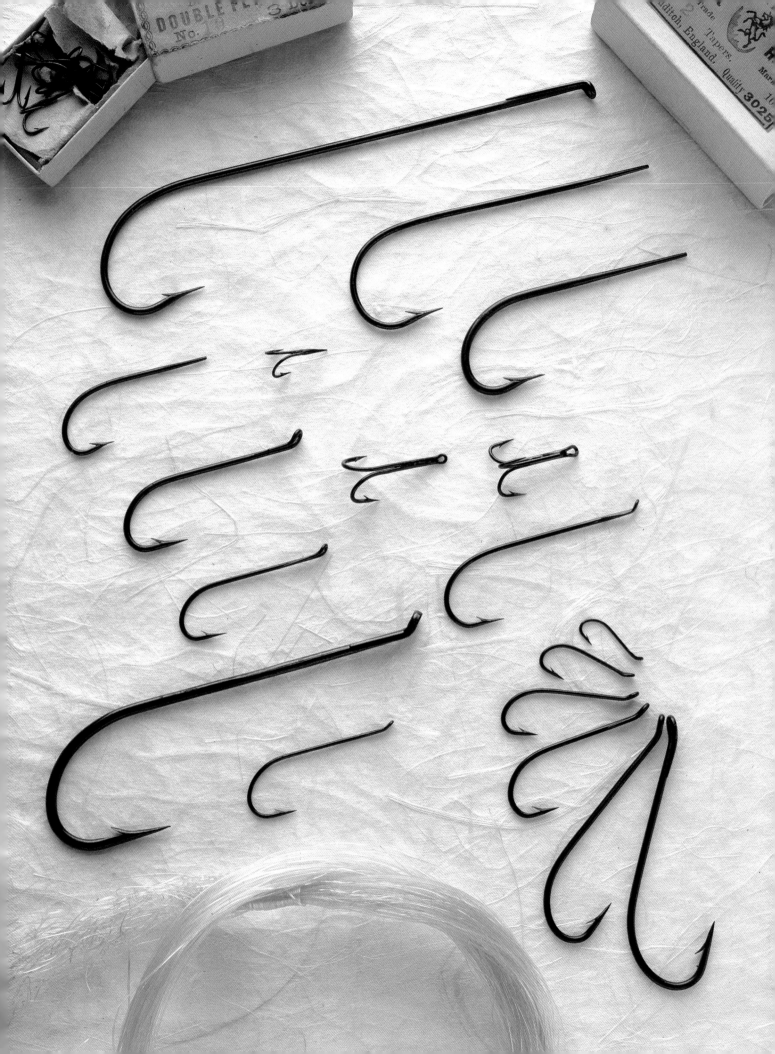

PLATE 14
CHARLIE DEFEO'S FLY WALLET

tumbled after barbs and points have been cut, prudent anglers sharpen them with a stone or, in the case of large hooks, with a small jeweler's file.

In addition to various patterns, there are several types of salmon hooks, of which we primarily are concerned with three: the low-water hook, the standard single hook, and the double hook, which is available in both standard and low-water weights. Long-shanked hooks also are used for streamers or bucktails and other types of patterns. In general, and within reason, the heavier the hook, the better it is, because heavier hooks are stronger hooks and tend to fish deeper.

Low-water dressings, usually occupying no more than the forward half of the shank, are very small in proportion to the hook and require a hook made with very light wire. This provides greater hooking and holding power when very small flies are needed.

The Wilson dry-fly hook, mentioned in some of the fly patterns, is a light-wire hook and basically is equivalent to a low-water hook. It is very satisfactory for salmon dry flies requiring a longer body, as well as for wet flies requiring hooks of this type. For short-bodied dry flies, the typical bronzed hook, such as the Model Perfect, is often used. Dry-fly hooks usually have a round bend.

The controversy regarding single hooks versus double hooks probably never will be settled, proponents being fairly equally divided between the two types.

One experienced angler says, "Double hooks provide sort of a keel to the fly and thus ride upright in the water and present the fly to the fish as it should be. With single hooks, you never can be sure. I believe there's more holding power, regardless of what some experts say about one of the hooks acting as a lever to work the other one loose. I have seen a lot more fish lost on singles than on doubles, all other things being equal. In several cases, I've had one of the hooks tear loose and the fish become hooked with the other before the fly got out of its mouth."

Another says: "It is not valid that the double hook will carry the fly deeper. Don't try to get the fly down by the weight of the hook. Use a line that will get the fly down, and dress the fly so that it will sink most readily. The crucial matter is how the fish takes the fly. Men who already fish double hooks undoubtedly will continue to do so. The newer anglers will fish them less often."

In my opinion, neither type of hook influences how the fly rides. That is decided by the dressing. Look at the fly down the hook's shank. If the wing is straight, the fly will ride straight. If the wing is tilted, even very slightly, it won't. The type of hook has little or nothing to do with its sinking ability, because that also depends on the amount of dressing. From my own experience, I am confident that double hooks hook and hold better than orthodox singles do, but perhaps not very much better. Anyway, I prefer doubles most of the time.

From the Old to the New in Salmon Flies

"Campfire"

We who enjoy collecting and fishing Atlantic salmon flies can learn much about how to select appropriate patterns for various conditions and how to use them properly if we know something of the ancient and honorable history of the most beautiful fishng flies in the world. It begins with the simple, expands to the sublime, and then reverts to the simple.

The first definitive book on fly fishing is the *Treatise of Fishing with an Angle,* printed in 1496 from an old manuscript dated 1406 or thereabouts. The origins and authorship of this treatise have been the subject of debate and conjecture among angling historians for almost five centuries. The controversy revolves around the mystique of Dame Juliana Berners, nun and noblewoman. Eminent angling historians of several generations have gone to painstaking efforts to verify or refute not only the authorship but the very existence of Dame Juliana. None has succeeded. Biographical notes referencing her life and lifestyle give credence to the fact of her existence, but none verifies her actual connection to the

"treatyse of fysshynge wyth an Angle." In spite of the scrutiny of historians, the legend of the "Dame of Dubbes" survives as a viable predecessor to all fine fish stories.

Ancient spelling and obsolete words make reading difficult, but the book has been translated into modern English by John McDonald in his masterly volume *The Origins of Angling,* published in 1963 by Doubleday and Company, Inc., of New York. This makes fascinating reading, because it describes the beginning of modern tackle and tactics, including rods, lines, hooks, and flies. Although dressing instructions leave much to interpretation, twelve seasonal flies are described, some evidently having been used for salmon. However drab and crude these flies may appear, their influence on modern favorites, such as the *March Brown,* is obvious.

The book tells how ancient hooks were made, from needles, large or small, and even from a shoemaker's awl. These were heated to remove the temper so that the barb could be notched with a knife and the point sharpened. After reheating, the hook

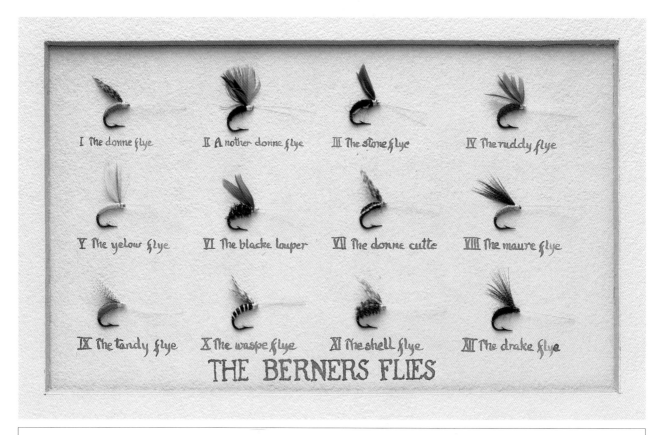

I The donne flye
II A nother donne flye
III The stone flye
IV The ruddy flye
V The yelow flye
VI The blacke louper
VII The donne cutte
VIII The maure flye
IX The tandy flye
X The waspe flye
XI The shell flye
XII The drake flye

THE BERNERS FLIES

PLATE 15
THE TREATISE TWELVE AS DRESSED BY BOB CAVANAGH

PLATE 16
CHETHAM TO CHAYTOR: FLY PATTERNS SPANNING TWO HUNDRED YEARS

Chetham's Gaudy Fly
dressed by Mark Waslick

Bainbridge's Summer Fly
dressed by Mark Waslick

Chaytor's White and Silver
dressed by Bob Warren

Bowlker's King's Fisher
dressed by Dorothy Douglass

Chetham's Horseleech
dressed by Maxwell MacPherson

was bent, then reheated and quenched to restore the temper. This process had to be repeated if the hook seemed too soft or too brittle. Hooks then were whipped to plaited horsehair "snoods," looped at their ends for attachment to lines. There are records of commercial hook making as early as 1560, in Redditch, England.

In 1725, this method gave way to the attachment of eyes made of loops of twisted silkworm gut. Metal-eyed salmon hooks were not known until 1845, when hook machinery was invented. Like the zipper and the wristwatch, it took time for metal-eyed hooks to become popular, and they weren't fully accepted until the turn of the century. Some anglers thought metal-eyed hooks sank too quickly or gave too stiff action between fly and leader.

Between 1496 and 1676, a few notable angling books were published. Izaak Walton wrote the *Compleat Angler* in 1676, but since he was a bait fisherman, he asked Charles Cotton and Col. Robert Venables to help him (in the fifth edition and hence) with the fly-fishing parts by combining their books, also published

in 1676, with his. In it, Venables says, "The salmon taketh the artificial fly very well." He describes fly types and recommends, "Use the most gaudy and Orient colors you can choose." Cotton explains fly-dressing methods of the day and gives dressings for sixty-eight patterns, mostly for trout and other fish, but some for salmon. Walton's book was revered mainly because of its style, a dialogue between "Piscator" and "Venator," teacher and pupil. Walton borrowed extensively from previous books, and just prior to 1956, the only known copy of W. Samuel's *The Arte of Angling* was discovered. Printed in 1577, it contained nearly identical dialogue between the same two contributors. Of course, Walton knew about it, because he "adopted" so much of it.

In 1700, a book by James Chetham describes the first named salmon fly, the *Horseleech,* with four to six wings and a contrasting body color embellished with silver and gold twist. In 1746, a book by Charles Bowlker mentions two salmon flies by name, the *Peacock Fly* and the *Dragon* fly. The first (hand-colored) plate of salmon flies, by George

Plate 17
Blacker Patterns, Dressed by Syd Glasso

No. 5: A Brown Fly

No. 8: A Gaudy Fly   *No. 13: The Ballyshannon*

No. 1: The Spirit Fly

No. 3: Another Spirit Fly

No. 1: The Spirit Fly

No. 1. I shall this The Spirit Fly, in consequence of its numerously-jointed body, its fanciful, florid, and delicate appearance. Its colours will be found most enticing to the fish, and is a sister fly to Ondine, in the "Book of Salmon," by "Ephemera."

The wings are made of six toppings, with a broad strip of wood duck on each side, a red Hymala crest feather at top, a cock of the rock feather, blue kingfisher feather at each side, a black head, and feelers of macaw. The body is made of joints of black orange floss, and a tip of gold tinsel at the tail, tail two smalltoppings, a tag of puce silk and ostrich, (it must be tied with very fine silk that the body may not be lumpy, but to show gradually taper from the tail to the head, and the hackle to be stripped at one side to roll even), and at each joint a scarlet hackle with a tip of gold tinsel under each joint, to make it lively looking. There is a purple hackle, or very dark blue, struck round the shoulder. The size of the book is No. 6 or 7. Salmon, B or B B.

No. 3: Another Spirit Fly

No. 3. This is another of the Spirit Flies that kill so well in the rivers of Ireland and Scotland, at high water, particularly the Spey and Tweed. The wings are made of the following mixtures of feathers, each side of the wings to be alike: Brown mallard, bustard and wood-duck; a topping, scarlet macaw, teal, golden pheasant neck feather, a strip of yellow macaw, and feelers of blue yellow tail; a head of black ostrich; the tail to be a topping, mixed with green and red parrot tail; the body is composed of joints, first a tip of silver, a tag of morone floss, a tag of black, a joint of brown, green and brown-red hackle, puce and red, green and yellow, blue and orange, with a tip of gold tinsel at each joint, a very small red hackle, and two red toucan feathers round the shoulder, and blue kingfisher's feather on each side of the wings. The hook No. 6, and No. 10 for Grilse.

No. 5: A Brown Fly

No. 5. A brown fly, a general favorite among the "old ones," on every salmon river in Ireland and Scotland, particularly the latter, and in rivers a good way up from the sea, on a dark day, with a good breeze blowing up the stream. The following fly, No. 6, may be used in a similar manner. The wings are made of the golden pheasant tail that has the long clouded bar in the feather, rather full, and two rather broad strips of light brown white-tipped turkey tail feather at each side; a good size peacock harl head, and feelers of scarlet macaw feather; tipped at the tail with gold tinsel—the tail a small bright topping, and a tag of gold-colour floss

silk; the body is made of cinnamon, or yellow-brown pig hair or mohair, ribbed with double silver twist; over the body roll a real brown red cock's hackle, and round the throttle roll on a bright red-brown small-spotted grouse hackle, or a brown mottled feather of the hen Argus pheasant's neck or back.

No. 8: A Gaudy Fly

No. 8 is a beautiful specimen of a gaudy fly. The wings, which are finely mixed of rich feathers are made of the following sorts:— orange, yellow, and blue macaw body feathers, three strips of each; teal bustard, and golden pheasant neck feathers broken in strips; silver pheasant tail, light brown golden pheasant tail feather, and a topping over all a little longer; a peacock harl head, and blue and yellow feelers. The body is formed in three joints, a tip of gold twist at the tail, a tag of peacock harl, and a bright small topping for tail; first, a joint of yellow floss, a joint of peacock, and two feathers of the red-tipped feather of the crest of the cock of the rock tied short above the harl and ribbed with gold; the next is a blue floss silk joint ribbed with gold, a peacock harl rolled on close, and two feathers of the crest of the cock of the rock tied close above it; and the third is an orange floss silk joint, a peacock harl tag, and ribbed with gold, two of the red-tipped feathers tied on close as above, and a blue jay round the shoulder. No. 8 hook on B. This is a famous grilse fly.

No. 13: The Ballyshannon

There is another good killer which I will here describe:— body yellow brown mohair, ribbed with silver twist, puce tag, topping for tail with a little scarlet ibis mixed, a good dyed yellow hackle rolled over the body, and a scarlet hackle round the head; the wings are four toppings with strips of summer duck, a sprig or two of pheasant tail and neck, a strip of dyed white tipped turkey tail, and a sprig of guinea hen and glede or kite tail, the tailfeather of the hen hymalean pheasant is as good as what is called in Scotland "salmon tail glede," and the topping or crest of the cock bird which is a transparent scarlet colour, and like a topping of the golden pheasant stands over all; blue kingfisher each side, and scarlet macaw feelers, black ostrich head, hook No. 9 or 8 in high water. This is a magnificent specimen of a salmon fly, and cannot be made properly at a small expense, either by the amateur himself who buys his foreign feathers, or by the fly-maker who get his bread by it. The three flies in the plates Nos. 1, 2, and 3, will be found to do the work well. With this one, see the gaudy jointed fly in the plate, with "picker" at top.

Instructions from *Blacker's Art of Fly Making,* William Blacker, London 1855.

Plate 18
Patterns by John Popkin Traherne

1   *Fra Diavolo*

dressed by Paul Schmookler

Tag	Silver tinsel and light yellow silk
Tail	A topping
Butt	Black herl
Body	In two sections as shown. The first being red-orange silk, ribbed with silver tinsel (oval), having four Indian crow's feathers, two above and two below, placed back to back, and butted as before. The second or lower part, light blue silk ribbed with silver tinsel (flat) and silver lace, having a light blue hackle along it
Throat	Yellow macaw
Wings	Two strips black turkey with white tips, Amherst pheasant, red macaw and swan dyed green macaw
Sides	Summer duck and jungle fowl
Horns	Blue macaw, and a couple of toppings over
Cheeks	Chatterer

Note: The fly shown is a variation of Traherne's pattern by Paul Shmookler. In it there is no white-tip turkey and the throat is orange hackle instead of yellow macaw.

2   *Lang Syne*

dressed by Mark Waslick

Tag	Silver twist, and golden topping coloured silk
Tail	A topping and two red crow
Body	In four equal sections—the first two of orange floss silk the same shade as the tippets, with two jay points top and bottom in each as shown and butted as before; the other two of red claret silk with jungle fowl instead of jay, and butted
Ribbed	Silver tinsel
Wings	Four Amherst pheasant tippets dyed a bright green
Cheeks	Two golden tippets extended, summer duck, and blue chatterer. Golden topping over
Horns	Blue macaw
Head	Black herl

3   *Golden Butterfly*

dressed by Michael Radencich

Tag	Silver twist, and light blue silk the same colour as a light blue chatterer
Tail	A topping
Butt	Black herl
Body	In five equal divisions, each terminating with a black herl butt. There are four tippets; two (back to back) tied in top and bottom of every section as illustrated over the golden floss which, silk is the same shade as the golden toppings
Ribbed	Oval tinsel
Throat	Blue chatterer feather (as shown)
Wings	Five or six toppings, according to size of hook
Cheeks	Blue chatterer
Horns	Blue macaw
Head	Black herl

4   *Chatterer*

dressed by Charlie Chute

Tag	Silver twist and light orange floss (tippet colour)
Tail	Topping
Butt	Black herl
Body	Two turns of purple silk, making headway for the chatterer's feathers closely packed and covering the whole of the body. A hook this size taking perhaps fifty or sixty
Throat	Gallina
Wings	Four red crows, in pairs, red points of the former extended, and one jay feather on either side. Toppings over
Cheeks	Blue chatterer
Horns	Blue macaw
Head	Black herl

5   *Nelly Bly*

dressed by Michael Radencich

Tag	Silver twist and green silk (the same shade as the green feather of the Macaw)
Tail	Topping
Butt	Black herl
Body	In four equal divisions of floss silk: No. 1, the same colour as the two feathers of the Red Crow, which are above and below, and butted with black herl, as also is each of the rest. No. 2, the silk is the same blue as the four Jays. The best idea I can offer of No. 3 is that the silk is the same in tone as that of a green Parrot and a few shades darker than the tag; and No. 4 of magenta silk, each having four Jungle Cock
Ribbed	Flat silver tinsel
Wings	Two red orange Macaw feathers, with one Jay feather on either side, as illlustrated, which are from the over-growth, having blue on both sides of the shaft; two golden toppings above
Horns	Blue Macaw
Head	Black herl

Patterns according to John Popkin Traherne and recorded by George Kelson.

1	
	4
2	
	5
3	

PLATE 20
ANTIQUE POPHAM, GIVEN TO THE
AUTHOR BY MEGAN BOYD

any of the trout flies, where salmon are plenty." (The first edition was written in 1747 by Richard and Charles Bowlker, but all later editions were written by Charles only.)

In 1842, William Blacker's *Art of Angling* (revised as *Blacker's Art of Fly Making* in 1843 and 1855) combined practicality with extravagance and established a principal standard in the style and character of salmon flies. Blacker's book in any edition is a cherished angling classic. His many "extravagant" patterns challenge even the greatest artists to properly reproduce these "jewels among salmon flies." This era featured intense competition between the local plain and simple patterns and the Irish (and other) gaudy and complicated ones. In every instance, the latter won.

Then, in the last half of the nineteenth century, everything seemed to break loose with the development of flies riotous with color and intricate detail. First in British publications (*The Fishing Gazette* and *Land and Water*), George Kelson served as scribe for Maj. John Popkin Traherne (1826-1901), described by Kelson as a "master of infinite elaboration." Although Kelson transcribed Traherne's patterns, he did not always credit them as such, and many remain relatively obscure. Those that are known exhibit the epitome of Victorian opulence and are a celebration of the use of materials available during this period. Traherne's dressings are some of the most intricate and brilliant patterns known today.

George Mortimer Kelson (1836–1920) personifies the peak of the golden age of the Atlantic salmon fly. His definitive book, *The Salmon Fly* (1895), is one of the most important works on the subject. Its 510 pages contain eight chapters on salmon flies and tackle, including about three hundred clearly described fly patterns of the time, of which fifty-two are shown in eight stone lithographed color plates.

Kelson and his book brought order and system (particularly as pertains to wing types) to the classification of salmon flies and the techniques of their dressings. Kelson has been called the "grand old man of salmon fishing" and the "high priest of the salmon fly," but he was a highly controversial figure who was

PLATE 19
THE SILVER DOCTOR
DRESSED BY TED GODFREY

photograph from *The Salmon Fly* by George Kelson

Bainbidge, appeared in 1816. It showed the *Spring Fly,* the *Quaker Fly,* the *Gaudy Fly,* the *Summer Fly,* and the *Wasp Fly.* Popular flies were generally somber patterns until the closing years of the century. Wings usually were of turkey feathers from birds raised for the purpose. These flies were known as the *Dun Turkey, Gray Turkey,* and so forth.

In the second edition of *The Art of Angling* (1774), Charles Bowlker says, "It is needless to treat of any more salmon flies; for salmon flies, in general, are made just as the painter pleases. Salmon, being fond of anything that is gaudy . . . will rise at almost

as maligned as he was applauded. His reputation suffered irreparable damage with the publicized feud he had with his editor and former friend and fishing companion, R. B. Marston, who took exception to the credit Kelson readily claimed or misappropriated regarding the origins of numerous patterns and the techniques used to tie them. Regardless of disputes and evidence of character flaws, one thing is clear: Kelson's masterful work, *The Salmon Fly,* remains a standard fly-tying reference and a cherished collector's classic. Favoring the simpler *Summer* patterns, Kelson was not a proponent of actually using many of the complicated dressings and regarded them as historical more than practical. On this point I might concur; although I am appreciative of the history and details of the handsome classics, I tend to use their hairwing counterparts when on the stream.

Kelson shared his father's belief that salmon most avidly took moths or butterflies, and the gaudy patterns of his era reflected this. Famous ones, still in use, include the *Thunder and Lightning, Green Highlander, Black Dose,* and the *Blue, Silver, Black, White, Red,* and *Helmsdale Doctors.* He was one of the first writers to give detailed instructions and to offer a system for tying salmon flies. These are nearly identical in style or shape, and they feature mixed (married) wing components, compound (built) wings, and often several butts with veilings of toucan, as in the *Jock Scott* (when properly dressed), or Indian crow, as in the very fancy *Popham.*

The developing salmon fly reached a burgeoning intensity during the days of Queen Victoria (1819-1901), ruler of the United Kingdom, empress of India (from 1876), and monarch of other lands beyond the seas. These were the days when British warships and merchantmen roamed the oceans, and when British regiments guarded the queen's domains in far-flung places.

British officers, hunting and trading in these exotic regions, sent home the skins of beautiful birds so that the gillies and their families could while away dreary winter evenings dressing flies for their lords and masters to use when they returned home. It is not surprising that intense competition rapidly spread to see who could create the most gorgeous and fruitful patterns.

In addition to the feathers of birds of almost every imaginable exotic species, these patterns were composed of mohair, camlet, and Berlin wools; chenille; fur from seal, rabbit, monkey, pig, and other animals; gold beater's skin; threads and silks of every conceivable color, embossed with gold and silver; round, oval, and flat tinsels; wire; and lace. Many of the fur and feathers were dyed in a complexity of shades and colors. These components, both common and exotic, were readily available to both professional and amateur tackle dealers and fly dressers. Today, many of the feathers called for in the grand old patterns are difficult to find, expensive, or even illegal, but substitutes can work just as well.

The classic patterns can be divided into two main groups. One is those dressed to hook salmon—which, after all, is really what this is all about. This group is composed of many popular favorites still used today: the *Doctors,* the *Rangers, Thunder and Lightning, Green Highlander,* and *Silver*

31

✠ SALMON-FLIES ✠

We are prepared to make the finest quality of Salmon-Flies. and shall take pleasure in giving careful attention to orders with which we may be favored.   Flies not on list can be made to order from sample.

PRICES, according to pattern, ... $3.co to $7.50 per dozen.

Baron.	Dirty Orange.	May Queen.
Beaufort Moth.	Dunkeld.	Nepenthian.
Benchill.	Durham Range.	Parson.
Black Dose.	Dusty Miller.	Phœbus.
Black Fairy.	Fairy.	Popham.
Black Ranger.	Fiery Brown.	Prince Wm. of Orange.
Blue and Brown.	Gitana.	Sailor.
Britannia.	Gordon.	Silver Doctor.
Brown Eagle.	Greenwell.	Silver Grey.
Brown Fairy.	Highlander.	Spey Dog.
Butcher.	Hill Fly.	Taile's Fancy.
Captain.	Harlequin.	Thunder and Lightning.
Champion.	Infallible.	Toppy.
Childers.	Jock Scott.	Wasp.
Colonel.	Lion.	White Miller.
Curtis.	MacNicoll.	Wilkenson.
Dawson.		

"The flies used for Salmon are more numerous and varied than those used for trout, and quite as uncertain and puzzling to those who use them.   *   *   *   There are, however, standard flies which experience has shown to be generally more 'taking' than others, and for this sufficient reason are always found in salmon angler's fly books; but no expert deems any fly, or any dozen flies, invariably adapted to all waters and all conditions of wind and weather. Without multiplying varieties indefinitely, it is yet necessary to have an 'assortment,' gaudy and sombre, large and small, but plenty of them.   It is very unpleasant to run short when you are two or three hundred miles away from the shop.' Those who have had any considerable experience know just what they want, and the only safe thing for the novice do do, when ready to lay in his stock, is to seek advice of some one who knows something of what may be required in the waters to be visited."—GEO. DAWSON.

Postage Prepaid on Flies.

Pre-1890 list of salmon flies for sale

PLATE 22
ORIGINAL EXHIBITION PATTERNS

1 *Impeyan Constellation*

dressed by Howard Biffer

Tag	Yellow silk floss followed by green silk floss and divided by fine blue-green oval tinsel
Tail	Golden pheasant crest
Butt	Black ostrich herl
Under-body	Green silk floss
Body	Tapered and symmetric layers of monal pheasant neck feathers
Throat	Green followed by blue hackle followed by black hackle
Wing	A pair of Lady Amherst pheasant tippet feathers dyed dark green topped by a pair of bright teal feathers over which are fibers of muscovy, speckled bustard, and red and lavender swan
Cheeks	Iridescent green feather from the upper body, topped by a red-tipped iridescent blue from the neck of a sunbird, topped by riflebird
Topping	Golden pheasant crest
Head	Black

2 *Stinger*

dressed by Dorothy Douglass

Tag	Fine oval gold tinsel, extra long, and lavender floss
Tail	Two golden pheasant crest feathers and two small jungle cock, back to back
Butt	Black ostrich herl, orange peacock herl and black ostrich herl
Body	In two equal parts: rear, olive green floss, veiled above and below with ring-necked pheasant back feather dyed olive green, butted as above; front half, lavender floss
Ribbing	Rear: medium oval gold tinsel and black silk thread; front: oval gold tinsel
Hackle	Ring-necked pheasant flank feather, dyed orange
Wing	Underwing: three pairs of metallic green feathers of Lady Amherst pheasant, staggered; married strands of black (1), olive green (3), black (1), orange (3), black (1), lavender (2), black (2), lavender (2), black (1), orange (3), black (1), olive green (3), black (1)
Sides	Gold peacock body feather
Cheeks	Jungle cock
Topping	Golden pheasant crest
Head	Black

3 *Opera*

dressed by Megan Boyd

Tag	Fine oval silver tinsel and scarlet floss
Tail	Golden pheasant crest over which are slips of red and green goose
Butt	White ostrich herl
Body	Flat gold tinsel
Ribbing	Green floss
Hackle	Orange from the third turn
Throat	Orange hackle
Wing	Two jungle cock, back to back, over which are two pairs of golden pheasant tippets, the outside pair shorter and to the second bar of the inner feather. Over this is a strip of barred wood duck.
Topping	Golden pheasant crest
Head	Black

4 *Prince Philip*

dressed by Jimmy Younger

Tag	Fine oval gold tinsel and light blue silk floss
Tail	Golden pheasant crest, over which are two small sections of light blue and red swan about half as long as the topping
Butt	White ostrich herl
Body	Royal purple silk floss, or wool
Ribbing	Flat gold tinsel, followed by heavy gold twist
Hackle	A claret cock's hackle palmered ahead of ribbing over front half of body
Throat	A few turns of a magenta hackle, forward of which are a few turns of a light blue hackle
Wing	Two strips of white-tipped brown mottled turkey, back to back, over which on each side are married strips of blue and black swan, set low, over which are broad strips of Amherst pheasant tail feather, set high, over which are strips of brown turkey or mallard set mid-wing
Topping	Golden pheasant crest
Shoulders	Jungle cock, of moderate length
Cheeks	Kingfisher, over the jungle cock, and shorter
Head	Black

5 *Deutschland*

dressed by Wilhelm Gruber

Tag	Oval gold tinsel and lime green floss
Tail	Golden pheasant crest veiled with barred wood duck
Butt	Yellow ostrich herl
Body	In three equal sections of embossed silver tinsel ribbed with oval gold tinsel. The first section is veiled with yellow hackle below and butted with red ostrich herl; the second section is veiled with claret hackle and butted witih black ostrich.
Throat	Black hackle
Wing	White tipped turkey over which are married slips of speckled bustard, yellow, red and black goose, and speckled bustard followed by bronze mallard
Sides	Jungle cock
Cheeks	Jay
Topping	Golden pheasant crest
Horns	Scarlet macaw
Head	Black

6 *Covent Garden*

dressed by Megan Boyd

Tag	Fine oval gold tinsel and golden yellow floss
Tail	Golden pheasant crest, over which are slips of black and yellow goose
Butt	Black ostrich herl
Body	Rear half: lilac-pink floss; forward half: black floss ribbed with oval silver tinsel
Throat	Black hackle followed by yellow
Wing	Married slips of black, lilac-pink, black, yellow, and Lady Amherst pheasant tail. Over this is a strip of barred wood duck
Horns	Red and blue macaw
Topping	Two golden pheasant crest feathers
Head	Black

```
      1
  2     3
          4
  5
          6
```

PLATE 23
ORIGINAL EXHIBITION PATTERNS

1	*Emerald Isle*

dressed by Charles Chute

Tag	Oval gold tinsel and golden silk
Tail	Golden pheasant crest veiled with peacock sword; this is veiled on either side with Indian crow, back to back
Butt	Scarlet wool
Body	In two equal sections: rear section, black silk ribbed with fine oval gold tinsel; a mid-body butt of scarlet wool veiled above and below with golden bird of paradise; the forward section, green silk ribbed with a strand of black silk on either side of which is a ribbing of fine oval gold tinsel
Throat	Long, fine black hackle
Wings	Long pair of quetzal feathers over which is another, shorter pair of quetzal feathers
Sides	Jungle cock
Cheeks	Indian crow and riflebird
Topping	Golden pheasant crest
Horns	Scarlet macaw
Head	Black

2	*Bronze Monarch*

dressed by Michael Radencich

Tag	Flat gold tinsel
Tail	Golden pheasant crest
Butt	Peacock herl
Body	In three equal sections of yellow, orange and red silk ribbed with fine silver tinsel. At each section above and below is a pair of impeyan pheasant feathers, back to back, each pair slightly graduating in length with a topping tied in over each pair, top and bottom. The bottom feather pairs and toppings should be very slightly shorter than the ones above. Each division is butted with peacock herl
Head	Peacock herl

3	*Pam*

dressed by Mark Waslick

Tag	Fine silver tinsel and purple-magenta silk
Tail	Golden pheasant crest and mot-mot
Butt	Black ostrich herl
Body	In three sections: the first section, light blue silk ribbed with fine silver tinsel and veiled top and bottom with jungle cock, back to back; the second section, green silk ribbed with fine silver tinsel and veiled top and bottom with jungle cock, back to back; the third section, claret silk ribbed with fine silver tinsel
Throat	Indian crow, back to back, and pitta, shorter
Wing	Peacock pheasant and jacamar
Cheeks	Indian crow and pitae
Topping	Two golden pheasant crest feathers
Head	Black ostrich herl

1

2

3

Gray. The other is those dressed as exhibition flies, sometimes called "vanity patterns," often composed of rare feathers and complex design. Although these patterns weren't necessarily intended to hook salmon, many of them did. To put things into perspective, in this country around the turn of the century a number of the most complicated patterns, including John Traherne's, were offered for sale in fly shops by the dozen for a little more than sixty cents each.

Another purpose of the more intricate patterns was to demonstrate prowess in fly dressing, and many of them were named for people their originators wanted to honor. Regardless of whether the flies were intended to catch fish or to catch the favor of *Homo sapiens,* nowadays they catch collectors, who treasure them for their history, their beauty, and their intricate construction.

One cannot dismiss the butterfly patterns of the Victorian era without paying tribute to the noted gillie Jock Scott, who originated the most successful perennial favorite of all time: the beautiful classic that bears his name and, ironically, that of his employer, Lord John Scott. Experience and legend tell us that the *Jock Scott* is a practical pattern as well as an honorary one.

Many accounts of Jock Scott, both the man and the fly, have appeared in angling literature, and the challenge, more than a century and a half later, is trying to separate fact from fancy. The most popular version, the "boat to Norway theory," was initially written by Charles H. Alston in the *Fishing Gazette* in 1895 and was subsequently repeated by Sir Herbert Maxwell in his 1898 book, *Salmon and Sea Trout.* Also mentioned by Lee Wulff in *The Atlantic Salmon,* this account dates the origin of the fly as

PLATE 24
THE JOCK SCOTT

dressed by Ted Kantner

"from a strand of which on one occasion a salmon fly was made, now celebrated amongst fishermen under the name of 'Jock Scott' "

1845. Gillie Jock Scott, accompanying his master Lord Scott on a stormy voyage to Norway, "to wile away the tedium . . . occupied himself with dressing flies for the approaching campaign; one result of his labours was the fly which has made his name famous among salmon fishers the world over."

Jock Scott's obituary, written in February 1893 under the pen name of Punt Gun, states, "It was while acting as fisherman to Lord John at Mackerston in 1850 that he set himself to devise something new and taking; the Jock Scott was the result." It has been generally accepted that the fly remained nameless for several years until Jock took it to John Forest of Kelso after his master's death. At that time, John Forest "thereupon named it after the inventor and, as 'Jock Scott,' it will remain while salmon swim in the Tweed."

The legend of the pedigree of this famous fly continues with a fascinating account of its origin by R. T. Simpson in a publication titled *The Collection of*

Wroth Silver. First published in 1884, expanded in 1910, and reprinted in 1927, it is a detailed chronicle of the history and customs of "The Lordship of the Hundred" (an old English term used before areas were split into parishes and districts) of Knightlow County, Waswick—and the only account of the fly I know of written before Jock Scott's death in 1893. This little volume states that "Lord John Scott greatly endeared himself to rich and poor alike on his estates and in the neighbourhood, as the monument to him at Dunchurch testifies. His tastes induced him to revive and continue the old customs and ceremonies connected with the estate, and he and Lady John repeatedly attended the collection of Wroth Silver, and did much to ensure the continuance of its observance." Hence, we can deduce that "Wroth Silver" was a ceremony and not a service in need of protection from tarnishing. Furthering the lore, and in its only reference to angling, Simpson states, "Lady John at the time of her marriage was a noted beauty, and had glorious Titian hair, from a strand of which on one occasion a salmon fly was made, now celebrated amongst fishermen under the name of 'Jock Scott' fly, an enlarged model of which was presented by the writer, to the Reading Room at Dunchurch, given by her Ladyship while resident at Cawston."

No mention is made of the gillie Jock, and there is no further description of the fly; however, it is fun to speculate that Lord Scott might have requested that this fly be dressed to honor his bride and that the gillie accommodated the request. Simpson's phrase "on one occasion a salmon fly was made" could indicate that the hair episode was brief and confined largely to the Scott family. Whether Jock adapted his pattern before or after the celebration of the "glorious Titian hair" is not possible to determine. It does seem logical, however, that the body of the fly would be the most obvious place to incorporate a strand of hair. Body descriptions in dressings written for the *Jock Scott* differ among resources, including Francis, Kelson, and Pryce-Tannatt, and all accounts of the fly (except Simpson's) were written after the death of both Lord Scott and his gillie, Jock. Some call for the rear half of the body to be gold, yellow, or buttercup silk—all shades that can vary from golden yellow to golden orange to golden red. This charming addition to the lore of such an important fly intrigued me enough to try to substantiate it. I studied a few dozen early *Jock Scotts* in my collection and found that in several the rear half of the body was orange, or more so than yellow.

The use of hair in fly bodies is rare, but not unknown. For example, Kelson caused himself trouble by claiming to have originated the *Little Inky Boy,* an almost forgotten pattern with a body of black horse hair, closely coiled. James Wright's *Garry* or *Yellow Dog* and the *Collie Dog* are examples requiring canine assistance, and Megan Boyd reported to me that she had been requested to dress a fly using a portion of a customer's ample eyebrow! At any rate, the lore continues and will perpetuate itself. We cannot, at this point, determine if the *Jock Scott* was in fact originated in 1845 or in 1850, if the body was originally more or less than orange, and if, indeed, the young water bailiff was inspired by the glorious tresses of Lady Scott. By chance or by design, however, Jock Scott originated a fly Kelson rightfully referenced as "the utmost triumph in harmony and proportion." The choice of the lore is left to the reader.

Mention should be made of the many fine angling references of the 1800s. Since this book is about Atlantic salmon fishing and its flies, they are not included here, but their omission is by no means a reflection of their importance. Many are discussed in some detail in my book *The Art of the Atlantic Salmon Fly,* and some are also included in the Bibliography of this book. In addition to others too numerous to list, authors such as Francis, Hale, and Maxwell are all worthy company. Those wishing to pursue the academic side of angling will find it rewarding to explore its invaluable literature.

When styles of most any sort seem to be reaching their peak, the pendulum swings the other way. The change in outlook from the sublime to the sensible began around the turn of the century, and the return to simplicity in salmon flies had ups and downs that still exist into the present day. We enjoy collecting, admiring, and often using exotic and complicated patterns, even though most of us know full well that simpler ones are as useful for enticing salmon, and perhaps even more so.

In the early part of the twentieth century, two men in particular were responsible for the developing road to simplicity. They were A. H. Chaytor, author of *Letters to a Salmon Fisher's Sons* (1910), and Ernest M. Crosfield, who wrote articles for magazines under the pen name of Poacher.

Chaytor's return to simplicity bordered on the parsimonious, even to the extent of advocating, on occasion, the use of a bare, lacquered hook. Lacking

Baker
dressed by Robert Hibbitts

Namsen
dressed by Larry Borders

Goldfinch
dressed by Larry Borders

Colonel
dressed by Paul Phinney

Black and Teal
dressed by Larry Borders

Beauly Snow Fly
dressed by Larry Borders

Laxford
dressed by Larry Borders

Sir Richard
dressed by Larry Borders

Baker

Another good general fly; dressed small it is a standard fly on the Dovey. Tag, gold twist and lightish blue floss; tail, a topg.; but, black herl; body, three turns of golden-cold. floss, dark orange, light blue, and red pig, broadish gold tinsel; medium red claret hackle, gallina at shoulder, with light blue over it; under wing, two gd. pht. tipt., springs of gd. pht. tail, bust., peack., red, bright green, and blue and yellow springs of swan over; the macaw ribs; black head.

Black and Teal

Tag, s. tt. and golden floss; tail, one tg.; blk. hl.; body, two turns of orange floss, the rest black (either floss, horsehair, mor., or unlaid sewing silk); broadish s. tin.; black hackle over three parts of the body; gallina (the dark feather with the large round spots, not the small speckled grey) on the shoulder; wing, doubled junk. with tg. over them, and two good sized teal, or the small feather of the black partridge, one on either shoulder to form a body to the wing; head, g. td. This is my own pattern of dressing this fly, and a very good one I consider it to be. The fly is a first-rate general fly, and should be kept of all sizes, as it will kill large lake and river trout or sea trout, as well as salmon, if regulated in size. The smaller patterns may be made with single junk. feathers, a trifle more teal being added. It is one of the best flies that can be used on the Spey. Some persons, however, dress it purely with a teal wing; it is good anyhow.

Colonel

There are two uniforms which the colonel rejoices in; the one a bright gold or yellow, and the other a red gold, or orange. Tag, g. tt. and two turns of bright yellow floss; tail, red and yellow sprigs mixed with gallina, and a g. pt. tg.; no but; body, yellow floss half-way up, and then orange pig's wool; over this is ribbed side by side, g. tt. and tin., and bk. floss (a bit of unravelled coarse sewing silk does better)—first the tt., then the tin., then the bk. silk; yellow hackle from tail to head, but, hackle at shoulder; under wing, g. pt. tipt., two feathers shortish; on either side of these strips of bust. and arg. pt. (the dark speckled feather); fibres of yellow throws in here and there, and over all a g. pt. tg. with blue macaw ribs; black head. For the orange variety read orange for yellow. Size various, from about No. 4 to 8.

Goldfinch

This is the handsomest and neatest specimen of a showy salmon fly I know of.... Tag, g. tin. and black floss; tail, g. pt. tg.; body, gold cold. floss, hackle, pale yellow, blue jay at shoulder, g. tin.; wing, composed entirely of tgs.; red macaw ribs and black head. Size 5 to 7.

Laxford

Tag, gold twist; tail, one topg.; body, gold-cold. floss silk; hackle, bright yellow; silver tinsel and gold twist; darkish blue hackle at shoulder; wing, a lump of peacock, over it sprigs of bustd and bastd. bustd., gold pht. topping over all, and blue macaw ribs; black head. Size 9 and 10.

PLATE 26
ERNEST CROSFIELD'S BROCKWEIR
AND BLACK SILK

Brockweir
dressed by Bob Warren

Black Silk
dressed by Mark Waslick

ple, he too believed that a fly's wings should show all the fibers given to it, because every fiber had a purpose and should fulfill it. Crosfield's flies and patterns exhibit an elegant simplicity, combining the beauty of the Victorian era with the innovative practicality of the twentieth century.

Following are two of Crosfield's patterns: the *Black Silk* and the *Brockweir*. Of the former, Crosfield wrote, "This is a very favourite pattern of mine, and with it I have caught fish in many rivers and in all heights and conditions of water, of course varying the size to suit the conditions. I look upon this pattern and the Thunder and Lightning as two of the best dark flies." Crosfield adds, "A single strip of mallard is one of the most difficult feathers to tie neatly on as a wing, but if two narrow strips are placed one on the top of the other before putting in position to tie in, they 'sit' without any difficulty."

The few examples and descriptions in the literature of these two flies differ, and we can only deduce that Crosfield, like Kelson and Pryce-Tannatt before him (commenting on the *Gordon* and the *Silver Wilkinson* respectively), might also have commented that no two people dress the fly alike.

Black Silk	
Tag	Fine gold or silver thread or wire
Tail	Golden pheasant crest and a few strands of tippet
Body	Black floss
Ribbing	Oval silver tinsel
Body	hackle Bright claret
Throat	Blue jay
Wing under-	
wing	Tippet in strands, the point of a golden pheasant breast feather and one or two golden pheasant crest feathers. Over this and on each side are six strands of golden pheasant tail fibers, two strands of Lady Amherst tail fibers and two narrow strips of dark mallard
Head	Black
	(Taverner)

Brockweir	
Tag	Fine round silver tinsel
Tail	Two small jungle cock feathers, back to back with golden pheasant crest (or Indian crow) between
Body	Claret seal's fur
Ribbing	Round silver twist
Body	
hackle	Optional, claret hackle
Throat	Guinea fowl
Wing	Strips of black and white turkey with bronze mallard over
Cheeks	Jungle cock

his predecessors' reverence for extravagance, Chaytor discarded all parts of the salmon fly for which he could find no reason—tags, tails, butts, and horns. His 285-page book is both practical and readable, and is recommended for even advanced modern anglers. The *White and Silver* shown in Plate 16 illustrates Chaytor's simplified approach.

This move to eliminate ornamentation that had no fishing value was taking place about fifteen years after Kelson's book was published—that is, about 1910. Examples of the new style include the *Blue Charm, Silver Blue,* and *Logie.*

Ernest Crosfield, acclaimed as the greatest salmon fly dresser of his day, was another disciple of simplicity. Crosfield followed some of Irish master tier Michael Rogan's (1833–1905) tenets; for exam-

Crosfield's flies characteristically feature economy of material, intentional translucence, and slimness of dressing. Most notable, perhaps, is his technique of tying in his wing materials in tiny groups, separating one from another by a turn or two of thread to aid in giving translucence to the fly and reducing bulk. This method is discussed at some length in both of Eric Taverner's fine books, *Salmon Fishing* (London, 1931) and *Fly Tying for Salmon* (London, 1942), and was Crosfield's legacy to future generations of tiers, including the revered Sydney Glasso (1906–1983), from Forks, Washington, who took his rightful turn in establishing a new tradition in fly-tying excellence.

For several years before Syd's death in 1983, I

was privileged to share a correspondence with him. His letters were humorous, self-effacing, and full of "good stuff." Mystified by the tiny heads of his flies, I asked him to divulge his secret. He replied, "I follow Ernest Crosfield's style, where much of the wing is tied in before the throat hackle, and therefore there is less material to tie in at the head. It is a legitimate construction, and what is good enough for Crosfield is certainly good enough for me. I think he was the greatest."

Syd never sold his flies for fear it would "spoil the fun" and usually turned down requests for flies. In 1981, Syd wrote: "Got a real winner about a month ago from a fellow in New Jersey which went as follows:

PLATE 27
SYD GLASSO

Dear Sir,

Please forward to me a dozen or so of your select salmon flies. I would like a couple for me to keep, the rest I will use for fishing.

Sincerely yours,

My reply, on the same sheet of paper went like this:

Dear Sir,

Mr. Glasso is hunting in Africa and from there goes to Egypt to fish for Nile perch in, of course, the Nile. With barbless hooks, he says, 'Who cares?' Hasn't tied a fly for months—says he has run out of glue. Anyway he doesn't sell flies—gives them to friends to hang on the wall. I am his housekeeper and believe me he needs one—feathers and beer cans all over hell and every morning moths coming in to look for his toucan feathers. Sorry.

Lola Willing

As we bartered back and forth, Syd admitted to "a pitiful weakness for Indian crow," saying, "It's good for my soul to just look at these feathers." In 1980, Syd wrote that "they're making the rivers more slippery nowadays"; however, in 1981, he graciously agreed to tie the Blacker patterns for *The Art of the Atlantic Salmon Fly.* In acknowledging this request, Syd said, "Thanks for your faith in my ability to do the Blacker flies. They make Kelson patterns look like child's play. Blacker was an expert in thinking up torture tactics!" We are privileged that Syd chose to dress these flies for others to appreciate; in doing so, he rejuvenated the honored tradition of Atlantic salmon flies, about which he commented, "Old flies, besides being truly beautiful, recall a time and a way of life that is gone for all time."

The exemplary style and elegance of Syd Glasso's full-dressed classics make each a treasure and an inspiration. He was a pioneer in the development of Scotland's Spey flies for fishing steelhead, adding to their somewhat somber appearance brilliant colors and his distinguished style. Possessing a modesty that excluded any ambition for fame, Syd was an innovative angler, ardent conservationist, and fine friend. He was a peer of the best who mastered the fine art of dressing Atlantic salmon flies—indeed, it is rare individuals such as he who are responsible for elevating the craft of tying flies to the art of dressing them.

The most lucid, concise, complete and authoritative book on dressing classic patterns is, in my esti-

PLATE 28
SALMON FLIES DRESSED BY
T. E. PRYCE-TANNATT

mation, Dr. T. E. Pryce-Tannatt's *How to Dress Salmon Flies* (1914). It tells nothing about tackle, tactics, or fly selection, but its precise instructions on fly dressing denote the best practices of the time. Historically, it is the final touch of Victorian splendor and about the last we will hear of the complicated classics, even though their influences extend into American salmon fly tying and fishing. Pryce-Tannatt's book, then, is a reversion from simplicity; the last gasp, so to speak, from Victorianism. Although Pryce-Tannatt may have been old-fashioned, his love for the beautiful classics is shared by many connoisseurs today. A Pryce-Tannatt statement sums up the very essence of salmon flies: "There is an indescribable something about a fly dressed by an expert amateur who is a practical salmon fisherman which the fly dressed by a non-angling professional fre-

William Cushner in his New York studio

quently lacks. I have heard this peculiar quality rather neatly referred to as 'soul.' The term is incomprehensible to the uninitiated, but is completely understood by the experienced man."

We regret the passing of the complicated classics as fishing flies partly on account of tradition; however, the resurgence of interest among fly tiers during the past few years is heartening. The renaissance of the classic salmon fly and its popularity as an art form may well result in its revival on the rivers, but more importantly, respect of the art of the Atlantic salmon fly assures its preservation. Joe Hubert, author of *Salmon—Salmon,* is one of the few modern anglers still wedded to the classics. His ambition is to hook a salmon on at least a hundred patterns

given in Kelson's *The Salmon Fly,* and he is well on his way to that goal! During the 1970s, my very good friend Bill Cushner shadow-boxed many of my favorite classics in protective frames. Often combining the flies with angling art or artifacts, Bill developed a style in framing flies that is often emulated today. The American Museum of Fly Fishing is fortunate to have in its collection a great many of these beautiful framings, and others can be seen at the museum Bill founded in Florence, Oregon.

on following pages
PLATES 29–32
BRITISH CLASSICS, DRESSED BY MEGAN BOYD
AND FRAMED BY WILLIAM CUSHNER, 1973

Black Ranger

Golden Eagle

Orange Parson

Colonel Bates

Thunder and Lightning

Durham Ranger

Benchill

Mar Lodge

Red Sandy

Sir Richard

Gray Eagle

Lord Migdale

Popham

Green Highlander

Silver Doctor

Blue Doctor

Salscraggie

Childers

Member

Wilkinson

Jock Scott

Glentana

Gordon

Torrish

Butcher

Balmoral

Dunt

Brora

Dusty Miller

The Thistle

Kate

Sutherland

Dunkeld

John Campbell

Beauly Snow Fly

Black Dose

Akroyd

Highland Gem

Silver Gray

Judge

PLATE 33
MOHAIR MANE FLY, CIRCA 1850
THE OWENMORE

PLATE 34
INNOVATIONS OF THE EARLY 1900S

Hardy's Demon
"Prismatic-Gut" Salmon Fly
Hardy's Aaro Fly (Silver Doctor)

After the early 1900s with tradition thriving, few advances in salmon flies were made in the British Isles. In North America, other innovations were taking place.

Not wishing to give up the classic favorites entirely, but also not wishing to bother with their complicated built wings and mixed wings, fly dressers began to look for a way to retain all or nearly all of the classics' components except for the multifeathered wing. In trying to maintain an effect similar to the original, simplification was one answer. Examples of these "reduced" classics are the *Black Dose* (reduced) and the *Dusty Miller* (reduced), which are from the bench of celebrated American angler and fly dresser Harry A. Darbee, of Livingston Manor, New York. These are pretty flies and relatively simple to put together. As adaptations, they have no standard pattern, and each dressing depends on whatever its dresser wants to put into it.

Each generation has its individuals whose contributions to the development of tying are unmistakable. Two such gentlemen of the mid-twentieth century are Preston Jennings and Charlie DeFeo.

Both were as prolific as they were innovative, and their flies exhibit a multitude of ingenious applications of color and materials.

As an academic, Jennings pursued a tireless study of the theories of reflection and refraction of light through a prism. His research into "how the fish see it" resulted in minnow imitations dressed in a spectrum of colors. In addition to using hackle tips in the wings of his flies, he also dyed golden pheasant crests brilliant colors and incorporated them in the wing. Keeping accurate accounts of his research, he amassed a tremendous collection of patterns, photography, paintings, and flies that is now housed at the American Museum of Fly Fishing.

PLATE 35
HARDY NORSK LURE, CIRCA 1920

PLATE 37
DARBEE REDUCED DRESSINGS

Dusty Miller

Black Dose

PLATE 36
HARDY "MONOPLANE" SERIES WITH
ARTICULATED HOOK, CIRCA 1935
THE AKROYD

The author at Bill Cushner's studio with Charlie DeFeo and Don Haynes

PLATE 38
SALMON FLIES, ORIGINATED AND DRESSED BY PRESTON JENNINGS

1   *Orange Stone #1 (Togoperla immarginata)*

Tag	Flat gold tinsel and yellow floss
Tail	Golden pheasant crest and Indian crow
Butt	Black ostsrich herl
Body	One-half orange floss, balance fiery brown seal's fur
Ribbing	Oval gold tinsel, over all
Hackle	Brown cock's hackle, from seal's fur
Throat	Guinea, dyed brown
Wing	Cinnamon turkey tail; red, orange, green and blue swan in order named from bottom up; wigeon and brown mallard
Sides	Jungle cock
Topping	Golden pheasant crest, dyed blue
Head	Black

2   *Iris Sedge #1 (Stenophylax)*

Tag	Flat gold tinsel and green floss
Tail	Golden pheasant tippet
Body	One quarter orange floss, balance orange seal's fur, both tied over flat gold tinsel
Ribbing	Oval gold tinsel, over all
Hackle	Claret cock's hackle, from seal's fur
Throat	Jay
Wing	White-tipped turkey tail; red, orange, green and blue swan; barred mandarin and brown mallard
Topping	Golden pheasant crest, dyed blue
Head	Black

3   *Medium Stone #2 (Neophasganophora ex perla capitata)*

Tag	Flat gold tinsel
Tail	Golden pheasant crest, dyed green, and kingfisher
Butt	Black wool
Body	One-half flat gold tinsel; one-half black seal's fur
Ribbing	Oval silver tinsel, over all
Hackle	Dark furnace cock's hackle
Wing	Cinnamon turkey tail; wigeon and brown mallard; golden pheasant crest, dyed red
Cheeks	Kingfisher
Topping	Golden pheasant crest
Head	Black

4   *Yellow Stone #1 (Acroneuria)*

Tag	Flat gold tinsel and pale yellow floss
Tail	Golden pheasant crest and Indian crow
Butt	Black wool
Body	One-half primrose floss; one-half a mixture of cinnamon and Naples yellow seal's fur; both tied over flat gold tinsel
Ribbing	Oval gold tinsel
Hackle	Ginger cock's hackle and brown partridge
Wing	Cinnamon turkey tail showing a light tip; red, yellow, green and blue swan; wigeon and brown mallard
Sides	Jungle cock, small
Topping	Golden pheasant crest, dyed blue
Head	Black

7   *Iris Spinner (mayfly of any genus: Hexangenia, Isoynchia, etc.)*

Tag	Flat green tinsel
Tail	Magenta and light blue cock's hackle
Butt	Blue swan
Body	Ruby red lacquer
Ribbing	Oval gold tinsel
Hackle	Magenta and light blue cock's hackle
Wing	Golden pheasant crest, dyed green; unbarred mandarin; golden pheasant crest, dyed blue, red and natural yellow, built from bottom in order named
Cheeks	Kingfisher
Head	Black

8   *Orange Stone (Togoperla immarginata)*

Tag	Flat gold tinsel and yellow floss
Tail	Golden pheasant crest
Body	One-half orange floss, balance fiery brown seal's fur
Ribbing	Oval gold tinsel, over all
Hackle	Brown cock's hackle
Wing	Cinnamon turkey tail, veiled with brown mallard
Head	Black

9   *Iris Sedge #2 (Stenophylax)*

Tag	Flat gold tinsel
Tail	Golden pheasant crest, dyed green, and kingfisher
Butt	Red wool
Body	One quarter flat silver tinsel, balance light blue seal's fur
Ribbing	Oval silver tinsel, over all
Hackle	Kingfisher blue cock's hackle from seal's fur
Throat	Magenta cock's hackle
Wing	White-tipped turkey tail; green, blue, white and red swan; barred mandarin and brown mallard
Cheeks	Kingfisher
Topping	Golden pheasant crest
Head	Black

10   *Yellow Stone #2 (Acroneuria)*

Tag	Flat gold tinsel
Tail	Golden pheasant crest, dyed green, and kingfisher
Butt	Black wool
Body	One-half flat gold tinsel; one-half a mixture of cinnamon and Naples yellow dyed seal's fur
Ribbing	Oval gold tinsel, over all
Hackle	Light furnace cock's hackle
Wing	Cinnamon turkey tail; wigeon and brown mallard
Cheeks	Kingfisher
Topping	Golden pheasant crest, dyed red, and natural golden pheasant crest
Head	Black

```
        1
      2   3   4
      5   6   7
     8  9  10
     11  12
         13
```

PLATE 38

Continued

11	*Blackstone #2 (a stone fly of the genus Hydroperla)*
Tag	Flat gold tinsel and golden yellow floss
Tail	Brown mallard and kingfisher
Butt	Black ostrich herl
Body	Black floss
Ribbing	Oval gold tinsel
Hackle	Natural black cock's hackle and guinea
Wing	Two red cock's hackles, veiled with swan dyed black; golden pheasant crest, dyed red
Topping	Golden pheasant crest
Head	Red

12	*Another Orange Stone (Togoperla immarginata)*
Tag	Flat silver tinsel
Tail	Golden pheasant crest, dyed green, and kingfisher
Butt	Black ostrich herl or wool
Body	One-half gray floss over flat silver tinsel; one-half black seal's fur
Ribbing	Oval silver tinsel, over all
Hackle	Black cock's hackle and guinea fowl
Wing	Gray turkey tail showing white tip; white and red swan; wigeon and brown mallard
Sides	Jungle cock
Topping	Golden pheasant crest, dyed red, and natural golden pheasant crest
Head	Black

13	*Murky Iris (Black-nosed Dace)*
Tag	Oval gold tinsel
Tail	Golden pheasant crest, dyed red
Body	Flat gold tinsel
Ribbing	Oval gold tinsel
Hackle	Cock's hackle, dyed vermillion
Wing	Two cock's hackles dyed vermillion, veiled with strips of red swan and narrow strips of orange swan; four strands of peacock herl over, green and blue swan on top of herl
Sides	Badger cock's hackle, fine striped
Cheeks	Jungle cock
Head	Black with a red ring

Patterns 5 and 6 are unidentified.

Preston Jennings

PLATE 39
THE YELLOWSTONE CREEPER AND DARK IRIS, ORIGINATED AND DRESSED BY PRESTON JENNINGS, WITH PAGES FROM HIS NOTEBOOKS

Yellowstone Creeper (creeper of the stone fly Perla capitata)	
Tag	Oval silver tinsel
Tail	Golden pheasant red breast feather
Body	One-half yellow floss; one-half black floss
Ribbing	Oval silver tinsel, over all
Hackle	Black cock's hackle and brown partridge
Wing cases	Jungle cock

Dark Iris (Black-nosed Dace)	
Tag	Flat gold tinsel
Tail	Golden pheasant crest, dyed red
Body	Crimson floss
Ribbing	Flat gold tinsel
Hackle	Cock's hackle, dyed crimson
Wing	Two crimson cock's hackles, veiled with red swan; four strands of peacock herl over; green swan, brown turkey and blue swan on top of herl
Sides	Light furnace cock's hackles
Cheeks	Jungle cock
Head	Black with a red band

Another first in the wings of flies was Charlie DeFeo's use of floss with combinations of hair and feathers. With the eye of an artist, Charlie DeFeo knew no bounds when applying materials to hooks —the hook was simply another palette. Seldom tying a fly the same way twice, Charlie is remembered for his style of tying rather than for actual patterns. Frequently he would add to the body of a standard pattern a wing of jungle cock body tips, thus creating the nymphs that many associate with him. His creative combinations of floss, feathers, hair, and hooks produced a multitude of unrecorded patterns and provide a superb model for the innovative tier of today.

Substituting hair for feathers was another step in the quest for simplicity and practicality. There are many theories and suppositions as to where and when the popular hairwing salmon fly patterns originated. Whatever authentic documentation ever may have existed seems to have been lost.

Part of the lore involves a story that is interesting regardless of its authenticity; it is the story of immigrants who came from the British Isles to Newfoundland in the eighteenth century, very early in the history of fly fishing. They brought with them cattle, sheep, and dogs, as well as other essentials of colonial life, including fish hooks. Although fishing then was mainly done with nets, the colonists occasionally fished with long fly rods for sport. Fancy flies were unknown: people used what they had, and they quite sensibly named each fly for its ingredients, so its name told the neighbors exactly what was used to catch the "big one" of the day. Flies bore

---

PLATE 41
SALMON FLIES DRESSED BY CHARLIE DEFEO

Black Cosseboom

Silver Doctor *Silver Satan (original)*

Purple, Red and White Spey (original)

Torrish *Black Heron (original)*

Jock Scott

Thunder and Lightning *Copper Killer*

Silver Spey (original)

PLATE 40
UNNAMED STREAMER FOR SALMON, ORIGINATED AND DRESSED BY TED NIEMEYER

"I never named it since it is a mix of many tiers that have gone before. If you look closely, you will see Preston Jennings, John Atherton, Charlie [DeFeo], Syd Glasso and lastly me in the dressing somewhere."

—Ted Niemeyer

Body	Flat silver tinsel from opposite hook point to head
Tail	Dyed hot orange golden pheasant tippet
Wing	Two dyed hot orange badger hackles followed by: married swan wing of (from bottom to top) red, orange, yellow, green and blue; followed by bronze peacock (this must be bronze and not green or blue), three strands each side; followed by jungle cock eye each side.
Beard	Hot orange saddle hackle applied in three bunches
Head	Danville red tying thread with black horizontal stripe laid over (my trademark on salmon and trout patterns)

PLATE 42
EARLY-NINETEENTH-CENTURY HAIRWING

names that left little question about their composition: the *Red Cow* fly, the *Ten Bear* fly, the *Ordinary
Bear* fly, and so on.

We do know that bucktail flies were commercially available as early as the 1880s. In a monumental work, *The Complete Fly Fisherman* (1947), John
McDonald endows us with the notes and letters of
Theodore Gordon, fondly considered America's
patron saint of fly fishermen, which include some
interesting remarks about a special fly. Gordon wrote
on January 24, 1903: "*Some years ago* we tried some
flies on an entirely different principle, our notion
being to turn out something that would have real
life and movement and resemble a small bright fish
in colouring. If you could see one of these large flies
played, salmon-fly fashion, by a series of short jerks
of the rod top, and notice how the long fibres
expand and contract, how the jungle fowl feathers
(in a line with the hook) open and shut, you would

see at once that it must be very attractive to any
large game fish. White and silver predominate, but
are toned down by long badger hackles and jungle
fowl feathers. . . . They will kill all kinds of game fish,
salmon included."

This fly, which Gordon said was tried some
years earlier than 1903, was called by him the *Bumblepuppy.* Literally translated "whist without rules,"
the *Bumblepuppy* was dressed in many variations, one
of which was often enclosed in Gordon's fly orders.
The reference to salmon may have been to landlocked salmon rather than to Atlantic salmon, and
the pattern has fallen into obscurity. It is, however,
an early, authenticated, and named example of the
use of a hairwing and thus is important historically.

Although I state in *Streamer Fly Tying and Fishing*
that a bucktail fly for bass was in use in the United
States as early as 1886, and that a rancher in Idaho
named A. S. Trude tied hairwing flies for trout in

PLATE 43
THE BUMBLEPUPPY, ORIGINATED AND
DRESSED BY THEODORE GORDON

1901, this date may be open to question. The June 1948 issue of *Fortune* quotes an article previously published in the *Bulletin* of the Angler's Club of New York: "While trout fishing in . . . Idaho back around 1890 the late Colonel Lewis S. Thompson met a fellow fisherman, one A. S. Trude. . . . Trude tied his own flies, and used hair instead of feathers. So far as is known, he was the father of the hair fly, which in the form of the 'bucktail' is known to most anglers. Colonel Thompson saved some of the flies Trude gave him, and later had other flies tied. These were all trout flies. At least he thought so until he tried them on salmon, on the Restigouche about twenty years ago (1928 or before)."

Colonel Thompson related that a big salmon no one could hook took his 5/0 *Abbey* fly on a casual

PLATE 44
THE RED ABBEY, DRESSED BY BOB WARREN

This American pattern, dating about 1913, was especially popular in the Restigouche area of Quebec, and later has become a favorite on Maine salmon rivers. A similar trout fly, called the *Abbey,* has a tail of golden pheasant crest, red silk body, gold tinsel tag and ribbing, and a wing of gray squirrel tail hair or gray mallard flank feather. The throat is brown, or natural red cock. For a black-winged fly with the same body, see the British *Black Bomber.*

loose cast; the *Abbey* he mentions is the *Red Abbey* and is dressed as follows:

Red Abbey

Tag	Flat embossed or oval silver tinsel
Tail	Slips of red ibis, swan or goose dyed red, or a very small bunch of red bucktail
Body	Red silk floss, or wool
Ribbing	Flat embossed or oval silver tinsel
Throat	Brown hackle
Wing	Light brown squirrel tail or brown bucktail
Cheeks	Jungle cock (optional)
Head	Black or red

Undoubtedly the colonel didn't mean to imply that he initiated hairwing fly fishing for salmon. The important thing is not when or where or by whom hairwings were first conceived, but rather that they have helped revolutionize modern concepts in salmon fishing.

Experimentation with modern hairwing flies went on independently in many different regions. On the Miramichi, for example, men such as Everett Price, Bert Miner, and Ira Gruber developed a simplified style in both featherwings and

PLATE 45
TYPES OF FLIES, DESIGNATED BY MATERIAL

Black Bear, Red Butt
dressed by Keith Fulsher

Black Spider
originated and dressed by Ira Gruber

Black Bear
originated and dressed by Harry Smith

Squirrel Tail
dressed by Keith Fulsher

hairwings, but seemed to favor the hairwing. In *Atlantic Salmon Fishing* (1937), Charles Phair stated, "Hair flies have been fished with conspicuous success by some salmon fishermen, notably Colonel Edmund P. Rogers, Walter C. Teagle and the late Lewis Thompson."

About 1920, Harry Smith, of Cherryfield, Maine, devised a simple all-black pattern with a black bear hair wing appropriately called the *Black Bear Fly,* evidently one of the first used for Maine rivers. This fly and others, such as the *Squirrel Tail,* are designated as types of flies and named for the materials in them; examples are the *Black Bear, Red Butt* and the *Squirrel Tail, Orange Butt.* These flies are shown in Plate 45 and the dressings for them are given in chapter 14.

The rudimentary *Black Bear* is famous for hooking salmon, and there now are countless patterns that have evolved from it. Dressers elaborate by adding ribbing, hackles, colorful butts, and synthetic materials. Charles "Chuck" Conrad added a tinsel tag and green fluorescent butt, thus creating the variation known as the *Conrad* that is popular on the Miramichi River. Other examples are the *Black Bear, Green Butt, Undertaker,* and *Preacher.* Decades later, the simple hairwing has flourished, and the popularity of tube flies in some regions has opened new frontiers for its use.

It is one thing to learn that hairwing flies will take salmon, and quite another to know what types and sizes will do it best. Whether or not they take salmon better than featherwings may be a matter of opinion. Many of us have chosen to fish hairwings almost exclusively. They are more available to the fisherman largely because the materials are more accessible and are easier for tiers, both independent and commercial, to deal with.

When hairwing patterns were first developed, they were large and bulky. Experience proved that they should be smaller and dressed more sparsely, with the wing hugging the hook shank. I cringe when I see the hairwings often sold in stores. The hair employed on a conventional hairwing should be fine enough to give the fly proper action in the water, reasonably straight and bright, with a natural gloss to yield translucency and brilliance to the fly.

The desire for beauty in hairwings and the nostalgic reverence for classic patterns led to dressing many classics with hair instead of feathers. The base

Charlie Krom and Keith Fulsher

of these adaptations, sometimes referred to as *conversions,* is in the wing structure of the feathered predecessor, and the wing approximates in hair the colors of the pertinent classic. A well-executed conversion can be as strikingly beautiful as its classic counterpart. Countless patterns and their variations have resulted in the reform to hairwing flies, and simplifications can be made at the discretion of the dresser. An excellent reference on this subject is *Hair-Wing Atlantic Salmon Flies* (1981), by Keith Fulsher and Charles Krom (1981).

The New Testament passage "many are called but few are chosen" could be applied to salmon flies. It is natural for fly tiers to make up new patterns or variations in hopes that theirs will prove successful. One of the chosen few is the famous *Cosseboom.* Its originator, John C. Cosseboom, from Woonsocket, Rhode Island, was a fascinating gentleman endowed with multiple talents. Not only a champion fly caster, he was also a poet, newspaper writer, and insurance agent.

In July 1935, John Cosseboom and Ai Ballou, originator of the *Ballou Special,* were aboard the SS *Fleuris* making the twenty-four-hour passage from Quebec to Anticosti Island. To pass the time, flytying gear was brought out, and Ai's wife, Annie, challenged Cosseboom to create a fly using a spool of olive green silk floss she had selected. He met the challenge, incorporating the floss for both the body and the tail, and hooked it in Mrs. Ballou's lapel. Later, Ai Ballou attached a note to the fly, "This is the original Cosseboom dressed by John Cosseboom on the S.S. Fleuris, July, 1935, and given to Annie Ballou." The fly is still in existence and exhibits a throat hackle rather than the collar that is usual on the pattern today (see Plate 138).

The success of the *Cosseboom* led to considerable experimentation and many variations, including the *Cosseboom* that is dressed as a streamer or bucktail. The *Miramichi Cosseboom,* with its dark green body rather than the olive green of the original, is one of the most popular flies on that river.

Two other significant names in North American salmon fly development are Ira Gruber and Everett

Price. Gruber was a cotton knitting mill owner from Spring Valley, Pennsylvania, who fished New Brunswick's Miramichi River in the Doaktown-Blackville area almost daily during every season from 1915 until his death in 1963. In 1930, Wilson "Bing" Russell became his guide and caretaker. Ira usually used two fly rods. When he hooked a salmon with one, he would hand that rod to Bing, who played the fish while Ira tried to hook another with a different fly on the other rod. Ira was more interested in the

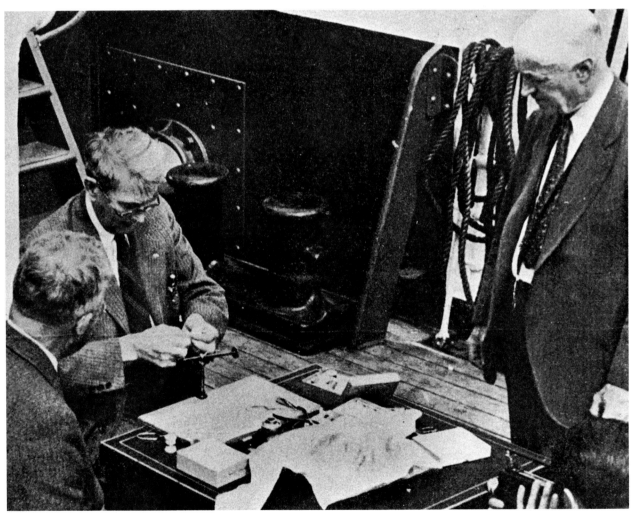

John Cosseboom aboard the SS Fleuris

PHOTOGRAPH BY MAINE FISH AND WILDLIFE

fish-taking abilities of fly patterns and fly sizes than in landing fish. He kept accurate records.

Gruber started dressing his own flies in 1935 under the tutelage of a local expert named Everett Price. Together they recorded over twenty patterns, many of which are Gruber originations or adaptations. Hairwings eventually became more favored because they seemed more interesting to the fish and were easier to tie. Ira's son, Edward, sent me nineteen of Ira's flies dressed in the 1930s that clearly exhibit Gruber and Price's influence on the popular Miramichi "butt patterns." The *Black Spider,* in particular, with its burnt orange butt has led many anglers to believe that Gruber fathered the black bear butted patterns; others insist that Harry Smith should have that credit.

Black Spider

Tail	A few hairs of black squirrel tail
Butt	Fine orange floss (short)
Body	Black wool
Ribbing	Fine oval silver tinsel
Wing	Black squirrel
Throat	Black hackle
Head	Black

This noteworthy Gruber pattern is evidence that "butt" flies were tied before they were called that. We now know it as the *Orange Butt,* and it may well have been the first of this type of pattern.

More than anyone else, Gruber was responsible for establishing the general conformation of the Miramichi-type salmon fly: a short, cigar-shaped body ribbed with close-turned fine tinsel and with a short wing that hugs the body. In addition to the simple methods and materials, another feature is the care with which throat hackle is tied or wound on.

Ira Gruber also was among the first to use bronzed straight or offset hooks for salmon fishing. Almost all of his flies were tied on Allcock Model Perfect hooks, and he seemed to prefer singles to doubles. He favored offset hooks because of their improved hooking and holding advantages and was an early proponent of this type of hook popular on salmon rivers in Maine and Canada.

Bing Russell, who also guided me before his death in 1970, claimed that in the early years anglers gave up fishing when the water became low and bright because salmon were too hard to catch although many could be seen. During these years,

---

PLATE 47
SALMON FLIES DRESSED BY
IRA GRUBER

Gray Buck		Black Hawk		Raleigh
Le Mac		Dr. Reamer		Gorilla
U-No	Baron	Moose Fly	Little Joe
Hermit		Stone Fly		Abe Mohn
		Sherman		
	Peacock	Male Stone Fly	
		Favorite		

---

big flies in sizes 4 and 6 (usually doubles) were thought necessary. Ira Gruber's experiments proved that salmon could be taken in warm, low-water conditions on flies as small as size 12. No mention is made of his using dry flies, although they were then becoming well known.

Most of Ira Gruber's patterns were originated and developed between 1935 and 1945. The *Oriole* and *Reliable* (chapter 14) are particularly noteworthy and are still used on the Miramichi and other rivers.

A few of Gruber's patterns had bodies where the rear third (or so), was of a different color, usually yellow, leading several old-time anglers to believe that he fathered the popular and productive butted patterns. The black body with yellow butt is nothing new, however. Many British featherwing patterns are dressed this way, including the *Black Fairy* and the *Jeannie.*

Abe Mohn (or Munn)

Tail	A few fibers of golden pheasant red body feather
Body	Medium yellow wool
Ribbing	Very fine oval silver tinsel
Throat	Brown hackle
Wing	Brown mallard (four sections)
Head	Black

Mohn may have been a misprint for *Munn,* but this pattern decidedly is a variation of the *Abe Munn Killer.* Abe Munn was a guide in the years around 1925 in the Boistown area of New Brunswick, on the Miramichi River.

PLATE 48
LEE AND JOAN WULFF: THE SURFACE STONE FLY AND THE LADY JOAN
ORIGINATED AND DRESSED BY LEE WULFF
Photograph by Stanley Bogden

Surface Stone Fly	
Body	Yellow preformed plastic
Wing	Natural brown bucktail, tied in flat and extending well beyond the bend of the hook
Hackle	Light badger, quite long and applied parachute style over a preformed stub

This is another of Lee Wulff's innovations. Designed for fishing the surface film, this fly has a silhouette that differs considerably from that of the higher-profile *Wulff* patterns. The preformed plastic body is dissolved with a solvent so that the deer hair and the hackle are bonded directly into the body without the use of tying thread.

Lady Joan	
Tag	Oval gold tinsel
Body	Orange floss
Ribbing	Oval gold tinsel
Throat	A few strands of the short, fluffy fibers found at the base of a yellow dyed-saddle hackle, mixed with a few strands of the soft hackle fibers found on the same feather
Wing	Gray squirrel tail over black bear hair
Head	Black

Originated by Lee Wulff and named for his wife, Joan Salvato Wulff, the *Lady Joan* was first tied during a trip to Canada to satisfy the need for a fly with orange in it. Joan Wulff is also a writer on angling subjects, an expert angler, and an ardent conservationist. Together they founded a fly-fishing school in Roscoe, New York.

Baron

Tag	Three turns of very fine oval silver tinsel and red floss, short
Tail	Golden pheasant crest, over which are a few fibers of bright red hackle of same length
Butt	Sparse black ostrich herl
Body	Rear half: fine flat silver tinsel ribbed with very fine silver oval tinsel. Middle butt: black ostrich herl with a few strands of very bright red hackle fibers under. Front half: black floss ribbed with very fine oval silver tinsel
Throat	A few bright red hackle fibers tied under, beard fashion. Over this is black hackle
Wing	Brown mallard (two double wings) tied low
Head	Black

This fly, a simplification of the British salmon fly of the same name, is often used at the mouth of the Dungarvon River.

Black Hawk

Tail	A few fibers of summer (wood) duck
Body	Light slate floss
Ribbing	Black tying thread
Throat	Black hackle
Wing	Slate tapered to off-white duck (four sections)
Head	Black

This fly was dressed primarily to be used in small sizes on Big Hole Brook Pool upriver from

PLATE 49
WOLF-HAIR SKATER, ORIGINATED
AND DRESSED BY CHARLIE DEFEO

PLATE 50
FLIES DEVISED FROM ESTABLISHED PATTERNS

1   *Pearl Heron*

originated and dressed by Bill Wilbur

Tag	Oval gold tinsel
Tail	Golden pheasant crest
Body	Flat pearl tinsel over flat silver tinsel
Ribbing	Oval gold tinsel
Hackle	Blue heron
Throat	Teal
Wing	Bronze mallard
Head	Red

2   *After Eight*

originated and dressed by Bob Warren

Tag	Oval silver tinsel and orange floss
Body	Blended synthetic seal's fur, from light to dark: fluorescent yellow, fluorescent lime green and olive dun
Ribbing	Oval silver tinsel
Hackle	Blue-eared pheasant
Wings	Bronze mallard
Collar	Guinea, dyed green
Head	Olive green

3   *Moisie Dunkeld*

originated and dressed by Bill Wilbur

Body	Flat gold tinsel
Ribbing	Oval gold tinsel
Wing	In the round: gold crystal hair followed by fox squirrel
Sides	Jungle cock
Collar	Hot orange hackle
Head	Black

4   *Green Prawn*

originated and dressed by Bob Warren

Tag	Oval silver tinsel
Tail	Fluorescent green polar bear
Body	Blended synthetic seal's fur from light to dark: fluorescent yellow, fluorescent lime green and olive dun
Ribbing	Oval silver tinsel
Body hackle	Dark olive
Body veiling	Applied *General Practitioner* style (see text): golden pheasant body feathers varying from rust red to metallic green, the last of which is predominantly green with a black bar
Head	Olive green

5   *Cutty Sark*

originated and dressed by Bob Warren

Tag	Copper oval tinsel and fluorescent orange floss
Tail	Golden pheasant crest
Butt	Black goose
Body	In two equal sections: green floss followed by bronze peacock
Ribbing	Copper oval tinsel
Throat	Black hackle
Wing	Three strands of floss: yellow, orange and green, veiled with teal
Sides	Jungle cock
Head	Black

6   *Merry Widow*

originated and dressed by Eric Baylis

Tag	Fine flat gold tinsel, long
Body	Rear third: golden yellow floss; remainder: peacock herl
Ribbing	Fine flat gold tinsel
Throat	Yellow macaw breast feather
Wing	Black squirrel or moose hair
Sides	Jungle cock
Head	Fluorescent green with red band at rear

7   *Tippet Shrimp*

originated and dressed by Bill Hunter

Tag	Oval gold tinsel
Tail	Red and orange bucktail and gold and pearl crystal flash, mixed
Body	Rear half: golden orange chenille Mid-body veil: two small golden pheasant tippet feathers, splayed around the hook shank. Cut the tip from each feather before tying on, and align the outer tips with the inside of the hook bend Front half: heavy application of spiky, sparkling dubbing very hot red in color
Ribbing	Gold oval tinsel over front half of body only
Hackle	Red body feather from a golden pheasant, applied as a collar
Head	Flame red

8   *Glitter Bear*

originated and dressed by Bill Taylor

Tag	Fine oval silver and fluorescent green wool
Tail	Golden pheasant crest
Body	Peacock herl
Ribbing	Fine oval silver tinsel
Wing	Several strands of fluorescent green crystal flash over which is squirrel hair, dyed black
Throat	Black hen hackle, applied as a collar
Head	Black

PLATE 50

Continued

9	*Glitter Bug*

originated and dressed by Danny Bird

The *Glitter Bug* is essentially a *Buck Bug* with a tail of crystal flash added.

10	*Bullock's Bar*

originated and dressed by Bob Warren

Tag	Oval silver tinsel and lemon floss
Tail	Golden pheasant crest
Body	Black floss
Ribbing	Oval silver tinsel
Throat	Blue hackle
Wing	Yellow and red polar bear hair, sparse, and black bear hair over which are a few strands of pearl crystal flash
Head	Black

11	*Gold Cosseboom, hair hackle*

originated and dressed by Rob Solo

Body	Fine gold mylar tubing tied off at rear with fluorescent green thread
Wing	Fox squirrel, dyed dark brown, over strands of fluorescent green crystal flash
Hackle	Deer hair dyed yellow, applied as a collar
Head	Black

	1	2	
		3	4
5	6	7	8
9	10	11	

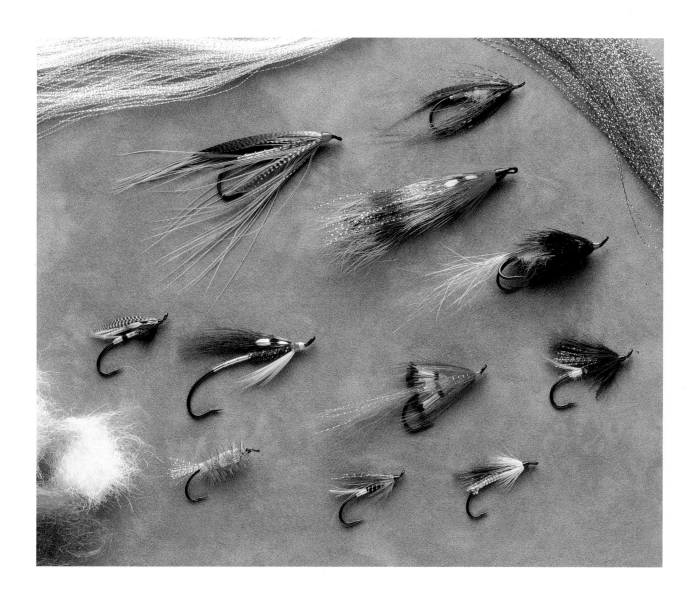

Doaktown, a very large pool, fed by springwater from Big Hole Brook, that was leased by Ira Gruber from Sherman Hoyt. Ira Gruber was one of the first to learn that even in the hottest part of summer, salmon could be hooked in this pool by using flies as small as size 12.

Dr. Reamer

Tail	A few fibers of the red body feather of golden pheasant
Butt	A few turns of very light red silk floss
Body	Very light brown wool
Ribbing	Black tying thread
Throat	Black hackle
Wing	Two right and two left sections of any black feather, such as crow, applied well down to hug the body
Head	Black

This was originated by a doctor from the Boston area and appears here as dressed by Ira Gruber. It is of minor value.

Favorite

Tail	Golden pheasant crest
Butt	Sparse black ostrich herl
Body	Medium flat silver tinsel
Ribbing	Fine oval silver tinsel
Throat	Plymouth Rock hackle dyed orange
Wing	Gray mallard (four sections)
Cheeks	Jungle cock, small
Head	Black

This is a minor variation of the *Blackville,* the primary difference being that the orange hackle of the *Blackville* is orange-dyed Plymouth Rock on the *Favorite.*

Hermit

Tail	A few fibers of the red body feather of golden pheasant
Body	Rear third: bright yellow silk floss. Forward two-thirds: black silk floss
Ribbing	Narrow flat silver tinsel, over whole body
Throat	Brown hackle
Wing	Underwing: several fibers of an orange-black golden pheasant feather. Overwing: gray mallard dyed green drake color
Head	Black

Ira Gruber often alternated this fly with the *Oriole* and used them in all levels of water. He used larger and more heavily dressed ones in high water, and smaller and more lightly dressed ones in low water.

Little Joe

Tail	A few fibers of a black and white barred feather, such as wood duck
Body	Black nylon wool
Ribbing	A copper-colored (brownish copper cast) thread
Throat	Very light dun
Wing	Brown mallard (four strips)
Head	Black

Little Joe was often used by Ira Gruber in the fall at the mouth of the Dungarvon River in New Brunswick.

Male Stonefly

Tail	A few fibers of the red-brown body feather of golden pheasant
Butt	Ostrich herl, black
Body	Yellow silk floss, slim, butted in the middle with black ostrich herl, under which are tied in three or four fibers of brown hackle, short
Ribbing	Very fine black tying thread, over both body sections
Throat	Brown hackle, extending halfway to bend of hook
Wing	Brown mallard (four sections)
Head	Black

This is a very effective fly, and one of Ira Gruber's favorites. Gruber's patterns were greatly simplified, as will be noted from other dressings.

Moose Fly

Tail	A few fibers of summer (wood) duck
Body	Moose hair that is cream colored with black edges, wound on as above, nymph-style. The body is clear lacquered
Throat	Light dun hackle
Wing	Very light slate duck (four sections) extending only two-thirds the length of the body
Head	Black

This unusual Gruber pattern has a clear-lacquered body, fat at the head and tapered toward the tail, nymphlike.

Peacock

Tail	Golden pheasant crest
Body	Rear third: bright yellow silk floss. Forward two-thirds: peacock herl
Ribbing	Fine bright green thread, over rear third only
Wing	Brown mallard (four sections)
Throat	Olive green hackle
Head	Black

This Gruber pattern usually was used in the fall but was considered good all during the season.

Raleigh

Tail	A few yellow hackle fibers
Body	Waxed cream-colored (nearly white) string
Ribbing	Black tying thread, wound on fairly closely
Throat	Yellow hackle
Wing	Cinnamon brown duck (four sections)
Head	Black

Being of moderately light color, this fly was most effective on bright days in medium or low water.

Sherman

Tail	A few fibers of summer wood duck
Body	Black floss
Ribbing	Very fine oval silver tinsel, wound closely
Throat	Light brown hackle
Wing	Slate duck
Head	Black

This was named for Sherman Hoyt, from whom Ira Gruber leased Big Hole Brook Pool.

Stonefly

Tail	A few fibers of Plymouth Rock, dyed yellow
Body	Bright yellow floss
Ribbing	Very dark green thread
Throat	Plymouth Rock hackle, dyed yellow
Wing	Gray mallard, dyed green drake color
Head	Black

This pattern uses the *Oriole* wing of gray mallard breast feather especially dyed by Ira Gruber in a green drake color (a dye obtainable from Veniard).

U-No

Tag	Gold floss
Tail	Golden pheasant crest
Body	A few turns of light gray floss, forward of which are a few turns of medium brown floss, both constituting the rear half of the body. The forward half is black floss
Ribbing	Very fine oval silver tinsel
Throat	Slate colored hackle
Wing	Slate duck (four sections), hugging shank of hook
Cheeks	Jungle cock, small
Head	Black

Ira Gruber never gave this one a name. When referring to it, he would say, "that fly—you know the one." He used it so often that his guide Bing Russell always knew what he meant.

Gruber's Hairwings

Following are three hairwing patterns originated by Ira Gruber.

Gray Buck

Tail	A few tips of very light blue dun hackle
Body	Very soft light green wool
Ribbing	Fine oval silver tinsel
Throat	Very light dun hackle
Wing	Badger hair, extending slightly beyond bend of hook
Head	Black

This is one of the more important Gruber patterns, with an extralong wing of the bucktail type.

Gorilla

Tail	A few fibers of black hackle
Body	Black silk floss
Ribbing	Very fine oval silver tinsel, wound closely
Throat	Black hackle
Wing	A small bunch of woodchuck guard hairs, fairly sparse and applied to hug the body
Head	Black

This is an early hairwing pattern used on the Miramichi.

Lemac

Tail	A few fibers of woodchuck body hair
Body	Black nylon wool
Ribbing	Fine oval silver tinsel
Throat	Plymouth Rock hackle, short and sparse
Wing	A very small bunch of woodchuck guard hairs, over which are a few bits of the cream-colored hair of white polar bear, about two-thirds as long as the underwing
Head	Black

This pattern was considered particularly effective in fast water.

Taking Atlantic salmon on the dry fly has become a standard and successful practice in North America, especially under low-water and warm-water conditions, although we have had quite a time convincing our friends across the sea of the fact. Adherents of the dry fly also now know that they can usually take salmon with the dry fly under the same conditions as are ideal for wet-fly fishing.

The history of catching salmon with the dry fly goes back farther than some may think. John McDonald tells us that "Pulman *(Vade Mecum of Fly-Fishing for Trout)* pulled the dry fly out of his hat, complete, in 1841, though for all anyone knew it might as well have been a rabbit." During the latter half of the nineteenth century, other references to the revolutionary practice of fishing the fly dry surfaced in the literature, and in 1890, Theodore Gordon wrote to Halford inquiring about the practice. Halford replied, "I can quite imagine that in some parts of your country fish could be taken on the dry fly where the more usual sunk fly would be of no avail." In an April 1906 letter, Gordon wrote: "A friend of mine took a 14-pound salmon on a dry fly tied like a *Coachman* but dry-fly style on a big Pennell hook. The line was slack, he broke his rod in striking the fish and was a long time killing it. This was on Restigouche and he got two more, a grilse and a small salmon, in the same way out of the same pools in three days."

George M. L. LaBranche, in *The Salmon and the Dry Fly* (1924), gives credit to Col. Ambrose Monell for being the first angler in North America to take a salmon on a dry fly (which may be incorrect in view of the foregoing): "Believing, as I did, that salmon do not feed in fresh water, I hesitated to introduce the subject of fishing for them with a floating fly. Divining, perhaps, what was in my mind, my friend (Colonel Monell) calmly announced that he had killed a fifteen-pound salmon two years before on a dry fly, and assured me that it was not an accident. He had seen the fish rising just as a trout would rise and, having failed to interest the fish with any of the wet flies in his box, he had deliberately cast across and upstream with a No. 12 *Whirling Dun,* floating it down over the fish, which took it at once. It was the taking of this fish, and the rising of six or seven others which he did not hook, that convinced him it would be possible to kill fish with the dry fly when the water was low." In the book, LaBranche gives four favorite dressings of dry flies that are heavily palmered over silk or dubbing.

The greatest exponent of dry-fly fishing for salmon is Lee Wulff, author of *The Atlantic Salmon* (1958), who designed the *Gray Wulff* and the *White Wulff* in 1929. He says, "In the early thirties, it was unusual to meet another dry-fly angler and it was quite common when moving to a new river to find guides and fishermen who had never seen a dry fly fished and who were frankly doubtful that a floating fly would have any attraction for salmon."

In 1962, Lee fished Scotland's Aberdeenshire Dee and demonstrated his ability to catch salmon on the dry fly. He caught only one, but proved it could be done. Either salmon are much harder to take on the dry fly in the British Isles than in North America, or British anglers are much harder to convince that it can be done consistently under favorable conditions. Could it be that the presumed reluctance of salmon across the Atlantic to take dry flies is in reality a reluctance on the part of anglers to use them because of the misconception that dry flies are ineffective?

In 1977, Angus Cameron, Bob Kuhn, Lewis Stone, and I were fishing Iceland's beautiful and productive Laxá í Kjós. Because of the weather conditions, the fish were less cooperative than usual. I was teamed with Angus and had fished down a pool without result. On Angus's turn at the rod, he gave me a sly look and dangled a size 4 *Gray Wulff* tied to his leader.

"You can't do worse than I did," I said. "Go ahead and try it."

On the third cast or so, a salmon rose to the fly and took it solidly. The fish took Angus downriver about a hundred yards before being tailed. It weighed 14 1/2 pounds.

To make the story short, we both took salmon on dry flies that day. Returning to the lodge, we met up with Bob Kuhn, who proudly exhibited two big salmon.

"Guess what I hooked them with," he asked.

"Dry fly," said Angus.

"Dry fly," I repeated.

"Dry fly," confirmed Bob proudly. "How did you guess that?"

The following July, Angus and I took salmon regularly on dry flies on the same river. It wasn't a coincidence. On some days the fish came to dry flies better than to the wet ones usually used on the river.

Lee Wulff's series of flies were a valuable contribution to dry-fly salmon fishing, as their bushy hair-wing dressings make them excellent floaters, even in fast currents. Many other floaters such as spiders, skaters, bombers, bugs, and heavily palmered patterns have since been developed.

Word of successful flies spreads quickly on the rivers and in the shops, and, as patterns become established, they are often modified. Some changes are quite by chance while others are made by the determined efforts of hopeful anglers. Combining the old with the new, innovative tiers alter tags, butts, bodies, and wings. With new techniques and new materials, variations of proved patterns are developed, this creating another generation of productive flies.

Throughout the history of the salmon fly there are countless examples of flies influenced by previously documented patterns, and elements of classics such as the *Doctors,* the *Parsons,* the *Jock Scott* and the *Thunder and Lightning* can be recognized in many patterns that appear in this book. Modern examples of flies and styles of flies often emulated are the *Black Bears, Rats, Cossebooms, Buck Bugs, Muddlers* and *Wulffs.*

Theories for Fly Selection

"Noon Break"

*I*n a vast area of the Atlantic ocean about a thousand miles east of Florida and far south of Bermuda, away from normal shipping lanes, an ages-old rite occurs annually that many authorities think helps explain why Atlantic salmon take artificial flies, as well as what types they go for most eagerly. This remote area, in or near the weedy Sargasso Sea, is the breeding ground of American and European eels, which travel as far as 5,000 miles from North American and European rivers in order to assemble at this particular place.

This place, in season, is a swimming, undulating, entwining mass of millions of adult eels, which exude countless billions of fertilized eggs into the sea so thickly as to resemble miles-wide blobs of tapioca pudding. Having done what they came to do, the eels die. The transparent drifting protoplasmic masses of eggs become caught in that majestic river in the ocean known as the Gulf Stream, wherein, as they grow, they are swept northward, and then westward by the North Atlantic Drift.

Since it takes two years or so to transform eggs to elvers there must be a place or places where the immature eels can rest and grow to prevent the Gulf Stream from delivering them to their destinations before they are ready to ascend the rivers. These places must be back eddies in the Gulf Stream, and one of them may be in the Davis Strait between Labrador and Greenland, where so many salmon have been caught by commercial long-liners and netters. In any event, when the smolt (young salmon) leave their rivers they travel with or against the currents (depending on which continent they come from) to meet the swarms of drifting immature elvers, feasting on them to such an extent that they may be a principal part of the salmon's diet in the ocean.

Now, let's look at the elvers in the stage of their growth when they are resting and maturing in the ocean's back eddies, where salmon have the greatest opportunity to devour them. At this stage, they are nearly transparent and blood-lined with prismatic or opal-like hues and glints of silver when viewed upward toward the light as salmon would see them drifting near the surface. Their shape then resembles that of melon seeds or almonds, fronted with prominent heads and eyes, and they usually are between 1 and 2 inches long—about the size and shape of

PLATE 51
THE ELVER
DRESSED BY MIKE MARTINEK

salmon flies in sizes between 2 and 8. It is interesting to note that the silhouette of the classic Atlantic salmon fly resembles that of the immature elver. Often exhibiting the elver's familiar glint or flash, salmon flies also can have mixtures of colors similar to those of the elver. At a later stage of growth, when the elvers have thinned out and elongated and are beginning to look like small eels, they can be represented by slim black or brownish bucktails or streamers, of which the *Collie Dog* tube fly (particularly popular in Iceland) and the *Elver* streamer fly are good examples.

Elver (or Blue Elver or Ransome's Elver)	
Body	Black floss, dressed thin
Ribbing	Oval or flat silver tinsel
Wing	Two blue vulturine guinea fowl feathers with white stripe, nearly twice as long as the hook and tied low, back to back, to cover the shank of the hook. (Vulturine feathers come from the African guinea fowl. They should be 2¹/₂ inches long for hook sizes 6 or 4.)
Hackle	Three or four turns of a plain blue vulturine feather (without the white stripe) ahead of the wing and tied to blend with the wing. The fibers should be very long, extending beyond the bend of the hook
Head	Red

This modern and unusual British fly of the streamer type was popularized by Arthur Ransome in a radio broadcast in England. He observed that elvers breed in the Atlantic off Bermuda and travel in the Gulf Stream to American and British rivers in astounding numbers and thought they must be a staple food for salmon. The young elvers, at one stage, are only about 2¹/₂ inches long, very fat, and translucently dark. Ransome indicates that this fly, dressed to resemble a young elver, is successful for salmon, and it should be equally successful in North American rivers, into which they migrate.

Bucktails or streamers are useful as salmon flies, particularly as "change of pace" patterns when salmon can't be tempted with anything else. In extremity they often are successful, especially when the fish have been shown so many classic patterns by so many anglers that they only will react to something more unusual.

At sea, the salmon attain their growth on a diet of a variety of oceanic foods. This would include the elvers, of course, as well as krill, crustaceans such as shrimp or prawns, and to a minor extent, squids. Thus, representations of shrimp and prawns make good salmon lures, as indicated by such patterns as the *General Practitioner* and the *Black-Eyed Prawn,* both often considered "deadly" (although I dislike the word). Squids are not represented in salmon fly tackle because of their size, although there are bucktail-type lures that might do it. Salmon also feed on smaller fish, but evidently as a last resort because they are harder to catch.

One of the very best imitations of the shrimp is Col. Esmond Drury's *General Practitioner,* which he originated in 1953 and which has been eminently successful ever since. The fly is not an easy one to dress, but if you follow the step-by-step instructions and look at the accompanying color plate, it should not present great difficulty. In the British Isles, treble hooks usually are used. In North America, we would use doubles or perhaps singles, preferably #2 long-shank, fine-wire, with red-orange tying thread. After

PLATE 52
THE BLACK-EYED PRAWN (FRANCES), ORIGINATED AND DRESSED BY PETER DEANE
Photograph of Peter Deane and Orri Vigfusson fishing in Iceland courtesy of Orri Vigfusson

each winding of hackle, the hackle on the top of the shank is clipped off to allow the golden pheasant neck feathers to lie as flat as possible. When the fly is completed, stroke the feathers backward so that they will lie flat and close to the body to give the effect of a shrimp's carapaces.

This dressing was sent to the author by Colonel Drury, and the fly in Plate 53 was dressed by him. The pattern was given in the first edition of *Atlantic Salmon Flies and Fishing* (1970) and started a wave of popularity in North America that has not diminished. Colonel Drury says, "If I wish to tie a smaller fly, such as size 6, I omit the golden pheasant neck feather number 12. I fish the large fly slowly on a sinking line and the small fly on a floating line, sometimes fishing it in fast by stripping in line."

Since I wrote my first book on salmon, an angling friend visited the manor house of Mary Saunders Davis, who owns both sides of 3 miles on the River Test. The conversation turned to Colonel Drury and his *General Practitioner*. She said, "He is a dear friend of mine and of my late husband and, indeed, the *General Practitioner* was devised right here in this house as a result of my husband's barring Esmond's use of the prawn. That creature, as you know, either takes every salmon in the pool or else frightens every fish right out of the pool. My husband's banning of prawns caused Esmond to create a fly to imitate the prawn and he did so, coming down the next morning with his new and ingenious creation. It proved to be most effective—indeed, almost as deadly as the prawn itself—and we dubbed the new fly originally the *Romsey Rascal* [Romsey is a village nearby]. Later its name was changed but originally we all called it the *Romsey Rascal,* as did Esmond himself."

A prawn imitation of equal repute, the *Black-Eyed Prawn,* was originated about 1970 by famous fly dresser Peter Deane, of Sussex, England. The success of the pattern has brought it international acclaim. It is immensely popular in Iceland, where it accounts for nearly half of all fly sales. Additional information about its origin and name is given in chapter 13.

Iceland's *Krafla* seems to be a copy of it, using a body of trimmed palmered hackle. In my opinion, the *Black-Eyed Prawn* and the *General Practitioner* are the two best shrimp imitations available. Deane's dressing for his *Black-Eyed Prawn* (or *Frances*) is as follows:

PLATE 53
THE GENERAL PRACTITIONER TYING STEPS, DRESSED BY BOB VEVERKA
Photographed on original artwork by Milt Weiler
from *Atlantic Salmon Flies and Fishing*

The steps for dressing the *General Practitioner* are as follows:

1. Wind tying thread to bend and tie in ten thick-rooted bucktail hairs dyed hot orange. (These represent the shrimp's whiskers and should project 2 inches beyond the bend of the hook.)

2. Tie in at the same spot, *concave* side upward, a small orange-red golden pheasant neck feather.

3. Tie in, *convex* side upward, another small orange-red golden pheasant neck feather. These feathers, 2 and 3, should lie one on top of the other. They represent the head of the shrimp.

4. Tie in a long hot orange cock's hackle and a strip of fine oval gold tinsel.

5. Dub tying thread liberally with pinkish orange mohair or seal's fur.

6. Wind dubbed thread to *A* and secure.

7. Wind about three turns of ribbing tinsel to *A* and secure.

8. Wind the hackle between the ribbing to *A* and secure.

9. At *A,* tie in, *convex* side up, a slightly larger golden pheasant neck feather long enough to cover feathers 2 and 3. Tie this down to lie flat.

10. Prepare the eyes of the shrimp by cutting a V from a golden pheasant tippet. Tie this in to lie flat on top of feather 9.

11. Dub a further length of tying thread and wind it to *B.* Wind three turns of tinsel and hackle to *B.* Tie these in and cut off.

12. Tie in, *convex* side up, a golden pheasant neck feather. This should be tied down to lie along the body so that it will veil, but not cover, feathers 9 and 10.

13. Dub a further length of the tying thread; wind this to *C* and secure it.

14. Tie in, *convex* side up, a golden pheasant neck feather. Tie this down so that it will lie flat along the body.

15. Finish the fly with a whip finish and apply red varnish to the head.

10th September

Dear Colonel,
  Thank you for your
letter o the a...

① ② ③ ⑨ ⑩ ⑫ ⑭

Side View

Ⓐ Ⓑ Ⓒ

Top View

Cement

Step 10

FIGURE XIII—21 (NO TITLE)

Black-Eyed Prawn (or Frances)

Tying silk	According to body color
Hook	Any size standard, double or single size 8 to 4/0 or low-water double or single size 2 to size 10
Whisks	Six large natural red cock hackles, stripped of all fibers and tied in so that they splay out nearly equidistantly from each other and extend at least 3 inches long
Rostrum (nose)	A fairly large bunch of cock pheasant tail fibers set over the whisks and nearly as long as the body
Ribbing floss	One strand, red
Eye floss	A double strand, red, waxed★
Ribbing	Flat gold tinsel, size 2, or wire
Hackle	A natural fox-red cock's hackle tied in at stem (*not* point)
Body	Bright red seal's fur★, thick at hook's bend and tapered to eye, in carrot or cone shape
Eyes	Two tiny black beads tied in near rear of body, on top, to resemble a pair of eyes. Red eyes are substituted for black when the body is black seal's fur.
Head	Red for red-bodied fly and black for all others

The famous *Frances* is dressed in four color combinations: red (as above), black, yellow, and "bottle green" (dark green). The green pattern has an egg sac of orange seal's fur applied as a small collar next to the eye of the hook. Since the dressing is rather unusual, let's review it by steps:

1. Attach the appropriate colored tying thread (according to body color) just short of the eye and wind down in close turns to the bend of the hook.

2. Tie in at the bend the six prepared hackle stalks so that they splay out equidistantly. Bind down butts and remove surplus. Take the thread back to bend of hook again.

3. Tie in at least five or six cock pheasant tail fibers; bind down, cut off surplus, and take thread again to bend of hook.

4. Tie in one longish strand of ribbing thread of appropriate color.

5. Tie in the ribbing tinsel at exactly the same place.

6. Tie in, again at the same place, a double length of the appropriate color thread for attaching eyes. (Wire is unsuitable.)

7. Double a fox-red cock's hackle and tie in by the butt at the same place (over bend of hook) as above.

8. Prepare the seal's fur dubbing; spin on at bend, and take down the shank just short of the eye. Build up the body into fat carrot shape, tapering to the front.

9. Rib with the tinsel down body and tie off.

10. Twist the doubled length of eye floss, and

thread on the two black beads, positioning them as eyes at top of body; then figure-eight with the doubled floss until both eyes are secure at the top of the body. Rib the rest of the body with the surplus floss and secure it at the eye end of the hook.

11. Take the ribbing hackle down the body behind each turn of tinsel. Make sure the hackle fibers are sloping back towards the bend and downward; trim off any sticking out at the sides or on top with scissors.

12. Wind the final strand of ribbing floss down the body to make the ribbing hackle secure. Whip-finish, and varnish head in appropriate color.

The pattern given above is for the red *Frances*, which is very popular. The others are done in the same manner, using appropriate colors where marked with an asterisk. An illustration of the fly dressed by its originator is given in Plate 52.

While the many theories of why salmon take artificial flies can be accepted or rejected as one chooses, there is a great deal more to it than what has just been said. The hypothesis of one astute angler is often rejected by another, but the fact remains that imitations of the salmon's oceanic diet are a viable alternative.

The first suggestion regarding salmon fly selection is to begin with the traditional style, but if this is unsuccessful, try something quite different, such as prawn or shrimp representations, or even streamers or bucktails. Anglers who prefer the classic featherwings, such as the *Jock Scott, Green Highlander, Durham Ranger, Silver Wilkinson, Thunder and Lightning, Rosy Dawn,* and the various *Doctors,* are becoming as rare as those who still prefer split-bamboo rods. The modern trend is toward hairwings and, in some cases, hairwing conversions and adaptations. In the matter of adherence to the classics, there is a middle ground. The bodies of the classic featherwings can be simplified, and the wings converted to hair in the same or similar mixtures of colors as the feathers.

Although no one can narrow down the field of fly selection exactly, accumulated experience is the angler's greatest asset. The first narrowing down can be done on fly size.

Fly Size

Since most salmon rivers are of average size and depth, let's consider them first. When the current is

Fast water on the Spey River

BOB O'SHAUGHNESSY

deep and fast, such as below falls, a larger fly is advisable for visibility—normally a size 2. When the flow widens out a bit and is more moderate, a size 4 pattern would be better. These larger flies also are more visible, and therefore are better takers, when water is discolored, such as after rain. Bright colors, such as orange and yellow, should prove superior for the same reason.

The most useful sizes in rivers of moderate size and depth are 6 and 8. When the current becomes from medium to slow, probably because the pool has widened still more, a size 6 pattern should be preferable. Size 8 should be ideal when the stream becomes thinner and more sluggish, such as in the tail of a pool where it widens out over the gravel before spilling downstream. Such a place always fascinates me, perhaps because longer and longer casts provide wider and wider swings, at any moment of which a salmon may take hold.

Never ignore the slow and thin water at the tail of a pool, perhaps thinking it isn't deep enough.

There usually are many depressions in the gravel in which salmon can lie comfortably. They often do this to rest after swimming up the fast water over the lip. These fish are resting preparatory to moving again, so they usually are good takers. Many anglers think size 8 is as small as anyone needs to go, but I like to fish 10s and even 12s in such places, even though they aren't supposed to hook as well as the larger sizes. A size 12 fly can be dressed on a size 10 hook, or a size 10 fly on a size 8 hook—in other words, fully dressed low-water patterns.

These are general rules for wet-fly fishing, but you may need to go a few sizes bigger on very large rivers, using the same size graduations with respect to river depth and current flow. On Canada's Grand Cascapedia and Restigouche, for example, 5/0s were commonly fished flies, normally with the longer and stiffer rods needed to cast them. With the advent of lighter tackle, however, this big-fly theory, often noted in older books, has largely been exploded, and the very big flies have become relics of the past; it is much harder to set the hook with them, not to mention the difficulty of casting them with modern lighter equipment.

It will bob up now and again in this book that trout fishermen must forget much of what they have learned, because it doesn't apply to salmon fishing. A case in point is the sizes of dry flies that salmon take best. You are not trying to match hatches! You are trying to attract salmon, which means that small dry flies usually are inferior to bigger ones—often, very big ones as large as one can cast conveniently. For example, Lee Wulff says, "I use 3/0 *White Wulffs* to wake up sleepy salmon under low-water conditions and often catch salmon on them." Usually, high-riding patterns between sizes 2 and 6 are better and can be considered standard sizes for salmon dry flies. Lee also mentions, however, that he enjoys using tiny tackle trying to hook and land salmon on dry flies as small as 16s or even 18s. His challenge to himself and to others is to hook the biggest salmon on the smallest hook.

My own experience has been that if salmon will come to dry flies at all, they will come most often to the bigger ones, and the patterns used are of minor importance. Of course, light-wire hooks are mandatory, such as the famous Wilson Dry Fly Hook.

Fly Color

As a collector of antique salmon flies and an admirer of the fine art of their construction, I've often wondered, in connection with the plethora of patterns both old and new, why there have to be so many. Does a salmon take or refuse a fly because it has or hasn't a certain ingredient or the proper blending of colors? How much time does a salmon take to inspect a fly? Would a salmon go for a *Silver Doctor* but refuse a *Wilkinson*? Would it bang a *Blue Rat* but turn up its nose at a *Hairy Mary*? Can selection be reduced to a sensible few that can be contained in a single fly book? Yes, but I, for one, will still carry far more than needed. Let's see if we can rationalize this ancient and still continuing controversy over fly colors and degrees of brightness.

Comments of three expert anglers in the first half of this century are indicative:

A. H. Chaytor (1910)
"If a fly is neat and workmanlike, well-shaped, and with wing and hackle dressed sufficiently lightly to play freely in the water, it is of comparatively small importance what pattern or of what colors the various parts are composed."

A. H. E. Wood (1933)
"As regards pattern, I do not believe that this matters at all. 'Blue Charm' and 'Silver Blue' are my stock, simply on the principle that one is more or less black and the other white, and so they give *me* a choice.

"I am in absolute agreement about particular shades of color being just so much nonsense, but I do like to have a dark fly and also a light one."

Richard Waddington (1948)
"The question of the value of various colors in salmon flies is one on which widely divergent views are held. I think that most fishermen have felt that to suppose that a salmon should differentiate between say a 'Black Doctor' and a 'Thunder & Lightning' was faintly ridiculous and that the more modern school of thought is tending all the time, largely as a result of the experiences of greased line fishing, to the belief that color is of little importance in the salmon fly."

Though color may be of little importance in salmon flies, it is of some importance during daylight hours. A fly pattern is a mixture of colors, and tone is the result of such blending. It is the tone—the graduation from light or bright to dark or opaque—that is of real importance.

In *Through the Fish's Eye* (1973), famous angler Mark Sosin and ichthyologist John Clark explain how fish see:

In our own eye we have an iris, or diaphragm, that opens or closes depending on the amount of light entering the eye. The iris in a fish's eye is fixed. It is an opaque curtain of tissue with a hole in the center. The iris admits light through the fixed center only. Adjustments to changes in the brightness of light are managed by receptor cells in the retina.

There are two types of receptor cells in the retina which are used alternately, depending on light levels: rod cells and cone cells. Each group sends messages to the brain describing any image flashed on the retina. The cone cells are the *color receptors* and are used in daytime or whenever the light source is brighter than about one foot-candle. At night, or when the light level falls below one foot-candle, fish change over to the rod cells, which are the super light sensitive receptors. In fact, the rods are about 30 times more sensitive than the cones, but they detect and record *only black* and *white*. The complete changeover may occupy two hours or more in the fish's normal daily cycle.

Another avid academic angler on the subject of both color perception and feeding habits of salmon was Preston Jennings. The conclusions he reached as a result of intense study differ significantly from the above. His findings include the following three statements: "1. Salmon do feed in fresh water after their return from the sea. 2. Salmon can distinguish colors, are especially sensitive to red. 3. Salmon take artificial flies which suggest the natural food produced by their native river." Jennings's studies concentrated on the manner in which light strikes and penetrates the water, and the resulting spectrum of colors surrounding objects in the water. Depending on the intensity and source of light, the bands of light surrounding the silhouette would vary with different colors dominating at different times of the day or year.

When a salmon looks up toward the light and sees a fly drifting or swinging by, it may see some color, but against the background of light, the color is more of a tone, or a brighter or darker silhouette, accented usually by a certain amount of sunlight. Thus, while we can diminish (but not eliminate) the value of color, we can't diminish the importance of tone and flash, which depend mostly upon the intensity of the sun and its position relative to the salmon's vision. This is echoed by the "bright fly, bright day; dark fly, dark day" theory advanced by some anglers and disputed by others. The theory is simple. On a bright day a bright fly sparkles, but it doesn't sparkle on a dull day. Salmon respond to bright flies, but lacking reflection from the sun, a darker one with more pronounced silhouette seems better. Even on a bright day, you should use a dark fly if the salmon is facing the sun, so the position of the sun relative to that of the salmon is more important than the above theory indicates.

Which flies are best for the different lighting conditions? Everyone has his favorites, and I have no intention of imposing mine on anyone else. For whatever it may be worth, however, let me suggest

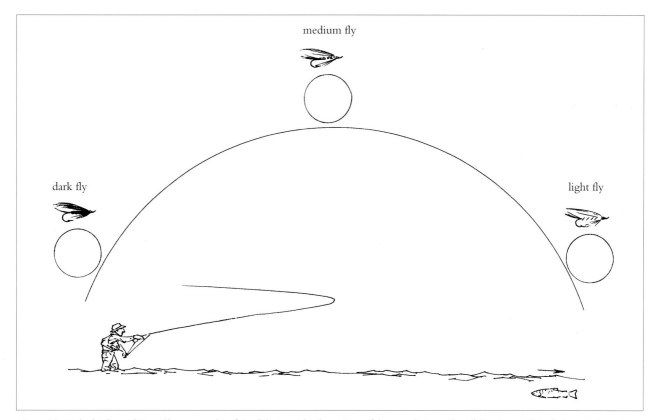

medium fly

dark fly

light fly

Figure 11. Under bright conditions, always use a lot of tinsel, but consider the position of the sun relative to that of the salmon. If the fly is cast before salmon facing the sun, use a darker fly because the salmon sees it against the sun and therefore sees it mainly as a silhouette. If the fly is cast before salmon whose tails are toward the sun, use a lighter fly because the salmon sees detail and flash more easily. When the sun is overhead, use a fly between light and dark shades.

two patterns for each of eight lighting conditions, including two for discolored water. Either one of each pair can be selected for a total of eight flies, which should be carried in at least the three most useful hook sizes of 4, 6, and 8. This totals two dozen flies, which could start a beginner's collection. Few of us will be content with only these, however, and extras are advisable in case of loss or damage. These are normal wet flies. You might also want as many dry flies in similar light reflective or silhouette classes, in addition to some low-water dressings. The choice between double and single hooks is a matter of opinion; if single hooks are used, offset ones provide better hooking advantages.

When a fly is presented to salmon facing the sun near the horizon, a *Silver Rat* or a *Night Hawk* would be appropriate under bright and sunny conditions. The latter can be simplified to just a silver body with black hairwing and black hackle. Under shady or cloudy conditions a *Black Bear* with green fluorescent butt or a *Black Rat* would be my choices. If I were confined to only one pattern for all conditions, it would be the *Black Bear* with a fluorescent butt. The butt color makes little or no difference. This fly is one of the simplest to tie and has an imposing reputation all around the Atlantic. The fancier *Black Dose* is the classic pattern.

When the sun is high in the sky, a fly of medium shade or tone is recommended. Under bright and sunny conditions this could be a *Blue Charm* or *Hairy Mary,* both general favorites of mine. There is an Irish version of the *Hairy Mary* that I like even better because it has a fluorescent orange butt. In this one, the wing is of Irish badger hair, a point rather inconsequential. Under shady or cloudy conditions, I would select the original *Muddler* or the *Rusty Rat.* The amount of tinsel when the sun is high doesn't seem to make much difference.

When a fly is presented to a salmon that is not facing the sun, a very light one is appropriate—mostly white, light gray, or any light color. Under bright and sunny conditions, I would select a *Silver Gray* or a *Silver Blue,* because both have light wings and tinsel bodies. If it is shady or cloudy, a *Gray Rat* or the *Priest* should be effective.

There is no sharp dividing line in any of these categories. Just memorize the general idea and use your own judgment. I often fish all day with a *Blue Charm* or a *Hairy Mary.* In theory, I would do better by changing flies for changing conditions. Though this may be true, I am sometimes lazy!

The above suggestions are for water that is clear, or very nearly so. When fishing discolored water, such as when rivers are peaty or after a rain, the prospects may not be as good, but get out on the stream anyway. You need a big fly with lots of red, orange, or yellow in it. If the day is bright and sunny, use a highly reflective pattern such as *The Chief* or a *Copper Killer;* it may be best to work them deep. As alternatives for less bright or cloudy conditions, try Colonel Drury's famous *General Practitioner* or the equally renowned *Cosseboom.*

Bucktails and Streamers

The importance of using bucktails and streamers in Atlantic salmon fishing is, in my opinion, too often diminished or overlooked. In summer fishing, they are valuable as a "change-of-pace" fly. For example, there are conditions when a pool has been fished by a large number of rods. The rods have been taking fish, but suddenly the action slacks off. At such times, these baitfish imitators prove effective because the fish have already seen conventional patterns. It doesn't matter what the salmon think they are, or why they take them. The fact is that they often do.

Streamer flies or bucktails can produce excellent results during a summer rise of water. Under these conditions, when the water is often discolored, salmon seem to have little difficulty seeing these "big fish flies" and are attracted to their large sizes and bright colors.

In bright salmon fishing, the streamer or bucktail can be very effective in the fall when the water temperature is 50 degrees or lower. Under such conditions they can outfish any of the standard patterns. They will work in deep water, in shallow water, in broken water, or in smooth water. The splash of a streamer, rather than flushing fish, seems to attract them. In this type of fishing, the streamer can be fished with either a floating or a sinking line. When the water is very cold, the sinking line is preferred. Under all conditions, the fly should be cast straight across the stream, allowing the current to make a considerable bag in the line and hence increase the fly's speed. Evidently, working the fly does not increase its attractiveness to salmon, although my opinion is that it does help to move it occasionally in imitation of the erratic manner in which a baitfish swims. Fly size is usually number 2 or 4, on 3X long hooks.

The interest in studying the uses of streamers and bucktails for effective salmon fishing is recent and is increasing. Some of the expert anglers in the United Kingdom snapped up the idea about as soon as we did. Their bucktails are very sparse—only a dozen hairs or so—and are up to 3 inches in length.

One of several reasons why bright salmon may be interested in these baitfish imitations was interestingly brought out by Colonel Drury in the autumn 1969 issue of the *Flyfishers' Journal*. In an article on how salmon take flies in flowing water, he explains: "In the autumn the situation is complicated by the fact that one may be dealing with two distinct categories of fish. There is the fresh fish which may, depending on conditions and water temperature, behave either like a spring fish or a summer one and there is the stale fish which, as the spawning season approaches may, particularly if a cock, come on the take again. When these stale fish are interested it is generally in a large fly, irrespective of water height or temperature, and they will often grab it with a ferocity that almost pulls the rod out of one's hand. To understand this 'killer' take one must remember that the male salmon parr can fertilize the eggs of an adult female salmon and that, if allowed to do so, this precocious youngster will take part in the nuptials.

"As the spawning season approaches, the cock fish do become restless and one can watch them chasing about in the pools. I suggest that they are beginning to feel jealous and to regard small fish as potential suitors for the favors of the hen fish, which they understandably regard as their special prerogative. They will kill these potential interlopers if they can catch them and this explains why a large fly which superficially resembles a salmon parr can be so effective. As the season advances still further toward spawning time all fish seem to lose interest in small flies to the extent that, one might almost say, 'They are on the parr,' but it is noticeable that the nearer it is to spawning time the less inclined are hen fish to take, but that the cocks when they take, take with an almighty bang!"

Fluorescent Butts
Previous comments about the effectiveness of fluorescent butts need expansion, because many of us are convinced that a bit of fluorescence is highly effec-

tive in salmon flies. A little is better than too much, except possibly in discolored water. I have studied learned dissertations about the relative effectiveness of the various colors under changing conditions, but experience indicates that no one color seems any better than the others. If pressed for an opinion, however, I would opt for green, followed by yellow and red.

Since the simple *Black Bear* has proved more effective with a fluorescent butt, I have been experimenting with various applications. Additions of a few strands of fluorescent thread in the *Black Bear's* wing have been very successful for me. After tying down the wing wrap in two threads of fluorescent material, such as red and blue or green and yellow, to let the two threads on each side act more or less as median lines, and cut the ends off as long as the wing. The *Black Bear* is an excellent pattern for fly tiers to play with, because it can be varied any way we want.

You can also use fluorescent monofilament in small diameters, such as in a pattern called the *Firefly*. Build up a fairly fat body, with the rear half being fluorescent monofilament and the front half black floss. The rest of the fly is the familiar *Black Bear*, with the rear half of the body substituting for the butt. You can make this a bit fancier by first winding the rear half of the body with flat silver tinsel and tying it off in the middle. Then apply the body, as above, and rib the black part with the remainder of the tinsel. The tinsel under the monofilament adds to flash.

Nymphs
Nymph fishing for salmon is an often neglected part of the game, but under suitable conditions—usually those of low, warm, and clear water—salmon may take nymphs while refusing everything else. Since parr fed on nymphs before maturing and going to sea, there is no reason why adult salmon shouldn't be conditioned to take nymphs as well as flies. They do, but no one knows why they so often can be so selective about it.

Fly dressers seeking perfection can dress nymphs with uncanny accuracy, but I know of no firm proof that these are more effective than cruder tyings. Wrap four or five strands of peacock herl around a #8 hook to make a cigar-shaped body. Using a hook of similar size, make a body of fine black chenille and wind on about two turns of a very narrow, soft black hackle at the head. This provides two nymphal imitations that seem to work as well as more complicated dressings. It is rarely necessary to go to sizes smaller than this.

Although these simple dressings are effective, many anglers will think that more lifelike ones should do better. Therefore, here are some lifelike nymph patterns.

DeFeo's Salmon Nymphs

The following patterns are by celebrated angler-artist Charles DeFeo, of New York. They are among his favorites. Dressings start on the hook shank above the middle of the barb.

Black Nymph

Tag	Gold tinsel and flourescent orange floss
Tail	Bronze mallard feathers
Butt	Peacock herl
Body	Black seal's fur
Ribbing	Fine oval gold tinsel
Throat	Bronze mallard feathers
Wing	Jungle cock hackle points, tent style
Head	Black

Gold Nymph

Tag	Silver tinsel and flourescent orange floss
Tail	Bronze mallard fibers
Butt	Peacock herl
Body	First half: oval gold tinsel; second half: peacock herl
Throat	Bronze mallard feathers
Wing	Jungle cock points, tent style
Head	Black

Green Cosseboom Nymph

Tag	Gold tinsel
Tail	Golden pheasant crest
Body	Green wool
Ribbing	Fine oval gold tinsel
Throat	Black hackle, long and sparse
Wing	Jungle cock hackle points, tent style
Head	Tan

Under normal conditions of good flow, average temperature, and reasonable water height, when fishing a pool fished by many rods, a simple nymph with or without hackle often is more effective than the fully dressed fly. This may be because the nymph is different from the types of flies usually used.

Nymphlike flies (which may be flies with the wings clipped off) also work well when salmon are "lying in," as they do for example in cold-water pools or in the tails of pools in the autumn. These fish have little motivation to move and usually are difficult to entice. Under such conditions, nymphs can be deadly if they are fished properly.

In the summer, cold-water pools should be fished by false-casting the line and delivering the fly straight across the stream. If the fish can be seen, as is often the case, the fly should be fished about 1 foot beyond and ahead of it. The rod should then immediately be raised with a slight tremor in the hand and with considerable speed so that the fly is practically breaking the surface while it moves several inches across and ahead of the fish.

If the fish moves to the fly, tease it by taking the fly away, casting it downstream, and waiting half a minute or so. Repeat the process and the fish might very possibly take the fly.

Charlie DeFeo   COURTESY OF PAUL SCHMOOKLER

PLATE 54
ORIGINAL NYMPH PATTERNS

Unnamed Nymph
dressed by Howard Clifford, Jr.

Junglestone
dressed by Ted Niemeyer

Schweimeyer
dressed by Wilhelm Gruber

Peastone
dressed by Ted Niemeyer

Black Nymph
dressed by Charlie DeFeo

Green Cosseboom
dressed by Charlie DeFeo

Gold Nymph
dressed by Charlie DeFeo

This technique is effective because the fish does not get as much opportunity to see the fly as it would if the fly were being fished by normal wet-fly methods. Fish are penned in these cold-water pools because other parts of the river are too warm, and there is very little current in these pools.

In the autumn, when a number of fish are lying in rather slow-moving water ("lying in," or staying for several days or perhaps weeks) and are being fished over extensively, these nymph imitations are very effective when fished in the following manner: Cast a long line straight across the stream. After several seconds, while the nymph sinks slightly, grasp the line just below the stripping guide and draw it moderately slowly until the pulling hand is straight down by your side. Repeat the process until the fly has fished the water to be covered. If a fish should boil for the nymph but not take it, rest it for a short period and then fish for it again in the same way.

Nymphs also should be productive as change-over flies during normal summer conditions and during low-water conditions before fish have gone into the cold-water pools.

Although nymph fishing for salmon has its skeptics, one angler who is not is Howard Clifford, Jr., from Portland, Maine. In October 1980, on a river he protectively declines to name, Clifford captured (and still holds) the U.S. record for salmon by landing a 28-pound, 1-ounce fish on a nymph he had tied the previous day. The fly, like the river it was so successful on, remains nameless. Following is the pattern:

Tail   Fibers from a ring-necked pheasant tail feather
Body   Dark gray mink, under fur
Ribbing   Gold oval tinsel
Wing case   Turkey tail, lacquered and tied in stonefly style (two
            strips, lacquered and folded back to imitate the stonefly
            in two sections)
Beard   Gray fox
Head   Dark brown tying thread

There are three basic types of wet flies. The simplest is the fly hook with a body, which is, of course, a nymph. Next is the fly hook with a body and front hackle. Finally, there is the conventional wet fly with a body, front hackle, and a wing. There can be variations of these, such as a hook with a body and a wing but no throat hackle, or a body with a palmered hackle rather than a mere throat hackle. There are times in salmon fishing when one of these

stages in fly dressing will work better than the others. There are also times when any one will be as successful as any other. Perhaps salmon fishermen should take greater advantage of these types, occasionally trimming off the wing of a wet fly and some or all of the hackle to see if this nymphlike simplification works any better.

While nymphs in part are low-water patterns, other ways to fish them will be noted later. The use of nymphs in salmon fishing seems to be a North American method that even we are too much neglecting.

Terrestrials

Terrestrials have been referred to by Lee Wulff as "the next and perhaps final step." He goes on to say that "in spite of the wide variety of flies that may work, I still think the basic urge to rise comes from a salmon's insect-feeding memories as a parr." In Lee's quest to always try something different, during one particularly difficult season he decided to experiment with imitations of terrestrials. His most successful fly for that year was the *Black Ant*. Other anglers report similar success with *Grasshoppers, Dragonflies,* and other such insects salmon might have fed on as parr.

Among anglers, salmon anglers in particular, transition from the traditional is often a reluctant process. Initially this was true in the general acceptance of the dry fly and for other innovations such as the *Bomber,* the *Surface Stone Fly,* and the *Woolly Worm.* Many scoff at streamers, nymphs, and terrestrials, but, as these "unusual" choices creep into our fly boxes, we may well find that the belief that one can find success with salmon with almost any fly—combining it with the more mystical elements of technique and timing—is valid.

PLATE 55
TERRESTRIALS

Dragon Fly
dressed by Mark Waslick

Hopper
dressed by Bob Warren

Ant
dressed by Keith Fulsher

Tube Flies

More popular on the European side of the Atlantic, another fly type that raised the eyebrows and of traditional anglers is the tube fly. In relatively recent years, it has become an important element in the salmon angler's arsenal, and some think the tube fly is one of the most important innovations in angling since Wood introduced the greased-line method. Sometimes resembling either an elver or a nymph, tube flies are generally rigged with treble hooks, which may be part of the reason for their lack of acceptance in this country. They are, however, still very effective with doubles or even singles. Long and slim, like bucktails, they evidently provide a different action that salmon seem to go for to such an extent that some anglers use them exclusively.

In addition to elementary tying materials, all that is needed is a supply of tiny tubes of metal or plastic—metal for fishing deep, plastic for near-surface. The bores of the tubes must be no larger than will allow the leader to pass through them comfortably. In some places, metal tubes may be considered weighted and therefore illegal. Either metal or plastic tube flies can be made that will fish near-surface or at any reasonable depth. Their lack of rigidity diminishes the tendency to wear a hole in the fish's jaw so that it could throw the hook.

One of the most significant advantages of the tube fly is its versatility, both for the tier and for the fisherman. An infinite number of adaptations and

PLATE 56
TUBE FLIES, DRESSED BY BILL WILBUR

Akroyd

Jock Scott

Black Bear, Green Butt

Blue Charm

Silver Grey

PLATE 58
STEPS IN TYING THE JOCK SCOTT
DRESSED BY MICHAEL RADENCICH

tube. Before using them, find out if they are legal on rivers you plan to fish. Double or single straight-eye hooks can be used, preferably with very short shanks. With single ones, the short-shank salmon egg type is recommended.

One of the most successful tube flies used for salmon in Iceland is the *Collie Dog,* a pattern that was adapted as a tube fly. Use a metal tube 1/2 inch long, or very slightly longer. Dress the head of the tube with a small bunch of the longest black collie dog hair, using black thread in the same way bucktail would be applied for a wing. Cut a piece of colorless plastic tubing 1/2 inch long, or very slightly longer, that can be pressed tightly over the rear of the metal tube (only enough to hold it in place). String this on the leader and tie on the (usually treble) hook. Now fit the rear of the plastic tubing over the eye of the hook, thus making a nonrigid connection between the dressed metal tube and the eye. If the eye is round, it may fit into the tube more easily if it is pinched into an oval shape carefully with pliers. The dressing is nearly twice as long as the rest of the lure.

Although there are accounts that predate this one, history tells us that tube flies were originated about 1945 by the noted fly dresser Winnie Morawski, when she was working for the tackle firm of Charles Playfair & Company, of Aberdeen. At first she used sections of turkey wing quills with the pith scraped out and with the shanks of the strung treble hooks inside the quill sections. She dressed orthodox flies (body dressing, wing, hackle, and so on) on these. A doctor named William Michie, when visiting the shop, suggested using sections of surgical tubing instead. Later the treble hook was left on the outside so that the tube could travel up the monofilament line, out of harm's way, when a fish was hooked. Also, the wing later was dressed around the tube, instead of in only one place.

Enduring Classics

The previous chapter traced the evolution in salmon fly design from the simple through the complicated to the sensible, the salient phases of which were sketched. Through evolution or through reason, or

PLATE 57
INTERCHANGEABLE TUBE FLY
SECTIONS, DRESSED BY BILL WILBUR

combinations can be created with reasonably limited materials. Tube flies can be tied with either a two- or three-dimensional wing, in the standard manner or in the round (360 degrees). The advantage of the latter is that the fly will appear the same to the fish from any angle. Tube flies also can be dressed in sections with interchangeable components.

There are two ways of rigging tube flies: with the loose hook, and with the hook secured in the rear of a plastic sleeve. Treble hooks for salmon fishing can be small, such as numbers 8 to 10, and sometimes smaller, depending on the size of the

whatever, a basic fly style has developed because it has been proven to be the style that usually gets the best results in hooking salmon. (This is in reference to patterns based on flies, as differentiated from others that could be more aptly termed lures, such as those made to represent developed elvers, prawns, shrimp, baitfish, and so on.).

Of the classics, the popular *Jock Scott* is one of the prettiest of those of the Elizabethan era, as shown in Plate 24 and in the dressing procedure in Plate 58. This famous fly contains about fifty components, including, when authentically dressed, several rare feathers. Here is the pattern, according to Pryce-Tannatt:

Jock Scott

Tag	Silver tinsel
Tail	Golden pheasant crest and Indian crow
Butt	Black ostrich herl
Body	In two equal halves: first half, golden yellow floss butted with black herl, and veiled above and below with six or more toucan feathers; second half, black floss
Ribbing	Fine oval silver tinsel over golden yellow floss, broader oval silver tinsel or flat silver tinsel and twist (in the large sizes) over the black floss
Hackle	A black hackle over the black floss
Throat	Speckled gallina
Wings	A pair of black white-tipped turkey tail strips (back to back); over these, but not entirely covering them, a mixed sheath of married strands of peacock wing, yellow, scarlet, and blue swan, bustard, florican, and golden pheasant tail; two strands of peacock sword feather above; married narrow strips of teal and barred summer duck at the sides; brown mallard over
Sides	Jungle cock
Cheeks	Blue chatterer
Topping	Golden pheasant crest
Horns	Blue and yellow macaw
Head	Black

The Victorian era boasted well over a thousand such patterns, more or less as complicated as this one. Together they constitute the ancestry of the salmon fly as we know it today, and although they cannot compete with the practicality of their modern counterparts, their beauty is unrivaled.

PLATE 59
POPULAR SPEY PATTERNS

Carron
dressed by Steve Gobin

Lady Caroline
dressed by Syd Glasso

Grey Heron
dressed by Bob Warren

The Spey type is an interesting variation in classic salmon fly style. Examples are the *Gray Heron, Carron,* and *Lady Caroline.* As shown in Plate 59, these flies have simple wings of soft feathers such as barred mallard or teal, but the most distinguishing characteristic is their long, flowing hackles of black or gray heron. I add this note because many popular simple patterns can be hackled this way. They should provide excellent mobility in clear but fast water on salmon rivers of North America as well as on Scotland's streams such as the famous Spey, where they were born.

6

Tips on Locating Salmon

"Spring Run"

Stream fishermen who can "read the water" (my 1974 book, *How to Find Fish—and Make Them Strike*) are better able to locate salmon when they confine their attention to areas of moderate flow rather than places of concealment and feed lanes. These are of value when seeking trout, but not salmon. Salmon are apt to lie off to the side of the current, herd up at the head or foot of a pool, or settle down in a "hot spot" beneath a fall of rapid water.

Salmon ignore security to the extent that they habitually lie in plain sight in places where the river's flow is moderate, but they may not take lures if they feel they are being observed. Since they have no desire for food, except possibly as a matter of curiosity or instinct, feed lanes are of no interest to them. The key to locating salmon can be given in two words: *moderate flow.* For the salmon, moderate flow is three-dimensional: It provides necessary oxygen, comfortable resting lies, and the path of least resistance to complete the journey to the spawning ground.

Understanding moderate flow is so important in salmon fishing that this entire chapter will be devoted to it. After absorbing what is presented here, you should be able to view any part of a salmon river and locate one or more spots that should hold salmon, even if conditions of the water are such that the fish can't be observed. Thus, almost instantly, you will be able to select the few likely places on which to concentrate and can ignore all the rest. You can put the fly where judgment says that salmon should be lying rather than wasting time over unproductive water. Judgment may not be correct all of the time, for reasons we will later explore, but it will be correct most of the time if you thoroughly understand the various situations of moderate flow.

Although trout fishermen are familiar with conditions of moderate flow, even experienced anglers who think they understand it can profit by reviewing moderate flow as it applies to salmon.

Exactly what is moderate flow? The best example is to imagine that you are facing upstream at least knee-deep in a spot where the river is flowing rather briskly. Put a hand down in the water beside one of your boots. There, without any barrier to slow it down, the stream flows at full force. Now put your hand just upstream of the boot, and then downstream of it. In these two places note that the

flow is much more moderate because the boot obstructs it. A rock in the stream has the same effect, and so do many other types of obstructions. Now note the water flowing around the boot. This obstruction forms a wake in the current in the form of a **V** extending downstream and widening as it gradually disappears. A smaller but similar disturbance also extends upstream where the current has to divide to flow around the boot. These visible wakes are called *edges.* Outside of them the current travels at usual speed, but inside of them it is slower—a place of relatively quiet water.

Notice these edges where the current separates to go around a midstream rock. Observe that where a rock, or any other obstruction, juts out into the current from the shore, there is one edge. There is a similar visible edge where an entering brook flows into the mainstream of the river, or perhaps where there is a small island or any other obstruction to the current's flow. The current travels at the usual speed outside these edges but is much more moderate inside of them. Salmon seek the insides of edges, but usually not so far inside that they form dead water. Where fish are visible, notice that they can lie inside the edges with so little exertion that they seem nearly motionless. These are called *resting positions* or *holding positions,* where salmon pause in their travels upstream. In them the fish are said to be *lying in.*

These are not the only resting positions, however. Any depression in the stream's bottom can be a resting position, because the current flows over it and there is moderate flow inside it. These depressions can be quite small, such as a rock on the bottom or an old salmon redd, and may be only large enough to hold one salmon. Where the current fans out and thins over the gravel at the tail of a pool, there can be many such depressions. They may not be visible to anglers, but provide enough moderate flow to satisfy salmon. We can only assume they are there and fan-cast the area to locate salmon. Salmon like these depressions at the tails of pools because they can rest there and regain strength after negotiating the fast water flowing over the lips. Such resting positions are used only temporarily, and fish lying in them usually are good takers.

The banks of a river, besides influencing the flow of the current as they narrow, widen out, and provide obstructions, also can tell us about the

"Evening"

nature of the riverbed. If the banks contain many boulders, the riverbed should also. Rocky banks indicate a rocky or graveled bottom, as do grassy areas with outcrops of rock. On the other hand, if the banks are grassy and the river's edge is sandy, the bed of the stream probably is sandy, silty, or fine gravel. Salmon like to lie over gravel, but not sand or silt, although along meadow stretches there are occasional exceptions, perhaps because the salmon have no alternative.

If you return to the same stretch of river year after year, keep in mind that large rivers that are not very deep may be affected by ice. Thus, lies may have changed and places that were hot spots a season ago may be hot spots no longer. Some pools may have been ruined, and good new ones may have been made. There may be good fishing in a place that formerly was no good. This may be a warning to anyone who is considering spending a large sum of money to buy or lease a pool on such a river.

Normal Summer Conditions

The resting or holding positions of salmon in pools vary with the height of water in the streams. When water is higher or lower than normal summer conditions, these positions will change. Let's first become acquainted with such positions during normal summer conditions, which is when we'll usually be fishing, and then look at where salmon may be located when rivers are too high or too low. Since there are typical situations applicable to almost any river, drawings are provided to help make them clear. These conditions will be encountered again and again.

Normal summer conditions generally are defined as when the temperature of water in the stream is 70 degrees Fahrenheit or below. Since 70 degrees is a rather critical temperature, and since air and water temperatures affect fishing success, carrying a thermometer is very helpful. Some rivers will produce fish in the regular pools even when the

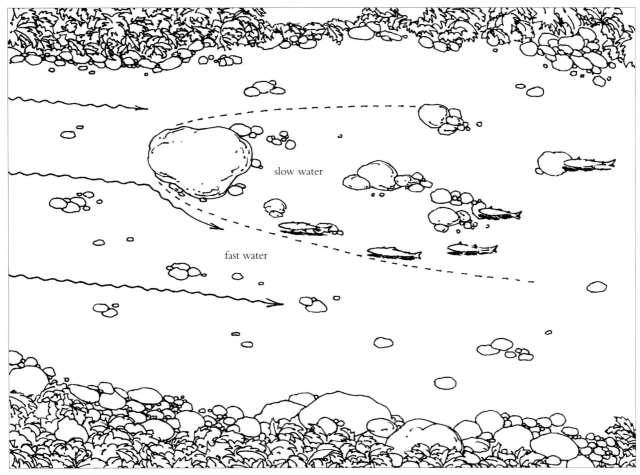

Figure 12. Salmon lie near a rock.

water is above 70 degrees, but this is true primarily when there is a heavy volume. When this situation exists, fishing is best very early in the morning and very late in the afternoon or evening rather than during the heat of the day. If the regular pools do not produce fish under such conditions, seek them in cold-water ones such as will be discussed.

Since summer fish like moderate flow, they are less likely to be in the deeper quiet water and will not stay in very fast water that has no current-breaking obstacles. Do not be fooled, however, by the *surface* speed of the water. The water on the surface moves faster than the water beneath. The bed of the river itself acts as an obstacle to speed, and therefore the narrowed tails of pools (where the water on the surface may be quite fast) will hold fish—more so if there are rocks or other obstacles in the tail.

Figure 12 shows a rock or boulder in a salmon stream. There are two edges, or conditions of mod-

erate flow, trailing downstream from the rock, as marked by the dashed lines. These edges can be lies for salmon. How good they are depends on the size of the rock in relation to the depth of the water. As a rule, a large submerged rock provides a better lie than a rock in shallower water. Rocks in shallow water tend to have sand and gravel piled at their heads, so whether or not there will be a suitable lie just above such a rock depends on how deep the water is. Of the two edges, one may be better than the other, as determined by which offers more ideal flow and the best streambed conformation. Salmon may lie in the edge nearest the inshore bank if the water is deep enough, but generally the best water is on the offshore side. Below this large boulder may be smaller rocks. Salmon may lie in the in-between water. Probably none will be in the water immediately below the large rock, because there the flow may be *too* moderate.

Figure 13. Salmon lie near a combination of rocks.

A better lie is one where another big rock is immediately below an upper one. In fact, a combination of several rocks, as in Figure 13, may provide an ideal pool. Salmon will lie in such a place for the same reason as in the preceding instance, but since two or more rocks provide more area of moderate flow, the place may harbor more fish. The shoreward lines of moderate flow (marked X) may or may not be suitable for salmon, depending largely on the amount of depth and the relative desirability of the edges. Too many rocks or boulders may slow down the current so much that the position will hold no fish.

In fishing a wet fly on an edge lie, it is better to present the fly just at the *inside* of the edge than to cast well beyond it.

Salmon will not lie in eddies even if they seem to present an edge. If an angler hooks a fish in an eddy, he may think that they stay there, but this evi-dently is not so. More likely the fish has left its lie and has followed the fly into the eddy and taken it there.

On some rivers, pools are made by one bar or ledge after another along the length of a large part of the river. A typical bar situation is shown in Figure 14. The shallow water on the bar causes the fish to hesitate before going over it, so some may be nosed up in shallow water on the lip of the bar and may take a fly there. In the shoal above the bar there may be little pockets or depressions in which salmon may lie. Pools made by bars often have rocks or boulders in the deeper water, and fish may lie in moderate flow areas below or near the rocks. The large rock to the right in the diagram indicates that fish may be in the edge of current on the channel side, but perhaps not on the upper edge where it shelves into shallows.

Another situation frequently encountered is a ledge in a stream. If certain conditions exist, this

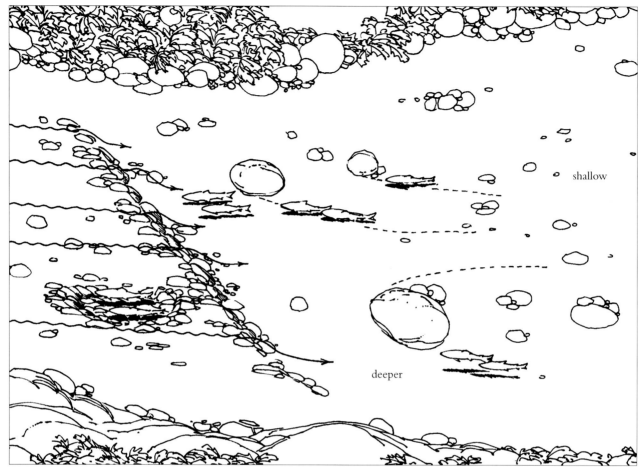

Figure 14. Salmon lie in a pool made by a bar or ledge.

could provide an ideal pool for salmon. The depth of water running over the ledge must be shoal. The water off the ledge must be of reasonable depth and afford a moderate flow. In cases resembling this, salmon may lie in the deeper water right off the ledge and along it. They also may lie in the edges of moderate flow below rocks in the pool and possibly in the pockets just above them.

In some pools, the flow of water will come from two different directions, as when a current flowing over a bar meets the main current or when a side channel meets a main channel, as with a brook entering a stream or a river rejoining itself below an island. The place where the two currents meet provides water of moderate flow and is a good lie for salmon.

In Figure 15, the deep current is entering the pool from the steep bank side while part of the same stream is running over a bar on the shallow bank side. Where the two currents meet, there is in-

between water, indicated by the dashed line. This may be ideal.

In another similar instance, two currents join and form two places where there is in-between water. One is where the two currents meet, which is very similar to the preceding instance. In this case, this is also called *decision water,* because salmon may pause there while deciding which of the two streams to follow. The other place is where the water from the entering stream at the left swings outward around the bend of the bank at the left. Here also is in-between water, because the strong current of the stream meets the water on the inside of the stream flow. If salmon travel up the inside, they will lie on the edge made by the turn of the current toward the bank. Often this edge is rather close to the shore, and fishermen who do not understand the situation may wade where the fish are instead of fishing for them there.

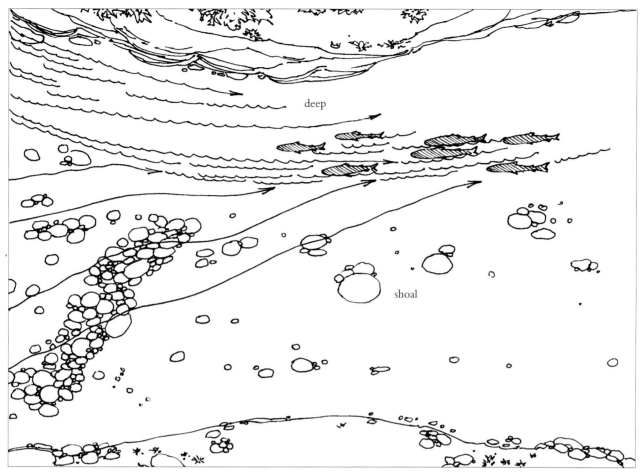

Figure 15. Salmon lie where two currents meet.

Fish will stay in all these places, perhaps for an extended time, if stream depth, rate of flow and other conditions are to their liking.

Sometimes a side channel will be the *main* course the fish will take. If the flow in the main river becomes slow and that in the smaller channel remains brisk, the fish will run the smaller channel.

Salmon often will lie in the narrowed tail of a pool even when the surface water is very swift. Very often beneath this swift water there are submerged rocks that brake the fast water into moderate flow. Tails of pools that are at the heads of strong rapids may be ideal. Do not judge current flow as it appears on the surface, because it is what lies underneath that counts.

Any major obstruction on a salmon river, such as a small dam, waterfall, or even a counting pen, will impede the salmon's normal ascent of the stream. In such situations, look for the first good

holding pool *below* this spot. It is the habit of salmon, upon reaching such an obstruction, to turn back to the first good lie. Eventually they will pass the obstruction, but they seem reluctant to do so when they first encounter it.

If there is a good flow and depth of water along the shore of a stream, and a protrusion is made into it by a rock, a large submerged log, or anything else that breaks into the flow, the downstream side of such a place may be a good lie for salmon. The obstruction makes an edge in the current, and fish will lie in the moderate water along such an edge.

There are stretches of water on many rivers that look hopeless—long, flat bars where there is a good uniform flow of water that, under normal conditions, may be about 3 or 4 feet deep. But though there may be no rocks or boulders, the bottom of the river probably will have large potholes in the gravel, and salmon often will lie in these protective holes. Even the rim of a big wagon wheel or a rubber tire lying on the bottom can provide a good lie wherein a salmon will rest. If the salmon is caught, another one may soon take its place.

High-Water Conditions

High water, often called a *spate,* changes the summer condition of moderate flow. The lies of salmon change as the volume and depth of the river increase, so you probably will not find salmon in the places where they used to lie. Fishermen often will doggedly fish a spot where they caught salmon a week or so earlier, not realizing that the increased volume of the river has changed the lies completely. Any attempt to generalize as to the effects of a spate on fishing would be questionable except to say that because there is more water, which also may be discolored, the prospects of hooking salmon usually are diminished. It is possible to achieve success in such conditions, however.

First, though there may be exceptions to this, particularly on small streams, let's rule out all fishing in the main current because it's probably too swift and too deep. Let's concentrate primarily along the banks.

I once was booked on a stretch of Canada's upper Matapedia and arrived there only to find the river several feet higher than usual. My guide was Henry Lyons, whose many years on the river during all conditions provided profound knowledge of how to hook salmon under spate conditions. Early morning found us stowing our gear in his boat, to which a powerful engine was attached. I looked down the river. Tall grasses that usually were on dry land showed their tips above the water.

"Looks pretty hopeless," I commented grimly.

Head of the run

R. VALENTINE ATKINSON

Henry shrugged but appeared cheerful. "I think you may hook a salmon within half an hour, and less than a hundred feet from here," he said, as he pulled the cord on the Johnson and headed the boat into the flow. "Use the rod with the sinking line and put on a bright fly with lots of red and yellow in it; about size 4."

Within a minute of our departure, Henry stopped the engine and lowered the anchor a moderate cast from shore. The shoreline was a narrow field, now waterlogged, with an edge of green showing along what usually was the bank.

"The bank here normally is about three feet above the water," he remarked. "Now the grass is covered about a foot, so just in front of that grass line is about 4 feet of depth. Cast upstream a bit and get the fly down as deep as possible, as close to the grass line as you can put it."

I noticed that the current was rather moderate near shore in comparison with the speed of driftwood rapidly coursing down the main flow of the river. I worked the fly down as directed, but several casts accomplished nothing.

"Sometimes under these conditions salmon lie close to the bank here," Henry said. "With all this water, we've got to do a bit of prospecting to find any. You've got to get the fly down close to them. They aren't in a chasing mood, but they're lying in and some should be takers. Anyway, this was only a warm-up. Your fly was fishing close to bottom where it should be. Now we'll go to a better place."

The better place was only a stone's throw downstream. A great clod of earth and sod had broken from the bank and showed nearly car-size just above the surface.

"You can see the edge of current making down from that pile of turf," Henry said. "Work the fly just a mite inside the edge, as deep as possible."

I cast quartering upstream to land the fly as close to the top of the edge as possible. It quickly sank from sight in the slightly murky water. When it had reached a quarter downstream position, there was a sharp yank, and a salmon was on. The fish raced out into the flow, taking the line well into its backing. It jumped once and headed upstream.

"Raise your rod high and tighten up some more so the line will clear that tree branch floating down," Henry warned. "That's a good fish!"

The salmon was brought to net in less than twenty minutes—a handsome bright cock fish weighing 14 pounds. About an hour later a second one was hooked and landed—a 9-pound hen that took the deeply fished fly from the current edge of a large boulder against the shore. The two were our limit for the day, and we were elated at such success under such adverse circumstances.

Thus, deep fishing of the edges created by shore obstructions is one way to tackle high-water conditions. Such obstacles provide moderate flow, and the best ones are only a few feet deep; these places, under normal conditions, would hold little, if any, water. Anglers casting from the bank in high water may slide into the stream to wade and may flush a salmon or two. It is not generally realized how closely fish lie under riverbanks during spates.

On another occasion, my guide and I parked our car in a field bordering Canada's Miramichi near Doaktown. Since the river was in near spate, we looked for places where the bank shelved steeply into a few feet of water. Any protrusion that formed an edge, even if ever so slight, was worth trying. A fair length of sinking line was necessary to get the fly down to the fish. Once it was deep enough, the trick seemed to be to work the fly down and back slowly as close to the bank as possible. Hooking salmon securely in this manner is difficult, because you may be working the fly in when a salmon takes, thus creating the tendency to take the fly away from it unless slack is momentarily given when even the slightest pull is felt.

One solution to better hooking under such circumstances is to give slack line when a pull is felt, and then to hurry along the bank to a position below the fish. Then, when you tighten, the fly may pull back into the hinge of the jaw instead of being pulled away from the salmon. Since a badly hooked fish probably will become detached anyway, this tactic is worth trying.

Another approach for spate conditions is to fish the shallower gravel bars, which may normally be dry. Many of these are at river bends, where the force of the current is along the deeper side, leaving more moderate flow over the bar. Like the widening and fairly shallow tail of a pool during normal conditions, these bars also contain depressions where salmon can rest in moderate flow. Fish them the same way from a position that allows the fly to swing and thus sweep over the promising water on gradually extended casts.

Finally, we should not overlook small back channels where, under normal conditions, there was little, if any, water. With the rise, such channels may have a moderate flow, and fish will run them.

The angler must learn to understand his river. On some rivers the fish will run primarily at night. On these rivers, you have to fish over whatever salmon have stopped in the pool. There will be no more until possibly toward evening, when some fish will start to move.

On other rivers, the fish may run all day long, whether the day is bright or dark. On these rivers, a pool may be empty for a short or a long period, and then suddenly fish will come in and all anglers are busy. When this happens and you are fishing a good pool, it is better to stay there than to move from one pool to another.

When fishing the sunk line, water height should have no influence on the size of the fly used. Fly size should be dictated by water speed, although I like to use a slightly larger one in discolored water on the presumption that it provides better visibility. The color of the water may also influence the choice of pattern. Many rivers in spate conditions are discolored, such as from peat from upstream. Owing to such impurities in suspension, the wavelengths of light toward the violet end of the spectrum become absorbed more than those at the red end, which tend to penetrate. Thus, regardless of light conditions, a fly with red, orange, yellow, or white dressing will show up the best.

Low-Water Conditions

Low water and warm weather impose entirely different challenges to salmon anglers, whether we like them or not. Seventy degrees can be a critical temperature. When warm weather and probably lower water make the stream's temperature reach or exceed 70 degrees, normal summer conditions change, and the salmon move into the more oxygenated and colder water that is more to their liking. This usually means cold-water pools, which can be a stretch of water below a spring-fed brook; a spring sending cold water from the bank of the stream; a spring feeding into the river in any other way, such as bubbling up from the riverbed; or even a pool in the spring-fed brook itself.

Most of these pools have a rather slow current. If they have a narrow section where the water flows more swiftly, and if there are suitable lies in it, the fish will take best in this faster water. There may be faster water where a cold brook pours water into a pool. In such cases, the salmon will work right up into this current and will take flies there better than they will elsewhere.

Most cold-water pools contain rocks and other obstacles, and salmon should be found around these, but under these cold-water conditions they may be anywhere. It is now less a question of their finding conditions of moderate flow than of their finding the *most available oxygen*. If these conditions prevail in certain places, fish will lie in them even if they are so shallow that parts of their backs are out of water.

Many experienced anglers think that when salmon lie in cold-water pools, this provides the most challenging angling, because it requires more skill and thorough knowledge of various angling techniques in order to coax them to take a fly. Usually this is the most difficult area of salmon fishing. Unfortunately, when salmon are in the shallow cold-water pools, they are at the mercy of poachers, who too often jig for them there. If a pool has recently been jigged for salmon, the remaining fish may be impossible to take with a fly.

The techniques for fishing in cold-water pools are discussed in chapters 7, 8, and 9. Under such conditions, if there is a sudden rise of water and if the fish begin to move, the fishing can be fantastic!

Autumn Conditions

A final condition in fishing for bright salmon has to do with their habits in the autumn, just before the close of the fishing season. Normal summer conditions may not prevail if the water becomes quite cold; then, in addition to their usual lies, under conditions of moderate flow the salmon will also seek deeper, slower water. Thus, in the fall there may be more potential lies than there are in the summer. Fall fish may hold lower down in what are called *ponds,* which are the deep, quiet stretches below the pools. They may work up into the pools from time to time, but such movements usually are in the early morning or in the late afternoon or evening.

Fall fish even will run into small brooks, so it is possible then to catch salmon in a trout brook! Some pools that are poor for summer fishing may be productive in the fall, so perhaps pools could be classed in three ways: those that are good in the summer; those that are good in the fall; and those that are good at both times. The trick is to learn to understand the water you are fishing. The basics that apply to normal summer conditions also apply to those in the fall.

Tidewater Fishing

Anglers seem to have been of the opinion that Atlantic salmon would not take flies in salt or brackish water. But the increasing number of fishermen on public streams induced a few of them to experiment with the idea of getting away from crowded waters and enjoying more sparsely populated areas. These few made the happy discovery that salmon would take flies in tidewater, even flies as small as 10s! In such waters there is a fly fishing only rule, and adept anglers found to their surprise that flies could be as productive as big Dardevles or other forms of hardware.

In areas where public salmon streams are crowded, this discovery has caused anglers to spread out, thus improving the fishing for all concerned.

Flies that are productive on the upper stretches of any given river seem to be equally productive in tidewater; this includes even dry flies. In North America we don't yet know much about how productive shrimp and grub imitations could be, but there seems to be no reason why some of the British patterns described in this book shouldn't turn out to be killers.

Salmon rarely will be caught on all tide conditions, and the best time of the tide on one river is not necessarily the best on others. The key to this depends on the presence of suitable lies where fish will congregate and rest for a while. These places may be in pools, near breakwaters, or in other locations where depth and the speed of tidal flow are to their liking. A good lie at one time of the tide may not be good at another because the ebb and flow constantly change conditions.

Thus, a good deal of experimentation is necessary to discover where the lies are and the time or times of the tide when they are occupied. Quite often local anglers are able to chart such knowledge, so visitors should try to get information from someone who knows and who will be straightforward about it. Some rivers have tidal areas where many good lies have been located; others have no fishable places at all.

7

Basics on Fishing the Sunk Fly

"Osprey"

*I*n younger years I had the mistaken notion that salmon fishing knowledge consisted primarily of acquiring equipment and arranging for a good place to fish. I thought that all one needed to do was to go there and work a fly in the water to hook salmon.

Consequently, many trips that could have been excitingly successful turned out quite the opposite. I caught a few salmon when they were "on the take," but I usually didn't during the more frequent periods when they weren't. I had failed to do my homework before going fishing—something like paying a lot of money for an automobile without learning how to drive it!

On these earlier forays I noticed that knowledgeable anglers often hooked salmon consistently while my efforts remained fishless. Some of these men, taking pity on an inexperienced angler, told me where and how to work the fly, so I gradually did better. Eventually it dawned on me that I shouldn't keep spending money on salmon trips until I learned what to do when I got there.

When this important fact soaked in, I began buying recommended books on salmon fishing, including many of the older classics, and spent winter evenings studying them. This interesting and profitable research brought to mind too many days on various rivers where I could have had successful fishing if I had learned what to do in the first place. Salmon fishing should include continuing study, because the more we learn, the more successful we will be.

When hapless salmon anglers excuse themselves by saying that salmon are unpredictable, and therefore sometimes can't be caught, they are only partly correct. What they mean is that under the conditions they encountered, they lack the know-how to be successful. The unpredictability of salmon is the name of the game, and it is one of the most intriguing games on earth. Sometimes you win, sometimes you don't. As in other games, knowledge and skill pay off. Knowledge can be found in books as well as astream. On days when the fishing was tough and I had worked over salmon without hooking any, the nagging question was "What could I have done that I didn't do?" Was there something? Probably! Probably that something can be found in books.

Therefore, in these next four chapters, let's see what can be done in the most typical situations that

so often come up. These aren't exact solutions but are suggestions that will often help. The type of situation you encounter will suggest what should work best at the time.

Basic Water Coverage

The elementary approach, which often is sufficient, is basic water coverage with the sunken fly, either by wading or casting from a boat.

The angler in Figure 16 doesn't know where the salmon are, but the stream is good gravel in depth between his knees and his waist, and it presumably contains depressions and rocks providing places of moderate flow where salmon should be resting. In such a case, the angler should explore all the water with the fly, paying particular attention to any rocks in the stream or protrusions from the banks that offer edges in the current. Since the stream flows moderately, his casts are quartering downstream at an angle of about 45 degrees. If the stream flows faster, his casts might be in a smaller arc; if slower, in a wider one.

His first cast in direction *A* is a very short one because salmon often are taken on short casts. The fly swings on a tight line until it starts to hang downstream at position *C*. Here, he pulls the fly in and lets it down a bit in case a salmon has followed it and could be hooked by changes in fly action. During the swing of the fly, the angler is not moving except to follow the direction of the fly with his rod tip. During the swing, the rod can be held quite low; many anglers keep it nearly horizontal. Thus, with the fly swinging on a taut line, any salmon striking the fly is pretty sure to be hooked.

If the water looks good on both sides of the angler, he next would cast to his left toward position *B*. If it looks good on only one side, he would cast to that side only.

Then the angler pulls a foot or so of line from the reel to extend his cast that much farther, fishing each cast as before, each one using an added foot or so of line until the casts extend as far as he wishes. After fan-casting several extending casts in this manner, he moves downstream a few feet and repeats the procedure.

An alternative to this method is to take a step downstream after covering an arc of the water. This option allows you to always use a comfortable

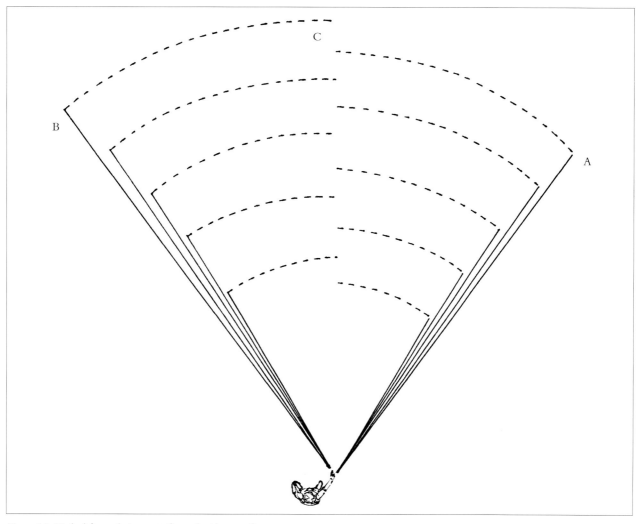

Figure 16. Method for exploring part of a pool with a wet fly.

length of line without having to shorten and lengthen it. The former method is handiest when fishing from a boat, the latter when wading. In casting from a boat, you don't want to keep dropping it downstream; pull the anchor and drop down a bit only when your casts have been extended as far as you wish. Avoid casting farther than is comfortable because long casts are tiring and less liable to hook salmon securely.

During these casting sequences, you may note places that look particularly good, such as rocks breaking the surface or boils in the current denoting large rocks below. If no sand has piled up on the upstream side of a rock, fish may be lying there. Note positions deserving special attention and worthy of varied casts. How much time you devote to

fan-casting and working special spots depends of course on how much water you have to cover and how much time you have to cover it. With a lot of stream available, we may want to confine attention mainly to the presumed hot spots.

When the water is above approximately 48 degrees F. and the air a bit warmer than that, salmon should be taking on or near the surface. A floating line is ideal for relatively thin stretches, because fly and leader sink enough. With this, dry flies and all-purpose ones such as the *Muddler* provide variety. If wet flies are to be used exclusively in water of moderate depth, the floating line with sinking tip or the intermediate line might be a better choice. This also is appropriate for moderate depths during colder air and water conditions. The sinking line seems neces-

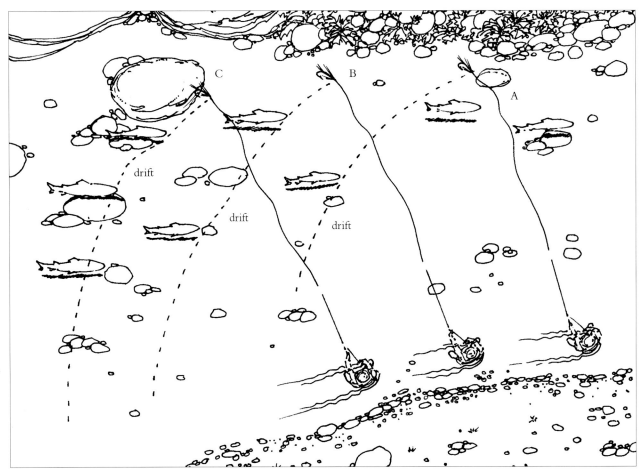

Figure 17. Another method for basic water coverage.

sary only in fast flows of more than moderate depth or when salmon lie deep in pools and can't be tempted to rise.

Now, let's look at another approach to basic water coverage as shown in Figure 17. This angler is fishing from a shallow bar near the bank and casting to deeper water on the far side that indicates good lies for salmon. He casts quartering downstream, more or less, depending on current speed and depth. In position *A,* his fly swings cross-current to a spot above the midstream rock in front of which a fish may be lying. He may or may not hook the unseen salmon over which his fly passes. The two fish at upper right are lying in the edge of the current that flows mainly between the two large rocks.

His next cast is to position *B* because he wants to work the fly in the current's edge in front of the ledge. He raises his rod slightly or strips in some line temporarily to avoid the rock near position *C.* The

fly swings over the midstream rock and may be taken by one of the salmon presumed to be lying there. His final cast, to position *C,* works the fly along the rock ledge and behind the midstream rock. He has exposed the fly properly to three of the five salmon shown and probably previously has done so to the fish lying in the edge of the current at upper right.

When casting from a fast current into a slow one, the faster current nearer the angler will sweep an increasing downstream belly in the line, causing the fly to speed up and to whip. Conversely, when casting from a slow current into a fast one, the line will lag behind the fly, causing the fly to slow down and nearly stop. These two conditions, shown in Figures 18 and 19, result in improper fly speed— speed either too fast or too slow to usually interest salmon.

So what is *proper fly speed?* It is the speed that

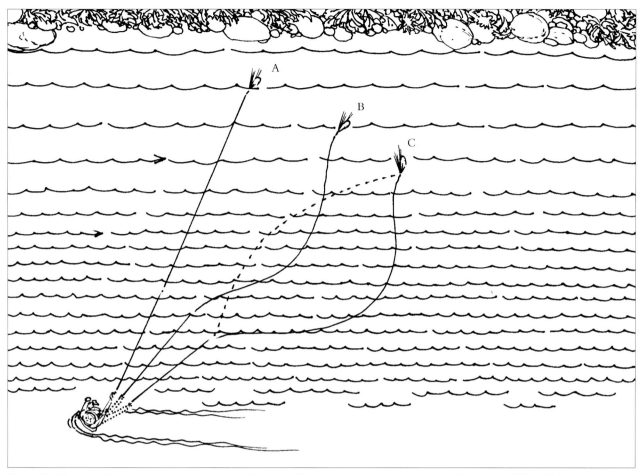

Figure 18. After the straight cast to A, the fast current near the angler will start to put a downstream belly in the line, as in B. When this begins to become pronounced, as in C, the fly will increase speed and start to whip. Mend the line upstream to retain proper fly speed. Numerous mendings may be necessary.

experience indicates normally excites salmon to strike. You will notice it by watching expert anglers. You can determine it for yourself by riffling a wet fly or by skating a fly on the surface. Proper fly speed is that which when the fly skims the surface makes small edges, or wakes, behind it, but not so fast that it throws spray.

When fishing in diverse currents that tend to fish the fly too fast or too slow, proper fly speed is maintained by *mending the line*. This is shown in Figure 20 and consists of an upstream or a downstream flip of the line to bow it in the opposite direction from that which the bow is making. It is sort of a sideways roll cast. In doing it you will observe that the rod should be pushed forward and the tip made to describe an arc like an inverted **U**. Mending the line may consist of an easy flip or a more energetic one, depending on how much line is on the surface.

The line must be lying on the surface, or very nearly so, and you should try to mend the line without disturbing the position of the fly.

Thus, in normal wet-fly fishing, the fly should be fished at a constant speed. No belly in the line should be allowed that causes the fly to whip (be pulled at excess speed by the bag in the line). When fish are lying in slack water the fly may not travel fast enough unless it is given added motion. Increasing the fly's speed can be done momentarily by lifting the rod tip or by swinging the rod tip upstream. It can be done more constantly by stripping in line, just as the speed can be slowed by lowering the rod tip or by letting out line. In slack water, the cast fly must be stripped in to give it adequate speed. Although salmon most often take flies at the speed described above, they sometimes show greater interest in a fly that is being fished slowly and often can

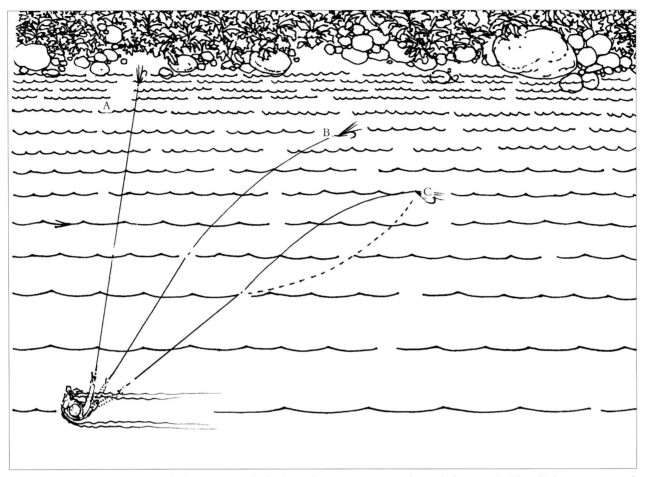

Figure 19. After the straight cast to A, the fast current near the far shore will start to put upstream drag in the line, as in B. When this becomes pronounced, as in C, the fly will decrease speed and tend to stop. Mend the line downstream to retain proper fly speed. Repeat mendings as often as necessary.

be made to take it if it is fished faster. Change speed only when normal speed doesn't work. Many anglers think that twitching the fly does no good, but on some rivers the guides recommend it, especially while the fly is swinging in an arc after being cast quartering downstream.

In wet-fly fishing, the speed with which the fly is fished can be a determining factor in success or lack of it. While traditional theories of fly speed may be subject to question, generally speaking it is true that in a strong flow the wet fly should be fished more downstream than cross-stream and that in a slow flow the fly should be fished more cross-stream than downstream. Experimentation is often rewarding, because there are times when fishing a wet fly somewhat upstream will be productive. There are times when it is most successful to give the fly hardly any drift at all, and there are times when very

fast stripping in of the line produces the best results. Usually, you should not give the fish time to inspect the fly closely.

Proper fly speed is very important in basic water coverage, but there are some exceptions to it that may tempt reluctant salmon to strike, which we will look at as we go along.

Although downstream fishing with the wet fly is the usual method, there are other ways to do it. You may need to cast cross-stream or even quartering upstream to get the fly deep enough when it reaches the proper quartering downstream position in situations when salmon lie deep and can't be tempted to rise.

How Salmon Take Flies

Anglers may get misconceptions about holding positions because they may cast to what seem to be

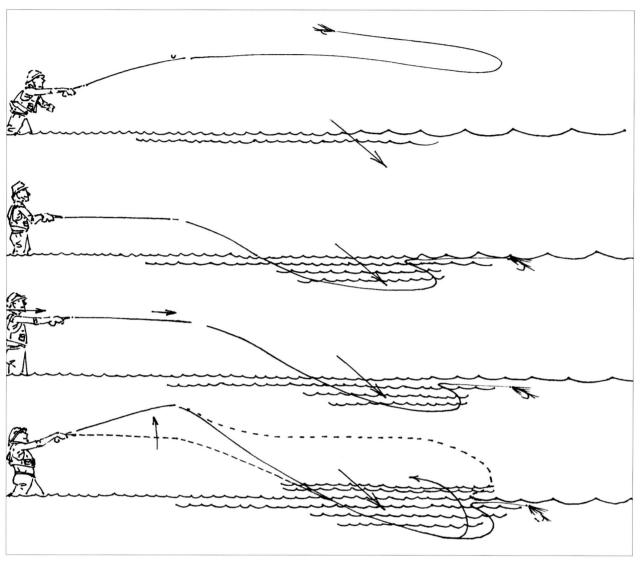

Figure 20. Mending the line.

good ones, only to hook salmon somewhere else. This brings up the question of how salmon take flies (and how to hook them).

Basically, salmon approach the fly in three different ways, as illustrated. They may (1) rise and take it almost at once. They may (2) leave the lie to follow the fly and take it after it has well passed them. They may (3) leave the lie to follow the fly until it is hanging downstream and take it after lying momentarily behind it.

The most usual way is the second. In this case, the fish may start moving for the fly, decide not to take it, and return to its lie—or it may start moving for it, and take it after the fly has swung past it. This means that the fish takes the fly as it turns and starts downstream—not upstream, as some of the older angling writers believed.

This action has been observed so often—by anglers spending considerable time watching them from a bridge while people are fishing the pool below—that it appears to be typical. Someone who watches from above can see what really happens, and there is a lot more going on than most people seem to realize! Generalizations are pointless, as salmon behave differently to the presented fly and don't always hook themselves; however, you will benefit from observing fish and noting various reactions. The important thing is to gently set the hook when

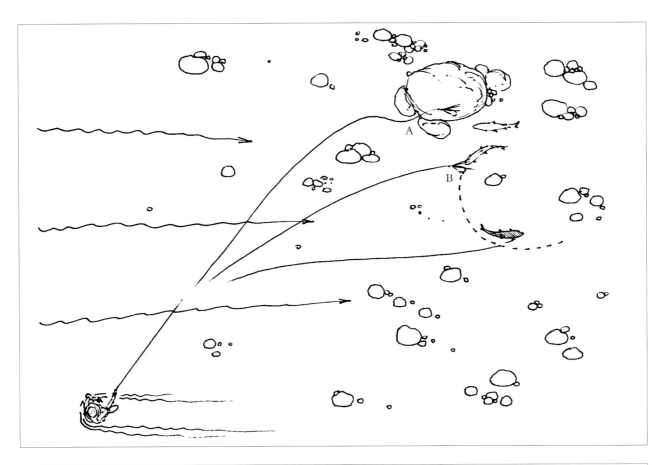

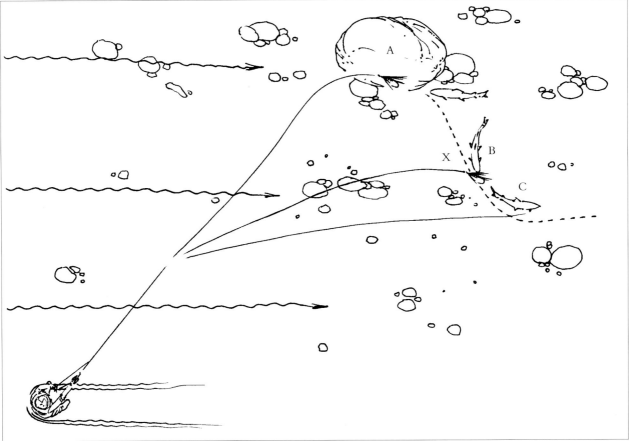

Figures 21–22. Two ways salmon take flies. In the top figure, the fly is presented (A) and the fish rises and takes the fly almost at once (B). In the bottom figure, the fly is presented (A), the fish follows the fly to X *(B), the fish takes the fly and turns downstream (C).*

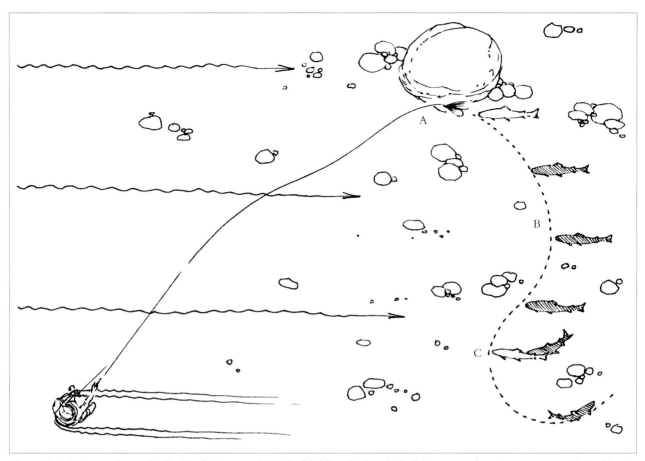

Figure 23. A third way salmon take flies. The fly is presented (A), the fish follows by dropping back in current and moving cross-stream (B), the fish nips or turns on the fly and takes it (C).

you feel a salmon on the line, to make sure you have connection.

Such observations refute the theory that loose line should be fed to the fish in order to cause the bag in the line (made by the current) to pull the hook into the back of the jaw. Since the fish is *not* going upstream at this point, but going downstream, the loose line more often than not prevents the angler from hooking the fish. It is true that a bag or belly of line in the current will tend to cause a salmon to move upstream, but this is *after* the fish has been hooked. Actually, the angler has little control over where the hook becomes embedded in the mouth.

In the third scenario, with the hanging fly, a typical situation is one in which the fly swings across the current and reaches a hanging position in a current that is rather slack. The salmon hesitates and then darts toward the fly, but merely nips it. In instances such as this, the fish either is not hooked or is hooked on the edge of the mouth. If hooked this way, it frequently becomes "unstuck" because there

is inadequate barb penetration. If you know the fly is moving into a slow current to hang there, it is wise to give added movement to the fly. When a fly hangs in a moderate current, however, the fish is more likely to turn on it and become properly hooked. If possible, you should avoid hooking fish on a hanging fly (also known as a dangling fly, or a fly "on the dangle"), even though it may produce rises. In order to prevent this, try not to wade out so far that you are standing immediately above a lie, or a possible lie. The chances of securely hooking a fish on a swinging fly are much better than on a hanging fly, regardless of current conditions.

In any case, when there is less than a moderate flow, the likelihood of good hooking will be improved by imparting added movement to the fly. Of course, there are many cases when a salmon will take a fly that is scarcely moving in very slow water, but chances are the fish will spit out the fly before the angler feels it and has a chance to tighten up enough to hook it securely. Even when a salmon's mouth is closed, there is a considerable gap through which a fly can slip out. For this and other reasons, many fishermen use offset and double-offset hooks.

The word *striking* often is used because it is a term familiar to trout fishermen who go fishing for salmon. This word probably is responsible for more lost salmon than any other in angling literature. If you strike, what happens? An angler strikes because something he sees (such as a boil) or something impeding the natural motion of the fly causes him to do it. There is a time lag involved in this reflex because of slack line, softness of rod tip, and other factors, affording ample time for the salmon to take the fly. To strike then only risks insecure lip hooking or taking the fly away from the fish altogether. Under normal conditions, the fish turns downstream as it takes the fly, and the current pushing against it provides added downstream velocity. Since you should keep your end of the connection fairly rigid (probably by pressing the line against the rod grip with a finger), the connection tightens up sufficiently to properly set the hook. So striking can

only do more harm than good, because the desired result has already been accomplished, and a smart strike may result only in pulling the fly from the mouth of the fish. The finer the wire of the hook, the less tension is required to set it. A moderate flow will produce better tightening than a slack current. The best you can do is to tighten—that is, to be sure there is sufficient tension to make the barb penetrate after the weight of the fish is felt. Then you can release the pressure on the line and play the fish in the usual manner.

Of course, many anglers will say that they always strike and they always catch fish, but there are times when the fish are so much "on the take" that it is nearly impossible not to hook them, no matter what the angler does. The anglers who say they always strike might pause to remember how many strikes have resulted in lost fish, many of which might have remained hooked if they had used the tightening process.

Regardless of what other writers may have said about it, the angler has little or no control over

Striking on a dry fly

where in the mouth the salmon is hooked. When a fish's takes a fly, even when the fly is swimming properly with the barb or barbs down, the hook may be turned sideways, downward, or upward by contact with the mouth of the fish. This may result in the fish's being hooked in the hinge of the jaw or in the lower or upper jaw. The hinge of the jaw is a good place. Sometimes the fish is hooked in the nostril, which is as good as the hinge, or better. The worst place is on the edge of the mouth because the bone structure is so close to the skin coverage that it is difficult to get hook penetration. Fish often are hooked through a piece of mouth skin. Summer fish have tender mouth skin, and they often break off. Autumn fish have much tougher mouth skin, and even the slightest hold may be enough to land them.

There are many different types of "connections" the angler can make with the fish in fishing the wet fly. For example, there is the sudden sharp jerk or pull followed by the line's going loose. This is caused by a fast-moving fish hitting the fly or contacting it with its body.

A pull by a salmon is when the fish seems to tug on the fly but isn't hooked. This may mean that it has hit the fly with head or tail in order to get it out of the way. It is an anger reflex, and it sometimes results in foul hooking. In this case, when the fish turns against the fly, the fly may become embedded in the body. The angler can't help this and has to try to bring in the salmon while its body is more or less sideways to the current. There is no real penetration, and there is nothing the angler can do about it.

The fast jerk is caused more often by fast-moving grilse than by the rise of a salmon. Again, there is a heavy pull, after which the line goes loose. This usually is caused by a salmon taking the fly without the hook penetrating.

Another situation is the boil caused by a salmon turning on a fly near the surface of the water. It may take the fly or it may not, so you may hook it or you may not. If there are many boils to flies and no fish are hooked, the answer could be to fish the fly a bit deeper.

When an angler gets a pull from a salmon without hooking it, he usually considers this as an expression of interest and an element of challenge. Some anglers say that such a fish should be rested before casting to it again; others don't. I think the fly should be put to it again without delay. When the salmon comes to the fly, we know how much line is out, and because this measures its distance from us, we don't reel in any line or change our position. We mark the fish's location against something on the far shore. The usual procedure is to rest the fish while changing the fly to a larger or smaller size. Then the angler presents the new fly in the same way in the same place. Sometimes this works and sometimes it doesn't. If one or two recasts don't get results, *then* the fish should be rested for a few minutes.

If we have been resting the fish, it is possible that it may have moved upstream a few feet. Therefore, we make the next cast to a point about 10 feet above it, judging the exact location by the landmark and by the amount of line that is off the reel. If the fish is more or less directly downstream, we do not cast the final 10 feet of line. If this brings no result, we continue casting, each time to a point a foot or so nearer its original position. If we have marked the spot carefully, we should by this time have hooked the fish. If we haven't done so, and if we want to continue to work on it, chapter 10 gives several other tactics that can be employed.

Some anglers think that during the resting period the fly should be changed. That is a matter of opinion. If you change the fly, the purpose would be mainly to occupy time; if a salmon came to a fly once, it will probably come to the same fly again and this time it may take it.

The drawings of how salmon take flies indicate that the fish often turn on the fly with or without taking it. Sometimes this results in *foul hooking,* and it explains why it happens. If foul hooking is not intentional, there is nothing you can do about it. When the fish turns on the fly, the leader (probably partially wrapped around the fish) can cause the barb to penetrate the body—usually the dorsal or a pectoral fin. Since these places are tough, the fish probably is securely hooked. The angler's first reaction is that he is into a big one, because of the side pressure of current on the fish. The sad truth soon becomes obvious because of this side pressure and because the fish often jumps. Getting it to beach may take more than the usual time, but it should be done as quickly as possible. Foul hooking is considered unsporting, and therefore it is customary—and in some places now *law*—to release an improperly hooked fish.

The Riffling Hitch

Because proper fly speed can be determined by riffling a wet fly on the surface, let's look at the simple *riffling hitch* (sometimes called the *Portland Creek hitch*) and how it was discovered. Since it evidently was popularized at Lee Wulff's former salmon fishing camp on Newfoundland's Portland Creek, it seems appropriate to describe it in Lee's own words, as published in *The Atlantic Salmon Treasury* (1975— limited edition of one thousand copies privately printed by the Atlantic Salmon Association).

Arthur Perry, able guide and devoted fisherman, introduced me to his 'riffling hitch' when I first fished Portland Creek (Newfoundland). It originated there and, having been taken into the repertoire of anglers who have fished there as the Portland Creek Hitch, it is spreading slowly to all salmon waters. It is a method of looping or 'hitching' the leader around the head of the wet fly and pulling it, skidded, across the surface instead of letting it sink under.

No one at Portland Creek claims to have been the originator of the riffling fly, but here is the accepted story. Long ago, warships of the British navy anchored off the stream, and officers came ashore to fish. They left a few old-style salmon flies, which had a loop of twisted gut wrapped to the straight-shanked hook to make the eye.

Soft and pliable when in use, the loop enabled the fly to ride more smoothly on its course and avoided the stiffness and canting which accompanied any solid attachment of the stout leader to the eyed fly. But the gut loops grew weak with age, and many a good salmon, when hooked on an old and cherished fly, broke away with the steel and feathers. . . . They made sure the fly would stay on by throwing those 'hitches' around the shank behind the wrapping. The fact that the fly skimmed, instead of sinking, bothered them not in the least, for they were practical fishers of the sea.

The making of the hitch is important. Arthur Perry, in common with most Portland Creek guides, makes his so the monofilament pulls away from under the turned-up eye at the throat. This will make both the single- and double-hooked flies ride correctly (hook down) on the retrieve. Such a hitch is effective on standard salmon fly hooks with turned-up eyes but is awkward if the eyes are turned down.

I use the same throat-hitch for double-hooked flies, but with my favorite (the single-barbed iron) regardless of whether the eye turns up or down, I shift the hitch forty-five degrees to one side or the other, depending upon which side of the current I cast from, so that on a cross-current retrieve the fly will always ride with the point on the downstream side. This position seems to give it much better hooking and riding qualities.

Using this method, it is easy to learn how to fish any wet fly correctly, whereas it usually takes years before you can watch the water under which the sunken fly is traveling and guess correctly just where it is and at what speed it is moving. Too much speed or too little will not draw a salmon's interest. The most perfect speed is that at which a hitched fly riffles best.

With the riffling hitch, fish are hooked about as readily and held just as securely as when the fly is tied on in the conventional manner. They are so sold on it at Portland Creek that ninety-five percent of all the wet fly fishing done there is with the hitched fly.

Many anglers with whom I have fished in Iceland consider the hitched wet fly the most effective way to fish for salmon. I am not of this persuasion, but my score might improve if I were.

As a footnote to Lee's remarks, others say that when the old classic gut-eyed flies became useless because of the weakening of the eyes, the flies were discarded as being worthless. The guides, thinking they were too pretty for oblivion, rescued them even if they had no eyes at all. They knotted the tip of the monofilament leader around the tail of the fly and then hitched it around the eye, as Lee describes.

Conditions That Affect Angling Success

Among added notes that may be elementary to experts but important to those less so, is one on how *shade and shadow* affect angling success. Americans who fly-fish for steelhead often won't work a pool when the sun is on it, so there are pools that fish best in mornings and others that are best in afternoons or evenings. Salmon also can become frightened of unexpected shadows—a cow or sheep on the bank, a person, or even shadow thrown by rod or line. Some shadows are expected, or considered normal, such as banks, trees, and clouds. When clouds obscure the sun, formerly unproductive pools may suddenly produce taking fish.

We thus should bear in mind that shade is our ally in salmon fishing but shadow is our enemy, and we should avoid throwing shadows on a pool, particularly when the surface is placid.

This brings up the point of *when* salmon are in a *taking mood,* and when they are not.

Temperature does have a decided effect, but we don't know exactly why, and the various conjectures are too voluminous to bother with here. A good condition is when air and water are of equal temperature, between about 48 and 70 degrees F. A similarly good or better condition is when the air is warmer than the water. When it is colder than the water, salmon usually are not in a taking mood.

The best conditions are when the river is steady at normal height and the air is no colder than the water. Good conditions should remain during and after a storm until water level changes appreciably. When it does change, the fish will be moving to

"Headwaters"

new lies and won't take very well. Resting fish usually are in a taking mood, but traveling ones are not. Sometimes you will find that your long-anticipated trip comes at a time of adverse temperature or water conditions. This is no excuse to stay in and play cards! It is a challenge to get out on the river to try some of the more unusual tricks that tempt reluctant salmon to take. One or more should work, and the decision to adopt these methods and use them properly should result in hooking a salmon or two. Such success under adverse conditions is the mark of the accomplished angler!

Handling a Hooked Salmon
When you have hooked your salmon, remember the following tips on how to handle it to bring it safely onto the beach.

The prick of the steel and the tension on the line will make the fish run. Hold the rod high and let it do so. The reel brake should have been set lightly enough to put only a moderate bend in the rod. More tension than this could, and probably

would, result in the hook's pulling out or in broken tackle. The first run of a big salmon may be a long one, taking you well into your backing, but the fish eventually will stop, partially exhausted. At this point the salmon may jump. At the first indication of a jump, push the rod hand forward and lower the rod nearly to horizontal. This provides temporary slack, which should prevent the fish from falling on an otherwise taut line and thus possibly breaking off. This is called *bowing to the fish,* a practice used with all jumpers, such as tarpon.

You can usually tell when a salmon is about to jump and be ready to handle it, and to enjoy the thrill of it. The indications are hard to describe, but at the end of a run, you probably will feel tremors like a shivering sensation transmitted to the rod hand by the tackle. The instant the fish returns to the water, return the rod to its former aloft position and restore tension.

The end of a run is the time to take control, because there is little you can do before this. Increase tension by squeezing the line hand around rod and line or by palming the rim brake of the reel (if it has one), and raise the rod higher in an attempt to induce the fish to return. The salmon probably now can be pumped in. *Pumping* means raising the rod high under safe tension and then reeling rapidly to recover line while you lower the rod. Then restore tension and raise the rod again, repeating this as much as necessary. While pumping, be ready for another run, and immediately relax tension when it starts.

Usually the salmon can be pumped in until it becomes aware of the cause of its predicament. Then it probably will run again, but not as far. The secret of handling salmon is to keep them busy, because an active fish is exhausting itself. This has little to do with the power of the tackle. Experts such as Lee Wulff and Arthur Oglesby can exhaust salmon with surprisingly light tackle, and less experienced anglers can learn to do it after a little practice.

When the angler thinks he is in control of the salmon he should get to a position quartering downstream of it, if possible, or at least abreast of it. This usually induces the fish to work upstream, where it will more rapidly become exhausted because it has to fight the current as well as the tackle. This position also provides line tension to pull the fish off balance (at an angle with the current), thus inducing it to move.

Sometimes a salmon will go deep and sulk. Make every attempt to prevent this, because the fish is, essentially, resting. Use maximum safe tension to pull it off balance. Strumming the taut line with the line hand sends annoying vibrations down to the fish, which may impel it to action. As a last resort, perhaps you can have your guide or someone else get near enough to the fish to make it move. Even throwing rocks at its position sometimes helps.

If a salmon is running downstream into dangerous territory, it sometimes can be made to stop, and perhaps to return, by giving it a lot of slack line. If this slack line bags downstream, the fish may return upstream because it will run against the pull of the line. Slack line may also indicate to the fish that it is free, and it may then return to its former position, where you can take control again.

If a freshly hooked salmon doesn't realize it is in danger, it is often possible to lead it to a favorable position, such as "walking it" from the tail of a pool to the head of it, as the following experience indicates.

My guide and I were fishing the tail of a pool from a boat on a big Canadian river. We knew that salmon were holding just inside the pool's lip, where it spilled into fast rocky rapids downstream.

"If I hook a fish here," I said to the guide, "it probably will run downstream, and we can't follow it."

"Perhaps we can walk it up to a safer place," the guide said. Noting my perplexity, he added, "You know—like leading a puppy dog on a leash."

I said I didn't understand. I had never walked a salmon then, but have done so several times since.

"If you get a pull," the guide advised, "set the hook very lightly and don't reel. Just hold the rod up under very light tension. Reeling sends vibrations down the line and makes the salmon run. The idea is that it shouldn't realize it has been hooked."

During the swing of the fly across the tail of the pool, I got a good pull and sensed that the barb was sufficiently embedded, so I merely held the rod up under such light tension that the line sagged a little. The guide quietly pulled anchor and poled the boat upstream. The salmon followed.

The guide brought the boat to the beach, and I stepped out. The big salmon finned placidly out in the pool, well in sight.

"Walk him up as far as you can," the guide grinned, smugly contented with the success of the maneuver. "Steady light pull. Don't jerk; don't reel until you want him to run."

The "puppy dog on a leash" description seemed apt because the salmon allowed itself to be led far up the pool. There, I began to reel in, curious to see how close the fish could be induced to come. I suspected that something might be wrong with it. None before had ever acted like that.

Suddenly the fish realized it was in trouble. With a mighty shake of its head, it streaked across the pool. There wasn't anything wrong with it. It was a lusty 14-pound cock, fresh from the sea.

When a salmon is wavering, exhausted, and showing the silver of its sides, it should be ready to be brought ashore. There are five ways to do this.

A favorite way under suitable conditions is to beach the fish—favorite because it is easy; it needs no equipment and no help. When a salmon is under control and the angler is ashore, he looks for a place to beach it. Ideally, this is a spot of quiet water and minimum slope, fairly free of rocks. Walking backward, the angler uses his tackle to pull the salmon to the beach. It takes surprisingly little pull to do this because the flopping fish works itself onto the beach in the direction of pull. Once there, it usually lies quietly, so the angler can grasp it or merely pick it up by the tail. When salmon are picked up this way they give little or no resistance.

If the angler is in the water and wants to retrieve his fish there, he can tail it by hand. He brings it alongside, where he can place thumb and fingers around the rear of the body just forward of the tail; quickly grasps it firmly there and raises it above the water.

Some anglers prefer a mechanical tailer and find it very useful when big salmon are encountered. This is a light metal tube about 1/2 inch in diameter and 30 inches long including the hand grip. A flexible metal cable of similar length fits inside the tube and has attached to it a much finer cable about a foot long that ends with a metal ring. The device is cocked by pulling out the cable and bending it to a U shape; it is held thus by the sliding ring on the tube.

When the salmon is ready for taking, the angler or his guide slips the tailer's noose around the salmon's tail and forward on the body to just behind the dorsal fin. A sharp upward yank secures the noose in front of the salmon's tail, the area referred to as the wrist. These methods of tailing are possible because, unlike soft-tailed fish, the salmon has a tail that is vertically rigid. A cocked tailer can be slung from the angler's shoulder, but it usually is kept handy ashore for use when needed or is carried by the guide.

In Canada and some other places, large, long-handled nets customarily are owned and carried by guides and are considered their badges of office, so to speak. When a salmon is ready for taking, the guide should lay the ring of the net as close to the stream's bottom as he can. The angler leads the fish over the net, and the guide merely needs to raise it to bag the salmon.

The fifth method is to use a gaff, and it merely will be mentioned here, because it seems repugnant to use such a device on the King of Fishes and is illegal in many places.

With salmon safely ashore, you need to know what to do with them if you don't want to take them to your lodgings soon. Of course, they shouldn't be allowed to become dry and warm. The usual solution is to make a corral at streamside in which to keep them wet and cool. This is quickly done by scooping out a small basin at streamside or by holding them in a circle of rocks made for them there. This should contain only enough water to float the fish. If water trickles through, so much the better. Cutting a few willow branches and laying them over the fish will keep them cooler.

Setting the Hook

No chapter on the basics of salmon fishing would be complete without again stressing remarks on what some fishermen call *striking*—when to do so and when not to. Since *strike* is too forceful a word, because to do so may rip the hook out or snap the tippet, this term is frowned on in favor of less drastic expressions such as *tightening* or *pulling,* which indicate that little force is needed to securely and safely set a hook.

When trout fishermen have their first experiences with salmon, they often "strike" at a sign of action before they feel the fish, with the result that they take the fly away from the fish instead of hooking it. With a few exceptions that will be discussed later, it is better to leave the business of hooking to the salmon, especially as far as the sunk fly is concerned. In his *The Art of Salmon Fishing,* Calcott quotes a Scottish gillie as saying, "When a salmon pulls at me, then I pulls back at 'im." It may not be necessary to "pull back," but I like to give the fly a gentle twitch to be sure the hook is set firmly, on the theory that a lightly hooked salmon will become unglued anyway, and I may as well learn this at the outset so as not to waste time.

Even with the sunk fly, there are anglers who correctly say there are exceptions to this. There are times when salmon sip in the fly very lightly, and then promptly spit it out. In such cases, when a fish is seen to take the fly, you should immediately set the hook. These situations seem to occur primarily on streams with very little current, but not in faster water.

This business of setting the hook is replete with conflicting opinions, including many that are erroneous. If any general rule can be drawn, it might be that on a tight line you shouldn't set the hook until you *feel* the fish, but on a loose line you should try to set the hook immediately when you *see* that the fish has taken the fly. In greased-line fishing, which is done with a more or less slack line, you should not tighten until you feel the fish.

How much force should be used in setting the hook? If the fly is small, such as size 6 or less, and the barb is sharp (as it should be), a slight twitch will do it. A double hook needs a little more force than a single one. The larger the hook, the more force is required. This is a matter of judgment that depends on the size of the fly and the strength of the leader. The usually used turle knot has about 80 percent breaking strength, so a 10-pound-test tippet actually has a strength of about 8 pounds. It has been noted that since salmon usually are not gut-shy, strong tippets of 12 to 15 pounds-test can be used if they swim the fly properly. These permit the use of considerable force, but strong jerks should be avoided, which is why the word *strike* is frowned upon. A strong jerk, on the part of either salmon or angler, can instantly snap a strong leader.

Many authorities think that when using the sunk fly, anglers should delay setting the hook upon feeling the fish. They advocate holding a few feet of loose line in the line hand and letting it go when a fish is felt or a rise is seen. The idea here is that this loose line will form a downstream belly that will pull the fly back into the hinge of the jaws of the fish, which is one of the most secure places to hook it. This theory has been refuted, however, by anglers who have observed that when salmon take the fly, they turn downstream with it, rather than continuing to face upstream, as this theory would require.

Sometimes a fish will pull at a fly but isn't hooked. This is often referred to as a *short-rising fish*. What usually happens is that since the line is under tension, the salmon follows the fly and takes it from behind. It is pulling one way and the angler is pulling the other, with the result that the angler takes the fly away from the fish. On feeling a nip or a pull such as this, you might hook the salmon if you immediately let a little line out.

The story goes that an angler was visiting a British gentleman who owned a good stretch of water. On returning to the house for tea, the very dignified wife of the gentleman asked the angler if he had had any luck.

"No," he replied, "but I had a good pull."

"Oh," she said, "that was probably only a lavatory fish—you know, one pull and it's gone." (We must assume that the estate had antique plumbing!)

Tracing the Trophy

Long after a big salmon is caught, the memory of its shape and size can be kept if you trace the trophy. Lay the fish on a section from a roll of wrapping paper and carefully trace around it with a long pencil. Then, with the fish in view, draw in parts such as gills, eyes, mouth structure, and fin rays, making the tracing in pencil, in ink, or in color as elaborately as desired. Letter in under the drawing the weight, where and when caught and by whom, fly used, and other data. Roll up the tracing and keep it as a souvenir. Few people realize how big a large salmon really is. An accurate drawing will provide interest for many years to come.

Fishing the Floating Line and the Patent

"The Salmon Guide"

The previous chapter's description of swinging the sunken fly is so basic, although often so successful, that sophisticated anglers often demean it as the "chuck and chance it" method. This is incorrect, however, unless you are doing just that. Choice of fly, proper fly speed and depth, and covering the best holding positions are so important that if addressed properly, chance is reduced and the system is very effective.

Since the unpredictability of Atlantic salmon is the lure of the game, you should understand and try other methods when basic ones don't work. Often an angler will fish down a pool without result, to be followed by another, using a different technique, who hooks one or more fish in the same amount of time.

Therefore, in this continuation of subsurface methods, let's explore two alternatives: first, Arthur H. E. Wood's revolutionary way of fishing the floating, or greased, line, and then Col. Lewis S. Thompson's method of using what he liked to call the Patent.

Greased-Line Fishing

While fishing an Irish river in July 1903, Arthur Wood discovered that salmon that had persistently refused sunken flies presented by the swinging method might take them if they were fished drifting broadside on or very near the surface without drag. Evidently Wood fussed with his method for about ten years before he thought it sufficiently perfected to disclose it to others. He called it *greased-line fishing* because, back in those days, it was necessary to grease the line to make it float. Now, with lines that can be made so buoyant that they can float naturally, we would call it *floating-line fishing* were it not considered more appropriate to retain Wood's appellation. Wood himself never disclosed his method in print, but he did relate all of it to a gentleman using the pen name of "Jock Scott," who wrote about it in *Greased Line Fishing for Salmon* (1937). He also discussed it with other famous anglers of the era, such as John Waller Hills, George M. L. LaBranche, Ernest Crosfield, Frederick Hills, Eric Taverner, Anthony Crossley, and others, some of whom referred to it in their writings.

Arthur Wood developed his method at his estate called "Cairnton" on the bank of the Aberdeenshire Dee, a bit upriver from the ancient town of Ban-

chory, where Bessie Brown dressed her famous salmon flies for some of the gentlemen mentioned above. From 1913 to 1934, by careful tally, Wood killed 3,490 salmon, most of them on the greased line. This is an average of 166 fish per season, which is a pretty good score for anybody! Certainly it is a recommendation for his method.

The basis of the greased-line theory is simple. Wood's first step was to discover where, in the sunk fly's course, most salmon take it. Next, he wanted to know how the fly was traveling at that point and how it appeared to the salmon. Finally, he needed to manage his tackle so that no matter where the fish were lying, he could offer the fly in the same way.

The most effective part of the fly's travel is when it is swinging around to its final downstream position, which answers the first point. There, the fly would be riding down past the salmon, not curving straight at them, which happens only when approaching the downstream position. It is not being drawn across them, as in the normal wet-fly swing, but, rather, *sidling past* them and floating downstream, which answers the second point. The third point is a matter of presentation, and Wood learned how to present the fly to wherever fish could be lying—straight downstream, at an angle downstream, straight across, or even across and upstream.

Theory and practice were united by the technique of mending the line. In this case, however, it is more important for mending to be done so as not to disturb the fly and the first few feet of the leader, a technique requiring some practice.

As "Jock Scott" explains it: "There are four points to remember. The mend is not a cast, but a lift with the arm extended and the rod held not high and not much out of the horizontal. It is made as much across stream as upstream; otherwise there is a pull on the fly. It must be made as soon as the fly lights, and it may have to be repeated two or three times in the fly's course. I should have said that cases exist where no mend is required; where the stream runs at an evenly increasing pace from angler to fly, but these are rare. To mend properly you must have a delicate touch. You must feel the line without pulling it. Very few people can make a mend right down to the leader without drawing the fly. The secret is to think of it never as a cast, and not even as a lift, but as a roll. Lead the line downstream by gently leading

156

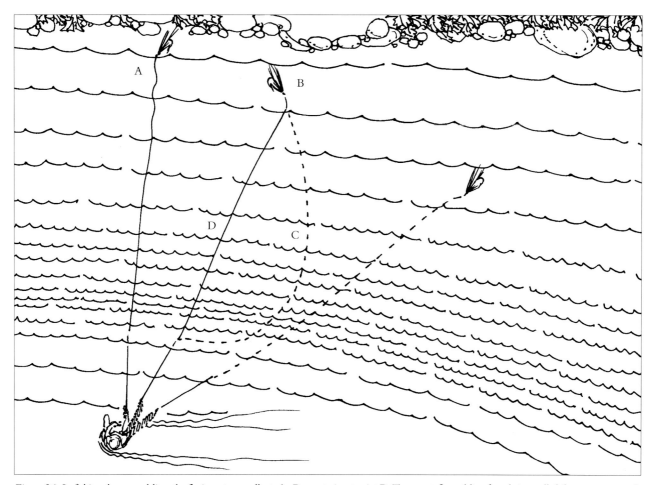

Figure 24. In fishing the greased line, the fly is cast normally to A. *Drag sets in at point* B. *To prevent fly and line from being pulled downstream, mend the line from* C *to* D. *The fly will then continue a natural drift. Continue to mend when necessary.*

the rod tip slightly downstream and continue rolling it over, not using the point as in a cast, but merely to keep you in touch with the line. Roll it over and place (not throw it) across stream as well as up."

Mending the line so as not to disturb the position or current speed of the fly is the basis of greased-line fishing, but exactly what is greased-line fishing, and how does it differ from swinging the sunk fly?

In greased-line fishing, the basic idea is to use the line as a float to control and suspend the fly just beneath the surface of the water in such a way that it swims diagonally down and across the stream, entirely free from pull on the line. The fly essentially is drifting broadside, or nearly so, to give fish a sideways view of it, rather than swinging on a tight line, in which case the fish would see the fly tailfirst. (Look at a wet salmon fly broadside, and then tail-

first, to see the pronounced difference.) To make this difference between the drifting and the swinging fly more obvious, let's compare the two methods as "Jock Scott" expressed them. *SF* means "sunk fly," and *GL* means "greased line."

1. (SF) The fly travels at midwater depth. (GL) The fly travels just, and only just, submerged.

2. (SF) The fly, being held by a taut line, travels far more across stream than down; it presents a tail-end view to the fish. (GL) The fly travels more down than across, because it is being fished on a more or less slack line. It presents a side view to the fish; that is, the whole of the fly is visible, not merely the tail end.

3. (SF) The fly is rigidly held against the current by a taut line. Hence, the only life shown by the fly is the play of wings and hackle caused by the action of the current in addition to any jerking motion imparted by the rod tip or by handling the line.

"Old Guide" courtesy of John Dreyer

(GL) The fly, being fished in such a way that it is entirely free from line pull, swims in a natural manner—wobbling, swimming, rising and falling with the play of the eddies exactly as would an insect or a little fish that is in trouble. The very light feathers work with the action of the water, and the *whole* fly is visible to the fish.

4. (SF) The fly is being held against the stream both before and after the instant at which the fish takes it.(GL) The fly is going with the stream, and with no tension on it, at all times.

5. (SF) The fish is taking a fly that is, at all times,

being held back from it. That is, it is taking against the line tension, and it feels an unnatural resistance. (GL) The fly floats naturally straight into the salmon's mouth, and the stream's tendency is to push the fly farther back toward the throat. There is minimum tension and resistance, and everything is easy and natural.

6. (SF) The line being taut, there is an instantaneous pull on the fly, tending to draw it out of the fish's mouth before it has closed. (GL) The line being slack, there is ample time for a fish to take.

7. (SF) The angler has no choice as to where

and when he may hook the fish. With the line being tight and leading upstream, pressure is automatically applied (unless the angler sees the fish come to the fly, which cannot always be the case when the fly is sunk) and the hook either comes out or takes hold. (GL) The angler always sees his rises, and gives slack. This slack line is swept downstream by the current and, in so doing, draws the hook into the back curves of the fish's mouth. It is always possible, therefore, for an expert angler to hook his fish in the part of the mouth that offers the most secure hold.

8. (SF) The sunk line is very largely out of control. (GL) The floating line is at all times (unless grievous errors are committed) *completely* under control.

9. (SF) In certain situations only a limited portion of the actual holding water can be fished, even if it is within casting distance. (GL) All of the holding water within casting distance can be virtually fished in a proper manner, and drag eliminated.

10. (SF) Drag is the bugbear of the sunk-fly fisherman. (GL) Drag can be completely eliminated.

Since Wood hooked and landed many times more salmon than I have, and spent many more days doing it, it may be impertinent for me to differ with him, but I do on a few of his points as outlined by "Jock Scott."

In the previous chapter, I noted how salmon usually take flies, and it is not in the ways Wood believed, so his practice of giving slack (point 7 above) is disputed, and it is left to readers to form their own opinions. If salmon, on taking flies, remained facing upstream, Wood's precept might be valid. If, however, they turn with the fly, as most anglers today believe, giving slack is inadvisable.

Wood propounded a method that he evidently favored nearly all of the time. I agree with fellow anglers that it may be the best one sometimes, but not always. When fishing the neck or tail of a pool, for example, the sunk fly probably would be the method to use because of the position of the angler, the fast water, or other reasons. On the other hand, when an angler is facing a pool, particularly when it isn't very fast flowing, such a situation may seem to scream for use of the greased line. The answer is to use the method that you judge most appropriate for the situation at hand. No one method is the solution to everything, which is why this book presents several.

When an angler is facing a pool in which the location of one or more fish is known, he should cast from a position opposite but slightly upstream of the fish and should drop his fly about 10 feet in front of and upstream from them. He should manage his line by mending and leading it so that the fly will drift down over the fish in a natural manner. Wood said that one should not strike when a fish takes, but should, instead, give slack so that the line will belly downstream and pull the fly into the secure hooking position at the apex of the fish's jaw. The pros and cons of this have been discussed; it's up to the discretion of the individual.

When an angler is facing a pool in which the location of fish is unknown, he should cover all of the good holding water, probably starting with shorter casts and continuing with longer ones. Fishing greased line is more fun than sunken fly because, somewhat similar to dry-fly fishing, the fly is near enough to the surface that most of the action can be seen. Ideally, the fly should be only an inch or two under the surface.

In fishing greased line, three requirements should be observed. The line must float throughout its entire length, with the leader-to-line knot visibly cutting the water. The fly must be fished directly across the pool so that it passes as nearly as possible at a right angle to the upstream direction in which the fish is lying, or presumed to be lying. And the fly must be moving at the proper fly speed the entire time, from the moment it drops on the water. If it seems to be moving too fast, this can be corrected by making an upstream mend. If it seems to be moving too slowly, this can be corrected by stripping in line, by allowing a proper amount of downstream belly to form in the line, by leading the fly, or by a combination of these methods.

It is obvious that proper line handling, or mending, is vital to complete success with greased-line fishing, and practice is needed to handle the line correctly without disturbing the fly. It is a good idea to practice this during lulls so that you can use the method with confidence when salmon are in a taking mood. Wood says the following about this:

Having made the cast and got a belly in the line, my hand and rod are close in front of my body in lifting, the point of the rod may be one foot or four feet from the water, it does not matter much, but it should not *be held high up.* I then lift the point of the rod with a stiff arm downstream and up [into the air] to clear it [the line] off the water without friction, then, continuing the swing *upstream* I keep the arm more or less stiff—after raising it from the shoulder in a horizontal position, simultaneously straightening the arm. This throws a slackness in the line between you and the fly.

Always mend to some particular spot down the line; that is, don't lift the whole line unless you have to, only down to the eddy or whatever it is that is causing the drag. The first thing to master is lifting without really dragging the fly any great distance. Once you get that right I think you will find the rest comes easy. Do not throw too tight a line when you cast, if the water is strong. Give yourself a foot or two of slack so as to be able to lift inwards before the point of the rod goes outwards and round. Finally, if the rod bends while you are mending, it means that you are using too much force. The whole thing is quite *gentle* and *slow*.★

A word about *leading the fly*. I find in practice that it is a great point to lead the line with the rod as soon as you can, and not follow it. By moving the rod in advance of the line [but not of course dragging it] you help the fly to swim more downstream than across. This dropping downstream is extremely valuable, and whenever you can do so you should allow the fly to drop as much downstream as you possibly can. Suppose you stood in the middle of a clock face [Digital watches are of no help here!] and cast to 12 o'clock. Throw a *slack* line and hold the point of the rod up after the fly has dropped on the water at 12 o'clock. By the time it has drifted to 11 o'clock the fly is still almost straight downstream from 12 o'clock instead of following the rim of the clock face in a circle. By 10 o'clock the fly is actually outside the clock face, and began to be so at 11 o'clock, finally ending up well outside the circle at 9 o'clock. Actually, while leading, the point of the rod is raised into the air. This lead in the air gives a belly in the line which enables the fish to take the fly upstream without getting an immediate pull from the rod. I generally throw a slack line, which gives me as much dropping downstream of the fly as possible.

This leading serves several useful purposes. If the rod were held steady the fly would come round in more or less a true circle but, when leading, the rod-point is going downstream in advance of the line, leading and coaxing it down as well as across. The rod is in the position it should be when you tighten the line on a fish; that is, in towards the bank, and not up in the air.

As soon as the fly gets round to your side it may pay you to keep the rod-point *behind* the line instead of in front of it, and gradually raise the point. This prevents a sudden snatch that sometimes occurs when a fish is lying below you and takes the fly when the line is taut.

I like to have a *very slight* downstream curve in the line as it drifts down, so that the fish can see the whole of the fly and, by leading and of course mending upstream if the curve becomes too pronounced, I often succeed in doing so. Try to more than get this curve, if you can, but never allow more than the slightest drag.

★Wood might have added that it is easier to mend when using a longer rod than a shorter one.

Tackle

Tackle for greased-line fishing is no different from that for any other method except that the floating line is mandatory and flies usually are very sparsely dressed on hooks of weights that will take the flies just under the surface film, but usually no deeper. In cold-water or high-water conditions, large flies as big as #4s, with ordinary dressings, are used. As water becomes warmer and clearer, the favored sizes gradually reduce to #6. Summer conditions may recommend sizes between #6 and #12, but these small sizes are used only when salmon are shy of the larger ones. Rather than using the smaller sizes, such as #10 and #12, better hooking can be obtained by using smaller dressings on the larger hooks.

Many greased-line anglers never, or almost never, start with hooks smaller than #6, but the hooks are of fine wire (such as Wilson dry-fly hooks) and the sparse dressings never extend beyond the point of the hook. These are commonly known as *low-water patterns*, where the body occupies no more than the forward two-thirds of the shank, with other parts of the dressing in proportion.

Wood had this to say about that:

I like the dressing to be as thin, transparent and misty as possible where low-water flies are concerned. The older and thinner a fly becomes through wear, the better the fish seem to like it, provided the weather is hot and the water clear. I have caught fish on a practically bare hook on which there was left no body and only the head and four fibers of the wings; also quite a number on a hook with only the body and no wing or hackle at all.

As regards pattern, I do not believe that this matters at all. *Blue Charm* and *Silver Blue* are my stock, simply on the principle that one is more or less black and the other white, and so give *me* a choice. I once fished through the whole season with a *March Brown* only, and got my share, and more, of the fish caught.

Blue Charm and *Silver Blue* I keep in all sizes from No. 1 to No. 12, ordinary weight of hook, and *March Brown, Blue Charm* and *Silver Blue* sparsely dressed on No. 4 to No. 10 light low water irons. These last I use only in warm weather and clear water. I always start with a *Blue Charm* and only change it if all the sizes I try prove no good. Then I try a *Silver Blue*. But if the water is very clear and the weather bright, I use a *March Brown,* and pick out the 'ripest' one in my box.

If you rise a fish to, for example, a No. 6, change to a No. 8 and you should get him, for that fish has shown you that No. 6 was on the large size for that pool, place or time. If you have the right size fly on it is very rarely that you get

PLATE 60
LOW-WATER PATTERNS

Silver Blue
dressed by Syd Glasso

March Brown
dressed by Mark Waslick

Blue Charm
dressed by Elizabeth Greig

merely a rise; the fish always means business if it comes. If, however, the fish rises and refuses, it is a clear sign that the fly is too big and too showy for it.

Wood approved a set of patterns for greased-line fishing that were included in Hardy Brothers' catalog for many years under the classification of "Wood Low-Water Flies." These included *Blue Charm, Logie, Jockie, Jeannie, March Brown,* and *Silver Blue,* plus four others now obscure. Modern anglers can't fault Wood on his choice of patterns, because those mentioned above are still very popular six or seven decades after he recommended them. The *Blue Charm* in particular is, even today, one of the most effective of all salmon flies, all around the north Atlantic.

In my opinion, for whatever that is worth, three low-water patterns should be sufficient for greased-line fishing: a darker one, a medium one, and a lighter and brighter one. The darker one, used primarily for silhouette when salmon are facing the sun, would be a simplified *Night Hawk* or *Black Jack.* The medium one, usually used when the sun is overhead, but good all the time, would be a *Blue Charm* or *Hairy Mary,* both as hairwings. The lighter

and brighter one, valuable primarily for glitter when salmon are not facing the sun, would be a *Silver Blue,* or Chaytor's *White and Silver.*

Chaytor's *White and Silver* is a historic favorite that, though extremely effective under the above conditions, unfortunately has become obscure. A. H. Chaytor, author of *Letters to a Salmon Fisher's Sons* (1910), said of this simple pattern, "This fly, called a 'White and Silver,' has a perfectly plain body of oval silver, a rather long white hackle, and wings of dark turkey, with a large jungle cock's feather over each wing. No tail, tag, butt, head, or any other adornment."

Arthur Wood often went to an extreme with sparsely dressed hooks. He said: "This small hook salmon fishing is done in low water and you do not want the fly to be too bunchy or create a big disturbance in the water. That is why I always had my own flies tied as flat to the hook as possible, and very little of them. In summer time and when hot weather comes and sport is the best, one often has to fish in strong, shallow water. Any fly that is bunchy or has stiff feathers is apt to skim on the surface or drag, and that is the reason why I personally like a bare hook, or very little indeed on it, and what there is should be sitting close to the hook; just a little thin bunch like a small, thin eel. Anything bigger, even a big eye or a big head often causes a skim or wave. This sometimes attracts the fish, but more often than not it will come to the fly and stop short."

The extreme Wood went to was to use a bare hook dressed only with tinsel or painted red or blue on the shank only. A few hairs or other very minor embellishment sometimes might be added. "Jock Scott" comments, "Personally, I cannot imagine many anglers having sufficient pluck to use them." Wood says that he took salmon on them, and I once fished with a Spanish angler who said he had taken salmon on a bare hook. I don't think he did it very often!

Wood also offers other comments:

The lowest water temperature at which I fish greased line and small fly is about 39 degrees or 40 degrees but, if there is a very cold wind I use a big fly and sink it. . . .

How much drag is permissible depends on circumstances, but there should be as little as possible. You should be able to tell by the feel of the rod if there is any drag, even with your eyes shut. Even in fastish water you should be able to take your hand off the line and none of it should run out through

PLATE 61
LOW-WATER PATTERNS

Lady Caroline
dressed by Syd Glasso

Blue Charm Hairwing   *Hairy Mary*
dressed by Keith Fulsher   dressed by Keith Fulsher

Jeannie   *Jockie*   *Baron*
dressed by Syd Glasso   dressed by Bob Veverka   *(antique)*

Black Jack   *Night Hawk*   *Logie*
dressed by Ralph Billingsley   dressed by Bob Warren   dressed by Elizabeth Greig

the rod guides. You should feel no weight on the rod at all; everything should be perfectly free and slack. . . .

Regarding using the greased line in very narrow rivers, I have fished 'ditches' not more than ten feet across, with parts only six feet between the rushes, and managed to get more fish than anyone else. The greased line is there to keep the fly near the surface, so it does not matter what size of water. A short line makes no difference, and I often prefer a short one to a longer one. I have caught fish within six feet of my legs. . . .

I have tried a No. 1 hook on greased line in floods when the water was so thick you could not see more than an inch

or two below the surface, and I find that even then the fish both see and take it. It does seem to me extraordinary how the fish can see the little fly in thick water but, in all waters except a really big flood [when heavy gear and big hooks are needed] I invariably fish small fly and greased line. . . .

To stir up a stiff [dour, or stale] fish lying in the tail of a pool it is not a bad dodge to let the fly down behind the fish and then suddenly draw it quickly upstream past it. Sometimes it will have a go for the fly! . . .

Why do I dress the body and wings of my fly so short compared with the length of the hook? I need a small fly in summer weather, say a No. 12, because the fish will not move to anything larger but, although the fish will take these small flies, they are no good at all for holding a fish. The hooks are so very small, and the eyes being also small, you have to use very fine gut; too fine. I found that salmon did not seem to mind the long, fine hook in the least, and it gave you a chance to hold the fish, and also to use gut of reasonable strength.

You also say that the dressing seems so very thin and would not show against the light. That is an advantage in fine weather. The more indistinct the fly is, the better, or so I find. If you have a sort of misty, indistinct fly, the fish will go for it when they would not touch a fully dressed, rather gaudy one, which looks unnatural.

When you are rigged for greased-line fishing— that is, with floating line—you have several other options. A long leader with ordinary fly lets one fish it swinging and sunk (as discussed in the previous chapter) when water is thin or when salmon will take flies near the surface. The same tackle lets one fish the dry fly, or the Patent, which now will be discussed. Thus, when salmon will come up to flies, or take them at their level in shallow water, this tackle seems to be the most versatile.

Fishing the Patent

Another method in the salmon angler's bag of tricks is one that has more or less been cloaked in mystery but is quite simple. It is called Thompson's Patent, or merely the Patent. Col. Lewis S. Thompson obtained some hairwing flies from an angler who pioneered them, A. S. Trude, and tried them on Canada's Restigouche River in 1928. The colonel wrote about his experiences in the March 1934 issue of a now-defunct magazine called *The Sportsman,* and here is the story in his own words:

> Five years ago I was fishing in Jimmie's Hole: a celebrated pool on the Restigouche. At that time there was in that pool an old he-salmon that we got to know as the 'Hobby Horse.' There he was in the middle of the pool, and all at once he would start in on his hobby, rolling up to the top of the water with his big, broad back, and doing it for twenty times or more at short intervals, always in the same place. Not a fly would he ever look at. We would always inquire at night from the one who had fished the pool, 'Anything doing with Hobby?' But there never was anything doing with that scoundrel! I was fishing the pool one day, and there was the old Hobby Horse doing his cavorting around much more than usual, I thought. But the fly meant nothing in his life, as I fished on to the drop below. I had on a 5/0 *Abbey* [see *Red Abbey.*] A large salmon rose to it away over near the bank. I let the fly come on around. There was some more time to

spare before the next cast, so I retrieved the fly and cast it away up the stream. As it floated down it looked like a large mouse. It drifted into the eddies and was then thrown out into the crystal-clear, mirror-like surface of the pool. It was slowly coming down to the home of the Hobby Horse and, by gracious, here came that horse! He grabbed it, and had gone for his last ride. And that was the birth of a new way to take a salmon, and a way that I think is far superior to any other method that I know about. We call it 'The Patent.'

> I have always been trying something new or different and have called whatever it was a Thompson Patent. The method is simplicity itself. The fly is thrown so that it lights on the water at the end of a loose line. Throw it up or down stream, at any angle, or straight across. Instead of having the line out straight, the rod will be stopped at about 45 degrees and the line pulled up before the fly hits the water. The hair fly instead of having its hair all in a line as it would be on the end of a taut line is spread out in an **A**-shape, and it looks like no other fly on earth or in the water. You can use it on a dry (sinking) or a greased (floating) line. I prefer the greased line on account of the easy pickup. You fish this Patent as you would fish for trout. You must strike the fish, and you can see every fish that comes. That is all there is to it. Let the fly float of itself without any pull at all from the line. Whether the water is high or low, or dark or clear, the salmon will come to this fly and will take it.

Later experience with this method recommends using a sinking line, or a floating line with a sinking tip, to allow the fly to sink gradually as it drifts downstream. The obvious purpose of the method is to make the fly fluff up to give maximum life to the hairs in the wing as they encounter action in the current.

Edward R. Hewitt, in *A Trout and Salmon Fisherman for Seventy-Five Years* (1948), adds this:

> The hair flies used for this type of fishing for salmon are not at all like the ordinary bucktail used in trout fishing. As fished with a slack line, they are not pulled through the water to a sleek, minnow-like form nor are they designed to imitate a small fish. They are tied and fished so that the hairs sprawl out and wiggle individually in the water.

> In fishing 'The Patent' it is well to have a variety of sizes of flies from 6's and 8's up and, with me, the larger sizes have been the more successful, say, from 1/0 and 2/0 up. Of these hair flies, I have never found a great variety of patterns to be necessary. Three will be sufficient, I think, until such time as the individual angler invents others to suit himself. These are: the *Abbey,* made of red-brown hair, a silver ribbed red silk body, and a red tail; the *Teagle Bee,* with a yellow and black [bee-like] body, red tail, and black and brown hair; and a third fly with a silver body, red tail and gray hair."

Some of the Rocky Mountain bucktails whose dressings are given in my book *Streamer Fly Tying and*

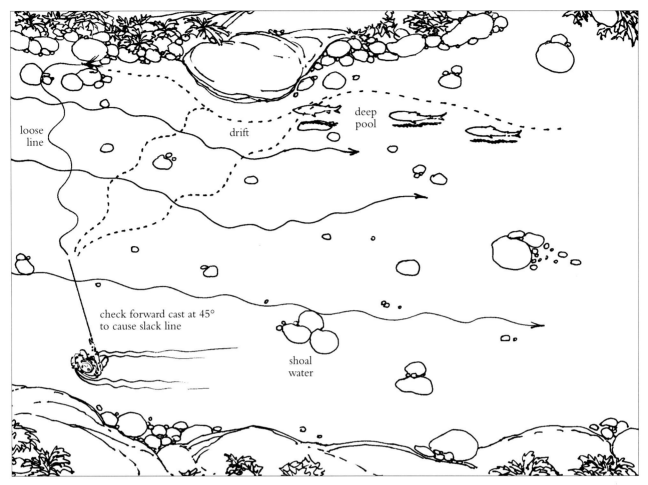

Figure 25. In fishing the Patent, cast a slack line up, across, or downstream. Allow hairwing fly to drift without any pull from the line, thus making it "work" or "fluff." Fish near the surface, or deeper down.

Fishing (1966 and 1995) are ideal for this purpose, mainly because of the method of dressing the hairwings for pronounced pulsating action.

Richard C. Hunt, in *Salmon in Low Water* (1950), gives these notes, by Walter C. Teagle and Bayard W. Read, which appeared in the October 1945 issue of *The Anglers' Club Bulletin:*

There would seem little doubt that the secret of The Patent's success is the action or movement of the hairs, giving the fly the appearance of being alive as it goes down through the swirls of the current. You can see this action for yourself by simply dropping a hair fly in the water beside you when you are next on the river. Let it float downstream, tail first, watch it as it goes by with no drag on the line, then pull it up and see how all the hairs are bunched together on top of the fly.

No one understands what makes this action so consistently enticing to the salmon, but it has been demonstrated time and time again when, after raising a fish two or three times on the ordinary wet fly, or even on a small fly fished on the greased line, only to have it turn away, it comes up and makes a grab for it the first time The Patent is floated over it.

In fishing The Patent, it must be remembered that you have to strike your fish, and tighten hard, just as you would a trout, or as in dry fly salmon fishing. This is only logical since your fly is at the end of a slack line. You must take up that slack and strike your fish before it realizes its mistake and ejects the fly. The amount of line you have out should be governed by the keenness of your eyesight. There is no point in fishing so much line that you cannot see the fish approach. You must see it to time your strike correctly. This may be difficult if the fish comes up slowly. Then you are apt to strike too soon and pull the fly away from it. Too, if the fish moves to the fly towards the end of the cast, you may not be able to see it clearly because by then your fly will be well down in the water. Usually, however, there will be a flash of silver, a swirl, or a wave, that will be your cue. Strike as the fish turns with the fly or, if you cannot see it clearly, strike when you see the boil in the water. If it seems probable the fish has not touched the fly, give it the customary four or five minutes rest, and then fish over it again with either another pattern or a different sized fly of the same pattern.

Unlike the orthodox wet fly and greased line fishing, The Patent is not a method to be used to find salmon. To cover all fishable or likely water by this method as you go downstream would take much too long. But once you can see the fish, or know them to be in the pool, The Patent will move them and bring them to the fly, in many cases after other methods have failed.

Of the three patterns mentioned above for fishing the Patent, there seems no reason for recommending the *Teagle Bee,* except that it is an adaptation of the well-known *McGinty* trout fly that was used for salmon by Walter C. Teagle, who popularized it with his friends on Canada's Restigouche.

The *Abbey* mentioned is the *Red Abbey,* a development of the well-known and formerly described *Trude,* which has no red tail of feather sections. A *Silver Abbey* also used in fishing the Patent is the same except for a body of flat or oval silver tinsel—

a good pattern to use when salmon are not facing the sun.

The third one, for similar use, calling for a silver body, red tail, and gray hair, is very much like the popular *Silver Rat,* which might be an even better pattern for this purpose.

Any hairwing pattern can be adapted to this method of fishing if the style is suitable. Note that Hewitt said that "the hair flies used for this type of fishing for salmon are not at all like the ordinary bucktail used in trout fishing." I don't know exactly how Hewitt did it, but the modern practical way is thus: Apply the wing in reverse style, which will cause it to stand up higher. This is done by tying in the wing *first,* with the hair tips pointing forward over the eye of the hook. When the rest of the fly is completed, the wing then is reversed to normal position and tied down *so that it flares widely.* This method also provides a much smaller and neater head, as well as a very secure wing. The hackle is wound on *after* this is done.

9

Salmon on the Dry Fly

"Miramichi Morning" courtesy of J. Louis Newell

$\mathcal{P}$erhaps the greatest thrill in all angling is to cast a floating fly above a salmon lie and to watch it merrily bob along on the current until, with a mighty swirling swoosh, a great salmon rises up to take it. In wet-fly fishing, the striking fish cannot always be observed, and never can be observed as well as when it takes the floating fly on the surface. In this chapter, we will look at new ways of causing this to happen more often; ways that make salmon fishing more challenging—and a great deal more fun.

Taking salmon on the dry fly is a North American development that, after more than half a century, remains pretty much so because anglers in other countries around the north Atlantic think, rightly or wrongly, that the method is ineffective there. Some give colder water temperatures as the reason, perhaps resulting in fewer insects on the streams, but I will venture the opinion that the more logical reason is lack of practice or experience.

According to George M. L. LaBranche, one of the first men to do it evidently was Col. Ambrose Monell, on New Brunswick's Upsalquitch before the outbreak of the first World War. LaBranche, his companion on many angling expeditions, describes it in *The Salmon and the Dry Fly* (1924), a classic that has been reprinted.

"Believing as I did, that salmon do not feed in fresh water, I hesitated to introduce the subject of fishing for them with a floating fly. Divining, perhaps, what was in my mind, my friend (Colonel Monell) calmly announced that he had killed a 15-pound salmon two years before on a dry fly, and assured me that it was not an accident. He had seen the fish rising just as a trout would rise, and, having failed to interest the fish with any of the wet flies in his box, he had deliberately cast across and upstream with a No. 12 Whirling Dun, floating it down over the fish, which took it at once. It was the taking of this fish, and the rising of six or seven others which he did not hook, that convinced him it would be possible to kill fish with the dry fly when the water was low."

LaBranche goes on to recount other salmon taken on dry flies during this trip and recalls that, in many instances, repeated casting over salmon proved fruitless until a certain sort of presentation caused one of them to rise and take. He says that in such effective casts, the angler—whether he realizes it or not—is drifting the fly in currents in which rising fish are coming up for "drift stuff" being carried downstream. Thus, he thinks, the reason for repeatedly ineffective casts over known lies is that these casts are not being placed properly in the "groove," and the reason for a rising take is proper placement. He considers this so critical that it could "be measured by fractions of an inch," which, of course, may require many casts to effect. (LaBranche calls them *grooves,* while this book calls them *edges.* No matter, let's proceed with this famous angler's thinking for a bit.)

He says, and most of us will have to agree, that a smooth flow of water, with few obstructions, presents an easy problem because such a flow contains

Col. Ambrose Monell and George LaBranche

few edges. A fly presented anywhere near a fish in such water may bring a rise, because the fish is not averse to traveling a short distance to take the fly. Thus, skillful,delicate casting over known or presumed positions should be adequate, because fish are not apt to change locations in such a situation.

Increasing numbers of edges present increasing problems. Consider, for example, the rush of water entering a pool over a succession of rocks. The flattening water below the entering water reveals on the surface a multiplicity of edges where currents meet. These edges contain more "drift stuff" than the currents from which they form, and the edges are constantly changing because of the varying paces of the currents that form them. Thus, a fish stationed in an edge always is in the edge, but is moved from side to side with the shifting edge in a snakelike manner or as a tethered skiff may swing because of wind action. The salmon lies in the wavering edge, and the fly must be presented in the edge (not near it) if the fish is to be made to rise, because it will not move out of the edge to take the fly—or so LaBranche evidently thought.

Well, as a student of salmon fishing, I have been increasingly conscious of the importance of edges in locating the probable lies of salmon, but I wonder if all this is quite as critical as LaBranche thought. Anyway, it may help to explain why repeated dry-fly casts over a fish fail to tempt a rise, and why one suddenly does so.

Casting the Dry Fly

Let's now consider downstream, cross-stream, and upstream casting with the dry fly—elementary approaches that some advanced anglers probably understand much better than I do, and therefore may elect to ignore.

Select a dry fly that rides high in the water and can be doped to stay that way as long as possible. In downstream casting, when a good edge is decided upon or the position of a salmon is known, the angler drops the fly several feet upstream of the known or suspected hot spot, pulling back on the rod a bit to provide slack for drift near the fly. Note that this slack should be more near to the fly than otherwise.

Before or directly after making the cast, some extra line can be stripped from the reel and fed out through the rod guides by wavering the rod tip, thus

providing more line for a longer float, if desired.

While doing this, you should be prepared for a take and should set the hook the instant a fish is seen to take the fly. Because of the amount of line out, the setting of the hook will be delayed slightly but, with proper line handling, probably not too much. If you try this before the action, the act of setting the hook will pull the fly in somewhat even when the line isn't straight. This should be enough, but when slack is under control, another good pull seems advisable anyway to ensure that the hook is set properly.

In this downstream fishing the fly precedes the leader, thus making the leader less obvious. If a fish boils to the fly but doesn't take, it may be refusing because of improper fly size, but probably not because of pattern. It also may refuse because the leader is too big at the tip, but salmon usually are not very leader-shy. Another reason for refusal may be that the fly was drifting improperly, such as with a bit of drag. Anyway, a rising fish is a probable taker and should be worked on. Try the same cast again. If this doesn't produce, rest the fish for a few minutes while changing the fly to a size larger or smaller and making sure the leader tip is suitable to fly size. An interested fish is a taking fish when the right combination is offered.

You may find yourself on a pool that you know holds salmon, but you have no indication of exactly where they are. Whether casting from a boat or wading in a suitable position, the "drift and draw method," as I like to call it, offers an efficient way of water coverage, as shown in Figure 26.

Make the previously discussed downstream dry-fly cast to position A, which is as far to the left as is convenient, and perhaps close to the bank. Using slack, cast line and, by feeding line, if advisable, let the fly drift downstream more or less as the dashed line indicates. This first cast should be quite close in, because salmon often are hooked very nearby. When the drift has extended as far as seems sensible, draw the fly in a bit to the right to a spot beside where the first cast was made, such as to position B. This is done by raising the rod tip and stripping in line. The fly is skated to its new position, and this different skating action (similar to a hitched fly) may tempt a take. In any event, the fly at position B is allowed to drift downstream as before, but along the new path.

It is less important to evenly space these lateral casts than it is to work the fly down promising edges. The lateral casts can be made at least four or five times, depending on water conditions.

This first series of casts should have been made quite close in. Now, extend the length of the next series of casts, and repeat them, as before. Rather than doing this a third time, it may be preferable to drop down the pool a bit so as not to have to fish with too long a line, because this diminishes hook effectiveness.

In dry-fly fishing for salmon, there are five things to remember. First, flies seem to do better when they float high, rather than riding somewhat waterlogged in the surface film, although this may vary depending on pattern. Second, though salmon are not usually leader-shy, there are times when they

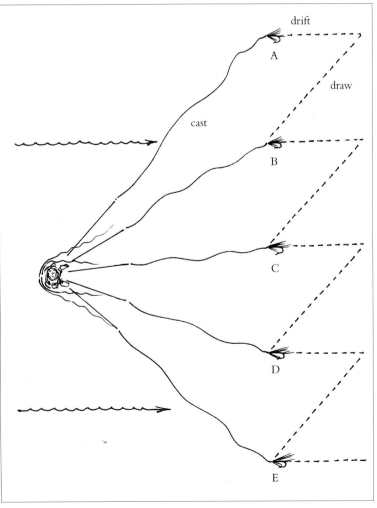

Figure 26. The drift and draw method for exploring a pool.

PLATE 62
DRY FLIES, DRESSED BY
GEORGE M. L. LABRANCHE

may be, so it is good to try to let the salmon see the fly first, not the leader. If salmon in certain instances are presumed to be leader-shy, smaller tippets within reason may do better. Third, the fly usually should drift down in the edge close over the lie, or presumed lie, of the fish, because salmon lacking the combative or protective instinct may not travel very far to take it. Fourth, avoid drag on the fly as much as possible, unless you decide to drag the fly intentionally—a last resort that often works. Finally, be very slow to give up when working on a reluctant salmon. A lucky cast, after many fruitless ones, often results in a take. This may be the cast you don't make after too soon becoming discouraged!

The size of the dry fly and its buoyancy are more important than the pattern, but a few patterns varying in character add to confidence, and sometimes to results. Colonel Monell and LaBranche settled on four: *Colonel Monell, Soldier Palmer, Mole Palmer,* and *Pink Lady Palmer.* In these more modern times, palmered flies no longer are very popular, but the dressings of these four, as well as later originations, are given later on in this chapter.

We all have our opinions about fly selection, so I'll venture to add mine, based on a few decades of experience. At a minimum, give me a *Wulff*—any *Wulff*—in sizes 2, 6, and 8. While larger flies for colder water and smaller ones for warmer may be a good rule, larger flies often prove best at any time. Above the minimum, give me three *Wulffs:* a very dark one, a very light one, and one in between, such as the *Royal Wulff,* which often gets my vote partly because it is so pretty. When *Wulffs* are properly made and treated, they are virtually impossible to sink. One angler I fish with less often than I'd like to likes the *White Wulff* because it's so easy to see on dull days. For this reason he also uses one predominantly yellow. There are seven *Wulffs* in the accepted series, a few of which are enough.

Then, for a change of pace or character, give me a *Bomber.* I have written about this one previously, because it has been my ace in the hole on many occasions. Don't confuse it with other flies of the

PLATE 63
BOMBERS, DRESSED BY
WARREN DUNCAN

across, across, or up and across, as desired. If it is fished down and across, with a reasonable amount of slack line shot through the guides, the fly will float freely for a time while the slack line is being used up. During the float, the line can be mended as need be.

When fishing upstream and across the slack line is being increased, but when fishing downstream and across it is being decreased. Slack line is being used up during the float, and to set the hook all that is necessary on the strike is to pull out whatever remains of it, if any.

In upstream fishing, you should try to keep the fish from seeing the leader (as little as possible) and to prevent drag on the fly. The basis of the loop cast to the left, sometimes referred to as the *Hewitt loop,* is to remember that whatever motion is transmitted to the rod by the angler in casting will be transmitted to the line, and thus to the leader and the fly. This cast throws a left curve in the leader and line end, thus letting the dry fly drift downstream with the leader *behind* it, the curved line end also drifting downstream naturally to prevent drag.

To make the cast to a certain point upstream, make a fake cast or two to measure distance and imagine you are casting to a spot 4 or 5 feet upstream of where you want the fly to land. When the final cast has straightened out, preparatory to dropping, pull the line with the left hand in a quick tug, or flip the rod tip a bit to the left, or even both simultaneously. This results, if done properly, in the cast's causing line end and leader to flip to the left, so that the leader will trail behind the fly as it drifts down over the fish, without drag. If an error in distance or direction is about to be made, the line can be kept in the air by another false cast, and this then can be corrected. The cast is made with the rod held between 45 degrees horizontal and horizontal; the lower the delivery, the wider the loop, or curve.

The loop cast to the right is done a little differently and is more difficult for the right-handed person. Forget that the tackle has leader and fly attached, because those several feet will curve to the right. Pay attention, in false-casting, to where the line end is, ignoring the rest. As the final cast straightens out, and just before you would shoot extra line, let the line go prematurely. This takes the life out of the forward part of the cast, causing it to collapse, with the line

same name. This one, as given later, is cigar shaped, of closely clipped deer hair, with a hackle of a contrasting color wound through it. The white one with red hackle is my favorite, in sizes 2 and 6. This gives four dry flies in a small selection of sizes, which basically seem enough. Some readers will insist that other patterns, such as the *Irresistible* or a skater, are important, but I haven't found this to be so. I'll have to admit, however, that the boxes I take astream contain many more than these.

Having digressed a bit because these notes seemed appropriate, let's go on with a few comments about cross-stream and upstream casting. The cross-stream part can be handled simply by referring to what has been said in the previous chapter about the Patent and greased-line fishing, except that dry flies are used. The fly is cast down and dropping first and the leader and fly dropping afterward, but at a right angle, more or less, to the right. This causes a greater curve than the loop to the left, and essentially is an incomplete forward cast. A bit of practice should make both of these clear.

Some very experienced anglers are very particular that when a salmon's lie is known, the fly must float down exactly over the fish. One of my fishing companions, the Reverend Elmer James Smith, of Prince William, New Brunswick, says about that: "The dry-fly principle that the fly must float right over the fish's head is not true when applied to salmon. If the fly is cast over its head and it doesn't come for it, the trick then is to cast above and beyond, allowing the fly to float only a very short distance. The fly then is picked up and cast back, allowed to float briefly, and the process is repeated, again and again if necessary. Some anglers do this in a very rhythmic manner, so that perhaps the salmon anticipates the moment when the fly will arrive again over its cone of vision. Part of the principle is not to let the fish see the fly too long at any one time, and casting in front of and a bit beyond it rather than directly over it sometimes is referred to as "taking him off his lie." One side may be tried and then the other. It is a principle similar to that which George LaBranche applied to brown trout, that of 'making a hatch,' and frequently the fish will come for the fly with an exciting surge!"

Anglers have refined this method of dry-fly fishing into a system that often works when a salmon's location is known:

Visualize the salmon lying under an imaginary clock face 7 or 8 feet in diameter. Twelve o'clock is upstream: the direction the salmon is facing. The fly, after false casts to measure proper distance, is first dropped at 1 o'clock, and then, with carefully measured timing, at 2 o'clock, and so on around the clock face. The fly should be on the water the exact amount of time that it is in the air, such as about five seconds for each.

For example, after casting to 1 o'clock and allowing a counted five seconds for a short drift, pick up the fly; allow a fully extended back cast; a fake forward cast; a second back cast; and then drop the fly at 2 o'clock. Using the countdown method, this casting should take five seconds, but whatever it takes, leave the fly on the water for that exact amount of time. My suggestion, if you are opposite the fish, is to stop the clockwise casting at 8 o'clock, then return to 1 o'clock, because I don't like to lay a leader over a salmon's back. If I were downstream from the fish, I would cast from 1 o'clock to 11 o'clock.

The idea behind these carefully metered presentations is to torment the salmon into striking—after a very few such casts, the fish has come to expect the fly and, seeing it drift past for so short a time that it has no chance to inspect it, will take it rather than let it escape again. The idea can work in any type of water that is of shallow to reasonable depth, and the short float prevents having to mend the line. The choice of dry fly is of no importance, although if a fish rises and doesn't take, it might be good to change to a smaller or larger pattern of a contrasting color and start over again.

I have experimented with this method too little to comment on its effectiveness; however, those who use it find it viable. Those who have watched from a vantage point say that after a few casts, a salmon will expect the next appearance of the fly to the extent that, if it should be caught up on a back cast, thus breaking the rhythm, the salmon will start to rise anyway in anticipation! As Father Smith says, under these conditions a salmon often "will come for the fly with an exciting surge!"

Conditions for Dry-Fly Fishing

What are the proper conditions for dry-fly fishing—when should you try it, and when should you favor another method?

One gentleman of great experience says, "Salmon rise best to the dry fly when the temperature of the water is in the neighborhood of 60 degrees, say from 57 degrees to 63 degrees, and when the air is warmer than the water. They will, however, take a dry fly in colder water provided the air temperature is higher."

Although others disagree, George LaBranche and Edward Hewitt, both anglers of exceptional experience, thought that salmon would take the dry fly as a function of water temperature itself, and they considered the actual temperature when salmon would take the dry fly to be 60 degrees F. or above.

Many years ago I learned the value of taking water and air temperatures as a clue to deciding fishing methods, and the men I often fish with are addicted to it. The first thing we do on reaching the river is to note the temperatures. We may or may not try the dry fly then, but if the water temperature has risen about 5 degrees an hour or more later, and if the air is no colder than the water, it is time for the dry fly. The actual water temperature makes little or no difference; we have had good success with the dry fly when the water was a bit under 50 degrees F., and the air temperature no less. It is the rise in water temperature that counts, and the air should be the same or, preferably, a few degrees warmer. (We agree with the maxim that when the air is colder than the water, the fishing will be difficult.) Of course, this indicates a day with some sun. Under these conditions, salmon should take dry flies as well as wet ones, or better. We would rather take one salmon on a floating fly than several on ones that have to be sunk.

Other Dry-Fly Tactics

Anglers have been taught that allowing a dry fly to drag is the wrong way to fish, but there are exceptions to that. If some of the methods that have been discussed don't work, another is to cast a bug-type dry fly with a decided drag. Cast it cross-stream and allow the current to put a bag in the line. This causes the fly to whip—to travel at high speed, making a wake. It is a tactic usually new to salmon, and it frequently incites one to chase the fly and grab it solidly while it is dragging.

If you raise a fish one or more times to a dry fly and the fish doesn't take, or if you know where a fish is that can't be made to rise, a trick is to cast the fly above and beyond the fish in such a way that the fly can be drowned by pulling it under the water. The fly should be pulled underwater so that it moves right in front of the salmon's snout. Many a fish has been taken by this method when others have failed.

Another trick is to skitter the fly, also discussed under wet-fly fishing, but here using a large dry one. You can do it blind if you don't know where the fish are, by using it anywhere where salmon are presumed to lie, but you can do it better if you can see the fish. In this case, the fly is cast on a tight line a few feet beyond and ahead of the lie of the salmon. It is immediately pulled into a skittering action with a wake so that it passes directly in front of the salmon. Another method when the location of fish isn't known is to cast it cross-stream and immediately pull it in fast and steadily, with a speed that leaves a wake on the water.

While orthodox patterns in the larger sizes such as the *Wulffs, Irresistible,* and *Rat Face* are good for these purposes, several special patterns are made specifically for them. Francois de B. Gourdeau's *Bottlewasher* is one, and its counterpart in hair body is another called the *Bomber*. Butterfield's *Whiskers* will do the job, and so will Hewitt's *Skater*. These are enough, and if I should suggest many more, it merely would confound the issue. If one or two don't work by any of these methods, it's time to go in and enjoy the happy hour.

These big and bushy flies are rather hard to sink. They will float jauntily on strong currents and can be dried quickly by a false cast or two. Using a waterproofing dressing to make them float longer is an individual decision that may not be a good one; after letting them float for a while, you may want them to sink so that you can fish the remainder of the cast wet. The *Bomber* often is used this way. Drift it or skitter it over the salmon. If they don't respond, work it in front of them again at a lower level.

Frequently salmon will come to these big floaters but won't take them. After resting the fish for a few minutes, try it again in the same way. If this doesn't work, at least you have located and interested the fish (which perhaps you couldn't have done by usual methods) and you will possibly be able to hook it by casting for it again after changing to a smaller dry fly or to a wet fly. Again, if you can cause the fish to show interest, you should be able to catch it, although this sometimes requires many casts and several changes of flies.

While salmon frequently take the big, bushy flies, the big ones often are used as "locators" that make a salmon show its position. When a fly makes the fish show its position, the usual procedure is, if the "locator" is a large dry fly, to try to tempt it with a smaller one, then perhaps with a wet fly, or by using one of the other methods discussed. If the fly that tempts it is a wet one, it is worthwhile to switch to a dry one. Dry flies are good under a broad range of conditions, but especially when a fish has been located. Since the angler can cover more water faster with a wet fly, many use it initially, switching to the dry fly when the position of a fish is known. Salmon often will take very small flies. Don't give up trying to tempt a good fish until you have tried the smallest sizes.

Until recently, the techniques of using dry flies and nymphs for salmon were largely ignored almost everywhere but in North America. My friend and editor Angus Cameron, for example, informed me that in seven years of fishing in Iceland, from 1976 to 1983, he had five different gillies who saw their first salmon taken on a dry fly while guiding him! Our friends across the sea should learn to benefit from them, because it seems inconsistent to suppose that salmon will accept them so readily on one side of the Atlantic while rejecting them everywhere else. There may be biological reasons that partially account for the lack of interest of European salmon in floating objects. Some anglers insist, for example, that British salmon will only play with dry flies and rarely can be hooked with them. We could ask in reply whether this may be, in part at least, the anglers' fault in fly selection and presentation.

Dry-Fly Patterns

While we may need, or think we need, a variety of color combinations in wet flies, the need for them in dry flies is very much less, perhaps confined to light and dark and maybe a shade in between. In dry flies, while floatability is important, what seems most necessary is a small collection of various shapes in a restricted range of sizes, some of which are very large.

This book offers dry flies in various shapes that can be dressed in as many color combinations as desired. Favorite color variations also are provided. If somebody's pet pattern has been left out, it may be because it is considered unnecessary. The popular *Wulff* patterns are essential, and so are the long cater-pillarlike floaters such as the *Bomber, Bottlewasher, Cigars,* and their close cousin, *Whiskers.* These last four can be fished by several different techniques, as we have seen.

Many anglers who have assembled a collection of these think that anything else is superfluous. A skater or a skittering fly or two may be handy, how-ever, and so might a few of the clipped deer-hair bodied flies like the *Irresistible* and the *Rat Face.* Another type listed under the *Silver Gray* is popular in some places. The formerly fashionable LaBranche palmers are included more for historic interest than necessity. Most anglers think that later developments are better.

Readers will note that patterns provided in this chapter are divided into five parts. Since most of these can be dressed in many color combinations and in a wide range of sizes, there should be more than enough to fill the boxes of even the most dis-criminating anglers everywhere in the world.

Bivisibles

These are thickly palmered dry flies in any colors desired, often with a short hackle tail of the same material as the rear of the body, and with the front quarter palmered in a brighter color (often white) so that anglers can follow them more easily while they are floating. Some, such as the LaBranche series and the *Pink Lady,* have bodies of silk, herl, dubbing, and so forth, and are lightly palmered to show body color. Others have only the thread base, with the body palmered to maximum thickness to conceal the dressing thread. Of the latter, for example, the rear three-quarters or so of palmering can be black for the *Black Bivisible,* or brown for the *Brown Bivisi-ble,* and so on, usually with the forward quarter heavily palmered in white.

Robert Jacklin's *Gray Bivisible* has a body heavily palmered with gray hackles, with a white forward quarter. The width of the hackling is optional and may graduate from narrower at the tail to wider at the head. Normally, the width of the whole hackle at the forward end of the fly is about the same as the length of the hook's shank. Most bivisible patterns originated when dry flies were in the experimental stages, and they have given way to the better floating properties of flies with clipped hair bodies or pat-terns of the *Wulff* type.

The LaBranche Series

In *The Salmon and the Dry Fly* (1924), George M. L. LaBranche gives the dressings of four bivisibles or heavily palmered dry flies that were popular when the book was written. Though these are not among current favorites (more effective patterns have since been devised), they are notable as being among the first named dry flies used for salmon.

In discussing the flies, LaBranche says: "Cock's hackles, being of finer quality than hen's hackles, were used exclusively. Dyed feathers were avoided because of an apparent tendency to absorb water, so the colors that could be used were limited to a few shades of brown and gray. While the hooks are small, the flies are large, looking much like pine cones, bottle brushes, and fuzzy caterpillars, certainly quite unlike anything the fish have ever seen before. Whatever the flies may look like to the fish, the fact remains that they are accepted, and that it is much more important to place them properly on the water than to consider what form or color they should possess. The four are merely adaptations of well-known trout flies [the one named for Colonel Monell being his favorite]."

Colonel Monell

Tail	Five or six whisks of gray Plymouth Rock cock's hackle
Body	Peacock herl, with a rib of red, lightly dressed
Hackle	Gray Plymouth Rock cock's hackle, tied palmer

Soldier Palmer

Tail	Five or six whisks of brown or brownish red hackle
Body	Red dubbing, with rib of tinsel, lightly dressed
Hackle	Brown or brownish red, tied palmer

Mole Palmer

Tail	Five or six whisks of dark brown hackle
Body	Brown dubbing or quill, lightly dressed
Hackle	Dark brown, lightly mixed with gray at shoulder, tied palmer

Pink Lady Palmer

Tail	Five or six whisks of ginger-colored hackle
Body	Light pink silk; rib of gold tinsel, lightly dressed
Hackle	Ginger-colored, with one or two turns of light yellow at head, tied palmer

LaBranche's comparison of these flies to bottle brushes is reminiscent of similar ones of double or triple length that are used effectively as this is being written, such as the *Gourdeau's Bottlewasher*. The LaBranche flies presumably were developed by one or more of several men who frequently fished together, who include LaBranche himself, Colonel Monell, and Edward R. Hewitt.

The next pattern isn't a true bivisible because it lacks a lighter color at the head, but it is included here because of its heavily palmered body and because it is a historic old floater closely related in development to the LaBranche patterns.

MacIntosh

Tail	A small bunch of red or brown squirrel tail hair showing a dark middle band, about as long as the hook's shank
Body	Heavily palmered with dark ginger furnace hackle, quite wide
Head	Black

Originated on the St. Mary's River in Nova Scotia by Dan MacIntosh, the MacIntosh represents a dry-fly style that was popularized during the 1940s. It has maintained its popularity and is now dressed in a variety of colors.

Gourdeau's Bottlewasher

Tag	A double tag, dressed thin. Rear part: black wool. Forward part: yellow wool
Body	Heavily palmered throughout with wide brown hackles, tapering slightly toward the tail
Head	Black

This is an elongated palmered dry fly originated in 1958 by Francois Gourdeau, an official of the Fish and Game Branch of the Department of Tourism of the Province of Quebec. He says, "I fish this dry fly upstream with four or five casts directly in front of the fish, leaving the fly on the water surface for about two seconds. It usually does not take long before the fish gets mad and goes for it. We have had success with this fly on most Gaspe waters. It always should be dressed on large, long-shank low-water hooks. It is especially successful [during low-water conditions] in August."

I also suggest using this as a "last-resort" fly, and sees no reason why it should not be tied in various colors. Like the preceding pattern, it lacks a lighter color at the head, but there is no reason why it shouldn't be dressed with one. Its principal distinction is its length, resembling a fat caterpillar.

PLATE 64
EARLY DRY FLIES

MacIntosh
dressed by Dave Lucca

Whiskers
originated and dressed by
Lew Butterfield

Bottlewasher
originated and dressed by
Francois Gourdreau

Colonel Monell
dressed by Herb Howard

Gray BiVisible
dressed by Bob Jacklin

Mole Palmer
dressed by Herb Howard

Skaters

This type is dressed on very short, very light, and usually very small hooks for maximum lightness and because the body primarily is very wide hackle. Sometimes sort of a tag is included, usually of finest tinsel, merely for a touch of glint. On a size 4 short-shank hook, for example, the hackle should be about an inch wide, providing a front view like a circular disc about 2 inches in diameter and not over 3/8 inch thick. The pattern takes the name of the color of hackle used. For example, the *Ginger Skater* would have ginger hackles.

The purpose of the type, as the name implies, is to skate across the surface, leaving a small wake propelled by wind action, by a slightly bagged line, or by hand manipulation. Given a slight breeze, the fly can be used for dapping. Since other more modern types, such as the *Wulffs,* can be made to skate as well, or perhaps even better, skaters as such have fallen into disuse. This is, however, a historic pattern that some readers may want to tie, and try. No book on dry-fly fishing could approach completeness without it.

Skater	
Body	Heavily hackled from a point above the tip of the barb forward to the eye with the longest, stiffest, and widest hackles obtainable (suitable to hook size), in any desired color, such as ginger, black, or white. The hackles at the front face of the fly are vertical to the hook shank (not tied back). Hackles should be tied in at their tip ends, making a widening taper toward the eye. Model Perfect hooks with short shank and turned-down eye are suggested because their light wire provides good floatability and their round bend decreases the chance of their pulling out after the fish is hooked
Head	Thread used

Skaters evidently were originated by famous angler and angling author Edward R. Hewitt in the 1930s. Originally they were trout flies, dressed to simulate butterflies skimming over the water, but they have been very productive for salmon also. You should give the fly a skating motion, a motion that excites all game fish and provides great excitement during the strike. The stiffest, and usually widest, hackles obtainable are necessary to ensure proper skating action.

PLATE 65
WOODCHUCK SKATER, ORIGINATED
AND DRESSED BY CHARLIE DEFEO

The Wulff Series
As discussed in the account of the LaBranche series of bivisibles, one of the greatest innovations in modern salmon fishing is the development of the dry fly and the various methods of fishing it effectively. Whatever its type of pattern, it must float "high" on the water and remain so for a reasonable time despite currents.

This didn't seem to make any very devastating impact on Atlantic salmon angling until the great American angler Lee Wulff developed his three *Wulff* patterns and proved to all who would pay attention that we really were missing something. Originally he developed these for trout, with the cooperation of another famous angler, Dan Bailey, of Livingston, Montana. He soon realized that if he made the flies bigger and bushier, they would float

PLATE 66
SKATERS, ORIGINATED AND DRESSED
BY EDWARD HEWITT

jauntily high on big salmon rivers, and there they would take salmon that were reluctant to bother with almost anything else.

My good friend, the late A. I. Alexander III, wrote about the genesis of the Wulff patterns in the spring 1968 issue of *Trout* as follows:

Most fishermen, I imagine, associate the *Gray Wulff* with a big, rough, rock-strewn salmon river in Newfoundland or Labrador. With its high degree of floatability, the *Gray Wulff* has become a favorite with Atlantic salmon fishermen who need a dry fly that will ride high on the water and require a minimum of attention to keep it afloat. It was conceived, however, not on a brawling salmon river but on a gentle trout stream, the Ausable, in New York State.

On Labor Day, 1930, Lee Wulff, dissatisfied with the then current dry fly patterns, sought to imitate a large grayish mayfly that was prevalent on the water. He was particularly interested in creating an artificial that had a larger and fuller body than the existent patterns and one that was not quite so susceptible to fish slime which, of course, is detrimental to the floating quality of a fly.

Wulff, whose inventive and original thinking has contributed much to American angling, made a radical departure from the traditional flies in his choice of materials. He used natural brown bucktail for the tail and wings and gray Angora rabbit fur [in the trout pattern] for the body. For hackles he used two blue-gray saddle hackles. One must remember that in 1930 the American fly-fisherman was still very much influenced by the English style of fly and the use of hair in any insect imitation was virtually unknown. It is still rarely used by English fly dressers. The result of Wulff's effort was a durable fly that would float, take trout, and still float after a few false casts.

Encouraged with his initial effort, Wulff then went on to create the *White Wulff* and the *Royal Wulff* in the same manner. The Wulff patterns that came later, the *Blonde, Grizzly, Brown,* and *Black Wulff,* were from the vise of another talented fisherman, Dan Bailey, who was Lee Wulff's partner that September day on the Ausable. It is the *Gray Wulff* that is important, however, in that it was the first, and it established a distinct American style of dry fly. The fact that it has been accepted as a standard fly pattern in such a relatively short time attests to its effectiveness.

This book illustrates original patterns by Lee Wulff and by Dan Bailey. Commercial tiers often substitute materials and thus sometimes lose the

original rough and bushy character that the flies should have. In salmon fishing, the flies are tied on light-wire hooks, usually in sizes from #4 to #10. Sometimes hard-to-cast giant sizes on larger hooks are employed as attractors.

As do some of the world's best fly dressers, Lee Wulff ties flies with his fingers, without bothering with a vise. He explained this in the sixty-eighth issue of the *Bulletin* of the United Fly Tiers Club, of Boston, Massachusetts. Whether or not the fly dressers who read this use a vise, they may be interested in his methods in order to obtain faithful reproductions:

In tying a Wulff dry fly I still prefer to use bucktail, the original material, although calf's tail is somewhat easier to use since it doesn't take the extra time to match up the hair ends and is just about as effective. Tying them in my fingers, my first step is to pick up the hook and start the dinging [attaching thread to hook] with a piece of thread long enough to tie the fly. For these flies the thread should be fairly strong as it takes a firm pressure and a small wall of thread around the base of the wings to hold them in position.

I hold the eye of the hook between the nails of thumb and first finger of the left hand, doing the winding of the thread with my right. When the shank is wound I can either hold the thread in place by pressure between thumb and finger below the eye of the fly, or take a couple of half-hitches to hold the thread in place.

Next I cover the wrapped shank with lacquer. I like to feel that the flies I tie will stay together for catching a lot of fish and so want the solid body permanence lacquer gives as well as the security against twisting. I use unwaxed thread as waxing prevents the lacquer from penetrating into the thread. The tail is cut to length and wrapped to the shank. I like a good thick tail to hold up the heavy end of the hook and having the bucktail run the length of the shank [IX long hooks preferred] starts building up the body as well as making the tail more secure.

Again the thread is clamped between the left thumb and finger, or the head of the fly may be put between my lips to keep the thread from unwinding while I pick up the Angora wool, or roll rabbit's fur around the thread to make the body. Normally, I use wool as it's easier to handle and, seemingly, just as acceptable to the fish. I wind the body from head to tail and back again, shaping it into a natural insect form, and winding over it with thread near the head.

The fly at this stage is either held between the lips or the thread is given two half-hitches to hold it while I cut the bucktail for the wings. I cut it long and then pull out the longer hairs and reset them until all the natural ends are approximately even and the hair is matched up. Then it's cut to length which is about 1/8 inch longer than the wings should normally be.

PLATE 67
THE WHITE WULFF, ROYAL WULFF, AND GRAY WULFF, ORIGINATED AND DRESSED BY LEE WULFF

Photo by Sadlier Dinger, courtesy of Joan Wulff

The hair is placed, facing forward, at the right place at the head of the body. It is wrapped tightly with several turns of the thread about 1/8 of an inch or less behind the winding. Then the hairs are lifted and thread is wound in front of the vertical hair until it stands upright and can be split by windings around the shank and a figure eight or two. The butt ends of the hair, protruding behind the first windings, tend to give a natural humpbacked look when the fly is finished.

Next, two saddle hackles are set in with two winds of thread. They face forward, on top of the hook, their bare butts fitting in between the rising wings. The fly, in all this tying, is still held between the nails of the left thumb and forefinger. A big drop or two of lacquer is then put on the base of the wings to penetrate well and set everything up when it dries. While it is still wet the two hackles are wound. The first wind is through the top between the wings, then two or three winds behind the wings and a wind back through between the wings. The tip is gripped between finger and thumb to hold it until ready to tie off. The second hackle is wound entirely in front of the wings and its tip secured along with that of the first hackle. Now the final wind or two at the head, three half-hitches to secure things, and a drop of lacquer goes at the head and the place where the tail joins the body to make everything secure.

These are the seven original dressings.

Gray Wulff		
Tail	Natural brown bucktail	
Body	Blue-gray wool	
Wing	Natural brown bucktail	
Hackle	Two blue-gray saddle hackles	(Wulff)

White Wulff		
Tail	White bucktail	
Body	Cream-color wool	
Wing	White bucktail	
Hackle	Two light badger hackles	(Wulff)

Royal Wulff		
Tail	White bucktail	
Body	Rear and front quarters are butted with peacock herl; middle half is scarlet wool or silk	
Wing	White bucktail	
Hackle	Two brown saddle hackles	(Wulff)

PLATE 68
THE WULFF STYLE OF FLIES, AN EXTENSION OF THE SERIES

Dry Cosseboom
dressed by Rod Yerger

Ausable Wulff
originated and dressed by Fran Betters

Grizzly Wulff
originated and dressed by Dan Bailey

Black Wulff
originated and dressed by Dan Bailey

Brown Wulff
originated and dressed by Dan Bailey

Brown Wulff

Tail	Brown impala hair	
Body	Cream angora	
Wing	Brown impala hair	
Hackle	Two badger hackles	(Bailey)

Black Wulff

Tail	Black moose hair	
Body	Pink silk, lacquered	
Wing	Black moose hair	
Hackle	Two furnace hackles	(Bailey)

Grizzly Wulff

Tail	Brown bucktail	
Body	Light yellow silk, lacquered	
Wing	Brown bucktail	
Hackle	One brown and one grizzly hackle, mixed	(Bailey)

Blonde Wulff

Tail	Light tan elk hair	
Body	Light tan angora	
Wing	Light tan elk hair	
Hackle	Two light ginger hackles	(Bailey)

As with other successful styles in flies, there have been many adaptations of the *Wulff* patterns (so named by Dan Bailey). One worthy of note was taken from the colors of the famous *Cosseboom* wet hairwing:

Cosseboom (Dry)

Tail	Gray squirrel, dark, with white tips
Body	Light olive floss
Wing	Gray squirrel, dark, with white tips
Hackle	Two bright yellow saddle hackles

Another fly of this type is the *Ausable Wulff,* originated by Fran Betters in 1964 for fishing New York's West Branch of the Ausable River. Betters's objectives in this pattern were to create a fly that would emulate as many of the major hatches of mayflies and stoneflies as possible, would be highly visible, and would float well in the heavy currents of the river.

Ausable Wulff

Tail	Woodchuck guard hair
Body	Australian possum, dyed rusty orange
Wing	White calf tail
Hackle	Grizzly and brown
Thread	Hot orange

When dressing these flies, to make hair tips even without manual adjustment, cut off the necessary amount and drop the bunch tip-first into a small, short vial or cup such as the cap on a lady's lipstick. Tap the container on a hard surface, and all hair tips become even immediately. (This method works best with straight hair.)

Here is another that is quite similar.

Black Gnat

This is dressed exactly like the *Wulff* patterns, and in the same sizes, except that it has a closely clipped fairly fat, bug-shaped deer-hair body. The tail, body, and hackling are jet black, with white *Wulff*-type wings that are somewhat longer than the hackle. My example was dressed by Harry Darbee, of Livingston Manor, New York.

Clipped Hair Patterns

Bomber

Tail	A fairly large and rather short bunch of the same deer body hair used for the body of the fly. (Other materials are often used, such as calf or woodchuck.)
Wing	A fairly short bunch of the same body hair tied so as to extend forward at an angle of about 45 degrees. (This forward and upward bunch of hair is called a "wing" for want of a better term. The upward slant keeps it free of the eye of the hook.)
Body	Natural deer body hair (gray, brown, or white) spun on, tightly massed, flared out, and clipped to a smooth cigar shape, tapering toward the tail and slightly toward the head. The body should be clipped so that about one-third is below the hook shank and two-thirds above it, to allow plenty of clearance between body and barb. To produce a dense body, rather small bunches of body hair should be used. Many anglers like the body rather roughly clipped
Ribbing	A large brown hackle (or one of any other desired color) tied in at the tail and palmered through the clipped body from tail to head
Head	Use any appropriately colored thread

This type is one of my favorites because it is showy, unusual, hard to sink, and very productive. The *Brown Bomber* calls for natural brown hair for tail and body, white wing (for better visibility), and reddish brown ribbing. The *White Bomber* (sometimes called the *Peppermint Bomber*) is all white with red ribbing. The *Black Bomber* is all black with white ribbing.

The *Bomber* dry flies should not be confused with wet-fly patterns of the same name. *Bombers* were developed in the 1960s for use on New Brunswick's Miramichi River and popularized by

PLATE 70
STEPS IN TYING THE BOMBER
DRESSED BY WARREN DUNCAN

PLATE 69
CLIPPED DEER–HAIR PATTERNS

Killer Whiskers
dressed by Rod Yerger

Hazel Fly
originated and dressed by Paul LaBlanc

Rat-Faced MacDougall, Hairwing
dressed by Dave Lucca

Bomber
dressed by Elmer Smith

Irresistible
dressed by Dave Lucca

Original Rat-Faced MacDougall
dressed by Dave Lucca

White-Winged Black Gnat
originated and dressed by Harry Darbee

the Reverend Elmer Smith, a great authority on salmon and a legendary figure on the Miramichi. Inspired by the success he observed a young boy having with a spun-hair mouse fly, Father Smith tied his first *Bomber* as a wet fly, trimming its bulky body and using a single grizzly hackle, dyed red, tied in at the bend and palmered forward over the body. Later, thinking the fly would be effective as a dry fly, he dressed it in several variations, preferring a body of spun deer hair, trimmed and tapered toward the eye, with two stiff hackles tied in by their butts and wound forward.

Some anglers say that if you can't catch a salmon with a *Bomber,* you shouldn't bother fishing. *Bombers* can be fished dry (the usual practice), dry and dragging (with a fast skittering motion), or wet (like any other sunken fly). They are effective in each technique.

Another pattern, quite similar to the *Bomber,* is the *Killer Whiskers.* It, too, is dressed with a clipped deer-hair body but has a chartreuse clipped deer-hair butt.

PLATE 71
CIGARS, DRESSED BY
WARREN DUNCAN

Cigars

Tail	A small bunch of white hair of moderate length
Body	Round with maximum density of white deer tail hair, clipped very short in thin cigar shape
Ribbing	A white hackle palmered through the clipped body from tail to head
Wing	A small bunch of white hair nearly as long as the body, tied in so as to extend straight forward. (This isn't a proper wing; it could perhaps more properly be called a snout!)
Head	Black

Hazel Fly

Tail	Gray fox
Wing	Gray fox, *Wulff*-style
Body	Deer hair, trimmed
Hackle	Red gamecock
Head	Black

Originated jointly by Hazel Maltais and Paul LeBlanc, the *Hazel Fly* has been successful in Quebec, New Brunswick, and Newfoundland. LeBlanc says of it, "I've taken a lot of nice fish in July with the *Hazel Fly.* Often when the salmon are not moving at all, they'll rise for that fly."

Irresistible

Tail	A moderate bunch of brown deer tail hair, tied in over tip of barb, about as long as the hook
Body	Gray deer body hair, spun on, tightly massed, flared out, and trimmed to egg shape except that the forward part is flat. The body is tapered toward the tail and occupies half the distance from point where tail is tied in to eye of hook
Wing	White calf tail
Hackle	Wide grizzly hackles, heavily applied as a collar from front of body to eye of hook
Head	Black or brown thread

This is another of the popular dry-fly patterns originally tied for trout but adapted in large sizes for salmon. It is an excellent floater, even on fast, broken water. Fly dressers make adaptations in various colors, similar to the *Wulff* patterns.

Very little is said in American angling books about this important pattern. Reuben Cross, in *The Complete Fly Tier* (1950), calls it a comparatively new and very effective trout fly, used with good success for salmon in sizes 10 to 4. His dressing is the same except that the hackling is blue dun.

Rat-Faced MacDougall	
Tail	A small bunch of straight ginger hair, about as long as the hook
Body	Clipped natural deer hair, trimmed to the shape of an elongated egg, tapering to the rear
Hackle	Ginger hackles, applied *Wulff*-style
Wing	Grizzly hackle tips, splayed upward at a 45-degree angle (V shaped)
Head	Thread used

This is the pattern for the *Rat-Faced MacDougall,* a popular dry-fly pattern on all salmon rivers in North America. Except for the wings, it is almost identical to the *Irresistible,* and it is dressed in several color combinations. A hairwing version of this pattern is dressed using white calf hair for the wings.

Teagle Bee (Dry)	
Tail	A small bunch of red hackle fibers
Body	Fine chenille, alternating yellow, black, yellow, black in four bands, occupying the rear half of shank
Wing	Mallard wing
Hackle	Brown hackle, heavily palmered, occupying the front half of the shank
Head	Black

This Canadian pattern was used in the 1920 era mostly on the Upsalquitch River. It was originated by Walter C. Teagle and was popularized by noted anglers who fished with him, including Richard C. Hunt, author of *Salmon in Low Water* (1950).

Whiskers	
Tail	A fairly large bunch of gray squirrel tail hairs, quite long
Body	Angora yarn of any color, such as brown, red, green, or black, moderately palmered with stiff, brown hackles. A turn or two of the yarn is made as a tip to hold up the tail
Wing	A fairly large bunch of deer body hair dressed fan shaped in a semicircle on top of the hook, upright and facing slightly forward. The deer hair is tied in first, over the forward two-thirds of the body, which then is covered by the yarn and hackles
Head	Black

This dry fly was originated by Louis M. Butterfield, of Stratham, New Hampshire, who owned a camp (now a club) on Black Brook, near where the Cains River flows into the Miramichi. He says that (over a great many years of salmon fishing) he has "caught thousands of salmon and grilse on *Whiskers.*" A way to describe the fly might be that it looks like a *Wulff* pattern (with the wing fan shaped but not separated) with a fairly long *Woolly Worm* body. As in most dry flies, the head is insignificant. Many color combinations and types of hair are used.

10

Methods for Hooking Reluctant Salmon

"Evening Grilse"

$\mathcal{D}$edicated salmon fishermen try to think that there are no bad days on salmon rivers because, despite adverse weather and water conditions, just being there turns bad days into ones that multiply the challenges of attempting to hook reluctant (or dour) fish.

If there are no bad days, we must agree that some are much better than others. The better ones often show blue sky liberally sprinkled with high cumulus cottony clouds, an agreeable temperature when the air is warmer than the water, and moderate river flow enabling the salmon to move upstream freely. Moving salmon rarely take flies, but all are forced to rest, even briefly, from time to time, and during these periods they usually become takers. They normally have to rest under conditions where they can't make themselves fully at home, such as in current edges or in depressions at the tails of pools just before they break into faster water. These *resting pools* normally may be empty but can provide fast action when salmon are running.

When salmon are not running, they are found in *holding pools,* usually larger ones suitable for prolonged stays, where they have adequate oxygen and protection from fast currents. In holding pools the fish may be lethargic, dour, or reluctant, although some will be more active than others. Salmon want reasonably deep water for their upstream journey. When a river's flow drops below their expectations, they refuse to move any farther and remain, dour and uncooperative, in these deeper pools until rains swell the stream enough to induce them to continue their ascent. The longer they remain in holding pools, the more reluctant they become to take any form of fly, no matter how presented.

Some anglers feel that when streams are low and salmon have penned themselves in holding pools, they may as well relax over a drink and a game of gin rummy. Others insist that no matter how bad conditions seem, salmon can be hooked if one discovers and uses appropriate techniques. That is what this chapter is about. It is only in small part a summary of what has been detailed before, because fishing for reluctant salmon should be a subject all to itself. If we could provide all the answers, then salmon fishing would become so cut and dried that it wouldn't be much fun. I can offer some suggestions, however—enough, perhaps, to make the challenge seem very worthwhile. You went on the trip to go fishing, so no matter how adverse the conditions may seem, stay on the river and try to make your trip exciting and successful!

Before wading into these deep, dark waters, let me assert that I have no pretensions about being an expert. I have fished for salmon around the Atlantic for many years; I have tried to do my homework with the literature, and my angling friends will affirm that I have been indefatigable about asking questions. From all this I have tried to separate the wheat from the chaff, and this is the result. Though some may bicker over a few details, I hope all will profit.

So you are at your lodge on the river, which is low, and the salmon are uncooperative. Some anglers frequently dip a thermometer and offer prognostications on what should be happening tomorrow because of water temperature changes. Others have placed markers at the river's edge to see if it is going up or down. One or two are reading or tying flies. What can be expected? First, a few thoughts to consider:

Under warm-water conditions the best fishing is very early or very late in the day. Salmon will seek spring holes or shady cold-water brooks and will be more inclined to take there. It pays to start as soon as allowable and not give up until you have to. The best fishing should be between sunset and dark.

Mist or fog that hangs low indicates that the air is colder than the water. If it persists, it can mean poor fishing, but salmon may take when it begins to lift.

When parr are taking the fly, salmon usually won't. When you land a salmon, go back to fishing at once, because this good taking time may not last long.

An abrupt change of climate, such as a thunderstorm, should improve fishing, especially during the first half hour after it starts. Other climatic changes, such as atmospheric pressure, temperature, light, or wind, may alter conditions.

When salmon are in a nontaking mood, some change in external conditions must take place before they become takers. Rising water will tempt them to move upstream, and the period just before a run starts should make them take well. Although running salmon rarely take flies, they often stop to rest, and then they are takers.

Barometric pressure is worth watching because salmon respond favorably to an abundance of dissolved oxygen. A rising barometer, which indicates greater air pressure, means that there is more free oxygen in the water, which, up to a certain point, makes salmon more active. Cool water holds more oxygen than warmer water does. After a long period of high pressure, however, salmon may start taking when the barometer falls.

Thus, a time when salmon likely will take is when the weather forecast predicts a break in the settled weather caused by an approaching low-pressure system. This usually is preceded by strengthening southerly winds, high cloud formations, and gradually darkening skies. Salmon seem to sense these conditions, which usually predict rain, and they become active.

The only time when one should be concerned about the position of the bright sun is when it is shining *downstream,* which may be early in the morning or near sunset, depending on which way the river runs. Then, with the angler facing downstream with the sun on his back, the sun is in the salmon's eyes, blinding them because they have no irises. They usually won't take flies then, and hang low behind obstructions or near cliffs or trees that cast shade.

If the sun is shining *upstream,* it doesn't matter how bright it is. It doesn't matter much if the angler is blinded by the sun, but it does matter if the salmon are. If the river is a winding one, this may suggest which pools to fish first or which bank to fish from. The only time when a dull day is better than a bright one is when the water is low and clear.

Reluctant salmon—that is, stale or dour fish—can be frightened easily, whereas nothing seems to bother fresh ones. Anything that distracts the attention of dour salmon may cause them to ignore flies, so the cautious approach one would use for trout is necessary. We may not realize that our approach has frightened them, and that our visible presence is why they won't take our flies. In addition to the cautious approach and disturbing the water as little as possible, finer leaders are recommended, as well as "fishing fine and far off."

With these generalities accounted for, let's get down to some specifics. Although it often may seem so, adverse conditions rarely are impossible ones. No matter how low and clear the water, nontaking fish may be taunted into taking by one or more of the methods described in previous chapters, which will in part be summarized here. It is very difficult to give an "old hand" ideas that differ from his own

practices, but the fact is that even a good salmon fisherman can become a better one by being willing to try new methods.

Previous chapters have detailed basic angling methods, including the sunken wet fly, the wet fly with the riffling hitch, the greased line and low-water flies, the Patent method, and the dry fly. To these now can be added a few notes as they apply particularly to hooking reluctant salmon.

When fishing the sunken wet fly for reluctant salmon, you usually must get it down to the fish because they are not inclined to rise to it. In many cases this means nearly dragging bottom, an unpopular method that may be necessary at times. When the usual flies don't work, you must try different ones, as well as different methods. The secret is *experimentation,* and the sequence of the experiments depends on individual judgment guided by weather and water conditions. Concentrate on the problem at hand, and determine what you will try first, next, and so on. Suddenly a particular method may work, and the problem is solved, at least temporarily.

Ira Gruber often solved it on New Brunswick's Miramichi by forsaking normal fly sizes and going to smaller ones, even as tiny as 12s, probably on leaders as long and light as seemed sensible. I have seen no evidence that Ira used low-water flies, but A. H. E. Wood did. The choice is a personal one. A size 12 fly can be dressed on a size 10 or 8 fine-wire hook, which may hold better.

The big-fly theory is a good alternative to trying very small ones. A neophyte once swept confidently into a lodge on the Miramichi when the river was low and the fishing so poor that the old hands had given up and were sitting on their porches playing cards. A big salmon was known to be lying behind a midstream rock, but no methods the old hands had tried could hook it, so they slyly told the beginner about it to rid themselves of his presence.

The young trout fisherman, in his ignorance of salmon fishing, tied on a size 4 *Gray Ghost* streamer fly, worked it in front of the dour salmon, and promptly hooked the fish. The point of the story is that dour salmon have been fished over so much that it is time to show them something new. They have lost their playful or curious instincts, and their aggressiveness has been dulled by having to stay for too long where they don't want to be. In other words, they are bored with the situation and won't be bothered by normal approaches. The answer, therefore, is to fall back on unusual methods—perhaps the more unusual, the better.

So the young man got a reaction by using a big streamer. The pattern probably didn't matter much, as long as it was big enough to stir the salmon's latent aggressive instinct to get something out of the way that bothered it. He could have tried large tube flies like the *Collie Dog,* or a big, bright bucktail. When nothing else works, the secret may be to "stir them up."

Ira Gruber had a habit of using two fly rods because his entire interest was in hooking salmon rather than in playing them. When one was hooked, he would hand the rod to his guide and promptly use the other. Some of us also carry two rods—a dry-fly one and a wet-fly one. When fishing over dour salmon that won't come to a wet fly, we sometimes can hook them on a large dry. Don't ignore the dry fly under such circumstances. It often works better than wet ones.

Bright flies, such as those predominantly red, orange, or yellow, usually are reserved for high or discolored water. They also can be productive under low and clear conditions over dour salmon. Colonel Drury's *General Practitioner* is a good one (probably drifted deep), but there are many others, including the simple *Mickey Finn* bucktail.

When you can get upstream of a reluctant salmon, there is another tactic that often works. Try a bright and bushy hairwing, or a streamer type dressed amply with marabou. Let it swing to hang in front of the fish, and leave it there, working it enough to make it active. Pull it in a bit, and then let it drop back to or behind the salmon's nose. Work it longer than you think should be necessary. Eventually the salmon's latent aggressive instinct may become goaded enough to make it take. As the Reverend Elmer J. Smith says, "There are instances where a literally hung fly will be the most productive technique. Wave it in their faces!"

The wet fly with the riffling hitch is another trick. The basic method was discussed in chapter 7, but there are some interesting variations to use over dour salmon. I confess that I do not enjoy fishing a riffled fly and do it very rarely, but it is a good trick, especially when experimenting over reluctant salmon. I prefer the skated fly instead, such as a big

dry one. This puts me in the minority in many areas, particularly in Iceland, where the riffled fly is popular and productive regardless of conditions. Since this discussion will get us into aberrations in fly speed, let's review what Lee Wulff says about it:

"If you use the Portland Creek (riffling) Hitch the speed is right when the fly skims the surface but doesn't throw spray. This speed is valid for both the hitched or normally fished wet fly. Tying on the hitch around the shank just behind the eye is a good way to check your speed and pick up an occasional fish that wouldn't have responded to any other method."

Famous outdoor author and columnist Gene Hill says on the subject: "Stu Apte and I fished Laxá í Kjós one morning in August without any action. When we came in for lunch we met a young and rather inexperienced Icelander who had six salmon. When asked, he said that on one lift for a back-cast, a rather slow lift, he skittered the fly, which was

The author and Father Smith

immediately taken by a salmon. He figured that if one would take that way another might. The result was that he took all six of his fish that way. Hearing this, we decided to use the Portland Hitch that afternoon. We did, and Stu took five fish and I took three."

While both wet and dry flies usually should be fished at the normal fly speeds that have been discussed, there are times when they should be fished faster, such as when experimenting over reluctant salmon where ordinary methods don't work. In such cases, pull the fly in with fast, long, steady strips or let the current bag the line to increase fly speed. The fast fly may work where the normal one won't. I have seen dour fish, presumably interested in nothing, suddenly wake up and streak for a fast fly, leaving an exciting bow wave. Long flies are good for this, such as the *General Practitioner,* or a tube fly or bucktail. No one knows why this works, except that it is a different approach—and different or unusual tactics can interest reluctant salmon!

Ernest M. Crosfield was an exponent of the fast fly and may have been the one who gave us the idea of the riffling hitch, because his method was basically that. Using a sinking line and a small, lightly dressed fly, he would hand-line the fly over the surface across the current at about current speed—fast in fast currents, and slower in slower ones. Thus, he could cover whatever parts of the water he wished, accurately and according to a definite plan. This, as in A. H. E. Wood's method, gives the salmon a broadside look at the fly, but Crosfield used a much shorter line than Wood did.

Sometimes these experimental methods can be combined, as when fishing a fly such as the *Muddler Minnow,* which can be drifted dry, then skittered, and finally pulled under for fast stripping in.

The other basic methods need no more elaboration than has been given earlier, except to remind the angler of their importance when fishing over dour salmon. The Patent method works well with the *wingless fly,* which so far has had scant attention. Although it has been said that traditional flies for use with the Patent method should be bushy so that their wings will sprawl out when being drifted on a slack line, they don't need wings to make them do so. Wingless wet flies are general-purpose ones, not restricted to any one method. They are distinguished by being well hackled, preferably with the

PLATE 72
WINGLESS PATTERNS, POPULARIZED
AND DRESSED BY PETER DEANE

Heather Moth
Camasunary Killer

softer saddle hackles, along the body or at the neck, or both.

Fishing wingless flies is no different from others. When using the Patent, they can be cast upstream, cross-stream, or downstream, as desired, and allowed to drift on a slack line. What the salmon think they represent is anyone's guess, but the following two American patterns were suggested by stoneflies seen on the screen door of a lighted lodge on the Miramichi. Rough representations have mobile hackles and seem to suggest bugs or nymphs. You usually can see the salmon come to the drifting fly and, of course, then should tighten on the loose line.

Here are the dressings of four typical wingless patterns that have unusual records of productivity.

Based on them, fly dressers can let their imagination roam. For example, I can visualize the *Heather Moth* in an all-black dressing and a hot orange one, among others.

Heather Moth	
Tag	Fine silver wire
Tail	Golden pheasant crest
Body	Gray squirrel fur, gradually thickening toward the head
Hackle	Plymouth Rock hackle palmered up the body
Ribbing	Fine silver wire or tinsel
Throat	Plymouth Rock hackle
Head	Black

This is an origination of the Hon. Edward Davies, who used it with great success on Scottish rivers in the Helmsdale region. The pattern has been popularized by Peter Deane, of Sussex, one of England's most noted authors and fly dressers. In Ireland, it is called *Deane's Miracle Fly.*

Camasunary Killer	
Tail	Medium blue wool, of moderate length
Body	Rear half: same blue wool as tail. Front half: red fluorescent wool
Ribbing	Fine oval silver tinsel
Throat	Black cock's hackle, as a collar, very long in fiber. The fibers are about as long as the length of the body from head to end of tail
Head	Black

The *Camasunary Killer* is another of Peter Deane's popular patterns; he says that it was an adaptation by Francis Williams of a fly known as the *Blue Fly.* Deane also recommends it for rainbow trout, saying, "In all the years I have been dressing flies, I have never come across anything to match the *Camasunary Killer* and the *Heather Moth* . . . although, they, of course, are not infallible."

Shady Lady	
Tail	Black hackle fibers
Body	Rear third: medium green fluorescent wool. Front two-thirds: black wool
Ribbing	Fine silver tinsel or wire over rear third only
Hackle	Black hackle palmered heavily over front two-thirds only, with an extra turn or two at the head. The forward hackling is nearly as long as to the end of the tail and is tied back only slightly
Head	Black

This pattern, by Donald F. Leyden, of Brookfield Center, Connecticut, and the late Charles DeFeo, of New York City, is essentially the familiar *Black Bear,*

Green Butt, with hackling substituted for the wing. It also is dressed with the rear of the body in orange, red, or yellow, sometimes with floss substituted for the wool, and with any sort of dark hackle.

Shady Old Lady

This variation differs from the above pattern only because several turns of a badger hackle (a black saddle feather with light fiber tips) are

PLATE 73
THE SHADY LADY
DRESSED BY DON LEYDEN

palmered near and to the head of the fly. Colors and widths of hackle can be varied. The green part of the body is used most often in clear water, and the orange or yellow in discolored water. These four patterns are most effective in moderate currents.

When working over stale fish in moderate currents, splayed wing patterns, such as *Ingalls' Butterfly,* offer another trick for inducing takes. If you decide to try a slow fly, one with splayed wings can be fished much slower than usual, the decreased fly speed being made up for by the pulsating wings. My favorite method of fishing this—one of my favorite flies—is to give it the conventional wet-fly swing and drift treatment while working it with short jerks of the rod tip to increase pulsation. If that fails, I go to the head of the pool, or run, to fish the fly directly downstream, letting it hang in the current while working the fly and, at the same time, drawing it in and letting it out.

PLATE 74
BEAUFORT MOTH AND
INGALLS' BUTTERFLY

Beaufort Moth
dressed by Vincent Engalls

Butterfly
originated and dressed by Maurice Ingalls

Ingalls' Butterfly (Ingalls' Splay-Wing Coachman)

Tail	Bright red hackle fibers fairly long
Body	Wound with rusty peacock herl. (Some instructions say that one turn of herl is added in front of the wing, but the original pattern does not show this. The body originally was tied with black wool, but Ingalls later preferred the peacock.)
Wing	A divided wing of white goat hair, slightly longer than the body and set a bit above the body, slanted backward at an angle of about 45 degrees. The wings are very sparse, and the hair should be from a small goat, as the hair from large goats is too brittle and too stiff
Hackle	Two turns of a brown hackle wound on as a collar, one turn behind the wings and one in front. The hackle is about half as long as the wing hair, is applied dry-fly style, and should be very sparse
Head	Black

This wet fly was originated by Maurice Ingalls, of Fort Lauderdale, Florida, in 1956, when he was in Blackville, New Brunswick. Wallace Doak, fly dresser and tackle dealer of Doaktown, New Brunswick, says, "For three years now, the *Ingalls' Butterfly* has outsold and outcaught all other wet-fly patterns. It has been tied in many different styles, but none have ever come up to the original fly."

Ingalls says of the fly: "The *Butterfly,* if tied with *goat* hair, is probably the best fly ever used on the Miramichi River. Because of its unusual appearance, it took time for it to gain popularity, but it seemed as though every time I dropped it in where salmon were, I'd get a strike! I have caught my limit a good

many times in four to six casts. My wife and I put it on every season and never exchange it except for another *Butterfly.*"

This is a breather-type fly tied in the color scheme of a *Coachman.* It can be cast and fished as a dry fly and then allowed to sink. When sunk, it is given slight action with the rod tip to make it pulsate, or "breathe." The design has been tried (not as successfully) in different color schemes, such as the *Cosseboom, Silver Rat,* and black-bodied flies with various-colored butts. Variations include adding a gold tag and ribbing and a red wool butt. Many are now tied with a green butt, and orange wings and yellow wings are also very popular.

Ingalls' Butterfly is reminiscent of the elderly *Beaufort Moth,* except that it is dressed using a red hackle tail instead of *Golden Pheasant* and using goat hair instead of splayed feathers for the wing. The *Beaufort Moth,* named for the Earl of Beaufort in the latter part of the last century, merely is the classic *Coachman* with "spoon" wings.

Beaufort Moth	
Tag	Fine oval gold tinsel
Tail	Golden pheasant crest
Body	Peacock herl
Hackle	Brown
Wing	A pair of whole white dense roundish body feathers, splayed
Head	Black

The splayed (or spoon-wing) white body feathers of course got chewed up, so Ingalls properly changed to hairwings. Both the *Moth* and the *Coachman* are from the late nineteenth century, and there is no need here to delve into them further. Author Arnold Gingrich, a northeastern angler, added to confusion by putting a hair wing on a *Coachman* and calling it the *Betsy.*

Our own Theodore Gordon, who fished with an inquiring mind if anyone ever did, evidently may well have been the first to dress a dry fly particularly for salmon, and to have it catch one. This fly was later known as the *Sailboat,* and its story, as quoted from *The Complete Fly Fisherman,* by John McDonald, was in an article in the *Forest and Stream* dated April 4, 1903, as follows: "It was tied with two stiff white wings, made of whole feathers, upright on the hook, peacock herl body, yellow butt, golden pheasant tail, silver tag, and a very full long brown hackle."

My own experiences indicate that when dour salmon are in a pool, a few fresher ones also may be there, and that these usually are takers, if they can be located. Sometimes they seem to frequent the faster water at the very heads of pools, but more often they may lie in the almost dead water near the tails. They don't seem to mingle with the dour fish. These are the few that recently have ventured upstream under prevailing adverse conditions, and they are brighter than the reluctant "lobster fish" that have penned themselves in the pools.

Joseph P. Hubert, author of the sumptuous *Salmon—Salmon,* calls finding them "salmon hunting." When we fished together in Iceland in 1979, I was impressed with his persistence, skill, and success. For many years, Joe Hubert has spent entire summers fishing for salmon all around the Atlantic, and he is regarded as one of the world's leading experts. Consequently, I asked Joe to provide his suggestions for solving what he calls "the dour salmon syndrome." These are his comments:

The Scots had a word for those salmon seemingly immune to the angler's most crafty presentations and finest patterns: *dour.* Every Atlantic salmon river, regardless of locale, will have at some time or place this assemblage of rolling, dolphining, jumping salmon that appear to the cast-weary angler to be deaf, dumb, and blind.

These are not running salmon nor those found at the foot of obstacles, but a congregation of slightly pink fish occupying lodges that at other times are renowned taking pools. This phenomenon has been experienced in high water and low, in bright weather and cloudy, and in warm or cold water temperatures.

Colonel Bates and I recently spent several days on a river in Iceland that simply turned off its ten rods. The river teemed with salmon, and the ability of the anglers present would normally yield respectable totals. Of the few salmon taken, the majority were fresh run with sea lice and taken in pools near the ocean. This wasn't the first time this has happened to me, and may the future give me many opportunities to run these risks again.

What happened, why, and are there discernible reasons and conditions? Even at this date those plaintive, long-unanswered questions remain unresolved. Many have tried to seek logical rational explanations: oxygen, water temperature and chemistry, and combinations of these and other environmental factors. I believe that each may prove to be significant, but overshadowing the physical reasons, perhaps there is a psychological one. Maybe these salmon have simply arrived at their resting places to await their moment to move to the redds. They essentially have become complacent. No longer is the salmon seeking to master the river currents and obstacles; river currents have been near consistent levels for an extended period, thereby eliminating the need for further movement or a radical change of lodge. The migrating salmon uses an extraordinary amount of energy, and once arriving at its goal, physical exhaustion must somewhat dull its otherwise keen senses. One too should bear in mind the physical and mental trauma that must accompany the shock in changing from salt to fresh water.

Irrespective of the causes, the result is a pool containing a cordwood assembly of salmon, jumping forward, sideways, backward, rolling at near predictable intervals, incessant activity, but all done within a restricted area. Each is seemingly oblivious to the most perfectly presented artificial.

The pool containing the dour salmon was made in hell for the angler but heaven sent for the sea gull in hip boots, employing snagging gear, Stewart tackle, and worms. The monarch of fish is vulnerable at this time to such conduct, and he deserves much better treatment. The factor of greed is in the Salmo salar equation, and that arithmetic is centuries old.

For the classic salmon angler a total checkmate? No, not in the least. Rest assured that not every salmon in the river has reached this state of complacency, but the angler now must readjust his goals and methods.

The angler must recognize that the salmon being pursued are in this apathetic state, but at varying degrees. The salmon did not all arrive at the same time, and some are still on the move. Certainly the majority of salmon observed will not be volunteer takers, so realistically the outlook for the fair-caught dour will be slim indeed.

Before giving hope to the salmon angler for a riverside resolution to this reluctant prize, the proposed campaign and its application have been gleaned from many years along Icelandic rivers. An universal adaptation may not be possible.

Iceland endows its salmon fisher with a most essential element in overcoming the "dour salmon syndrome": the availability of extra water, and lots of it. Most Icelandic rivers contain many miles of fishable water, and when divided into beats, the upper two-thirds or so generally represent the longest stretches of the river. It is generally in these upper zones that the dour salmon is found.

The salmon angler faced with this situation must now become overcritical of his skills and must assume the role of the hunter.

Let's set the scene. The conversation at dinner is nearly consistent in that the pools contain large numbers of salmon rolling and jumping, and after hours of trying, the results are great big goose eggs. Frustration is at every level, as the logbook shows fine catches from these very same locations just days earlier. This is a flies-only river, and talk goes to tube flies with lead, and as the week progresses, foul-hooked salmon become more evident and maybe just a little more rationalization is tolerated. A sad scenario for the lover of salmon from a distant land who arrived with purest of heart. Now stark reality has shown that the months of anticipation and great expense have been blunted by bad timing. "You should have been here last week" has no greater chilling effect than on the fisher for the Atlantic salmon.

Be that as it may, the fisherman well schooled in the basics and confident of his skills and his fly box will invariably make an entry or two in the logbook each day, and there will not be a hint of tarnish on those silvered trophies.

The proposed tactics, using the sunk fly, are designed for Iceland, and an even more limiting factor is self-imposed in that only the near-surface presentation is employed. Such obstinacy is a matter of personal choice, however, and my friend and fishing companion Haraldur Stefansson has repeatedly shown me the folly of my ways. Halli's proficiency with a salmon rod is well known by residents and foreigners alike. Although he prefers the surface strike, he can immediately diagnose the "dour salmon syndrome" and administer his curative prescription: the sunk fly, using split shot with

tube flies or the infamous *Black Sheep* pattern. As I have been witness to many such exhibitions, Halli's performance can best be described as "deadly." Halli generally restricts the use of the sunk fly to the center of all incessant activity, right where the jumping, dolphining hordes are located, and rare is the first or second trip through not rewarded without at least a "pull." These salmon are fair hooked, have no doubts on that score. So when in these circumstances, don't do as I do but do as I preach. Be prepared for the sunk-fly technique to possibly save an otherwise barren day. I don't even own a tube fly, much less split shot, and the original *Black Sheep* has been put aside for posterity. I called it the *Black Sheep* as it was so out of place among the *Jock Scotts, Bulldogs, Torrishes,* and *Sir Herbert Maxwells* in my fly boxes.

Admitting the effectiveness of the sunk fly in the hands of a skilled practitioner, and even recommending it for employment for these salmon, I find that the floating-line presentation will produce many salmon, although these catches will be small. My standard need not be compromise.

The near-surface presentation of the British classics will take salmon in rivers exhibiting the dour salmon malady, but the angler must be content with reduced numbers. For me, salmon grassed under these circumstances have a significantly higher appeal. Each salmon reestablishes the confidence in one's ability and can be regarded as documentation of an advanced degree in the school of Atlantic salmon angling.

Whether the angler chooses the greased line, *Patent,* Crosfield, riffle hitch, and/or the floating line for the near-surface presentation, the expertise in its application must be honed to perfection. Anything less and the fisher will be extremely handicapped, and little sympathy can be sincerely accorded to his fruitless day. Remember Richard Franck's advice to the fisherman too lazy to learn his trade: "Let him angle for oysters."

Quite another matter are the conditions found at riverside. The angler has no control over howling winds, rivers in spate, extreme temperatures, and the multitude of other factors that Mother Nature can inflict on these rivers in the North Atlantic. So temper once again your outlook for success. No veteran ever said pursuing salmon was easy.

So let's assume the extraneous conditions are within reason—water levels, clarity and temperatures, winds and weather. An angler can then proceed with a modest amount of probability for success.

The campaign strategy is concerned with where to fish, not how. Each fishing beat generally has several pools containing these reluctant salmon, and the two assigned rods can work out the time schedule to assure coverage of the available water.

I believe the salmon that have been in these pools for a couple of weeks or more are really impossible to fair-hook at the surface. Oh, I've been told one can "work up" a salmon with constant casting, but I sincerely believe that singular fish just happen to arrive on the scene and the fisherman happens to "hook" into it. There is patience and then there is *patience,* and that type doesn't fit into the campaign plans. The fisher must now take his best angling skills and become a hunter, and a very astute hunter at that.

The water available to you during your time period must be combed; you have to locate an active migrating salmon—a salmon that has yet to make it to his holding pool. The later in the season and the farther upstream you are, the lower the chances of finding such salmon.

Ideally, the lowermost "active" pool is where the hunt begins. Using almost a set procedure for these pools, a fishing plan of a very short duration will either produce a salmon or free up the angler for the upriver continuation of his fishing.

The active pool invariably reveals the location of its many dour salmon by their jumping and rolling. The pool has been rested and you believe the pool has not been "put down" in near-recent time by fishing. No one has to be told the best chance to get a salmon is where there are a lot of salmon, and these active pools possess at three locations the best odds for doing just that.

Most fishers eliminate immediately the choicest spot in the pool for taking a salmon by going straight to the area containing the showing fish. The fisherman has bypassed and revealed himself to that area at the extreme head of the pool right where the fastest currents enter. Very often this seemingly unlikely spot contains asalmon about to leave the pool. It's active, and it's a taker. Use the right daylight pattern and a #2 double hook.

Next, fish your way down to where the hordes are making all that commotion. Reduce hook size as determined by the water velocities, grading down to #8 doubles at the tail. Work over those rising fish very carefully, even change patterns a time or two, but leave the area if you feel that its coverage has been precise and accurate and you haven't had a roll or a tail. This is your second best possibility.

The remaining near-surface chance is just downstream and to the quiet-water side from the area of all that splashing and jumping. Should a salmon be just passing through and has momentarily paused in the pool, it will generally divorce itself from that area, as all that commotion is disturbing and the best lies are taken by the residents. Again, this is an area easily overlooked, and it will produce the odd salmon if carefully fished.

Now, after all of this and if you are so inclined, go through the pool with a sunk fly presentation. If the pools have been covered properly, and with care, nothing has been done to put the salmon down to the degree that it would adversely affect the sunk fly. A fifteen-minute rest would not be out of order, however. Be certain to offer the lure at the level of the salmon and that the fly, streamer, or tube is 22 inches or more. If the pool is covered in this manner, you may be rewarded with a salmon, but if not, you can feel confident that the salmon there are not takers and continued effort would be a waste of your valuable time.

Start moving upriver to the next active pool to repeat the procedure. The hunt continues. Clean those Polaroid glasses and begin searching every likely spot, no matter how small the area. By hunting upriver, you are approaching the salmon from its blind side. Every little trick helps. You are looking for a salmon that is between holding pools and will pause en route in some very strange places. Chances are that such a fish is an eager taker, and it often will be taken on the first drift. These are the salmon marked in the logbook as being taken in strange pools or in no known pool at all, and very often will be the only salmon taken on the beat.

Cover those active pools, but be disciplined and confident enough in your ability to leave that dead horse and go and try to make something happen. The entire river must become suspect, and the only way it can be explored is by a step at a time.

The "dour salmon syndrome" is part of Atlantic salmon fishing, but you need not compromise your standards to meet this finny grail on classical terms. The angler turns hunter, and mobility is the key to success. The worst that can happen is that you'll spend a small fraction of your life exploring new water with a salmon rod in hand in the wondrous pursuit of Salmo salar.

Another highly proficient expert is the Reverend Elmer James Smith. Since Father Smith was my earliest mentor in salmon fishing, I know he would agree with much of what has been said, but in a tape he sent to me, he advances additional suggestions:

There are many different cultures of Atlantic salmon, and all do not behave in the same way. Because of their great variations in behavior, no written work can encompass all of them. When salmon are reluctant, it is essential to experiment with fishing at different depths until the proper one is established. Use the longest and finest leader that seems sensible under the circumstances. A secret of success that often works is to pay more attention to fly movement than to fly speed. Learn where the fish are, and skim the fly over them across the water.

Move the fly quickly, but don't let the salmon see it for too long. Cast, move the fly at constant speed for only a foot or two, and then pick it up and cast again. Vary the speed and the length of strip. Salmon will respond to different actions, so it is necessary to *experiment* until the key is found. When the sun is up, go to the dry fly in any size, even very big or as small as #16. Give it only a short float on each cast.

Try a *commotion fly*—a wet pattern such as *Ingalls' Butterfly*—or a try one such as the *Bomber,* fished as above so that it breaks the surface in the manner of a riffled fly. Impart movement and vary it. Try changes in fly size, and try unorthodox patterns such as streamers. For best results, give the flies rapid exposure, because the more the salmon see a fly, the less liable they are to take it."

Finally, let's note the partially divergent methods of Jean-Paul Dubé, a well-known Canadian authority who has fished Quebec's famous rivers season-long for several decades. I have seen him frequently hook reluctant salmon after other anglers had given up. According to Dubé:

"Miramichi Evening"

It is said that so-called dour or stale salmon most often are those that have been in the river a long time, but this isn't quite true, because the same salmon may take readily when they move elsewhere. It is also verifiable that a newcomer to the same pool may be as obstinate as those that have been there for several days or weeks.

Since this phenomenon occurs only in certain pools and is seen mostly in specific parts of those pools, the explanation may not be in the fish, but in their lies. Again, as many of those salmon that have been sulking all day will strike savagely very late in the afternoon or just before dark, even when they stay in the very same spot, this would seem to indicate that the sulkiness is caused more by light or visual conditions than by the fish's moods.

This contention is also supported by the fact that in many, many pools, an hour of fishing after sunset may provide better returns than a full day of constant casting.

When asked if I have any system or methods for hooking reluctant salmon, I am more or less at a loss to find an answer. Of course, there are basic principles that apply especially to late-season or low-water fishing. One is that we should be extremely careful not to alarm the fish, which are more easily disturbed than earlier in the season. A soft, feathery presentation of a smaller fly at the end of a longer line is indicated.

It is easy to attribute the lack of interest in a fly to the salmon's diminished vitality as they fast in fresh water, but

this is an oversimplification. They still have plenty of energy as, once hooked, they may prove even better fighters than fresher fish. This means that we still have the problem of visibility to cope with: The fly we offer or its way of presentation does not create proper illusion to provoke a strike.

I do not believe in harassing a reluctant salmon with wet flies, as this usually will only prolong its period of sulkiness. I have seen a large fly get a good reaction when suddenly cast after a series of low-water fly presentations, but otherwise, when a salmon is hooked after continual casting, it may be that the angler has been at it long enough that the light conditions have changed. In other words, it's not the nagging that has teased the fish into striking, but the altered visual conditions that have caused the fly to create a different illusion that is more tempting to the salmon.

During the latter half of the season, when salmon become more reluctant, dry-fly fishing can undoubtedly be more effective. I mention it second because it is generally habitual to try wet flies first. Why? It may be that when wet flies fail, a dry can still do the job, whereas if a dry fly under proper conditions does not raise a fish, a sunken one is much less likely to do it.

Another reason may be that a dry fly is a poor locator. It tends to disturb the water more and isn't pleasant to use unless one sees the fish or knows exactly where one should be.

When I first started dry-fly fishing, I was taught to float a fly as long as possible while avoiding drag. In ensuing years I have found that it is preferable not to give the salmon time to examine the fly. I do much better now by dropping the fly on their noses, or slightly above, and drifting it not much more than their body length. Then I retrieve and cast to the same spot again.

In this way the pickup of the line is easier and it does not disturb other fish on nearby lies. Not disquieting the other salmon in the pool while concentrating on a particular one is of the utmost importance, as you may want to cast to them later. This is an advantage only dry-fly fishing has to offer.

While repeatedly showing a wet fly to a salmon seems only to disinterest it, teasing it with a floating fly will irritate the fish, goading it to strike. This can be seen when a salmon merely rolls over the fly to sink it, or bats at it with its tail, not making any effort to take it in its mouth. When the fly appears on a later cast, the irritated salmon then may take it solidly.

It is advisable to rest your fish. If your line has not been drifting through the pool over and over again, you can now address your efforts to another salmon with good chance of success. By this I do not mean resting a salmon that has come up to look at the fly, or has tried to take it and missed. In such cases, I believe in presenting the fly again, right away, while the fish is interested, because later on it may no longer be in the mood to react to it. I have often had the experience of rising a salmon to seven or eight successive casts before hooking it, whereas in earlier years I was regularly losing fish that would not come up again after the conventional truce.

If this be a system, I would call it "fishing a pool *fish by fish.*" The same applies even if conditions are such that salmon can't be seen. Then I work the pool *lie by lie.* This requires precision in casting, but it is a self-rewarding exercise that eliminates much of the pure luck aspect of simply "fishing at the pool."

Most of the protagonists of fishing the *Patent* are no longer casting their flies on this planet, so we don't often hear about the method anymore, but it is still a good way to cope with reluctant salmon. I have caught several fish using the *Patent* when they were lying deep in slack, lukewarm water, but since my preference is for dry-fly fishing, I haven't used large bucktails in later years except in cases when all else has failed. That is not giving the *Patent* much of a chance! It gives the bucktail a lot of action, and it can reach fish lying deep. Whatever illusion the fly, thus presented, creates for the salmon, that mass of erect and individually pulsating hair coming straight at the fish is known to tempt many that otherwise would be extremely difficult to catch."

Dubé's short-float method with the dry fly is similar to the method discussed in chapter 9. His causing the fly to create different illusions is reminiscent of Colonel Drury's method of using a different fly and/or method, such as fishing the wet fly (often a *General Practitioner*) upstream, as discussed in chapter 7.

Thus, these highly experienced anglers agree with the majority on many points while disagreeing on others regarding methods of hooking reluctant salmon—probably the most frustrating subject in Atlantic salmon fishing! How can the average angler solve it? He should have all these divergent methods firmly embedded in mind so that for each fishing situation he encounters, he can try the one or more that seem suited. There is no solution applicable to all conditions, and I hope none ever will be found, because a sure one would decrease the fascination and challenge of this entrancing sport.

So although there is no panacea for hooking reluctant salmon, there are different methods, one or more of which should work at one time or another. All you need to do is find the right one. To put it in a nutshell, be as unobtrusive as possible, fish fine and far off, size up the situation to decide which of the various methods to try first, and then experiment, experiment, experiment! For unknown reasons, even dour fish will suddenly go on the take for a time. Will you have your fly in the water then?

11

Fishing the British Isles

"British Isles"

The snug little isles of Britain, currently with the exception of Ireland, shine out as an example of how salmon fisheries can be restored following abuses so drastic that they were all but ruined.

Until the first half of this century, fishing in the British Isles had been affected by the ages-old rape of the salmon caused by increasing pollution, dams and other obstacles, excessive netting along the coasts and in the estuaries and rivers, and rampant poaching. Poaching used to be a traditional practice usually regarded as a sport. Chemicals and all sorts of implements were used to stun or kill the fish in numbers almost beyond comprehension. One such device was the leister, a three- or five-barbed spear mounted on

a long pole also used to propel the boat. Usually, three people manned each craft: one to guide it, another to operate the light for night location of salmon, and third to wield the spear. At certain places and times, so many boats were operating that they gave the impression from shore of scores of fireflies flickering in a field. Nets of all types also were used, and so were grapnels, or large, weighted treble hooks, cast out and dragged over the salmon to snag them. Anything went, and little was done about it until the fisheries had declined to such an extent that commercial fishermen regarded them as nearly worthless.

Late in the last century, it began to dawn on parliamentarians, landowners, fishermen, and the public at large that this precious but sorely abused

PLATE 75
ANTIQUE BRITISH CLASSICS

Highlander	*Dallas Fly*
Claret Major	*Thunder and Lightning*
McMillan	*Childers*
Thunder and Lightning (Irish)	*Pale Lemon Grey*

PLATE 76
ANTIQUE BRITISH CLASSICS

Butcher   Blue Jock Scott

Dusty Miller   Childers   Bittern

Logie

Silver Grey   Black Fairy

Durham Ranger

resource was in such a depleted condition as to be in danger of extinction. Starting in 1860, and increasingly to this day, various salmon fisheries acts, river pollution acts, water resources acts, and other acts and boards restricted or eliminated these excesses to the extent that Atlantic salmon fishing in Scotland, England, and Wales has recovered, or nearly so, on some—but far from all—of the rivers. The present situation is complicated by the Danes netting salmon off the west coast of Greenland, which they have done for many years—a practice that can be likened to milking a cow they neither own nor feed.

The prolific rivers of the British Isles are privately controlled by landowners, clubs, associations, and fishing hotels. Thus, rods are regulated; the rivers are guarded and poaching is minimized. This doesn't prevent anyone, citizen or visitor, from fishing for salmon, however, except perhaps to excess. Tickets can be purchased, usually at reasonable or low cost, allowing anglers beats on rivers for half a day or more, depending on arrangements made and availability of spaces. Crowding, as seen on some North American rivers, is unusual. Funds from the sale of fishing tickets (permits) normally are used for river improvements and propagation of the salmon. The system doesn't please everybody, but most agree that it's the best solution available because it is the one that works most efficiently.

I will not attempt to give specific information about fishing in the British Isles, or anywhere else, because I've had my fingers singed by such before! Since rivers that are good one week can be blank on another, giving such advice can be dangerous. The British publication *Trout and Salmon* (often available in libraries) contains advertisements of fishing hotels and fishing schools that own or lease beats on good rivers, but some weeks are better than others. Fishing schools run by well-known anglers may be the best choice because they usually are conducted during good fishing weeks. All arrangements are made for guests, and instruction is provided only when desired.

Scotland offers the best fishing for visiting anglers. Its most important rivers are the Dee, Spey, Tay, and Tweed; the Helmsdale and Oykel are also good at times. There are many other productive salmon rivers in Scotland, but the variability of their fishing makes it imprudent to recommend them on a long-term basis.

Notable runs of salmon come up rivers regularly, often during every month of the year. The fabled Tweed, nearly 100 miles long and with about 20 miles of it bordering England, has such runs every

PLATE 77
ANTIQUE BRITISH FLIES
BY P. D. MALLOCH

month, regardless of weather, as also does the Tay. Fishing in the Spey begins about February 10 and continues until the end of September, with big, fresh "springers" (two-sea-winter fish) appearing in January, but such forecasts depend on water, weather, and the fish being off the coast in the first place. The Aberdeenshire Dee and some other rivers on the far northeastern coast have good spring runs. The Don, meeting the Dee at Aberdeen, has been choked with pollution near its estuary, but reports indicate that this is being cleared up, so this beautiful stream may be a good producer in the future. Northern rivers, such as the Spey, yield good runs in March and April, but May and June offer more comfort. Grilse appear in June and July. Visiting anglers should find late spring or early autumn ideal because water levels and temperatures are more reliable then and more conducive to consistent and comfortable fishing.

The Spey River countryside

BOB O'SHAUGHNESSY

British fly rods are normally over 10 feet long, and even as long as 20 feet, whereas American rods are usually under 10 feet (see chapter 1). Both have their good points, and the choice often depends on water level and river size. If you can wade or are fishing from a boat, the shorter rods are adequate and, in my opinion, more fun to use. If, however, you are required to fish from the bank, the longer ones are nearly obligatory, because there often is such heavy growth streamside that overhead casting is impractical. Such tackle can be rented locally. You must learn to "Spey-cast" (essentially a roll cast) using the longer sticks of 12¹/2 to 15 feet. In Spey casting, it is important to use the double-tapered line because weight-forward tapers don't work nearly as well. These long rods are also helpful in pushing flies out into the wind and in making longer casts more effortlessly than is possible with the shorter ones. Leaders about as long as the rod and tapered to 10 to 15 pounds-test are ideal for both types; use the strongest taper that will swim the fly satisfactorily. Large flies up to 2/0 may be necessary for heavy water, such as in spring fishing, but sizes between 4 and 10 otherwise are standard. On streams where wading is practical, this is preferable to using a boat. Carry a folding wading staff for safety and wading comfort.

England's best salmon river probably is the Wye, followed by the Avon and Eden. English and Welsh rivers are relatively small, meandering around hills, through towns and valleys, usually without the excitement of waterfalls and fast rapids.

In Wales, the River Conway in Carnarvonshire may have the best salmon fishing. The Welsh Dee, one of the longest in Britain, originates in the Merionethshire Mountains and snakes placidly through about 100 miles of countryside in northeastern Wales and England. It and the Dovey, also in Merionethshire, are excellent salmon rivers. Many rural inns in these areas hold leases on these rivers and cater to anglers.

Ireland, which could be reaping rich rewards from visiting salmon anglers, is a disaster, primarily because of flagrant overfishing and poaching on the high seas off its coast, in its estuaries, and in its rivers. Many formerly famous salmon streams no longer exist as such. The lordly Atlantic salmon has been considered by politicians as good only for votes. As an example of this, there were only 363 drift-net licenses issued in 1962. Drift-net men demanded more licenses, and despite a rapidly declining fishery, the politicians issued them. Ten years later, nearly four times as many licenses were issued, and the figures evidently are much greater today.

You can still find salmon fishing in Ireland if you are not overly optimistic. A friend of mine fishes the Blackwater nearly every year and always hooks a few fish, perhaps because he is an expert. He enjoys the country inns and Ireland's beautiful scenery, the whole adding up to pleasant vacations, as far as he and his wife are concerned.

The Cork Blackwater rises near the County Cork border and flows nearly 100 miles past hills, woods, and quaint villages to reach the sea on the southeastern coast. Another important river, still productive to an extent, is the Shannon and its tributaries. From its source in the Cuileagh Mountains, it passes deeply and slowly through three large lakes to flow in a winding course southwesterly to the sea near the city of Limerick.

From an angling standpoint, the importance of the British Isles rests largely in the fact that these islands are the motherland of the salmon fly, the most beautiful fishing fly in the world. Chapter 4 traced the rise of the salmon fly from the somber British flies to the opulent Irish patterns, followed by the elegant patterns coming from Scotland and England, and finally the return to simplicity. All of this took place over a period of approximately fifty years—from the very complex patterns of Traherne, for example, to the extremely simple and effective *Black Bear* from New England. During the next fifty years, a melding of these two extremes took place as the conformation and components of the salmon fly became modernized. The progression continues, and it is gratifying to note the resurgence of interest in the classics and the art of tying them.

The return to simplicity in salmon flies by no means should mandate the decline of the classics. The beautifully feathered classics had, and continue to have, a profound influence on the development of the salmon fly. Many tradition-bent but practical anglers, rather than give up the classics entirely, creatively convert them to hairwing versions of their predecessors. Roughly following the coloration of the classic dressing, today's tier can eliminate nonessentials as desired and emulate any given pattern simply by substituting hair and floss for feathers. Although the simpler hairwing reduces the necessity of the fancy featherwing, many anglers who appreciate fine tackle enjoy using exotic patterns and probably always will.

The importance of the classics is twofold. Although to a lesser extent today, the first aspect concerns their value to fishing. Many anglers cling to the charm of the classics (and modernized versions of them) with the nostalgic feeling that only the exquisite is suitable for the King of Fishes—and "the tried and true" of salmon flies continue to charm the salmon as well as salmon fishermen. The second aspect is the appreciation of the rich heritage of the salmon fly as an entrancing art form. Many fly tiers seek inspiration in the challenge of intricate patterns without necessarily considering the original intent of the pattern. And growing groups of collectors covet the ultimate in precise assemblies of fine tinsels, flosses, and feathers. Indeed, it seems a fitting tribute to the salmon that we also treasure the art of the Atlantic salmon fly.

Listed in alphabetical order, the following patterns are representative of a 100 years of salmon fly development. They are an interesting study in contrasts; however, there is one constant—all of these patterns, regardless of the complexity of design or availability of materials, were originally devised to be fished. It is assumed that the reader understands that today substitutes are used for many of the original called-for materials.

Ally's Shrimp

Tail	Orange bucktail
Body	First half: red floss. Second half: black floss
Ribbing	Oval silver tinsel
Throat	Gray squirrel hair
Wing	Gray squirrel hair with golden pheasant tippet over
Hackle	Orange cock
Head	Red

This internationally popular fly originated on the Spey River. In addition to the predominantly orange original dressing, it is tied in many variations, including red, yellow, black, and purple.

Arndilly Fancy

Tag	Oval silver tinsel
Tail	Golden pheasant crest
Body	Yellow floss
Ribbing	Oval silver tinsel
Throat	Bright blue hackle
Wing	Black squirrel tail
Cheeks	Jungle cock (very small)
Head	Red ostrich herl (but usually a ring of red Cellire next to wing, with rest of the head black)

This fly was originated by Megan Boyd, Scotland's leading professional fly dresser. Until her retirement in the mid-1980s, Boyd took pride in dressing flies for fishermen. Now they are sought by collectors—in fact, revered by those who appreciate such things.

Avon Eagle

Tag	Silver tinsel	
Tail	Golden pheasant crest and the tip of a golden pheasant breast feather	
Body	In equal sections: lemon, bright orange, scarlet and fiery brown seal's fur	
Ribbing	Broad silver tinsel and twist	
Hackle	Eagle's hackle (substitute), one side stripped	
Throat	Wigeon	
Wings	A pair of golden pheasant sword feathers, back to back	
Sides	Jungle cock	
Topping	Golden pheasant crest	
Head	Black	(Pryce-Tannatt)

Beauly Snow Fly

Body	Pale blue seal's fur or floss, dressed thin
Ribbing	Broad, flat silver tinsel edged with fine oval gold tinsel or gold twist
Hackle	A black heron's hackle wound forward from third turn of tinsel, quite full at throat, the longest fibers extending to bend of hook
Wing	Green peacock herl in strands, extending to full length of hook
Ruff	Orange seal's fur or mohair
Head	Black

With large bunches of strands of peacock herl composing the entire wing, the Beauly Snow Fly is the leading example of a herl wing fly. It was first known simply as the *Snow Fly,* presumably named for its originator, Mr. Snowie of Inverness. Beauly, the river of its origin, was later added to the name to avoid confusion with other flies.

The ruff is unusual on salmon flies and could be termed a very short collar. On some accepted dressings, the ruff is wider than dubbed seal's fur would allow, and could be done by applying a collar of the very narrowest orange hackle. This is a classic Spey fly, used mostly in the snow waters of early spring. The hackle should be arranged to conceal the body as little as possible.

Benchill

Tag	Gold tinsel
Tail	Golden pheasant crest and the tip of a golden pheasant's breast feather
Butt	Black herl
Body	Orange, scarlet, claret, and pale blue seal's fur, well picked out
Ribbing	Flat silver tinsel and twist
Throat	A pale blue hackle
Wing	A pair of tippets, back to back and veiled with married strands (or, in large sizes, narrow strips) of peacock wing, scarlet and blue swan, golden pheasant tail and bustard
Cheeks	Strips of speckled gallina wing and jungle cock over
Topping	Golden pheasant crest
Head	Black (Pryce-Tannatt)

Beresford's Fancy

Tag	Silver twist and claret-magenta silk
Tail	Golden pheasant crest
Body	Blue and orange silk, in equal sections
Ribbing	Fine, oval silver tinsel
Hackle	Natural black hackle, from the second turn
Throat	Claret-magenta hackle and jay
Wings	Tippet in strands; bustard; swan dyed claret-magenta, blue, and orange; and mallard
Horns	Blue macaw
Head	Black ostrich herl (Kelson)

PLATE 78
BRITISH CLASSICS, DRESSED LOW WATER

Silver Grey
dressed by Arthur Elkins

Beresford's Fancy
dressed by Bob Veverka

Black Doctor
dressed by Mark Waslick

Black Bomber

Tag	Silver tinsel
Tail	Golden pheasant crest
Body	Rear third: lemon yellow floss. Front two-thirds: black floss
Ribbing	Oval silver tinsel
Throat	Natural black hackle
Wing	Black bear hair
Head	Black

This is the British version of the *Black Bomber* and a hairwing version of the *Jeannie*. The Canadian version is the same except that the yellow floss is used as a tag, with the body all black floss. This version also calls for jungle cock cheeks and a topping of a golden pheasant crest feather. Another North American fly, called the *Black Star,* is exactly the same, without the topping. Jungle cock eyes often are added.

This general dressing, with or without the embellishments, is one of the most popular flies on Canada's Miramichi River. There, following early traditions, it is called by a descriptive name such as *Black Bear, Yellow Butt.* On the Miramichi and other rivers, the butt or tag or rear third of the body is in a choice of colors, such as yellow, orange, green, and red. These often are fluorescent colors, which seem to make the fly much more productive. The wing should be sparse and applied close to the body.

Another British pattern, called the *Black Maria,* is the same as above except that a black hackle is palmered from tail to head and the throat is a small bunch of guinea fowl hackle fibers.

Black Brahan

Tag	Oval silver tinsel
Body	Red Lurex or mylar, or red floss
Ribbing	Oval silver tinsel
Throat	Black (sometimes hot orange) hackle fibers
Wing	Black squirrel
Head	Black

This fly was designed by John MacKenzie, a gillie on the River Conon, and is named for the Brahan beat on that river. It is a Welsh border salmon fly, popular on the Wye and the Usk. Another version, in bucktail form, was sent to me by Geoffrey Bucknall, of London. It has a red head; a tail of a small bunch of black squirrel tail, about as long as the body; same body, ribbing, and throat; and a wing of a small bunch of black squirrel tail extending to the end of the tail, which is quite long.

PLATE 80
THE DOCTORS

Helmsdale Doctor
dressed by Megan Boyd

Red Doctor
dressed by Belarmino Martinez

White Doctor
dressed by Bob Veverka

Blue Doctor
dressed by Bill Wilbur

Black Doctor
dressed by William Wilsey

Black Doctor
(antique)

Silver Doctor
dressed by Ted Kantner

Silver Doctor
dressed by P. D. Malloch

Few realize that John MacKenzie originated three other *Brahans.* They are interesting patterns productive all around the Atlantic. The *Bloors Brahan* has a tag of copper tinsel, a tail of golden pheasant crest, a body of yellow floss ribbed with copper twist, a magenta throat, and a wing of hot orange hair. The *Brahan Badger* has a tag of copper twist, a tail of golden pheasant crest, a body of red Lurex ribbed with copper twist, a magenta throat, and a wing of badger hair. The *Brahan Victor* has a tag of copper tinsel, a tail of golden pheasant crest, a body of flat silver tinsel ribbed with copper twist, a black throat hackle, and a wing of black hair, short and lightly dressed. Hook sizes are 2 to 10 on the first two and 6 to 10 on the third, regular irons.

The Doctors

This lovely series of patterns consists of the *Blue, Silver, Black, Red, White,* and *Helmsdale Doctors.* The first one, created in about 1850, was the *Blue Doctor,* originally called merely the *Doctor* until its variations were produced. Among the angling references of the last century there are a number of differing patterns given for the *Doctor* series, and this family of flies has retained its popularity into modern times.

Chronologically, the *Blue, Silver,* and *Black Doctors* are the first of the series. James "Jemmy" Wright (1829–1902), lauded as "the most innovative and artistic tier for miles around," evidently was the first to dress them. Although some of Wright's patterns may have been inspired by ideas given to him by his

customers or competitors, he is generally credited with the *Black Doctor* as well as several other prominent patterns. These include the *Black Ranger,* the *Thunder and Lightning,* and the *Silver Gray.*

Jemmy Wright was the third son of George Wright, also an angler and fly dresser. He was not satisfied with patterns as they existed and studiously studied the work of others to learn their secrets and improve their methods. His little cottage and tackle shop in Sprouston on the River Tweed was a daily gathering spot for anglers interested in the latest news about flies and fishing. Of all the proficient nineteenth-century English and Scottish fly dressers, James Wright was the one who gained the most enduring fame.

The Pryce-Tannatt pattern that follows for the *Black Doctor* differs from Wright's original dressing that calls for chatterer instead of Indian crow in the tail, blue hackle instead of claret, a jay throat instead of gallina, a different wing structure and components, blue macaw horns, and chatterer cheeks.

Black Doctor

Tag	Silver thread and lemon yellow floss
Tail	Golden pheasant crest over which is Indian crow
Butt	Scarlet Berlin wool
Body	Black floss
Ribbing	Oval silver tinsel
Hackle	A cock's hackle dyed dark claret
Throat	Speckled gallina
Wing	(Mixed wing) An underwing of strands of a golden pheasant tippet with strips of golden pheasant tail over it; a sheath of married single swan strands dyed (from bottom to top) scarlet, blue and yellow, with florican, bustard, peacock wing, mottled and cinnamon turkey tail, married narrow strips of teal and barred wood or summer duck fastened in across the sheath; and narrow strips of bronze mallard edging the top of the sheath
Topping	Golden pheasant crest
Head	Scarlet Berlin wool (Pryce-Tannatt)

The wings of the *Blue, Silver,* and *Black Doctor* are the same. The *Silver Doctor* differs from the *Black* in that the body is flat silver tinsel, the tail topping is blue chatterer, and the throat is a pale blue hackle followed by wigeon. The *Blue Doctor* differs in that the tag is golden yellow floss, the tail is a topping and tippet in strands, the body is pale blue floss, the hackle is pale blue, and the throat is of jay fibers.

The *Helmsdale Doctor* is the only other of the *Doctors* with a silver tinsel body. It is similar to the *Silver Doctor,* but instead of blue and teal for the throat a bright yellow cock feather is used. The *White Doctor*

is more obscure but can be found in Hale's *How to Tie Salmon Flies.* Even more unusual but certainly interesting is the *Red Doctor;* it is included (as dressed by P. D. Malloch) in the color plates of Hodgson's *Salmon Fishing.*

It might be appropriate to note here that kingfisher or blue hackle tip can be substituted when blue chatterer is called for. A good substitute for Indian crow is to dye the small white neck feathers of a male ring-necked pheasant yellow-orange and dip the tips in red, or use red-orange hackle tips.

The most challenging aspect of the *Doctor* patterns is the wing, and it can be simplified (or converted) into a hairwing by applying a small bunch of gray squirrel tail hair, over which are hairs dyed medium blue, with yellow hairs over these, in proportions of half gray and a quarter each of blue and yellow. Horns and toppings are usually eliminated in hairwing versions; other simplifications are a matter of individual judgment.

Black Dog

Tag	Silver tinsel and canary floss
Tail	Golden pheasant crest and ibis
Butt	Black herl
Body	Black floss
Ribbing	Yellow floss; silver tinsel (on each side of floss)
Hackle	Black heron (or substitute), from third turn
Wing	Two red-orange hackles, enveloped by two jungle cock; unbarred summer duck; light bustard; Lady Amherst pheasant; scarlet and yellow swan
Topping	Two golden pheasant crest feathers
Head	Black (Hale)

Kelson cites this elegant combination of materials as one of his father's old patterns, and Francis Francis recommends it for the River Tay. Patterns differ among the standard resources; the one given above is according to Hale.

Black Dose

Tag	Silver thread and light orange floss
Tail	Golden pheasant crest and married narrow strips of teal and scarlet swan, back to back
Body	Two or three turns of pale blue seal's fur; the rest black seal's fur, left smooth
Ribbing	Oval silver tinsel
Hackle	A black hackle
Throat	A light claret or fiery brown hackle
Wing	A pair of tippets, back to back, veiled with married strands of scarlet and green swan, light mottled turkey tail, and golden pheasant tail; peacock herl in strands above
Horns	Blue and yellow macaw
Head	Black (Pryce-Tannatt)

PLATE 81
THE BLACK DOG, DRESSED BY SYD GLASSO

The whole featherwing Pryce-Tannatt pattern given for the *Black Dose* is very different from that of Kelson, who attributes this fly to a Mr. Bernard and again credits his father. There is considerable confusion between the *British Black Dose* and the *Canadian Black Dose,* as well as their hairwing counterparts. To distinguish between the two, note that the British pattern often has a blue butt that emulates the pale blue seal's fur in the rear section of the body in the Pryce-Tannatt dressing. The *Black Dose* has been Americanized in various ways, including giving it a mostly black hair wing. The North American patterns, including my personal favorite, can be found in chapter 14. This useful pattern was also simplified in the 1930s by Roy Steenrod and later by Harry Darbee.

	Black Dragon
Tail	Black bucktail, as long as the body
Body	Black chenille
Ribbing	Narrow, embossed silver tinsel
Wing	Black bucktail, extending to the end of the tail (both tail and wing are very sparse)
Hackle	About two turns of a stiff black hackle, wound on as a collar, extending outward at right angles to the hook in all directions
Head	Black

This is another of the few British bucktail-type salmon flies, usually used on low water. A companion fly called the *Red Dragon* is the same except that the head and all other elements are red, and the ribbing is narrow, embossed gold tinsel. These two flies were dressed by Geoffrey Bucknall, of London, and are listed in his catalog.

	Black Fairy
Tag	Fine round gold tinsel and golden yellow floss
Tail	Golden pheasant crest
Butt	Black ostrich herl
Body	Black seal's fur or floss
Ribbing	Oval gold tinsel
Throat	A black hackle
Wing	Strips of brown mallard
Head	Black

Another version eliminates the butt in the above dressing and uses the tag as a butt. This dressing, popular on Canadian rivers, is almost identical to the popular *Jeannie,* whose hairwing versions include the *Black Bomber* and the *Black Star.*

Black Goldfinch

Tag	Silver thread and deep orange silk
Tail	Golden pheasant crest and Indian crow
Butt	Black herl
Body	Black floss
Ribbing	Oval gold tinsel
Hackle	Golden olive hackle
Wing	Tippet in strands, covered by strips of orange swan, set upright
Cheeks	Indian crow
Topping	Golden pheasant crest
Horns	Blue and yellow macaw
Head	Black (Pryce-Tannatt)

Black Marie

Tag	Gold tinsel
Tail	Golden pheasant crest
Body	Black floss
Ribbing	Fine oval silver tinsel
Throat	Scarlet and yellow hackle
Wing	Stoat's tail hairs or any fairly straight black hair
Head	Black

This is a British pattern, attributed to a Brigadier Gibson.

Blue Baron

Tag	Silver twist and claret silk
Tail	Golden pheasant crest and chatterer
Butt	Black herl
Body	In two equal sections; the first, oval tinsel, butted with toucan, above and below, and black herl; the second, blue silk having a blue hackle along it
Throat	Teal
Wing	Golden pheasant tippet and tail in strands, swan dyed blue and claret, and mallard
Topping	Golden pheasant crest
Sides	Jungle cock
Head	Black

This lovely British pattern with all the components of a classic is from the mid nineteenth century. The above pattern is from Kelson. Pryce-Tannatt suggests a slightly different wing construction and adds Indian crow to the tail. Some patterns call for a herl head and some do not.

Blue Charm

Tag	Silver thread and golden yellow floss
Tail	Golden pheasant crest
Butt	Black ostrich herl
Body	Black floss
Ribbing	Oval silver tinsel
Throat	A deep blue hackle
Wing	Mottled brown turkey tail strips, set upright, and narrow strips of teal along the upper edge
Topping	Golden pheasant crest
Head	Black (Pryce-Tannatt)

PLATE 83
STEPS IN TYING THE BLUE CHARM
DRESSED BY BOB WARREN

When fashions on the Dee turned to smaller, simpler flies, patterns such as the *Blue Charm* evolved. A. H. E. Wood claimed he always started with a *Blue Charm* and only changed it "if all the sizes I try prove no good." Elegant in its simplicity, this British classic remains a great favorite today all around the Atlantic.

The pattern given is from Pryce-Tannatt. Again, dressings differ among the classical authors. Kelson, for example, calls for a claret floss body and a black Berlin wool head. I prefer the Pryce-Tannatt pattern, which is more commonly used. It is shown in Plate 83 with the steps for tying the fly.

The low-water version is dressed very sparsely and simply on long-shanked, light-wire hooks usually in sizes from 4 to 10, the body occupying no more than half the length of the hook shank. Presumably, if an international poll were taken of anglers' favorites in low-water patterns, the *Blue Charm, Logie,* and *Black Jack* would rank at the top, and probably in that order.

PLATE 82
THE BLUE BARON
DRESSED BY TED KANTNER

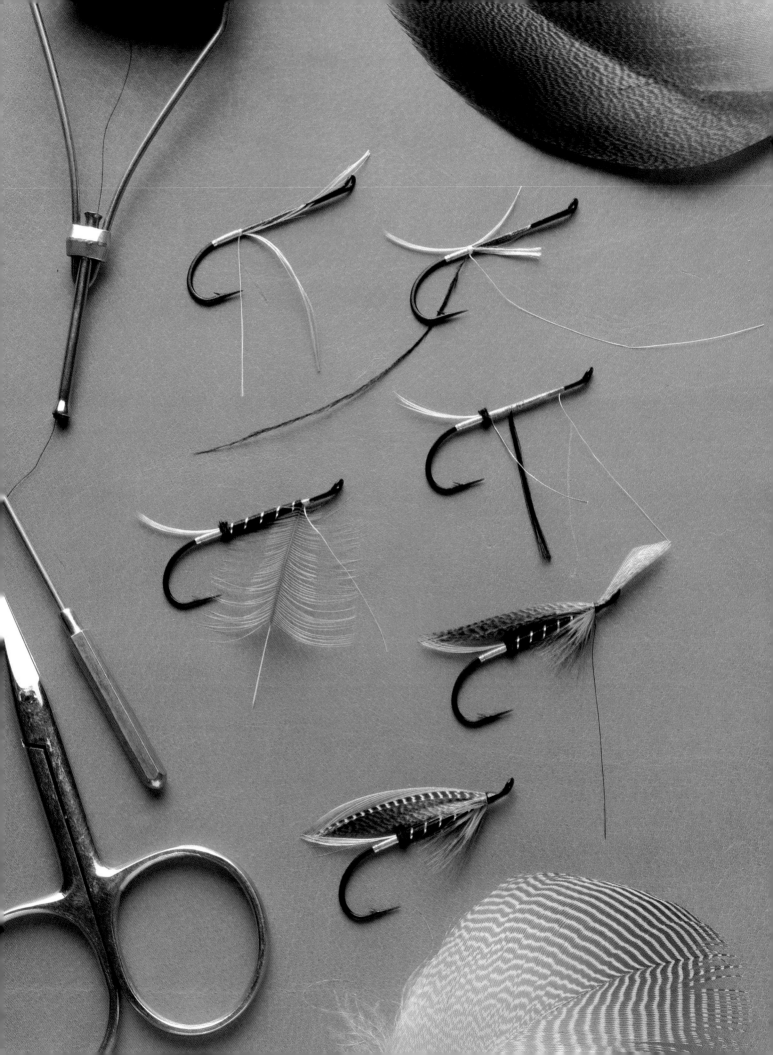

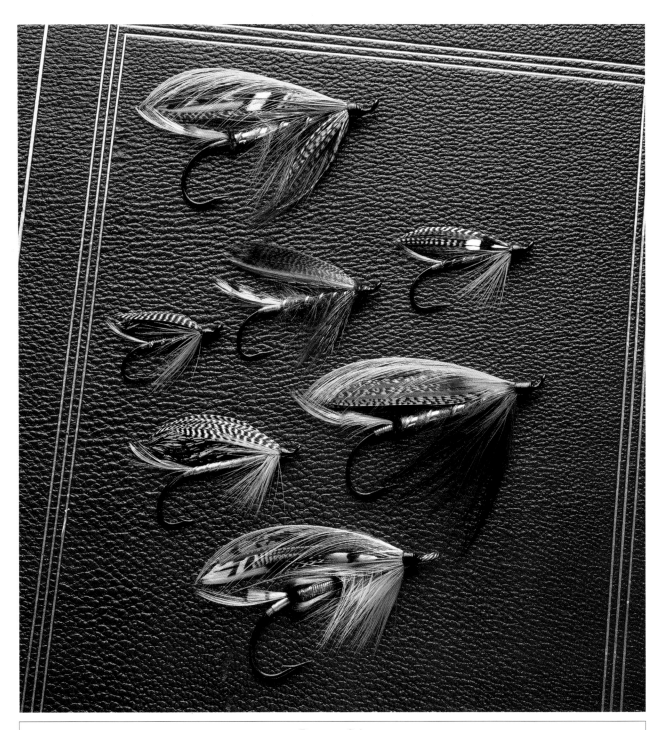

PLATE 84
BRITISH CLASSICS, DRESSED BY MEGAN BOYD

Childers

Sir Charles (Hill's Version)   *Fiery Brown*   *Musker's Fancy*

Sir Charles   *Sutherland*

Torrish

PLATE 85
BRITISH HAIRWING PATTERNS, DRESSED BY JIMMY YOUNGER

Garry

Bourach   Dunkeld   Tosh

Ally's Shrimp

Munro Killer   Stoat's Tail (low-water)

Thunder and Lightning
(low-water)

The *Blue Charm* hairwing is the same as the featherwing but with a wing of gray squirrel; however, tag, butt, or topping is often eliminated. The simpler hairwing version has nearly superseded the featherwing, and many consider it more effective. Essential to every salmon angler's fly box, the *Blue Charm* is particularly popular in Iceland, where "something with blue in it" is considered most necessary.

Other similar patterns are the *Hairy Mary* and the *Irish Hairy Mary,* the latter being the same except that a fluorescent orange butt is added to a wing of Irish badger hair. Of these I prefer the latter, perhaps because I think small fluorescent butts add to effectiveness. The fourth is the *Blue Rat.* The choice between the four is mainly a matter of confidence; any one should do as well as the others.

Bourach	
Tag	Oval silver tinsel
Tail	One or two bright blue hackle tips
Body	Embossed or flat silver tinsel
Ribbing	Oval silver tinsel
Throat	Bright blue hackle
Wing	Yellow bucktail, extending a bit longer than the hook
Head	Black

This simple and popular pattern came from Megan Boyd in Scotland. From the Gaelic word for "mess" or "muddle," *bourach* means no one thing or another, but a mixture of things. This fly is a very good choice for bright conditions and is also popular in Iceland.

PLATE 86
BRITISH HAIRWING PATTERNS

Watson's Fancy
dressed by Jimmy Younger

Jerram's Fancy
dressed by Harry Willcox

Black Bomber
dressed by Megan Boyd

Stoat's Tail
dressed by Rod Yerger

Stoat's Tail
dressed by Peter Deane

Silver Blue
dressed by Rod Yerger

Red Dragon
dressed by Geoffrey Bucknall

Blue Doctor
dressed by Pam Richards

Bucktail and Gold
dressed by Harry Willcox

Black Dragon
dressed by Geoffrey Bucknall

Black Dose
dressed by Bill Wilbur

Arndilly Fancy
dressed by Jimmy Younger

Jock Scott
dressed by Jedde Waterman

PLATE 87
BRITISH HAIRWING PATTERNS, DRESSED BY PETER DEANE

Brahan Badger	*Old Charlie*	*Yellow Fairy*	*Black Brahan*
Thunder and Lightning	*Brahan Victor*	*Brahan Shrimp*	*Brown Turkey*
Pot Scrubber	*Tish*	*Delfur Sweep, original*	*Bloors Brahan*

Brahan Shrimp

Tag	Copper tinsel
Tail	A pheasant rump feather, dyed black
Body	Red Lurex
Ribbing	Copper tinsel
Throat	Hot orange hackle fibers
Wing	Two very small jungle cock feathers, back to back
Head	Red Cellire

This is another of the *Brahan* series (see *Black Brahan*) designed by John MacKenzie, a gillie on the River Conon, and was named after the Brahan beat on that river. Many salmon in northern Scotland have been taken on these flies, which are also popular for sea trout.

Brora

Tag	Oval silver tinsel and lilac-pink floss
Tail	Golden pheasant crest, over which are a few fibers of blue kingfisher, half as long as the crest
Body	Rear half: oval silver tinsel, veiled at the front with gold toucan, top and bottom. Front half: black floss, ribbed with oval silver tinsel
Hackle	About two turns of a black heron feather, extending to the bend of the hook
Wing	Two cinnamon turkey strips, outside of which are married strips of blue and white swan, outside of which are strips of pintail two-thirds as long as the inside strips. The swan is not quite as wide as the turkey, and the pintail is not quite as wide as the swan
Head	Black

This pattern was sent to me by Megan Boyd, noted fly dresser of Brora, Sutherland, Scotland, who thinks it was originated by Charles Akroyd, also of

PLATE 88
BRITISH TUBE FLIES

Collie Dog
dressed by Bill Wilbur

Willie Gunn
dressed by Bill Wilbur

March Brown   *Silver Doctor*

Silver Blue
dressed by Rod Yerger

Tadpole
dressed by Bill Wilbur

PLATE 89
BRITISH FEATHERWING PATTERNS

Black Fairy
dressed by Belarmino Martinez

Jeannie
dressed by Megan Boyd

Little Inky Boy
dressed by Bob Warren

Ray Mead
dressed by Keith Fulsher

Silver Blue
dressed by Bill Hunter

Parson
dressed by Jan Londal

Dunkeld
dressed by William Wilsey

Butcher
dressed by Bill Wilbur

Mar Lodge
dressed by Bessie Brown

March Brown
dressed by Al Brewster

Black Dose
dressed by Al Brewster

Brora. It is a beautiful fly somewhat like the much simpler predominantly black patterns so successful on North American rivers, such as the Miramichi. Akroyd was the originator of the *Akroyd* pattern, which the *Brora* resembles slightly.

	Brown Fairy
Tag	Gold tinsel
Tail	Golden pheasant crest feather
Body	Fiery brown seal's fur, brown wool yarn, or brown floss
Ribbing	Oval gold tinsel
Hackle	A brown hackle palmered over front half of body
Throat	A small bunch of brown hackle fibers, tied full under the wing (if the palmering is insufficient or has been omitted)
Wing	Brown (bronze) mallard, in strips
Topping	Golden pheasant crest (sometimes omitted)
Head	Black

This (with the *Yellow Fairy*) is a variation of the *Black Fairy*. In the above dressing, a butt of black ostrich herl is often included. In another variation of the same fly, the tinsel is silver and the hackle and throat are black. This relates it more closely to the *Black Fairy*, which is also done in a more complicated dressing. It is a favorite fly on many rivers, especially the Miramichi in Canada.

	Brown Turkey
Tag	Very narrow flat silver tinsel
Tail	Golden pheasant crest
Body	Rear third: yellow-orange mohair. Middle third: scarlet mohair. Front third: black mohair, not built up
Ribbing	Flat silver tinsel
Hackle	Black hackle, of moderate length and fullness
Wing	Sections of brown turkey, medium width
Head	Black

In his authoritative *Fly Dressers' Guide*, John Veniard gives a slightly different dressing. It has no tag, and the rear half of the body is yellow seal's fur; the front half, claret seal's fur, ribbed with oval silver tinsel. The hackle is brown and the wing is com-

posed of sections of golden pheasant tippet veiled with strips of light cinnamon turkey. This, evidently, is the English dressing. The one given above is favored in Scotland.

Two other similarly named flies of a later date, the *Gold Turkey* and the *Silver Turkey,* are of North American origin and are described near the end of chapter 14.

Bucktail and Gold

Tag	Fine round or oval gold tinsel
Tail	Golden pheasant crest
Body	Flat gold tinsel
Ribbing	Oval gold tinsel
Throat	Medium blue hackle. The longest fibers extend nearly to the point of the hook
Wing	Brown bucktail, with a bit of blue bucktail on each side, extending to the end of the tail
Head	Black

This fly was originated in 1962 by Harry Willcox, of Alnwick, England, and is used extensively in Scotland. He prefers to dress it on double hooks.

Butcher

Tag	Silver thread and lemon floss	
Tail	Golden pheasant crest and blue chatterer	
Butt	Black ostrich herl	
Body	Fiery brown, pale blue, claret, and dark blue seal's fur in equal sections and picked out	
Ribbing	Flat silver tinsel and twist	
Hackle	A dark claret or black hackle	
Throat	A lemon hackle followed by speckled gallina	
Wing	A pair of tippets back to back, covered by a pair of pheasant breast feathers, and these by a pair of broad strips of teal; married narrow strips of yellow swan and bustard, scarlet and blue swan, orange swan, and golden pheasant tail; rather broad strips of brown mallard over	
Cheeks	Blue chatterer	
Topping	Golden pheasant crest (optional)	
Horns	Blue and yellow macaw	
Head	Black	(Pryce-Tannatt)

Campbell

Tag	Silver twist	
Tail	Golden pheasant crest and chatterer	
Butt	Black ostrich herl	
Body	In two equal sections: the first, silver tinsel, ribbed with fine oval silver tinsel and butted with black herl; the second, light claret seal's fur, ribbed with oval silver tinsel	
Hackle	A yellow hackle for the center	
Wings	Two strips of cinnamon turkey, narrow strips of swan dyed red, yellow, and light blue, married; bustard, golden pheasant tail, and teal	
Sides	Jungle cock	
Topping	Golden pheasant crest	
Head	Black	(Kelson)

PLATE 92
THE DUNT
DRESSED BY MARK WASLICK

Tag	Silver thread and pale blue floss
Tail	Golden pheasant crest and a pair of jungle cock feathers, back to back
Body	Yellow, orange, and fiery brown seal's fur in equal sections, dressed thin and well picked out
Ribbing	Flat silver tinsel and twist
Hackle	Black heron (or substitute), from the third turn of tinsel
Throat	Teal
Wing	A pair of brown turkey tail strips, with black bars and white tips, set flat
Cheeks	Jungle cock, drooping

This pattern, originated in the early nineteenth century by a Mr. Murdock, is typical of the Dee strip-wing style. The above pattern is Pryce-Tannatt's. Hardy, Hale, and Kelson all call for red claret in the body rather than fiery brown, and teal instead of jungle cock in the tail.

Carron

Body	Orange Berlin wool
Ribbing	Flat silver tinsel followed by scarlet floss, with silver thread applied reversed
Hackle	A black heron's hackle from the fourth turn of tinsel. This hackle extends at least to bend of hook
Throat	A turn or two of a mottled teal feather, nearly half as long as the heron
Wing	Brown mallard strips set low and roofed, extending to bend of hook
Head	Black

This is one of the famous Spey flies, distinguished by their long, flowing heron hackles and triple ribbing. Others include *Gray Heron, Green King,* and *Purple King.* Dressing this family of flies presents two difficulties. One lies in the number of ribbing materials that, with the usual heron hackle, have to be tied in at the end of the body and wound up the shank. A Spey fly usually has three tinsels: a narrow flat and fine oval being wound in the usual direction, with the remaining oval or flat reversed. To avoid an ugly bunching at the tail, these materials are spaced out as they are tied in, leaving two turns of the body wool between each tinsel. Between the last two tinsels, the heron hackle is tied in by its butt. The reversed tinsel is tied in last, over the hackle to protect it.

The other problem lies in winging because, although these are simple strips of brown mallard feather, they do not sit on the hook shank in the

usual wing position. They have to sit down lower on the shoulder of the shank. The usual procedure is to tie in the farther wing, then reverse the thread to tie on the matching nearer strip. Perhaps an easier way is to tie in both wing strips together. With care, the wings can be held in the normal upright position, then the pressure eased slightly while the wings are worked gently down onto the shoulders of the shank. The turns of thread are brought over the wings in the usual way. After a little experience, perfect results should be obtained.

Childers

Tag	Silver thread and pale blue floss
Tail	Golden pheasant crest and Indian crow
Butt	Black ostrich herl
Body	Golden yellow floss, orange and fiery brown seal's fur in equal sections
Ribbing	Flat silver tinsel and twist
Hackle	A badger hackle dyed lemon yellow
Throat	Golden pheasant breast feather followed by wigeon
Wing	Mixed: a pair of golden pheasant breast feathers, back to back; married strands of scarlet, blue, orange, and yellow swan, bustard, florican, golden pheasant tail, cinnamon and mottled gray turkey tail
Sides	Barred summer duck strips
Cheeks	Blue chatterer
Topping	Golden pheasant crest
Horns	Blue and yellow macaw
Head	Black

This Pryce-Tannatt pattern again differs somewhat from the other classic sources. This pattern was originated in about 1850 by Colonel Childers. Kelson commented that it is "one of the best old standard patterns."

Curry's Red Shrimp

Tag	Flat silver tinsel
Tail hackle	Golden pheasant red breast feather
Rear body	Red floss with fine oval silver ribbing and veiled with Indian crow at the sides
Center hackle	Badger cock
Front body	Black floss with oval silver ribbing and veiled with Indian crow at the sides
Wing	A pair of jungle cock, roofing the black floss
Collar	Long gray badger cock
Head	Red

This fly was originated by Patrick Curry, who claimed it was one of three flies that he limited his stock to and that it was responsible for taking 95 percent of all area salmon.

Dunkeld

Tag	Silver thread and light orange floss
Tail	Golden pheasant crest and a pair of jungle cock points, back to back, veiled by a pair of Indian crow feathers, back to back
Butt	Black ostrich herl
Body	Flat gold tinsel
Ribbing	Fine oval silver tinsel
Hackle	A bright orange hackle, wound forward from the second turn of tinsel
Throat	Jay
Wing	Golden pheasant tippet in strands; married strands of scarlet, yellow, and blue swan, peacock wing, bustard, florican, golden pheasant tail, and mottled brown turkey tail. Over this are strips of brown mallard
Sides	Jungle cock
Cheeks	Blue chatterer
Topping	Golden pheasant crest
Horns	Blue and yellow macaw
Head	Black

The above mixed-wing dressing is Pryce-Tannatt's; Kelson gives a simpler version and says, "This old standard pattern has undergone considerable change and now universally is dressed as above. Formerly the body was made with gold embossed tinsel, which I prefer. I believe it was invented by W. J. Davidson."

Durham Ranger

Tag	Silver tinsel
Tail	Golden pheasant crest
Butt	Black ostrich herl
Body	In equal sections: lemon floss, orange, fiery brown, and black seal's fur
Ribbing	Flat silver tinsel and twist
Hackle	A badger hackle dyed yellow
Throat	A light blue hackle
Wing	A pair of jungle cock feathers, back to back covered for three-quarters of their length by two pairs of tippets, back to back
Sides	Jungle cock
Cheeks	Blue chatterer
Topping	Golden pheasant crest
Horns	Blue and yellow macaw

For the *Black Ranger,* the butt, ribbing, wing, sides, cheeks, topping, and horns are identical to those of the *Durham Ranger,* but the following differ:

Tag	Silver thread and lemon floss
Tail	Golden pheasant crest and Indian crow
Body	Black floss
Hackle	A black hackle
Throat	A deep blue hackle

PLATE 93
THE DURHAM RANGER, DRESSED BY SYD GLASSO

James Wright originated the *Black Ranger* although it seems that he did not originate the *Durham Ranger*. Inspired by the *Parson* patterns, other variations of this distinctive whole feather-wing include blue, red, silver, and gold. It is known to have been fished in 1846, thus challenging claims that the *Jock Scott* was the first fly to have jungle cock incorporated in the wing.

Patterns with this type of wing are often dressed incorrectly. The inner bars of the inside tippets should be directly over the butt. The outer bars of the outside tippets should cover the inner bars of the inside tippets. The inner light spots on the two long jungle cock feathers should be visible behind and between the two outer bands of the tippets, and thus the jungle cock will extend from them slightly. The ends of the tippets should be straight rather than curved. This is correct also for other patterns with similar wings, such as the *Lady Amherst*.

Dusty Miller	
Tag	Silver thread or oval silver tinsel and golden yellow floss
Tail	Golden pheasant crest, over which is Indian crow
Butt	Black ostrich herl
Body	Rear two-thirds: embossed silver tinsel. Front third: orange floss
Ribbing	Fine oval silver tinsel
Hackle	A golden olive hackle over the orange floss only (this hackle sometimes is omitted)
Throat	Speckled gallina (guinea hen)
Wing	A pair of black, white-tipped turkey tail strips, back to back; over these, but not entirely hiding them, a mixed sheath of married narrow strips of pintail and barred summer duck; narrow strips of brown mallard over
Cheeks	Jungle cock
Topping	Golden pheasant crest
Horns	Blue and yellow macaw
Head	Black (Pryce-Tannatt)

The *Dusty Miller* is one of the oldest standard built-wing British classics that has endured through the generations. The above is the famous classic dressing; following are two simplified ones.

PLATE 94
THE EVENING STAR

Evening Star

dressed by Larry Borders

Tag	Silver thread and lemon floss
Tail	Golden pheasant crest
Body	Black seal's fur (picked out toward the shoulder)
Hackle	A black hackle
Throat	A deep blue hackle
Wing	Three pairs of jungle cock feathers, back to back, each pair shorter than the preceding
Topping	Four or five golden pheasant crest feathers
Head	Black (Pryce-Tannatt)

Evening Star

dressed by Harry Willcox

Tag	Silver tinsel and yellow floss
Tail	Golden pheasant crest
Butt	Black ostrich herl
Body	Black floss, not built up
Ribbing	Oval silver tinsel, with a black cock hackle palmered between the ribbing of the front half
Throat	Dark blue hackle
Wing	Four jungle cock feathers, the inside pair extending to the end of the tail, the outside pair somewhat shorter to expose the eyes of the inside pair
Topping	Golden pheasant crest
Head	Black

This is an old standard British pattern sent to me by the famous English fly dresser Harry Willcox, of Alnwick, England.

PLATE 95
THE EVENING STAR

dressed by Mark Waslick

Tag	Silver twist and tippet-colored silk
Tail	Golden pheasant crest
Butt	Black ostrich herl, at each section
Body	Four equal sections: the first three of silver tinsel, with two jungle cock above and below each; the fourth of blue rock-colored silk
Ribbing	Silver tinsel, on the last section only
Throat	Two jungle cock, as before. These feathers slightly increase in length from the opposite end of the body
Wing	Four Lady Amherst pheasant tippets, back to back
Cheeks	Summer duck followed by two Indian crow feathers
Topping	Golden pheasant crest
Horns	Red macaw
Head	Black ostrich herl (Traherne)

Although Hale attributes the *Evening Star* to Kelson in his first edition (1892), credit belongs to the supremely talented and somewhat obscure John Popkin Traherne. This beautiful pattern with its four graduated veilings of jungle cock above and below is entirely different from Pryce-Tannatt's dressing, which calls for three graduated pairs of jungle cock in the wing and several toppings. As is evident in Plates 94 and 95, both patterns are worthy gems for any collection.

Dusty Miller (Reduced)

Tag	Fine embossed silver tinsel
Tail	Golden pheasant crest
Body	Rear two-thirds: embossed silver tinsel. Front third: pink floss
Ribbing	Fine oval silver tinsel
Throat	A very small and short bunch of gray guinea hen fibers, tied under the hook
Wing	Fairly narrow strips of bronze mallard, extending to the end of the tail
Cheeks	Jungle cock, very small
Head	Black

This adaptation is the work of famous angler and fly dresser Harry A. Darbee, of Livingston Manor, New York. It was developed in 1950 and since then has been used on rivers in Nova Scotia, Labrador, Newfoundland, and elsewhere. This is a sparse dressing on a light-wire (Wilson dry-fly) hook, but the pattern also is dressed in regular and low-water styles. It has been very successful also on 1/0 hooks and larger.

A hairwing conversion of the *Dusty Miller* (such as shown in Plate 46) can be made by substituting hair for feathers. The components are the same as in

PLATE 96
THE FLOODTIDE, DRESSED BY SYD GLASSO

Tag	Fine oval silver tinsel and crimson silk
Tail	Golden pheasant crest and summer duck
Butt	Black ostrich herl
Body	Canary, yellow, dark orange, and crimson seal's fur
Ribbing	Silver tinsel and silver lace
Hackle	Yellow eagle (marabou), from dark orange
Throat	Two turns of gallina, dyed crimson
Wing	Two golden pheasant sword, back to back and enveloping two extended jungle cock, back to back; bustard, Lady Amherst pheasant tail, and swan, dyed yellow and crimson

Topping	Golden pheasant crest
Sides	Jungle cock
Cheeks	Jungle cock points
Head	Black

Aptly named, the *Floodtide* was designed and recommended to be fished at the highest tidal level of water. This late-nineteenth-century Kelson pattern is unusual with its combination of whole feathers, mixed sides, and cheeks of jungle cock.

the classic dressing from the tag through the throat. The wing has an underwing of gray squirrel followed by monga ringtail, dyed yellow, scarlet, and orange. Over this is European red squirrel, and on each side is gray squirrel. The fly is finished with jungle cock cheeks and a topping. Hairwing conversions and adaptations of any of the classics can be made at the tier's discretion.

PLATE 97
BRITISH CLASSICS
DRESSED BY SYD GLASSO

Jock Scott

Golden Parson

Purple Emperor

Pitcroy's Fancy

Queen of Spring

Turnbull's Sir Richard

Fenian

Fiery Brown

Tag	Silver thread and golden yellow floss
Tail	Golden pheasant crest and tippet in strands
Body	First quarter: bright orange seal's fur. Second quarter: light blue seal's fur. Remainder: fiery brown seal's fur
Throat	Jay
Wing	Mixed: tippet in strands; married strands of scarlet, blue, yellow, and orange swan, florican, bustard, golden pheasant tail; married narrow strips of teal (or pintail) and barred summer duck; strips (rather broad) of brown mallard over
Head	Black herl

The *Fiery Brown,* originated by Michael Rogan in Ballyshannon, Donegal, is a nineteenth-century Irish classic. Rogan was a master at dying feathers and dressed this fly to emulate autumn colors. The *Fiery Brown* has several variations, depending on the materials the gillie or fly dresser happened to have on hand. All, however, feature the fiery brown coloration. Some of the dressings are quite complex, including the above pattern from Pryce-Tannatt. Kelson's description (1895) differs slightly from other patterns, with a tag of light orange silk, body of fiery brown seal's fur, and head finished with black herl (other elements are the same).

Fenian

Tag	Silver tinsel
Tail	Golden pheasant crest
Body	First quarter: bright orange seal's fur. Remainder: bright green seal's fur
Ribbing	Oval gold tinsel
Hackle	A golden olive hackle over the green seal's fur
Throat	Jay
Wing	Mixed: tippet in strands; married strands of green, yellow, and orange swan, florican and golden pheasant tail, married narrow strips of pintail and barred summer duck; brown mallard strips over
Head	Black ostrich herl

Gardener

Tag	Gold thread and crimson floss
Tail	Golden pheasant crest and tippet in strands
Body	In three equal sections: yellow, green, and dark blue seal's fur, dressed thin and well picked out
Ribbing	Flat silver tinsel and twist
Hackle	Pale orange hackle
Throat	Black heron (or substitute)
Wing	A pair of cinnamon turkey tail strips, set flat
Cheeks	Jungle cock, drooping

One of the lesser known but lovely Dee strip-wing patterns, the *Gardener* is attributed to Dee angler W. Garden, who is also credited with the *Glentana* and *Balmoral.* The above pattern is from Pryce-Tannatt and varies slightly from Kelson's pattern.

PLATE 98
SPEY FLIES

Green King
dressed by T. E. Pryce-Tannatt

Miss Grant
dressed by Syd Glasso

Glen Grant
dressed by John Olschewsky

Red King
dressed by Syd Glasso

Gold Riach
dressed by Bob Veverka

Garry (or Yellow Dog)

Tag	Fine oval silver tinsel
Tail	Golden pheasant crest and tipped in strands
Butt	Black ostrich herl (optional)
Body	Black floss, with a black hackle palmered the forward two-thirds of the body, tied in at the tip
Ribbing	Oval silver tinsel
Throat	Guinea hackle, dyed blue
Wing	Yellow goat hair or bucktail, with a few strands of red hair underneath
Cheeks	Jungle cock often is used, but the pattern doesn't call for it
Head	Black

In John Veniard's excellent book, *Fly Dressers' Guide,* he says that the *Garry* was originated by the late John Wright, son of the noted fly tier James Wright of Sprouston, near Kelso-on-Tweed, in the mid-nineteenth century. It was named for the local minister's dog, a golden retriever, which happened to walk into the shop when some black-bodied flies were being tied. A few hairs were cut from its tail, and the result was the original of this pattern. The minister caught many fine salmon with it, and it became a firm favorite of Tweed fishermen, eventually becoming popular everywhere. Golden yellow floss was later added to the tag as an embellishment to the original pattern.

General Summer

Tag	Gold twist and gold silk	
Tail	Golden pheasant crest	
Body	Claret seal's fur	
Ribbing	Oval gold tinsel	
Hackle	Claret, from the second turn	
Throat	Jay	
Wing	Mallard	
Horns	Blue macaw	(Kelson)

PLATE 99
THE GREEN HIGHLANDER

Classic
dressed by Megan Boyd

Classic (antique)

Classic
dressed by Mike McCoy

Classic
dressed by Mark Waslick

Classic
dressed by Belarmino Martinez

Floss Wing
dressed by Bob Warren

Hairwing Conversion
dressed by Bob Warren

Reduced
dressed by Harry Darbee

Polar Bear
dressed by Bill Wilbur

Hairwing
dressed by Carmelle Bigaouette

Badger Hair
dressed by Jedde Waterman

Waddington
dressed by Bob Veverka

Hackle-wing
dressed by Al Bovyn

Tube
dressed by Bill Wilbur

Glen Grant

Tail	Golden pheasant yellow rump (point)
Body	Three turns of yellow wool and black wool
Ribbing	Silver lace and silver tinsel
Hackle	A black Spey cock hackle, from the end of body, but wound from root the reverse way, crossing over ribbing
Throat	Teal
Wing	Two long jungle cock, back to back, two reaching halfway and two still shorter, and teal
Head	Yellow wool (Kelson)

Kelson describes this fly as "an old standard on the Spey."

Gold Riach

Body	Three turns of orange Berlin wool
Ribbing	From different starting points, of narrow gold tinsel, gold twist, and silver twist, wound toward the head (in reverse), placed an equal distance apart
Hackle	A red Spey cock, from end of body, wound from the root feather instead of from the point, and crossing over the ribbing the entire way
Throat	Two turns of teal
Wing	Two short strips of mallard with brown mottled points and gray mottled roots (Kelson)

In 1872, A. E. Knox's *Autumns on the Spey* was published, contributing eighteen Spey patterns, some of which have stood the test of time. The *Gold Riach* is among these, along with the *Silver Riach, Gold-Green Riach, Silver-Green Riach, Gold-Green Fly, Silver-Green Fly, Gold Speal, Silver Speal, Green King,*

Purple King, Black King Culdrain Fly, Black Heron, Gold Heron, and *Carron.*

These flies all have bodies of Berlin wool, flowing cock or heron hackles, close-set downward-curved wings of mallard, and the fancy ribbings peculiar to so many of the Spey patterns. Confusion exists between the *Reeach* series of flies presented by Knox in 1872 and the *Riach* series later presented by Kelson. Although Kelson attributes the *Gold Riach* to a gentleman by the name of Riach, the difference may simply be a spelling error.

The *Golden Butterfly*, although certainly not the first, is perhaps the most famous of the so-called "gaudy" flies that evolved gradually but blossomed out early in the nineteenth century. Considered the progenitor of the *Parson* series, the first *Golden Butterfly* with a reversed topping wing was originated by Pat McKay. It is one of a group of Irish flies that John Younger described in *River Angling* (1840) as "made like butterflies, of parrot, golden pheasant and other bright fancy feathers." He stated that they were known in Scotland thirty years previously, about 1810.

Later John Traherne devised a far more complicated pattern of the same name (a variation of which is called the *Tippetiwitchet*) that appeared in Kelson's book.

Golden Eagle

Tag	Gold twist and gold floss
Tail	Tippet in strands
Butt	Black ostrich herl
Body	Equal parts of gold and fiery brown pig's wool
Ribbing	Gold tinsel
Hackle	Eagle hackle (substitute), dyed gold
Wings	Two strips of silver mottled turkey
Head	Black

Golden Parson

Tag	Silver tinsel and mauve floss
Tail	Two golden pheasant crest feathers, a few sprigs of tippet, and a kingfisher
Body	Two turns of golden floss silk, then golden pig's wool, merging into orange
Ribbing	Silver twist
Hackle	Golden orange hackle over the wool, red orange hackle over that, and two, three, or more short toppings tied in at the breast, instead of a throat
Wing	A tippet feather with a cock-of-the-rock (not the squared feather) on either side, and one above; strips of pintail or wood duck on either side, and as many toppings as you can pile on—seven or eight, or more if you like. These are often tied on with the turn bent inward at the Ballyshannon, and it gives them more play in the water
Cheeks	Kingfisher feathers on either cheek
Horns	Blue macaw (Francis)

Sometimes called the *Yellow* or *Orange Parson,* the above pattern is from Francis Francis. In describing the fly, he said, "This, however, is decidedly a topping parson, a sort of bishop or archbishop parson, in fact, and not for every day use; we only bring him out when the feelings of the salmon, having resisted all ordinary persuasiveness, require to be very strongly appealed to." Francis gives several changes and substitutions in the dressings of the *Parsons,* indicating that many were considered types of flies rather than specific patterns.

The *Parson* series of flies originated on the Erne, which was an ideal river for big salmon, with all sorts of limpid or challenging stretches, before being ruined by a hydroelectric dam. It lives on as a salmon river, however, in the beautiful *Parson* flies. Although correspondence tells us that others preceded it, the first *Parson* is generally credited to Pat McKay. This fly was dressed with its toppings on edge, sticking out at the sides like a butterfly with cock-of-the-rock tied in the same way. The fly was evidently passed on to a reverend, who aptly dubbed it the *Parson.*

Green Highlander

Tag	Fine oval silver tinsel and yellow floss
Tail	Golden pheasant crest, over which is barred summer duck
Butt	Black ostrich herl
Body	Rear quarter: yellow floss. Remainder: green seal's fur or floss
Ribbing	Oval silver tinsel
Hackle	A green hackle palmered over green part of body
Throat	Yellow hackle
Wing	Golden pheasant tippets, back to back; outside of this are married strips of yellow, orange, and green swan, florican, peacock wing and golden pheasant tail, with married narrow strips of teal and barred summer duck at the sides; over this are two slips of bronze mallard
Sides	Jungle cock
Cheeks	Indian crow
Topping	Golden pheasant crest
Horns	Blue and yellow macaw
Head	Black

This is one of the most famous of the British classic patterns and one of the few that are primarily green. It is still very popular throughout the world and has been adapted to the various forms and styles of flies that have evolved since its origin. Reduced, hairwing, and other versions follow. The fly was designed by a Mr. Grant, of Wester Elchies on Speyside in the late 1800s. Francis Francis's 1867 book presents a midcentury forerunner to this pattern called the *Highlander.*

When green is mentioned in the dressing, it should be the special shade now known as *Green Highlander* green, which is a very bright grass green color. This popular, successful and famous pattern is mentioned in many of the British classics, Kelson, Hardy, and Hale again differing from Pryce-Tannatt.

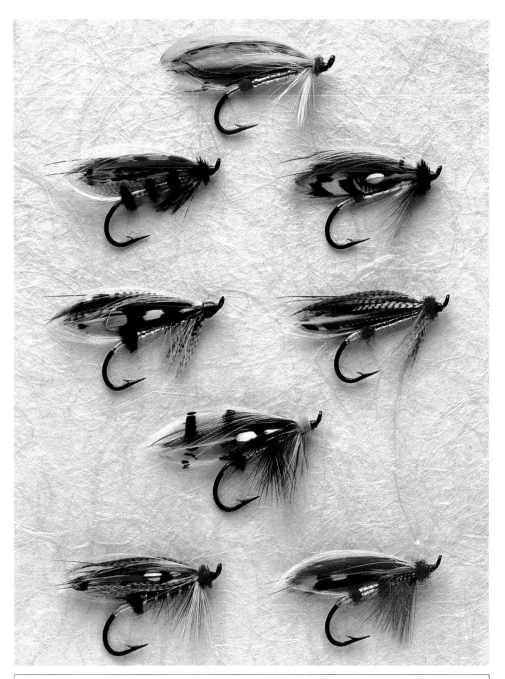

PLATE 100
SALMON FLIES DRESSED BY HELEN SHAW

Helmsdale Doctor

Popham   *Wilkinson*

Silver Grey   *Silver Doctor*

Rosy Dawn

Kate   *Red Sandy*

Green Highlander (Reduced)

Tag	Very fine oval silver tinsel or silver wire
Tail	Golden pheasant crest
Body	Rear half: golden yellow silk floss. Front half: bright green spun fur, all thinly dressed
Ribbing	Very fine oval silver tinsel or silver wire
Throat	About two turns of a bright yellow hackle, applied as a collar and pulled down, the longest fibers extending nearly to the point of the barb
Wing	Strips of brown speckled turkey wing, of moderate width, extending to the tip of the tail
Shoulders	Jungle cock, medium size and length
Head	Black

This simplified adaptation of the classic pattern is by Harry A. Darbee, of Livingston Manor, New York. It is a special dressing on a light-wire (Wilson dry-fly) hook and is often used as a "riffling" fly. It is also tied in regular and low-water dressings.

Green Highlander (Hairwing)

Tag	Fine silver tinsel and yellow floss
Tail	Golden pheasant crest and barred summer duck
Butt	Black ostrich herl
Body	First quarter: yellow floss, followed by green floss
Ribbing	Oval silver tinsel over both sections
Hackle	A green hackle of same shade as the forward part of the body, palmered over front two-thirds of body only
Wing	A very small bunch of golden pheasant tippet fibers, over which is a small bunch of medium to light colored deer tail hairs, or sparse green and yellow bucktail, mixed
Throat	Yellow hackle
Cheeks	Jungle cock
Head	Black

This is a hairwing version of the classic British featherwing pattern. It is dressed with whatever combinations the dresser considers will best imitate the featherwing, of which two favorites are given above. This hairwing version is an international favorite, used extensively in North America and especially in the Matapedia-Restigouche area of Quebec. A bright fly such as this usually is very effective on bright, sunny days.

When dressing very small sizes, the green palmered hackle in the body can be omitted because it could make the fly look too bulky.

Green King

Body	Green Berlin wool	
Ribbing	Flat gold and silver tinsels and gold thread	
Throat	Wigeon	
Wing	Brown mallard strips, short	(Pryce-Tannatt)

PLATE 101
ANTIQUE JOCK SCOTTS

Grey Eagle

Tag	Silver twist	
Tail	Red breast feather of a golden pheasant	
Body	Yellow, light blue, and scarlet seal's fur	
Ribbing	Silver lace and silver tinsel	
Hackle	Gray eagle (substitute), from blue fur	
Throat	Wigeon (teal for large patterns)	
Wing	Two strips of brown mottled turkey, with black bars and white points	(Kelson)

Grey Heron

Body	Rear third: lemon Berlin wool. Front two-thirds: black Berlin wool
Ribbing	Flat silver tinsel, oval silver tinsel, and fine oval gold tinsel
Hackle	A gray heron hackle, doubled, tied in at the point and wound forward from the rear of the body between the flat silver tinsel and the oval silver tinsel, with the oval gold tinsel wound in an opposite direction between the fibers, one turn of the tinsel covering each turn of the hackle
Throat	Speckled gray gallina (guinea fowl)
Wing	On each side, narrow brown mallard strips (showing brown points and light roots) set low and tied on points down, extending to the bend of the hook
Head	Black

First presented by A. E. Knox in 1850, the *Grey Heron* is the oldest of the regal Spey classics, which include *Lady Caroline, Carron, Black King,* and *Gold Riach,* among others. These patterns are distinguished by long, flowing hackles, which offer the "something different" often needed when salmon are off the take. The three ribbings provide a very attractive body, particularly when set off by the long hackles.

Hairy Mary

Tag	Silver flat tinsel
Tail	Golden pheasant crest
Body	Black floss (black wool is sometimes used)
Ribbing	Oval silver tinsel
Throat	A bright blue hackle (*Blue Charm* color)
Wing	Natural brown bucktail with a few fibers of yellow bucktail on top
Head	Black

The above is the original dressing sent to me by Peter Deane. Other dressings specify gold rather than silver tinsel, and some call for reddish brown

fitch tail for the wing. In small sizes, brown barred squirrel tail or calf tail can be substituted. There is also a *Black Hairy Mary,* which is identical except for a black hair wing. In Iceland, the pattern is varied to include gray and orange as well as brown, with a silver ribbing and light blue hackle.

The *Hairy Mary* was originated in the early 1960s by John Reidpath, who had a small fishing tackle shop on Ingles Street, in Inverness. It is one of the first, and probably the best known, of the British hairwings. It is a particular favorite in Iceland and the Scandinavian countries. Irish anglers brought to Iceland their version of it, called the *Irish Hairy Mary*—in my opinion an even better fly. It is the same except that a butt of fluorescent orange floss is added, and the wing is of Irish badger hair. Tag and ribbing usually are silver, but that is a minor matter. If I could have only one pattern for the countries mentioned above, this would be it!

Helmsdale

Tag	Fine oval silver tinsel and orange floss
Tail	Golden pheasant crest and Indian crow
Butt	Black ostrich herl
Body	Rear quarter: yellow floss. Remainder: yellow seal's fur
Ribbing	Flat silver tinsel and silver lace tinsel
Wing	Strips of cinnamon turkey
Cheeks	Indian crow
Topping	Golden pheasant crest
Head	Black

Highland Gem

Tag	Silver twist and yellow silk
Tail	Golden pheasant crest, ibis, and summer duck
Body	In two equal sections: the first half, yellow silk, ribbed with narrow oval silver tinsel and butted with golden bird of paradise or toucan above and below, and black ostrich herl; the second half, blue silk ribbed as before alongside broad, flat silver tinsel
Hackle	Black heron, from the center of the blue silk
Throat	Gallina
Wing	Amherst pheasant strips
Topping	Golden pheasant crest
Horns	Black cockatoo tail
Head	Black (Kelson)

Jeannie

Tag	Silver tinsel
Tail	Golden pheasant crest
Body	Rear third: lemon yellow floss. Front two-thirds: black floss
Ribbing	Oval silver tinsel
Throat	Natural black hackle (sometimes wound on as a collar)
Wing	Two strips of a brown mallard feather, set upright
Cheeks	Jungle cock
Head	Black

PLATE 102
BRITISH CLASSICS
DRESSED BY TED KANTNER

Wilkinson

Kate

The *Jeannie* is internationally popular both as a standard pattern and as a low-water dressing. As with the *Jock Scott,* the enduring popularity of this old pattern may be influenced by the yellow and black body. A wing of black or brown hair (or a combination of these) is used in modern hairwing versions, and the yellow part can be fluorescent.

There are several hairwing patterns where straight black hair (such as black bear hair) is used as a wing instead of the mallard. In the British Isles, this version is called the *Black Bomber,* which is similar to the *Black Maria.* It is the same as North America's *Black Star,* except that the yellow floss is used as a tag and the body is all black floss. With the addition of a few peacock sword fibers mixed into the black hair wing, it would be a simplified version of the popular hairwing *Black Dose.*

Jerram's Fancy

Tag	Silver tinsel
Tail	A section of dark blue floss, as long as the bend of the hook, and cut off
Body	Rear half: scarlet red floss. Front half: black floss
Ribbing	Oval silver tinsel
Throat	Dark blue hackle
Wing	Black hair
Head	Black

This was a favorite of Tom Jerram, a druggist of Turriff, Aberdeenshire, who was known as "a gentleman in business and a true sportsman on the river." He developed the pattern in 1965 for fishing on the Deveron River. The original dressing had a black crow wing, but Jerram later found that the black hair wing was "more deadly." He liked the fly dressed on double hooks in sizes 8 to 12.

A hairwing pattern called the *Watson's Fancy* is almost identical to the *Jerram's Fancy* except that tag and ribbing are gold and the tail is a golden pheasant crest feather. The throat is of black cock's fibers and jungle cock eyes are added.

Jockie

Tag	Silver tinsel
Tail	Golden pheasant crest and Indian crow
Body	First third: golden yellow floss. Remainder: dark claret floss
Ribbing	Oval silver tinsel
Throat	A coch-y-bonddu hackle
Wing	Brown mallard strips, set upright
Cheeks	Jungle cock
Head	Black (Pryce-Tannatt)

Jock O'Dee

Tag	Silver tinsel
Tail	Golden pheasant crest and Indian crow
Body	Two-fifths: lemon floss. Remainder: black floss
Ribbing	Flat silver tinsel and twist
Hackle	Gray heron (or substitute) from the third turn of tinsel
Throat	Wigeon
Wing	A pair of cinnamon turkey tail strips, set flat

This is a Dee strip-wing pattern.

Jock Scott

Pryce-Tannatt's dressing for this famous classic pattern is given at the end of chapter 5, and the steps in applying the many components of the *Jock Scott* are shown in Plate 58. Following is a pattern for a simplified hairwing version:

Tag	Fine oval silver and yellow floss
Tail	Golden pheasant crest and golden pheasant tippet in strands
Butt	Black wool
Body	First half: golden yellow floss, butted with black wool and veiled above and below with toucan (or substitute). Second half: black floss, ribbed with flat silver tinsel and silver twist
Hackle	Black hackle over the black floss only
Throat	Guinea
Wing	Underwing: tippet in strands; over this, yellow, red, and blue badger followed by red squirrel
Cheeks	Kingfisher (or substitute)
Head	Black

The subject of substitutes for feathers that are difficult to obtain or expensive is too complex for the purpose of this book. Note here, however, that dyed ring-necked pheasant is a reasonable substitute for toucan and kingfisher and was used in the hairwing *Jock Scott* shown in Plate 86.

PLATE 103
STEPS IN TYING THE LADY CAROLINE
DRESSED BY BOB VEVERKA

John Campbell

Tag	Silver twist and orange silk
Tail	Golden pheasant crest
Butt	Black ostrich herl
Body	Black silk
Ribbing	Silver lace and silver tinsel
Hackle	Natural black, from the center
Throat	An orange hackle
Wing	Golden pheasant tippet in strands; pintail, florican, light and dark bustard, pheasant tail, swan dyed yellow, and mallard
Topping	Golden pheasant crest
Horns	Blue macaw
Cheeks	Blue chatterer
Head	Black ostrich herl (Kelson)

Judge

Tag	Silver thread and light orange silk floss
Tail	A golden pheasant crest
Butt	Peacock herl
Body	Silver tinsel
Hackle	A golden-olive or yellow-orange cock's hackle (the color is between the two)
Throat	A red-orange hackle with blue jay over
Wing	Mixed: peacock wing and bustard, with a few fibers of golden pheasant tippet
Topping	Two golden pheasant crest feathers
Horns	Blue macaw
Head	Peacock herl (Francis)

Kate

Tag	Silver thread and lemon floss
Tail	Golden pheasant crest and blue chatterer
Butt	Black ostrich herl
Body	Crimson floss
Ribbing	Oval silver tinsel
Hackle	A crimson hackle
Throat	A lemon hackle
Wing	Mixed: golden pheasant tippet in strands, married strands of scarlet and yellow swan, golden pheasant tail, and bustard; married strips of teal and barred summer duck; brown mallard strips over
Sides	Jungle cock and blue chatterer
Topping	Golden pheasant crest
Horns	Blue and yellow macaw
Head	Black (Pryce-Tannatt)

PLATE 104
LESSER-KNOWN BRITISH PATTERNS

1   *Spey Green*

dressed by Belarmino Martinez

Tag	Silver tinsel and golden yellow floss
Tail	Golden pheasant crest and Indian crow
Butt	Black ostrich herl
Body	Green Lurex
Ribbing	Silver embossed tinsel with oval silver and gold
Throat	Black heron
Wing	A pair of tippets, back to back, veiled with married strands of red, green, yellow, and blue goose
Sides	Jungle cock
Topping	Golden pheasant crest
Head	Black

The *Spey Green* is a Freddie Riley pattern, given in the appendix of the 1977 reprint edition of Pryce-Tannatt's book *How to Dress Salmon Flies.*

2   *Beryl*

dressed by Maxwell MacPherson

Tag	Silver twist and yellow silk
Tail	Golden pheasant crest, ibis, and powder blue macaw
Butt	Black ostrich herl
Body	Silver tinsel
Ribbing	Oval silver tinsel
Hackle	Light blue hackle from second turn
Throat	Light orange hackle and wigeon
Wing	Two extended jungle cock, back to back, veiled with wigeon, gallina, bustard, peacock herl, ibis, parrot, mallard, and a topping
Horns	Blue macaw
Cheeks	Chatterer (Kelson)

3   *Dr. Donaldson*

Tag	Silver twist and yellow silk
Tail	Golden pheasant crest, a few strands of tippet and points of toucan
Butt	Black ostrich herl
Body	First section: blue silk, ribbed with fine oval silver tinsel, butted with blue chatterer fibers above and below, and black herl; second section: dark claret silk, ribbed with silver lace and silver tinsel, and a claret hackle along it
Throat	Orange hackle and wigeon
Wing	Two extended jungle cock slightly tinged with Bismark brown, golden pheasant tail, light and dark bustard, swan dyed red and yellow and a topping
Sides	Jungle cock
Horns	Blue macaw (Kelson)

4   *Euphrosyne*

dressed by Larry Borders

Tag	Gold tinsel and orange silk
Tail	Two golden pheasant crest feathers
Body	Bronze peacock
Ribbing	Gold tinsel
Hackle	Claret, closely wound from tail to wing
Wing	Brown Argus pheasant tail, golden pheasant tail and long golden pheasant crest feathers
Sides	Short pieces of silver pheasant tail feather
Head	Green peacock herl (Fitzgibbon)

5   *Bronze Pirate*

dressed by Ted Godfrey

Tag	Silver tinsel
Tail	Toucan
Butt	Black ostrich herl
Body	Silver tinsel ribbed with oval silver tinsel, partially butted in three equal sections with impeyan pheasant cheek feathers, increasing in size
Wings	Impeyan pheasant (doubled, crest) and two toppings
Head	Black ostrich herl (Kelson)

6   *Alexandra*

dressed by William Wilsey

Tail	Scarlet ibis
Body	Flat silver tinsel
Throat	A black or badger hackle
Wing	Peacock sword feather in strips
Cheeks	Jungle cock (Pryce-Tannatt)

7   *Kelly*

Tag	Gold tinsel
Tail	Ibis
Body	Brown seal's fur
Hackle	Dark red hackle
Throat	Dark red hackle
Wing	Bronze peacock sword and tail feathers
Horns	Red macaw
Head	Black (Hardy)

8   *Lemon and Grey*

dressed by William Byrnes

Tag	Silver thread and golden yellow floss
Tail	Golden pheasant crest and Indian crow
Butt	Black ostrich herl
Body	Gray seal's fur (or gray squirrel or silver monkey)
Ribbing	Oval silver tinsel
Hackle	Grizzly hackle
Throat	Lemon hackle
Wing	Mixed: tippet in strands; married strands of green, yellow, and orange swan, bustard, glorican, golden pheasant tail; married narrow strands of teal and barred summer duck; brown mallard strips over
Head	Black ostrich herl (Pryce-Tannatt)

9   *Silver Ardea*

Tag	Silver twist and yellow silk
Tail	Golden bird of paradise
Body	Silver tinsel
Hackle	Bright red-claret (a white coch-y-bonddu, dyed)
Throat	White heron, dyed light blue
Wing	Mixed: peacock wing, bustard, golden pheasant tail, Amherst pheasant tail, black, and white mottled turkey, red macaw, swan dyed yellow and blue and a topping
Sides	Jungle cock
Head	Black herl (Kelson)

1	2
3	4
5	6
7	8
	9

Lady Caroline

Tail	A very small bunch of red-brown golden pheasant breast feather fibers
Body	Olive-green and light brown Berlin wool wound together in the proportion of two brown to one olive-green
Ribbing	Flat gold tinsel, oval silver tinsel, and fine oval gold tinsel
Hackle	A gray heron hackle tied in at the point and wound forward from the rear of the body between the flat gold and the oval silver tinsel, with the fine oval gold tinsel wound in an opposite direction between the fibers, one turn of the tinsel covering each turn of the hackle
Throat	Two turns of a red-brown golden pheasant breast feather
Wing	On each side, brown mallard strips (showing brown points and light roots), set low and extending to the bend of the hook, tied on points down
Head	Black

Spey flies, originally designed for use in the fast currents of the Spey River, are tied on light-wire (low-water) hooks, which are one size longer in the shank than ordinary salmon hooks. Flies of this type have thin, drab woolen bodies palmered with very long, flowing, doubled heron hackles (or other extremely long-fibered rump feathers) and nearly horizontal slim mallard wings. The *Lady Caroline,* the oldest and most recognized of the Spey-type flies, was famous before the days of Kelson (1895) and is still popular on fast rivers in Europe as well as (more recently) in North America.

Little Inky Boy

Tag	Two turns of silver tinsel
Tail	Golden pheasant crest
Butt	Three turns of scarlet ostrich herl
Body	Black monofilament, closely coiled
Hackle	Badger dyed yellow, at throat only
Wing	Swan dyed yellow, or goose, with wood duck partially covering
Topping	Golden pheasant crest
Head	Black

The famous Catskill fly dresser Harry Darbee says in his excellent book *Catskill Fly Tyer:* "This is a modern variation of a hundred-year-old salmon pattern that was tied with black horse-hair. We substituted dyed monofilament, which is not as tractable but is stronger than hell. When tying the Little Inky Boy, flatten the tip of the monofilament with pliers and tie it in by the flat tip after you have tied in the tag and the tail. Get the monofilament really tight. Then wind the [tying] thread all the way to the shoulder very tightly. Then put a little cement all

PLATE 105
THE LORD MAYOR OF LONDON
ORIGINATED AND DRESSED BY
MEGAN BOYD

Tag	Oval silver tinsel and ruby floss
Tail	Golden pheasant crest veiled with slips of yellow, red, and blue goose; guinea in strands
Butt	Black ostrich herl
Body	In four sections: golden yellow floss followed by golden yellow seal's fur, scarlet seal's fur and blue seal's fur
Ribbing	Flat silver tinsel and silver lace
Hackle	Badger, dyed red
Throat	Red hackle and teal
Wing	Bucktail in three sections: one-quarter, orange; one-quarter, red; and one-half, yellow
Topping	Three golden pheasant crests, over
Head	Black

The *Lord Mayor of London* was designed by Megan Boyd of Brora, Scotland. It is now part of the Cushner Collection, which is housed at the American Museum of Fly Fishing.

along this foundation; bring the monofilament around in touching coils on top of the wet cement to the shoulder, and tie it down. Tie the hackle on and set on your wings and topping, and you've got a salmon fly."

In *Atlantic Salmon Fishing* (1937), Charles Phair says, "The Inky Boy has a body wound with gut dyed black and with very thin wings." The dressing can be found in some of the old British classics.

Logie

There are several somewhat similar dressings for this famous pattern. One of the earliest (1895) is from Kelson, as follows:

Tag	Silver tinsel
Tail	Golden pheasant crest
Body	Dark claret floss
Ribbing	Oval silver tinsel
Throat	Light blue hackle fibers
Wing	Two strips of swan, dyed yellow, set upright and slightly covered by broad strips of brown mallard
Cheeks	Jungle cock
Head	Black

Pryce-Tannatt's dressing is essentially the same except for the body. The first two-fifths of the body is pale primrose (light yellow) floss; the remainder is ruby red floss. His dressing does not call for jungle cock cheeks. Veniard agrees with Pryce-Tannatt. Leonard's dressing is the same as Kelson's except that he adds a tag of orange floss, calls the body "brown-red," and dresses the wing with brown (bronze) mal-

lard, without the yellow swan strips. He does not include the jungle cock cheeks.

Of the three, I like Kelson's dressing best, and it probably is the most authentic. It would make a good hairwing pattern if a small bunch of yellow under dark brown hair should replace the feathered wing. Kelson says that his dressing is "an excellent summer pattern in dull weather on the Dee. It is dressed on small double hooks."

Lord Migdale

Tag	Oval silver tinsel and scarlet floss
Tail	Golden pheasant crest and slips of barred wood duck
Butt	Black ostrich herl
Body	Golden yellow floss
Ribbing	Scarlet floss edged with light blue floss on each side
Throat	Light blue hackle followed by scarlet followed by golden yellow hackle
Wing	Married slips of golden pheasant tail; red, yellow, and blue swan; and Lady Amherst pheasant tail
Cheeks	Jungle cock
Topping	Golden pheasant crest
Horns	Red and blue macaw
Head	Black

March Brown

Tag	Round gold tinsel
Tail	Golden pheasant crest
Body	Fur from a hare's face, spun on and well picked out
Ribbing	Oval gold tinsel
Throat	Partridge (from the back for small sizes; from the rump for larger sizes)
Wing	Strips from a hen pheasant tail
Head	Black

A favorite of A. H. E. Wood, this early nineteenth-century simple strip-wing pattern has maintained its popularity through the generations. Some think it is reminiscent of the dun fly recommended for March in the Treatise Flies mentioned in chapter 4.

Veniard's dressing is the same as above except that silver tinsel is used instead of gold. This salmon fly pattern is adapted from the trout fly pattern, which is dressed as a dry fly, as a standard wet fly, and as a low-water pattern. There is a dry-fly hairwing version with barred brown squirrel tail as a wing. In this one, the throat is brown and grizzly cock, mixed (or cree hackle, which has brown, black, and white bars). This could be tied *Wulff* fashion, and it also is tied as a wet fly. In all its variations, the *March Brown* is a popular salmon fly pattern on many rivers.

Mar Lodge

Tag	Silver twist	
Tail	Golden pheasant crest and a pair of jungle cock feathers, back to back	
Butt	Black ostrich herl	
Body	Wide silver tinsel, jointed at the middle with two or three turns of black floss	
Ribbing	Narrow oval tinsel	
Throat	Speckled gallina	
Wing	Mixed: golden pheasant tippet in strands; married strands of white swan, bustard, florican, cinnamon, mottled gray, and mottled brown turkey tail, and golden pheasant tail	
Sides	Broad strips of barred summer duck	
Cheeks	Jungle cock	
Topping	Golden pheasant crest	
Horns	Blue and yellow macaw	
Head	Black	(Pryce-Tannatt)

Member

Tag	Silver twist and yellow silk	
Tail	Golden pheasant crest	
Butt	Black ostrich herl	
Body	Chocolate silk	
Ribbing	Silver tinsel	
Hackle	Light orange hackle, one-fourth of body	
Wing	Golden pheasant tippet, golden pheasant tail, and pintail	
Topping	Golden pheasant crest	
Sides	Jungle cock	
Collar	Light orange hackle	
Head	Black	(Kelson)

Miss Grant

Tag	Silver twist	
Tail	Teal, in strands	
Body	Two turns of orange silk followed by olive green Berlin wool	
Ribbing	Silver tinsel	
Hackle	Gray heron, from the second turn	
Wing	Two strips of golden pheasant tail	(Kelson)

Kelson described the *Miss Grant* as "a modern Spey pattern."

Munro Killer

Tag	Oval gold tinsel
Tail	None
Body	Black floss, slim
Ribbing	Oval gold tinsel
Throat	Orange hackle and blue guinea fowl
Wing	Yellow bucktail over which is black bucktail, very sparse. (Bronze peacock is sometimes added over the wing.)

Jimmy Younger

PLATE 106
MISS MEGAN BOYD, ORIGINATED
AND DRESSED BY JIMMY YOUNGER

Tag	Oval silver tinsel and blue floss
Tail	Golden pheasant crest and blue hackle tip
Butt	Black ostrich herl
Body	One-third yellow seal's fur; two-thirds blue
Ribbing	Oval silver tinsel
Hackle	Blue cock hackle over blue seal's fur
Wing	Golden pheasant tippets, married strips of yellow and blue goose, bustard or brown turkey and bronze mallard
Cheeks	Jungle cock
Topping	Golden pheasant crest
Head	Black

Both dressings and spellings for the *Munro Killer* vary. Some dressings call for a double ribbing of fine oval gold tinsel and orange rather than yellow bucktail in the wing. It is generally attributed to J. A. J. Munro, who operated a tackle shop in Aberlouor on the Spey River in Scotland. Gaining popularity in the early 1980s, the *Munro Killer* (although I dislike that word when applied to salmon) is similar to Joe Hubert's *Black Sheep,* so named because it is the only nonclassic he uses.

Another pattern quite similar to the *Munro Killer* is the *Thunder Stoat,* which is usually dressed with a shorter wing, a tail of golden pheasant crest, and a bright orange throat. Yet another variation has a gold tag and ribbing, a short and spare throat of orange hackle, and a wing of red squirrel instead of black.

These patterns can be considered interchangeable and are an extension of the *Thunder and Lightning* simplifications.

Moonlight	
Tag	Silver tinsel
Tail	Golden pheasant crest and a pair of jungle cock feathers, back to back
Body	In two equal parts: the first half, silver tinsel, veiled above and below with one or two pairs of blue chatterer feathers, back to back; the second half, black floss
Ribbing	Fine oval silver tinsel over flat silver tinsel; broader oval gold tinsel over black floss
Hackle	Black heron (or substitute) over black floss
Throat	Speckled gallina
Wing	A pair of cinnamon turkey tail strips, set flat

Above is Pryce-Tannatt's dressing for this lovely classic Dee pattern. Evidently it is not as old as the *Tri-color* also given in Pryce-Tannatt, but it should be noted for its distinctive composition.

Musker's Fancy (No. 1)

Tag	Silver tinsel
Tail	Golden pheasant crest
Body	Fairly thin. Rear third: black floss. Middle third: red floss. Front third: oval silver tinsel
Ribbing	Oval or round silver tinsel
Throat	Light blue hackle, extending nearly to the point of the barb
Wing	Teal and mallard, mixed
Cheeks	Jungle cock
Head	Black

The *Musker's Fancy* was originated in 1943 by Frederick Hill, the English author of *Salmon Fishing—The Greased Line on Dee, Don and Earn,* and was named by him in honor of his employer, Capt. H. T. Musker. It was made to represent a combination of the *Blue Charm, Logie,* and *Silver Blue.* In the British Isles, it is favored especially for the greased-line method of fishing.

There are two other variations of this fly, also by Hill. *Musker's Fancy,* No. 2, is the same as above except that black hackle is used instead of blue, and there is no jungle cock. For *Musker's Fancy,* No. 3, brown hackle is used instead of blue (with jungle cock).

In North America, this fly is dressed as a hairwing using red-phase squirrel (dark in color). The No. 1 version then is called *Cole's Modified Musker.*

Old Charlie

Tag	Flat gold tinsel
Tail	Golden pheasant crest
Body	Claret floss
Ribbing	Wide oval gold tinsel
Throat	Hot orange cock's hackle
Wing	Natural brown bucktail, with black tips, if possible
Cheeks	Jungle cock
Head	Red

This simple and successful hairwing pattern was devised by Douglas Pilkington, of Stow-on-the-Wold, in 1954. In writing of its origin to author and professional fly tier Peter Deane of Sussex, England, he said: "In 1954 I had the good fortune to be one of a party of five rods . . . who fished the Lower Oykel in May and we had a superb time. We broke the existing record for the river (203 fish in a fortnight, best day 38 fish: the best being 21 lbs, very fresh, which luckily took my fly). . . . The fishing was then owned by Lady Ross . . . When Lady Ross heard of our good fortune she left a bottle of whisky for us on the hall table . . . especially distilled for Sir Charles Ross of Balnagowan. There was at that time

a brand of whisky called 'Old Angus'—perhaps there still is. I christened our bottle 'Old Charlie.' It was powerful stuff and when my cousin flung the dregs of his glass into the fire, he nearly blew the place up. I decided to make a fly to celebrate our success and call it 'Old Charlie.'

"The dressing of this fly has an alcoholic theme as follows: Tail: Golden pheasant topping (Chateau Youem); Body: Wine-coloured floss silk (Taylor's #27 port); Ribbing: Gold tinsel (Veuve Cliquot Champagne); Hackle: Dyed orange cock hackle (Apricot Brandy); Wing: Deer hair (Grand Marnier); Sides: Jungle cock (Black & White Whisky); Head: Scarlet sealing wax (Pedlar Sloe Gin)."

Veniard says that this is a first-class, all-around hairwing salmon fly. It is equally good as a low-water fly, used on the Spey and many other rivers.

PLATE 107
THE POPHAM
DRESSED BY SYD GLASSO

Orange Parson

Tag	Silver thread and lilac floss	
Tail	Golden pheasant crest and tippet in strands	
Body	Orange floss, orange, scarlet, and fiery brown seal's fur in equal sections, picked out	
Hackle	A lemon hackle	
Throat	Cock-of-the-rock	
Wing	A pair of tippets, back to back and veiled with cock-of-the-rock	
Sides	Barred summer duck strips	
Cheeks	Blue chatterer	
Topping	Golden pheasant crest	
Horns	Blue and yellow macaw	
Head	Black	(Pryce-Tannatt)

Parson

Tag	Gold tinsel and light orange floss	
Tail	Golden pheasant crest and chatterer	
Butt	Black ostrich herl	
Body	Bright claret floss	
Ribbing	Gold tinsel	
Hackle	Bright claret	
Throat	Blue hackle	
Wing	Tippet in strands, married slips of dark turkey; swan dyed yellow, red, and blue; peacock wing; speckled bustard; golden pheasant tail; bronze mallard	
Sides	Slips of teal and wood duck	
Cheeks	Blue chatterer	
Topping	Golden pheasant crest	
Horns	Blue and yellow macaw	
Head	Black	(Hale)

Pitcroy Fancy

Tag	Silver twist
Tail	Golden pheasant crest and strands of tippet
Butt	Scarlet wool
Body	Silver tinsel
Ribbing	Oval silver tinsel
Hackle	Gray heron (or substitute), from center
Throat	Gallina
Wing	Large strips of tippet, light mottled turkey, pintail and mallard
Topping	Golden pheasant crest
Sides	Jungle cock
Head	Scarlet wool (Kelson)

Kelson commented that the *Pitcroy Fancy* was "a modern Spey standard." He attributed this late-nineteenth-century pattern to Turnbull, along with several other patterns, including *Turnbull's Sir Richard*.

Popham

Tag	Gold twist
Tail	Golden pheasant crest and Indian crow
Butt	Black ostrich herl
Body	In three equal sections: the first, dark red-orange silk, ribbed with fine gold tinsel, butted with Indian crow, above and below, and black ostrich herl; the second, yellow silk, ribbed and butted as before; the third, light blue silk, ribbed with oval silver tinsel, and Indian crow above and below
Throat	Jay
Wing	Golden pheasant tippet and tail, gallina, parrot, light brown mottled turkey, red macaw, bustard, and mallard
Topping	Golden pheasant crest
Cheeks	Blue chatterer
Horns	Blue macaw
Head	Black ostrich herl (Kelson)

Originated by F. L. Popham, this pattern is one of the most complicated, beautifully constructed and noteworthy among the fine company of the great British classics. A challenge at the vise and a fine addition to any collection, the *Popham*, with its veilings of tiny Indian crow feathers, is indeed a gem. Megan Boyd concurs and says that if she had to pick a favorite, the glorious *Popham* would be her choice. I am privileged to have several "lovely wee *Pophams*" that she sent me some time ago, one of which is shown in Plate 20. Another prize is that from the talented hands of Sydney Glasso in Plate 107.

Patterns in the classic references differ and are interesting to compare; the above is from Kelson.

Pot Scrubber

Tag	A few turns of oval silver tinsel
Tail	Golden pheasant crest
Body	Flat copper tinsel
Ribbing	Oval silver tinsel
Throat	Brown hackle
Wing	Gray squirrel tail showing brown, black, and white parts
Head	Black

This hairwing pattern was designed in 1961 by John MacKenzie, a gillie on the River Conon, in Ross-shire, Scotland. It was so named because the original body was made from a copper pot scrubber.

Purple Emperor

Tag	Silver twist and yellow silk
Tail	Tourocou, strands of summer duck and powder blue macaw
Butt	Black ostrich herl
Body	Fine oval silver tinsel with four turns of violet seal's fur at throat
Ribbing	Oval gold tinsel
Hackle	A silver coch-y-bonddu from butt
Throat	A hen pheasant dyed yellow
Wing	Two jungle cock, back to back, wigeon, swan dyed yellow, golden pheasant tail, tourocou, and gray mallard
Topping	Golden pheasant crest
Head	Black

Queen of Spring

Tag	Silver twist and canary silk
Tail	Golden pheasant crest and summer duck
Butt	Black ostrich herl
Body	Silver tinsel and black silk, equally divided
Ribbing	Gold lace and silver tinsel
Hackle	Black, from silver tinsel
Throat	Jay
Wing	Golden pheasant tippet, Amherst pheasant and golden pheasant tail, gray mallard, swan dyed canary yellow, red, and light blue; mallard
Topping	Two golden pheasant crest feathers
Horns	Blue macaw
Sides	Jungle cock
Cheeks	Blue chatterer
Head	Black

Another fly, the *Queen of Autumn,* is the same except that it is dressed with gold twist and gold tinsel. Kelson cited this old pattern as being a favorite of his on most rivers.

PLATE 108
THE RED SANDY (PRYCE-TANNATT), DRESSED BY BOB WARREN

Red Sandy

Tag	Silver thread and golden yellow floss
Tail	Golden pheasant crest, Indian crow and blue chatterer over
Butt	Scarlet Berlin wool
Body	Flat silver tinsel
Ribbing	Fine oval silver tinsel
Hackle	A badger hackle dyed deep orange
Throat	Jay, or speckled gallina dyed blue in the larger sizes
Wing	A pair of white-tipped turkey tail strips, back to back; over these, but not entirely covering them, a mixed sheath of married strands of peacock wing, yellow and scarlet swan, bustard, florican, and golden pheasant tail; two strands of peacock sword feather above; married narrow strips of teal and barred summer duck at the sides; brown mallard over
Sides	Jungle cock
Cheeks	Indian crow with blue chatterer over
Topping	Golden pheasant crest
Horns	Blue and yellow macaw
Head	Scarlet Berlin wool (Pryce-Tannatt)

Red Sandy

Tag	Silver twist
Tail	Golden pheasant crest and Indian crow
Butt	Scarlet wool
Body	In two sections of oval silver twist; the first section is butted with Indian crow and scarlet wool
Hackle	Scarlet, along the second section
Wing	Indian crow: four double feathers overlapping each other and enveloping extended jungle cock, back to back
Topping	Golden pheasant crest
Horns	Red macaw
Head	Scarlet wool (Kelson)

These are two dramatically different patterns for two flies of the same name. Kelson's pattern is of an unusual whole featherwing construction using four double sections of Indian crow and jungle cock, back to back. Pryce-Tannatt's dressing is mixed-wing in style, and the wing is similar to that of the *Jock Scott* except that the blue swan is omitted and blue chatterer is added to the cheek.

Ray Mead

Tag	Silver twist and light blue silk
Tail	Golden pheasant crest, ibis, and summer duck
Butt	Black ostrich herl
Body	One-quarter of yellow silk, followed by oval silver tinsel
Ribbing	Oval gold tinsel
Hackle	Large Irish gray from oval tinsel
Throat	Three turns of teal
Wing	Alternate married narrow strips of swan dyed yellow and black and summer duck
Topping	Golden pheasant crest
Sides	Jungle cock
Cheeks	Blue chatterer
Horns	Blue macaw
Head	Black

In *The Salmon Fly,* Kelson cited this pattern as "one of my oldest and most successful patterns at the present time (1895)." In its original dressing Kelson evidently used a wing from one of his father's patterns with body section of silver and blue.

Red King

Body	Brick red Berlin wool
Ribbing	Gold from far side, narrow silver tinsel from near side, wound the reverse way an equal distance apart
Hackle	A red Spey cock hackle from end of body, but wound in the usual direction from the root instead of from the point, thus crossing over the ribbing at each turn given
Throat	One turn of teal
Wing	Two strips of mallard, showing brown points and light roots
Head	Black (Kelson)

The *Red King* is another Spey pattern of the *King* series mentioned previously.

Rosy Dawn

Tag	Gold tinsel
Tail	Golden pheasant crest and tippet in strands
Butt	Black ostrich herl
Body	In two equal halves: first half, embossed silver tinsel; second half, oval gold tinsel, butted at joint with a magenta hackle
Throat	A magenta hackle, followed by a pale blue hackle
Wing	A pair of tippets, back to back, veiled with married strands of yellow, blue, and scarlet swan and golden pheasant tail
Sides	Jungle cock
Topping	Two or three golden pheasant crest feathers
Horns	Blue and scarlet macaw
Head	Black

This is Pryce-Tannatt's dressing for a pretty fly with a pretty name. It is of whole featherwing construction and appears to have been developed around the turn of the century.

Silver Blue (or Silver and Blue)

Tag	Silver tinsel (optional)
Tail	Golden pheasant crest
Body	Flat silver tinsel
Ribbing	Fine oval silver tinsel
Throat	Pale blue dyed hackle (Cambridge blue)
Wing	Two strips of barred black and white teal breast feather (sometimes brown mallard is used)
Topping	Golden pheasant crest
Head	Black

The *Silver Blue* is an old British pattern most popular as a low-water fly, the dressing then being very sparse and occupying only the forward half of the long-shanked light-wire hook. As such, it is one of the principal patterns in North America and in the British Isles. It also is tied as a hairwing pattern, using a very small bunch of gray squirrel tail hairs for the wing.

PLATE 110
FEATHERWING PATTERNS AND THEIR HAIRWING CONVERSIONS

Thunder and Lightning, classic
dressed by Keith Fulsher

Thunder and Lightning, hairwing conversion
dressed by Keith Fulsher

Rosy Dawn, classic
dressed by Keith Fulsher

Rosy Dawn, hairwing conversion
dressed by Charlie Krom

Silver Grey

Tag	Silver thread and golden yellow floss
Tail	Golden pheasant crest and barred summer duck, in strands
Butt	Black ostrich herl
Body	Flat silver tinsel
Ribbing	Fine oval silver tinsel
Hackle	A badger hackle
Wing	Mixed: tippet in strands: married strands of white, yellow, and green swan, bustard, florican, and golden pheasant tail; married strips of pintail and barred summer duck; brown mallard strips over
Topping	Golden pheasant crest
Cheeks	Jungle cock
Horns	Blue and yellow macaw
Head	Black (Pryce-Tannatt)

Attributed to James Wright in the mid-nineteenth century, this very traditional British standard is, along with the *Silver Doctor,* perhaps the most popular of the tinsel-bodied patterns. It is consistently recommended by angling authors and is effective both as a featherwing and as a hairwing.

The pattern above is as given by Pryce-Tannatt and, as usual, has a wing construction different from Kelson's.

Sir Charles

Tag	Round silver tinsel
Tail	Golden pheasant crest, over which is a section of Indian crow (or substitute), half as long
Body	Fairly thin, of golden floss
Ribbing	Fine oval silver tinsel
Throat	Pale blue hackle, almost as long as the body
Wing	Several peacock herl tips, over which are two strips of black and white barred teal, of equal length. (Some dressings call for two strands of peacock sword instead of the larger number of herl tips.)
Head	Black

This is the classic standard dressing. The noted British author and angler Frederick Hill gives a variation he likes better. He fishes the above dressing only in bright sunlight and uses the following variation "in all weathers, from May onwards." It is the same in wing and proportions as the above, but with a tag of gold tinsel, tail of golden pheasant crest feather (only), body of olive green floss, ribbing of embossed gold tinsel, and throat of pale navy blue hackle.

PLATE 111
THE SHANNON
DRESSED BY BOB VEVERKA

Tag	Gold tinsel and lemon yellow floss
Tail	Golden pheasant crest, scarlet ibis, and blue macaw
Butt	Black ostrich herl
Body	Silk floss, in four equal sections of pale blue, orange, puce, and pea green and separated by ostrich herl; over this, hackle on each section and of the same color
Ribbing	Gold thread, on each section
Throat	Golden pheasant rump feather
Wing	Two bright yellow macaw feathers with black streak down the center and a strip of dark speckled argus pheasant and strips of tippet on each side
Sides	Two or three slips of ibis
Cheeks	Small feathers of purple lory (a Polynesian parrot)
Horns	Blue macaw
Head	Black
	(Blacker, as per Francis)

Sir Richard

Tag	Silver thread and dark orange floss
Tail	Golden pheasant crest and Indian crow
Butt	Black ostrich herl
Body	Black floss
Ribbing	Flat silver tinsel and twist
Hackle	Black hackle
Throat	Speckled gallina
Wings	Mixed: married strands of scarlet, orange and blue swan, bustard, florican, mottled gray turkey tail, and golden pheasant tail; a short strip of speckled gallina wing over
Cheeks	Blue chatterer
Topping	Golden pheasant crest
Horns	Blue and yellow macaw
Head	Black (Pryce-Tannatt)

Stoat's Tail (or Stoat Tail)

Tag	Fine oval silver tinsel
Tail	Golden pheasant crest
Body	Black floss, not built up
Ribbing	Fine oval silver tinsel
Throat	Stoat's tail or black cock's hackle, tied underneath only, of moderate length
Wing	Black points of a stoat's tail
Head	Black

This is a British pattern with numerous variations, reminiscent of the variety of black-bodied butted hairwings so popular on the Miramichi River. Essentially, it seems to be anything with a black hair wing. Variations may eliminate the tag,

tail, or both; use dark claret floss for the body, since it becomes almost black when wet; wind on a fluorescent thread or fluorescent "Stren" monofilament beside the ribbing, or include it as a tag.

Among other variations of this pattern are the *Silver Stoat's Tail,* dressed with a body and ribbing of silver tinsel, and the *Gold Stoat's Tail,* a gold-ribbed pattern with blue hackle at the throat rather than black. Except for the color of the wing, this fly is very similar to the popular *Hairy Mary.*

The *Stoat's Tail* is another fly with yet another story, which I will pass along here for interest's sake. British author Peter Deane writes: "Some forty years ago an Edinburgh surgeon was operating on the innards of a patient and using, so we are told, some plastic tubing. Being a salmon fisherman, he took a piece of the tubing home, cut it into small lengths and on the end of one of them, attached some hair, as it happened it was the dark end of a stoat's tail. He stuck a leader through it and tied on a small treble which naturally became buried in the end of the hair and so was born the first modern salmon tube fly. Note I say modern as the North American Indians had been using a similar fly for salmon 100 or more years previously, successfully at that.

"From the Stoat's Tail tube came the Stoat's Tail fly on the hook with various types of body and hackles. The paradox is, rarely if ever these days is stoat's tail hair used but black squirrel, natural or dyed."

Sutherland

Tag	Oval silver tinsel
Tail	Golden pheasant crest, over which is Indian crow half as long
Butt	Black ostrich herl
Body	Burnt orange wool
Ribbing	Flat silver tinsel followed by silver twist
Hackle	From the third turn of tinsel, black heron
Wing	Five married strips of speckled bustard and orange swan, alternating and beginning with bustard (three bustard and two orange swan)
Cheeks	Indian crow
Topping	Golden pheasant crest
Head	Black

Sweep

Tag	Oval or silver tinsel
Tail	Golden pheasant crest
Body	Black silk
Ribbing	Fine oval silver tinsel
Throat	Black hackle
Wing	Any black feather, such as crow or dyed goose
Cheeks	Blue kingfisher
Horns	Blue and gold macaw
Head	Black

This is a favorite pattern in Scotland. Correctly dressed, the throat is of a Spey cock's hackle obtained from the lateral tail feathers of the bird. These are scarce, especially in the United States, and black heron's hackles are often substituted.

Peter Deane gives his own dressing of the *Sweep,* which he calls the *Delfur Sweep.* It is the same except that he doubles the black cock's hackle and ties it in at the point. The wing is dyed black calf tail hairs with jungle cock sides, and he eliminates the kingfisher and the horns, the latter being unnecessary anyway.

Another dressing for the *Sweep* is listed in Hale. It is more elegant than the other two patterns and is given below as a matter of interest.

Sweep

Tag	Silver tinsel	
Tail	Golden pheasant crest	
Butt	Black ostrich herl	
Body	Black floss	
Ribbing	Silver tinsel	
Hackle	Black	
Wing	Black crow	
Topping	Golden pheasant crest, optional	
Cheeks	Jungle cock	
Horns	Red macaw	
Head	Black	(Hale)

Tadpole

Tail	Yellow hair, tied long
Body	Rear half: yellow floss; front half: crimson floss
Wing	Collie dog hair, extending to the end of the tail
Head	Red

This pattern is a more colorful variation of the versatile and simple *Collie Dog,* tied with a wing of long black hair and a plain silver body.

Thistle

Tag	Gold twist and yellow silk	
Tail	Golden pheasant crest, with Indian crow above and below	
Body	Equal parts of light fiery brown and black pig's wool	
Ribbing	Flat gold tinsel	
Hackle	Black, from the second turn	
Wings	Teal, dark bustard, fibers of golden pheasant breast and of Amherst pheasant, and mallard	
Sides	Jungle cock	
Horns	Red and blue macaw	
Topping	Golden pheasant crest	
Head	Black ostrich herl	(Kelson)

Thunder and Lightning	
Tag	Fine oval silver tinsel, or wire and golden yellow floss
Tail	Golden pheasant crest, over which is a shorter section of Indian crow (or a hackle point dyed salmon red)
Butt	Black ostrich herl
Body	Black floss
Ribbing	Oval gold tinsel
Hackle	A deep orange hackle, wound forward from the second turn of the tinsel
Throat	Jay
Wing	Strips of brown mallard, set upright
Cheeks	Jungle cock
Topping	Golden pheasant crest
Horns	Blue and yellow macaw
Head	Black

Perennially popular, Kelson called the *Thunder and Lightning* "the great storm fly." He went on to say, "This fly is exceedingly popular and has a well-earned reputation for its destructive qualities when

PLATE 112
THE SWEEP

dressed by Bob Veverka
dressed by Steve Gobin

rivers begin to rise after rain. General B puts an underwing of tippet, and brown mottled Turkey strips."

Originated in the mid-nineteenth century by James Wright, the *Thunder and Lightning* is probably the most popular of his patterns. Tradition-bent but practical adaptations appear in fly boxes wherever anglers fish for salmon.

Above is the classic dressing from Kelson, with whom Pryce-Tannatt basically agrees. Following is an excellent hairwing version, which can be further simplified:

Thunder and Lightning (Hairwing)	
Tag	Oval gold tinsel and claret floss
Tail	Golden pheasant crest
Butt	Black ostrich herl
Body	Black floss, not built up
Ribbing	Oval gold tinsel
Hackle	A deep orange hackle, palmered over front third of body
Throat	A small bunch of blue gallina (guinea hen) fibers
Wing	Orange under brown under yellow bucktail in layers, quite sparse
Cheeks	Jungle cock
Head	Black

This hairwing version of the British classic is by the celebrated British fly dresser Peter Deane. He writes, "On all hair wing Thunders I tie, I only use the orange cock hackle round the throat in small sizes. In big sizes it's palmered along the body and in both cases with a false throat of blue (dyed) Gallina."

Another popular way of dressing the wing is to use a section of a dark brown turkey feather, over which is dyed brown polar bear hair, over which is polar bear hair dyed yellow.

Jimmy Younger, a modern Scottish authority, sent me a very simple dressing without tag, butt, topping, and horns (as in the classic featherwing pattern). The throat is a very small bunch of orange cock fibers, forward of which is a very small bunch of blue gallina fibers. The wing is squirrel tail, dyed brown, and jungle cock eyes are included. A further simplification is the *Bastard Thunder and Lightning,* originated by Roger D'Errico and included with the flies of the Penobscot in chapter 14.

Tish

Tag	Fine silver wire or twist
Tail	Golden pheasant crest
Body	Flat silver tinsel
Ribbing	Black thread
Hackle	In three equal sections of palmered hackles over the body: rear, orange; middle, red or scarlet; front, sapphire blue
Wing	Dark turkey
Head	Black

The unnamed genius who thought this up evidently had in mind another pattern named the *Tosh,* although there is no resemblance except for the paired names, *Tish* and *Tosh.* The pattern is more interesting than prominent and is well known in Scotland.

Torrish

Tag	Silver thread or tinsel and golden yellow floss
Tail	Golden pheasant crest, over which are a few strands of golden pheasant tippet or red ibis, half as long as the crest feather
Butt	Black ostrich herl
Body	Rear two-fifths (or half): oval silver tinsel, butted forward with black ostrich herl veiled above and below with Indian crow. Forward three-fifths (or half): oval silver tinsel palmered with a lemon yellow hackle and ribbed with fine oval silver tinsel
Throat	A deep red-orange hackle, the color of Indian crow
Wing	A pair of black, white-tipped turkey tail strips (back to back); outside of which but not entirely concealing them is a mixed sheath of married strands of teal, yellow, scarlet, and orange swan, bustard, florican, and golden pheasant tail; outside of which are married narrow strips of pintail and barred summer duck; outside of which are narrow strips of brown mallard
Cheeks	Jungle cock and/or Indian crow
Topping	Golden pheasant crest
Horns	Blue and yellow macaw
Head	Black

This dressing essentially is the one recommended by Pryce-Tannatt. Megan Boyd gives a somewhat different and simpler formula for the wing. In addition to the turkey, she uses bustard, peacock wing, golden pheasant tail, married strands of red and blue swan, and gallina, plus the mallard. She also sent me a different and very popular "cousin" of this fly, the *Pale Torrish.*

Pale Torrish (or Salscraggie)

In this fly, the head, tag, tail, butt, and topping are the same as for the *Torrish.* The rear section of the body is oval silver tinsel butted forward, with a turn or two of yellow hackle and ostrich herl. The forward part is yellow seal's fur ribbed with oval silver tinsel.

The underwing is cinnamon turkey, outside of which are married strands of red, yellow, and blue swan, plus Amherst pheasant, gray mottled turkey tail, and pintail. The throat is a deep yellow hackle, and the cheeks are jungle cock.

These two flies are named after places in Scotland's Strath of Kildonan, through which flows the famous Helmsdale River. Though the flies were made chiefly for use there, their popularity is worldwide. The *Torrish* is included in the Hardy Brothers' most popular twelve classic patterns.

Tosh (or The Devil or Spey Tosh)

Head	Black
Body	Black floss, sparsely dressed
Wing	Black and yellow bucktail, very sparse and long

This is a relatively recent British pattern first tied by Ned Ritchie, the head gillie of the Delfur beat of the Spey. Owned by the Mountain family, the Delfur beat is the first holding water up from the estuary and is considered by many the best water on the river. Named for the dog that provided the wing material, the *Tosh* is one of the few British flies dressed in the form of the American bucktail. It was tied on the riverbank for fun, but it proved to be a good fly that often does extremely well in low water. The very simple dressing is body and wing only.

The fly evidently is tied in several variations, so the name is more for a shape than for a pattern. Regarding this, Colonel Drury says: "A new addition to the killer range is *The Devil* or *Spey Tosh.* This is a simple fly, tied with either yellow or blue Badger or Squirrel hair or black bucktail with a polythene body. It is tied very thin indeed, a dozen fibers, no more. It is not an attractive fly to look at, but is very attractive to salmon. The only thing these modern spring flies have in common with their Kelson ancestors is size. They are used up to three inches in length, but there the resemblance ends."

Tricolor

Tag	Silver tinsel
Tail	Golden pheasant crest and the tip of a golden pheasant's breast feather
Body	Equal sections of pale yellow, light blue, and scarlet seal's fur
Ribbing	Flat silver tinsel and twist
Hackle	A gray heron hackle from the third turn of tinsel
Throat	Teal
Wing	A pair of cinnamon turkey tail strips
Head	Black

This early-nineteenth-century Dee pattern is typical in construction of the Dee flies but is distinguished by a gray hackle rather than the more generally used black hackle. The pattern given is from Pryce-Tannatt.

Turnbull's Sir Richard

Tag	Silver twist and golden yellow silk	
Tail	Golden pheasant crest and Indian crow, above and below	
Butt	Peacock herl	
Body	Black silk	
Ribbing	Silver lace and narrow silver tinsel	
Hackle	Gallina, one-third of body	
Throat	Jay, and one turn of gallina over it	
Wing	Two broad strips of swan dyed scarlet, veiled with bustard, mallard, gray mallard, and parrot	
Topping	Golden pheasant crest	
Sides	Summer duck	
Horns	Blue macaw	
Head	Black herl	(Kelson)

Usk Grub

Tag	Fine round silver tinsel
Tail	Fibers from a red golden pheasant body feather, protruding as long as the body
Body	In equal halves: rear half, hot orange seal's fur with a suggestion of yellow mixed in; front half, black seal's fur
Ribbing	Fine oval silver tinsel
Middle hackle	Between both halves, a small hot orange hackle followed by a small white hackle, both tilting slightly backward, one turn of each only
Front hackle	Coch-y-bonddu hackle with fibers as long as the body
Wing	A pair of jungle cock feathers of the same length as the front hackle, tied one on each side to form an upward V of about 45 degrees
Head	Red tying thread or red varnish

Grub flies are especially popular in the British Isles, where most regions seem to have their favorite wingless, or grub, patterns. England and Wales seem

PLATE 113
SHRIMP PATTERNS

General Practitioner
originated and dressed by Esmond Drury

Usk Grub
dressed by Jimmy Younger

Golden Shrimp
dressed by Jimmy Younger

Curry's Red Shrimp
dressed by Jimmy Younger

to favor the *Wye Grub*, Scotland has its *Black Shrimp*, and Ireland its *Hicks Grub*. The pattern above is for the *Usk Grub*, popular with anglers in Wales and very similar to the *Hicks*. Another similar pattern is the *Usk Silver Grub*, which is the same as the above dressing except that the entire body is flat silver tinsel that is ribbed with silver wire. These flies are extensions of very old and simple Welsh patterns.

PLATE 114
ANTIQUE SUMMER PATTERNS

Blue Boyne

dressed by Ted Godfrey

Tag	Silver twist
Tail	Two Indian crow
Butt	Black ostrich herl
Body	Small silver tinsel intersected with four sets of chatterer, slightly increasing in size toward the throat
Wings	Double strips of yellow macaw and golden pheasant crest
Head	Black ostrich herl (Traherne)

Bo Peep

dressed by Ted Godfrey

Tag	Silver twist
Tail	Toucan and two small chatterer, back to back
Butt	Black ostrich herl
Body	In three equal sections of fine oval silver tinsel: the first butted with toucan above and below, followed by black herl; the second butted with Indian crow above and below, followed by black herl
Throat	(Third section) Double chatterer feathers, back to back
Wings	Ibis and red macaw in fibers and three golden pheasant crest feathers
Horns	Amherst pheasant
Head	Black ostrich herl (Kelson)

Yellow Baronet

Tag	Silver tinsel and light blue floss
Tail	Golden pheasant crest and wood duck
Butt	Black ostrich herl
Body	Three turns of light orange floss followed by medium orange seal's fur
Ribbing	Silver tinsel
Throat	Green parrot
Wings	Two strips of orange and yellow swan, cock-of-the-rock and two golden pheasant crest feathers
Cheeks	Blue chatterer
Horns	Red macaw
Head	Black (Hale)

Kelson, a great proponent of wingless flies, created grub variations of classic patterns by using the same body construction and simply eliminating the wing and adding hackles.

Watson's Fancy

Tag	Fine oval silver tinsel, or silver wire
Tail	Golden pheasant crest
Body	Rear half: red floss. Front half: black floss or dubbing
Ribbing	Fine oval silver tinsel, or silver wire
Throat	Black cock's hackle
Wing	Black squirrel tail
Cheeks	Jungle cock
Head	Black

This is a British trout fly pattern, now used without change for salmon. The original trout pattern has a wing of sections of a crow's wing feathers. The hairwing version uses any fairly straight black hair.

PLATE 115
EAGLES

Avon Eagle Variation (antique)

Grey Eagle
dressed by Megan Boyd

Avon Eagle (antique)

Golden Eagle (antique)

Wilkinson

Tag	Silver twist
Tail	Golden pheasant crest, tippet, and Indian crow
Butt	Scarlet wool
Body	Silver tinsel
Ribbing	Oval silver tinsel
Throat	Magenta and light blue hackle
Wing	Tippet, teal, peacock wing, golden pheasant tail, swan dyed red, yellow, and blue, and mallard
Topping	Golden pheasant crest
Horns	Blue macaw
Sides	Jungle cock
Head	Black ostrich herl

Although Kelson stated that the *Wilkinson* was "one of my Father's earliest patterns and is patronized on most rivers," it seems that this fly is a later adaptation of the *Silver Wilkinson*. James Wright shared responsibility with P. S. Wilkinson for the early version of the *Silver Wilkinson*, each devising a fly with a body of silver tinsel. Except for its distinctive magenta and blue throat, the *Silver Wilkinson* is much like the *Silver Doctor*. Many believe that this is the first pattern with a silver body; others argue that the *Aglaia*, noted by Fitzgibbon, was.

Willie Gunn	
Body	Black floss
Ribbing	Silver tinsel
Wing	Evenly mixed: yellow, red-orange, and black hair
Head	Black

Named for the Sutherland Estate's head keeper on the Brora, the *Willie Gunn* is dressed as a tube fly with its three colors evenly distributed rather than tied in separately. It has proven to be a highly successful pattern in a variety of sizes and weights.

Yellow Fairy	
Tag	Silver tinsel
Tail	Golden pheasant crest
Body	Yellow seal's fur or yellow floss
Hackle	A yellow hackle palmered over front half of body
Ribbing	Oval silver tinsel
Throat	Yellow hackle
Wing	Brown (bronze) mallard, in strips
Topping	Golden pheasant crest (optional)
Head	Black

This seems to be a variation of the *Black Fairy*, which is dressed both in a simple version similar to the above, and in a more complicated dressing that can be adapted to this one, if desired.

12

Continental Europe and Scandinavia

"Norway Fire"

SALMON FISHING IN FRANCE AND SPAIN

France

Before and during the Middle Ages, and from then until the French Revolution in the last part of the eighteenth century, all fishing rights in France belonged to the Crown. The rivers, being for the most part clean and unobstructed, teemed with salmon, as well as eels and shad. To indicate the abundance of this silvered wealth, the fishery in Brittany alone in good years produced about 4,500 tons of salmon.

During these lush years, the king assigned most of the fishing rights to the clergy and the nobility, who often sublet them to landowners along the streams. These rights eventually became hereditary. The owners, who derived considerable revenue from them, were careful to keep the streams clean and unobstructed, providing passageways for the fish around dikes and mill dams. Various laws were enacted to protect the fishery, these varying widely from place to place. These laws, as they became more and more widespread and complicated, tempted excessive illegal fishing and poaching, but until the Revolution of 1789, the authorities saw to it that the rivers remained unpolluted and that there were no barriers to prevent ample runs of fish from reaching their spawning grounds in order to maintain an abundant fishery.

After the revolution, all this began to change for the worse. The new republic abolished the hereditary rights and allowed free fishing for all people on all rivers. As has happened in so many other countries around the Atlantic, too many people became imbued with the "grab it while you can get it and to hell with the future" syndrome. The rivers became neglected. Industry dammed them for mills of various kinds without bothering to erect fish ladders or bypasses for the salmon. Pollution from mills and factories did further damage.

By the middle of the nineteenth century, less than a hundred years after the revolution, the decline of the French salmon fishery became so serious that authorities finally were aroused to action. Laws were passed to avert the increasing damage, but

again, as in so many other countries, they lacked adequate definition and sufficient penalties for non-conformance. Failure to enforce the laws resulted in the disappearance of salmon from more and more of the rivers. Rivers became sprinkled with mill and hydroelectric dams not equipped with fish passages, thus condemning them to sterility. Mills formerly equipped with fish ladders allowed them to go to ruin while the authorities once more turned blind eyes and deaf ears to the decline of the salmon, a decline that then would have been neither too difficult nor too expensive to avert. Added to all of this, and again as in so many other countries, the plethora of nets in the sea, along the coasts, in the estuaries, and blockading the rivers themselves made it almost impossible for salmon to return to their former spawning grounds.

In the rapid decline of the salmon fishery in France, which I hope all salmon conservationists will carefully note as an example to be avoided, the destruction by poachers also was of paramount importance. These were more or less organizations of water pirates and thieves who used every effective means, from nets to tridents to explosives to poisons, to decimate the very small percentage of salmon lucky to have run the gauntlet of nets and dams into their rivers.

The poaching situation in France may have been no better or no worse than it is in some other countries; however, it could have been minimized if authorities had been more interested in the protection of salmon than in the acquiring of votes.

In fairness to some of the officials, the protection of the salmon and the regulation of the rivers were made more difficult because authority was divided among at least four different bureaus that often conflicted with each other at the expense of conservation as opposed to industrialism. Before World War II, increasing but feeble and more or less futile attempts were made to pass more stringent laws to protect the salmon, but by then, the fishery was in such a sad state that most of France's salmon had to be imported from overseas, including considerable amounts of canned fish from the Pacific coast of the United States.

During the middle of this century, France underwent unprecedented industrial development. The traditional type of agriculture that operates in harmony with the land and the waters practically disappeared. It was replaced by highly mechanized farming requiring the use of chemical fertilizers for high yields. The effect of these changes on the environment was severe, and salmon habitat was not spared.

This grim résumé only rapidly skims the situation in France; it can serve as a warning of what can happen, or what may be happening, elsewhere. Readers who wish to pursue this in greater detail are referred to Anthony Netboy's erudite, factual, and monumental book, *The Atlantic Salmon: A Vanishing Species?* (1968).

It would be unfair to conclude without offering what may be a ray of hope provided largely by the growing strength and dedication of nongovernment organizations such as angling groups and nature protection associations. An example is that of the Association Pour la Protection du Salmon en Bretagne (Brittany), which works with local anglers' associations. This group of dedicated sportsmen and nature lovers has, almost alone, cleaned up the majority of the better Breton rivers, which were in a shocking state of abandon when it started back in the early 1970s.

In Brittany the picture is quite bright, and there has been a definite upward trend from the catastrophic low point of the early 1970s. The cleanup work started by various agencies is paying off handsomely, with many disused spawning areas now in use again. Logjams, derelict dams, and other obstructions have been removed or provided with fish passes.

Breton rivers are mostly small or medium-sized, and many offer good fly-fishing water. Rod-catch figures fluctuate from year to year; however, the following rivers might well be worth the visiting angler's attention: the Aven and its tributaries; the Aulne, which flows into the Bay of Brest; the Pense; the Scorff; the Elorne, which meets the sea at the Finistere, a department in Brittany occupying the westernmost tip of France; the Blavet; and the Elle. Some salmon catches are also reported in the other north-coast rivers.

In Normandy there are four rivers that have some runs of salmon and spawning areas in use. These are the Couesnon, the Selune, the See, and the Sienne. These rivers flow into the Bay of St. Michel, where netting and poaching have been a problem in the shallow waters. Both the Breton and Normandy stocks of salmon, as well as those headed for the Pyrenees, are vulnerable to drift nets off the Irish coast that they have to skirt on their homeward migrations.

Once the greatest salmon rivers in France, the Loire and its major tributary, the Allier, still offer good fishing, but only as shadows of their former selves. With the work of a special salmon mission on the upper Allier to improve fish passes, count and evaluate stocks, and mark smolts, the quality of the water has improved, but industrial and domestic pollution are still serious problems. To these have been added those created by extensive gravel workings in the riverbed, thus causing siltation, lowering of the beds, and the destruction of food animals that would nourish parr and smolts.

Although heavy concentrations of local anglers have been a problem, the Allier perhaps offers the best prospects for rod fishing. In part, this is due to an exceptional group of sportsmen who not only initiated the practice of catch and release, but also operate (at their own expense) a small hatchery for rearing smolts, which are released in the Allier. The potential for this river still is great, but the future is uncertain.

In the Pyrenean area, only the Adour, which meets the Atlantic at Bayonne, and two small coastal rivers, the Nivelle and the Bidasoa, still have salmon runs. In the Adour system, only the Gave d'Oloron still has runs. The Gave de Pau has been dammed and polluted and holds no salmon. The salmon runs that formerly ran up the Nive also have been blocked in the lower reaches by an impassable dam, and the native stock is on the point of disappearing. The runs in the Saison, a major tributary of the Gave d'Oloron, and the best potential fly water in France, were wiped out in the same way some years ago. As the biological potential of these rivers is still largely intact, it is to be hoped that something will be done about these dams, which were illegally installed by private parties.

The Gave d'Oloron has also had its problems, but various agencies are doing good work, especially with smolt restocking and a hatchery for rearing smolts. The Gave is not reliably good fly water because it is subject to prolonged snow-water runoff, and its levels can be too high for fly fishing right through the season. Nevertheless, under low-water conditions it can be excellent. Fish that enter the Adour in February can be quite large, although not numerous. Smaller salmon and some grilse follow, swimming upriver late in March and providing good fly fishing after the mountain snows have melted early in June if the river level allows.

The Nivelle enters the sea at St. Jean de Luz and is the site of an intensive salmon restoration program. At St. Pee, on its middle reaches, is the chief freshwater research station in France, Centre de Recherches Hydrobiologiques (an agency of the Ministry of Agriculture), which is well equipped with laboratories, rearing ponds, and so forth. The river itself was partly cleaned up in the Clean Rivers Program, but unfortunately, some of the worst pollution is in its upper reaches, in Spain, and progress in remedying the situation is slow. A smolt-rearing operation has been somewhat successful, and numbers of returning salmon have been identified as having been released as smolts by the Centre. A spawning and rearing channel as well as other facilities are planned. For some time, salmon fishing was prohibited on the Nivelle in order to protect the stocks, and the river cannot yet be considered a fishing water.

The Bidasoa, mostly in Spain, is not really considered a French fly-fishing river. Only the estuary and part of the tidal reaches are international, with the right bank in France.

Salmon Flies of France
The salmon flies of France are simple dressings, usually with ribbed and hackled bodies of wool or silk and wings of dark mallard shoulder feathers, golden pheasant tail, or badger hair, sometimes throated with a bit of hackle. Hairwings seem to be taking the place of featherwings. Simplified British classics are popular, usually with wings of hair in color schemes resembling the original complicated feathered ones. Feathered wings are set upright but sometimes, particularly in commercial dressings, look more or less bunched and ragged. Patterns are often referred to by types and numbers or named for regions or rivers.

Since we have looked at the salmon fishing of France by the three areas of Brittany, Normandy, and the Pyrenees, favorite flies are listed for each of the three regions. Of course, the patterns popular in any one of these three regions often overlap with those favored in the other two.

Brittany. The following seven patterns were originated by the famous French angler and fly dresser Francois Le Ny (incorrectly spelled as "Leny" in Ragot's catalog) and further developed by Henry Clerc. These, and other Brittany patterns such as the Elle and Aulne series, are dressed commercially by Mouches-Ragot, in Loudeac, France, and can be found in its catalog.

Andre Ragot originated a trout fly, later popular for salmon, called the *Ruz-Du,* which is Breton for red and black. Dressed in sizes 6 to 10, this simple pattern has a body of which the rear half is red (or orange) and the front half is black tying thread or wool. Both throat and wing are black.

Bretonne #3

Tail	Golden pheasant crest
Body	Orange wool, not built up
Hackle	Light brown, over front half only
Ribbing	Fine flat gold tinsel
Wing	Strips of golden pheasant tail fibers

Bretonne #7

Body	Lemon wool
Hackle	Yellow or very light brown, over front half only
Wing	Strips of golden pheasant tail fibers

Bretonne #15

Body	Olive wool
Ribbing	Yellow thread
Hackle	Black
Wing	Strips of golden pheasant tail fibers

Leny #21

Tag	Crimson wool
Tail	Golden pheasant crest
Body	Gray wool, not built up
Hackle	Light brown, over whole body
Wing	Two strips of reddish orange breast feather of golden pheasant, outside of which are strips of golden pheasant tail fibers

PLATE 116
FRENCH SALMON FLIES, MOUCHES–RAGOT

Gave #1   Bretonne #3

Bretonne #15   Leny #21

                                                Lemon Gray

Bretonne #7

Leny #23   Leny #24   Leny #22

Leny #22	
Tag	Olive green wool
Tail	Golden pheasant crest
Body	Dark gray wool, not built up
Ribbing	Medium flat gold tinsel
Throat	A bunch of brown hackle fibers
Wing	Two golden pheasant tippets, outside of which are strips of mottled brown pheasant feathers, leaving most of the tippets showing

Leny #23	
Tag	Olive green wool
Tail	Golden pheasant breast feather
Body	Dark green wool, built up forward and slightly picked out
Ribbing	Crimson thread
Throat	Brown hackle
Underwing	Peacock sword over which are strips of mottled brown pheasant
Wing	Strips of gray mallard flank feathers, outside of which are about six peacock sword fibers on each side

PLATE 117
SALMON FLIES OF BRITTANY
ORIGINATED AND DRESSED BY
YANN LE FEVRE

Le Fevre #6

Le Fevre #4   *Le Fevre #7*

Le Fevre #5

Le Fevre #3   *Le Fevre #1*

Le Fevre #2

Leny #24

Tail	Golden pheasant crest
Body	Black wool, not built up
Ribbing	Medium flat gold tinsel
Throat	A small bunch of light brown hackle fibers
Wing	Two golden pheasant tippets, outside of which are strips of golden pheasant tail fibers, leaving most of the tippets showing

Normandy. Flies popular in Normandy often are hairwings adapted from British classics such as *Lemon Grey, Black Doctor, Black Dose, Kate, Silver Gray, Thun-* der and Lightning, Fiery Brown, and *Dusty Miller,* in sizes usually between 1/0 and 4, but in early season as big as 6/0 and in low water as small as size 12. These may vary somewhat from the British classics; following is one typical variation to indicate how others may be adapted. Additional information can be found in *Le Saumon de l'Allier,* by P. Boyer.

Lemon Gray

Tag	Oval silver tinsel and yellow floss
Tail	Golden pheasant crest and slips of red goose
Butt	Peacock herl
Body	Gray-blue wool, not built up
Hackle	A gray hackle from third turn of tinsel
Ribbing	Flat silver tinsel
Throat	Yellow hackle fibers
Wing	Badger hair

Pyrennes. Pyrenean patterns differ only slightly from those given above, the difference being principally that local ones are preferred to adaptations of the British classics. A constant feature is the wing of badger hair and/or strips of mallard flank feathers. Bodies are somewhat fuzzy rather than with the sleek look provided by silks or floss. They are made with such substances as seal's fur or boar's wool, usually in colors such as natural, yellow, green, or brown. Following are two examples:

Gave #1

Tag	Silver tinsel and blue floss
Tail	Golden pheasant crest
Body	Gray wool, as above
Ribbing	Fine flat silver tinsel
Throat	Yellow hackle, followed by light brown
Wing	Two golden pheasant tippets, veiled with bronze mallard
Topping	Golden pheasant crest

The above pattern is so similar to another called the *Gave #2* that only one is needed. They are varied to suit individual tastes. For example, the wing can be made of badger hair with or without some mallard, and the body and throat of colors in subdued tones. Red tags or butts often are used, with hackles of brown or black.

Most of the French patterns are in the midrange of color tones or brilliancy, almost none being very dark or very bright. Might the salmon of France sometimes prefer flies with more flash, such as with all-tinsel bodies, or with wings of black or more brilliant colors? Evidently they sometimes do, because anglers in France report the use of many of them in Pyrenean rivers, including British classics or adaptations such as *Lemon Grey, Black Doctor, Silver Doctor,* and *Jock Scott.*

Spain

Spain's salmon rivers meet the sea on the northwestern coast where the Atlantic ocean joins the Bay of Biscay. They originate in towering mountain cliffs as high as 9,000 feet and, fed by abundant rainfall, tumble fast and cold down waterfalls, over ledges, and through deeply graveled pools ideal for spawning. About fifty of these rivers formerly were abundant with salmon. Now there are less than ten where anglers can fish with much hope of success. At best, Spain's salmon fishery is but a faint shadow of its former abundance.

The causes of this drastic decline during the past two hundred years are so similar to those of France that they need not be repeated in detail: obstruction by dams, pollution, diversion of water for agriculture, commercial fishing, poaching, and inadequate enforcement of what few conservation laws existed.

In 1936, when Spain was involved in its Civil War, all protection of the salmon was withdrawn, and the destruction of the fishery rapidly accelerated. By the end of the war, when Gen. Francisco Franco came into power, whatever was left of the salmon fishery was in desperate straits.

Fortunately, General Franco was a salmon angler who loved the sport intensely. He couldn't do anything about the excessive netting of Spain's salmon as they passed along the Irish coast on their way home, but he did what he could to mend the sorely depleted fishery in Spain. In 1942 he was instrumental in passing laws designed to prevent further deterioration. All netting was banned in estuaries and in the rivers themselves.

He handed over the entire fishery to rod fishermen, some of them professionals. He turned three of his favorite rivers, the Eo, Narcea, and Sella, into national fishing preserves and placed them under the management of the State Tourist Bureau.

General Franco also inaugurated an extensive restocking program. He saw that fish passes were erected around useful dams, and he had useless dams and other obstructions dynamited. He enlarged the groups of wardens and gave them greater prestige and power. He decreed that prison sentences up to

ten years should be given to people convicted of poaching and other forms of illegal fishing.

He also dictated that every salmon that was killed must be registered and tagged by a warden. He divided sections of rivers into two types, called *cotos* and *free areas.*

The cotos are supposedly select areas that are restricted zones requiring special permits specifying the dates and/or hours when their holders can fish. Salmon taken in these areas receive a blue tag and cannot be sold, under a high penalty for doing so.

In the free areas, anyone with a license can fish as often during the season as he wishes, using any sort of terminal tackle that can be handled with rod and reel, including hardware and bait. Fish taken in free areas are registered with a red tag and can be sold.

One might assume that these improvements and regulations should go far toward remedying the drastic decline in Spain's salmon fishery. They did help some, but they didn't go far enough.

The free areas, which permit unrestricted fishing with anything that can be used on rod and reel, became overrun with market fishermen to the extent that twenty times as many licenses were issued than had been formerly. These market fishermen became experts who were taking at least 80 percent of all salmon killed in Spain. The fish are shipped to markets, such as Madrid, and are auctioned at such high prices that the market fishermen are ruthless and put salmon runs into grave danger from overfishing. In addition to this, the expanding economy conflicts with stream improvement by demanding more dams for power and manufacturing.

Of Spain's fifty or so rivers that formerly were abundant with salmon, only six now seem worthy of mention, going clockwise from west to east around the northwestern coast.

The Eo has had the smallest runs of salmon because of former overnetting and dams. It should provide fifty thousand fish per year but offers only a few hundred. It has characteristics like the Narcea but is much less rapid. There are good pools in the lower stretches. Fly fishing is best from March to May. The Eo is a national fishing preserve under the management of the State Tourist Bureau.

The Navia is similar to the Eo, except that fishing has been a little better.

The Narcea offers the best conditions for fly fishing of any river in Spain, or even in continental

Europe, excluding the Scandinavian countries. It is also a national fishing preserve, with seventy-five pools and many beautiful fly-fishing stretches. It formerly was polluted by mines and damaged by over-netting, so its capacity of about fifty thousand salmon has been reduced to less than a thousand. Fly fishing generally starts by the end of April, according to the lowering of spring runoff, and lasts until the third week of July.

The Sella was once a very productive river but has suffered similar decline to the others. It is the one least suited for fly fishing, and the greatest number of salmon are taken with artificial lures or with natural live bait. It also is a national fishing preserve supervised by the State Tourist Bureau.

The Deva-Cares also yields only a tiny fraction of its former production. It is beautiful like the Narcea, but more turbulent and with stronger rapids. It is excellent for fly fishing, especially toward the end of May.

The Ason, the farthest east, has been the most productive of all Spanish salmon rivers.

Licenses and special permits for fishing in Spain are inexpensive, and arrangements can be made in advance by contacting the Servicio de Pesca Conti-nental, a department of the Caza y Parques Nacional, in Madrid. Salmon tackle for Spain is the same as for other countries.

Salmon Flies of Spain

Classic patterns of flies such as *Jock Scott, Green Highlander, Dusty Miller, Silver Wilkinson,* and so forth, which still are popular to an extent, are giving way to simpler hairwings or hairwing versions of the classics. Some anglers use flies as large as 5/0 to size 2, with smaller ones as the rivers recede and the season advances. Others rarely go above size 2, with sizes 6 or 8 a good average.

A discussion of Spain's fly fishing would not be complete without mentioning a man whom many call the greatest contemporary fly dresser in the world—certainly one of the greatest. He is Belarmino Martinez, who lives in Pravia, in Asturias. Excelling in classic featherwing patterns, he works without assistants and specializes in innovations of his own, many of which are named for rivers in Spain. His classic salmon flies are so perfect that they are sought by collectors for framing as well as by anglers for fishing. Following are salmon fly patterns originated by Belarmino Martinez:

Good holding water on Spain's Narcea River

BELARMINO MARTINEZ

Black Orange

Tag	Oval silver tinsel and golden floss
Tail	Golden pheasant crest and teal
Butt	Black ostrich herl
Body	Black floss
Ribbing	Silver oval tinsel
Hackle	Orange hackle
Throat	Blue dun hackle
Wing	Badger
Head	Brown lacquer

Cares River

Tag	Oval silver tinsel
Tail	Golden pheasant crest over which are two small jungle cock, back to back
Butt	Magenta-red wool
Body	Two-thirds embossed silver tinsel; one-third green chenille
Ribbing	Oval silver tinsel
Throat	Green hackle followed by guinea
Wing	Brown bucktail over which is peacock herl followed by three small bunches of yellow, red, and green bucktail
Sides	Married strips of teal and barred summer duck
Cheeks	Jungle cock
Head	Red and brown lacquer

Deva River

Tag	Oval silver tinsel and light orange floss
Tail	Golden pheasant crest, veiled with red ibis
Butt	Magenta-red wool
Body	In three equal parts: blue floss, blue seal's fur, and black seal's fur
Ribbing	Oval silver tinsel
Hackle	Claret
Throat	Guinea dyed blue
Wing	Broad strips of Amherst pheasant tail and married slips of mottled turkey, yellow, red, and blue swan. Over this are several fibers of peacock herl. The entire wing is veiled with married slips of teal, barred summer duck, and bronze mallard
Sides	Jungle cock
Cheeks	Kingfisher
Topping	Lady Amherst pheasant crest
Head	Brown lacquer

Eo River

Tag	Oval gold tinsel
Tail	Golden pheasant crest over which are two small jungle cock, back to back
Butt	Magenta-red wool
Body	Rear three-quarters: embossed gold tinsel. Front quarter: yellow chenille
Ribbing	Oval gold tinsel
Throat	Claret hackle followed by guinea
Wing	Brown bucktail hairs, over which is green peacock herl followed by yellow and red bucktail
Shoulders	Married slips of teal and barred summer duck
Cheeks	Jungle cock
Head	Brown lacquer

Esva River

Tag	Oval gold tinsel and yellow floss, fairly wide
Tail	Golden pheasant crest with golden oriole, above and below
Butt	Black ostrich
Body	First half: yellow wool. Second half: orange chenille. Separated by a black ostrich butt
Ribbing	Both sections, oval gold tinsel
Hackle	Yellow, over yellow wool
Throat	Yellow followed by red hackle
Wing	Broad strips of gray heron, mottled turkey, yellow, red, and blue swan, and peacock herl. The entire wing is veiled with married strips of teal, barred summer duck, and bronze mallard
Sides	Jungle cock
Cheeks	Kingfisher
Topping	Golden pheasant crest
Head	Brown lacquer

PLATES 118–119
ORIGINAL PATTERNS BY BELARMINO MARTINEZ

Navia River	Pas River	Esva River	Ulla River
Deva River	Silver Martinez	Narcea River	Martinez Special
	Eo River		Cares River

	Martinez Special
Tag	Oval gold tinsel and yellow floss
Tail	Golden pheasant crest and two very small jungle cock tips, back to back
Butt	Magenta-red wool
Body	Rear three-quarters: flat gold tinsel. Front quarter: pale yellow chenille
Ribbing	Oval gold tinsel
Throat	Magenta hackle, followed by guinea
Wing	Golden pheasant tippets, outside of which are married strips of yellow, red, and green swan. The entire wing is veiled with married strips of teal, barred summer duck, and bronze mallard
Sides	Jungle cock
Cheeks	Kingfisher
Topping	Golden pheasant crest
Head	Brown lacquer

	Narcea River
Tag	Oval silver tinsel and yellow floss
Tail	Golden pheasant crest, over which is a red hackle tip
Butt	Peacock herl
Body	First half: mixed yellow and green chenille. Second half: red mohair. Separated by a peacock herl butt
Ribbing	Oval silver tinsel, over front half of body only
Hackle	Green, over front half
Throat	Guinea
Wing	Two large jungle cock feathers, back to back and veiled with golden pheasant tippets, outside of which are married strips of yellow, red, and green swan. The entire wing is veiled with married strips of teal, barred summer duck, and unbarred summer duck
Sides	Jungle cock
Cheeks	Kingfisher
Topping	Golden pheasant crest
Head	Red and black lacquer

PLATE 120
THE SILVER ORANGE AND THE HOT ORANGE
ORIGINATED AND DRESSED BY BELARMINO MARTINEZ

Silver Orange

Hot Orange

THE FLIES AND THE PATTERNS

277

Navia River

Tag	Oval tinsel and red floss
Tail	Golden pheasant crest, over which is barred summer duck
Butt	Peacock herl
Body	In three equal parts of yellow, olive green, and blue floss. The first section butted with yellow hackle and peacock herl; the second section butted with purple hackle and peacock herl. All sections ribbed with silver oval tinsel
Throat	Olive hackle and unbarred summer duck
Wing	A pair of Lady Amherst pheasant tippets, back to back, and married strips of yellow, red, purple, and green swan. The entire wing is veiled with teal, barred summer duck, and unbarred summer duck. Outside of this is a wide slip of unbarred summer duck veiled with married slips of teal and barred summer duck
Sides	Jungle cock
Cheeks	Kingfisher
Topping	Golden pheasant crest
Head	Red and black lacquer

Pas River

Tag	Oval silver tinsel and red floss
Tail	Golden pheasant crest with two slips of barred summer duck over
Butt	Peacock herl
Body	First half: embossed silver tinsel veiled with yellow hackle tips and butted with peacock herl. Second half: red floss ribbed with silver oval tinsel and wound with a green hackle
Throat	Guinea
Wing	Four red hackles, over which is a pair of golden pheasant tippets
Sides	Lady Amherst pheasant tippets
Cheeks	Very small Lady Amherst pheasant tippets
Topping	Golden pheasant crest
Head	Brown lacquer

Silver Martinez

Tag	Oval silver tinsel
Tail	Golden pheasant crest, over which are two small jungle cock, back to back
Butt	Magenta-red wool
Body	Flat silver tinsel
Ribbing	Oval silver tinsel
Hackle	Green
Throat	Guinea
Wing	A pair of large jungle cock feathers veiled with golden pheasant tippets, outside of which are slips of green swan. The entire wing is veiled with teal, barred summer duck, and unbarred summer duck
Sides	Jungle cock
Cheeks	Kingfisher
Topping	Golden pheasant crest
Head	Red and black lacquer

Silver Orange

Tag	Silver oval tinsel
Tail	Golden pheasant crest and tippet
Butt	Scarlet wool
Body	Flat silver tinsel
Throat	Magenta and dark blue or purple hackle
Wing	Two jungle cock, back to back and veiled with four golden pheasant tippets
Sides	Jungle cock and kingfisher
Topping	Golden pheasant crest
Head	Black

Ulla River

Tag	Fine gold oval tinsel
Tail	Golden pheasant crest, with strands of peacock sword over
Butt	Peacock herl
Body	First half: red floss. Second half: peacock herl
Ribbing	Oval gold tinsel
Hackle	Yellow hackle over red floss
Throat	Blue dun hackle
Wing	Lady Amherst tippet in strands, over which are married slips of green swan, mottled turkey, and white and lavender swan. Outside of these are slips of barred summer duck and bronze mallard
Sides	Jungle cock
Cheeks	Very small gray pigeon
Topping	Golden pheasant crest
Head	Brown lacquer

The above original patterns by Belarmino Martinez represent the highest standard in the dressing of classic salmon flies. The creativity and complexity of the patterns devised by Martinez have captured the interest of accomplished fly dressers around the world. Since *Atlantic Salmon Flies and Fishing* was published in 1970, many students of the art of fly tying have expressed curiosity about the methods employed by Martinez; it is for their benefit that the following information is included. According to Señor Martinez:

"I obtain the thread for tying the flies by unraveling ladies' nylon stockings without the seams. It's a job that at first looks difficult, but it's not that bad once you find the trick. Not all nylons are good for taking apart. Some have too much thread and turn out to be too thick. The ones that are ideal have two or three threads. The chenille for the tying of the fly *Narcea River* can be taken from strips of silk ribbon, one green and one yellow. Unravel one-half to three-fourths of the ribbons and wind them together.

PLATE 121
MARTINEZ FLIES FROM THE AUTHOR'S FISHING BOX, SIZES 4 TO 10
Photo courtesy of Belarmino Martinez

"I also design my own simple tools, vises that are manual. My system of tying is a bit different from the traditional way. I insert the eye of the hook into the vise when tying the bodies, and to put on the wings, I reverse and insert the hook into the vise in the traditional way."

Martinez uses few, if any, commercial fly-tying tools. Instead, he fashions what he needs out of wood or adapts common tools, such as pliers, for his purposes. Many of his flies are distinguished by a burnt sienna head, for which he uses automotive paint that also serves as a cement. The resourcefulness and ingenuity of Belarmino Martinez should be an example to the growing ranks of contemporary fly tiers—particularly to those who rush, with bulging wallets, to purchase the latest contrivance with the hope it will improve their results at the vise.

Norway

Since many who read this book would like to hook and land a gigantic Atlantic salmon of 40 pounds or even bigger, let's go first to the famous Vosso River in Norway, which has the reputation of harboring the biggest salmon in the world. Here, single-handed casting does not have the same sporting reputation it does in the United States, and a great percentage of the fishing is done by a method called *harling,* a back-trolling procedure for which surflike rods with large reels are used. Visiting Americans will find the approach quite different and lacking the traditional guidelines and constraints they may be accustomed to.

The lure of salmon fishing in Norway is due as much to the magnificence of the scenery as to the size of the fish. The granite-like mountains along the coast appear to have been ripped, split, and smashed by the violent gargantuan claws of nature to form a myriad of island peninsulas, fjords, lakes, and rivers nestled deep in rocky gorges whose glistening cliffs often rise vertically to a few thousand feet above the rippling waters. On more sloping places, and where trees can cling by root holds to the rock, the country is densely green with pines, firs, and birches. Above the treeline the mountains are baldly gray except for the greenish tinge of mosses. From these escarpments, waterfalls cascade from ledge to ledge, fed by small glaciers and patches of perpetual snow.

Down in the valleys, neat farms perch on hillsides and small towns colorfully display clusters of buildings whose red, blue, yellow, and white roofs protect those who make their living from the bounty of the sea. In every valley there is a stream, many harboring salmon, flowing through lush countryside where verdant fields are dotted with cattle and sheep. The fields are green with grasses and gardens and are colored in blues, yellows, and pinks by bluebells, clover, buttercups, and thistle. One feels the pervading influence of peace, quiet, and neatness. There is no litter because the careful always pick up whatever the careless have thrown away.

Those who have traveled extensively often refer to Norway as the most beautiful and most majestic country on earth. To see it, you can take a costly cruise in one of the luxurious ships that explore the wide and deep fjords, gazing up at the jagged cliffs and stopping here and there in small towns along the way. You can do it also by taking the Bergen to Oslo railway, an engineering marvel extending 295 miles and reaching an altitude of 4,300 feet at Finse, with two hundred tunnels bored through hard granite and three hundred bridges crossing the many rivers. The rail bed is blasted into the precipices of the mountainsides, where the train hums doggedly through the blackness of tunnels and suddenly appears in daylight to flash a kaleidoscope of awesome and ever-changing views of towering mountains, deep valleys, and tumbling waterfalls.

If you do this, do not miss riding the spur line from Myrdal to Flam, which is even more spectacular. This little railroad descends in 12 miles from 3,000 feet at Myrdal (on the Bergen to Oslo line) through various switchbacks and twenty tunnels (3.7 miles of them) down to the little town of Flam, on the Aurlandsfjord, which joins the Sognefjord, 112 miles in length and Norway's greatest. The *Viking Queen* was anchored there when we arrived.

Across from the railway station is the white and neat Fretheim Hotel, which looks across the wide fjord to a background of towering peaks. We went there for the fishing, both sea trout and salmon, but we soon put away our fly rods in favor of a drive along the fjord and up into the mountains. People who have been there refer to this as "seeing Norway in a nutshell."

So much for Norway's beauty. Now, how about Norway's fishing on the brawling Vosso River, reputed to hold the biggest Atlantic salmon in the world?

About an hour and a half's travel on the Bergen to Oslo railway brought us to the little town of Bolstad Oyri, where the Vosso flows into the Bolstadfjord, which is an arm of the Veafjord, which joins the Sorfjord. The lower 2 miles of the river, consisting of seven beats, has been leased for many years from farmers along the river by Odd Haraldsen, one of the world's greatest anglers for Atlantic salmon.

My fishing companion on this trip was Lewis Carr Stone, an M.I.T. fraternity brother and fine friend with whom I have fished in Iceland for several years. As the little train departed from the tiny Bolstad Oyri station, a car drove up to take us to Odd Haraldsen's lodge, "Oddsbu," a mile or so upriver. Odd and his people welcomed us there, and we stowed our gear, had a bite to eat, and got ready for the evening's fishing, which lasts from six o'clock to ten.

"Oddsbu" merits a description. The principal building, used by guests for eating, meeting, and sleeping, is of thick gray slabs of fieldstone, split from the mountainside. Its roof is of sod, on which grow grass, flowers, and tiny birches. Back of this, and looking across the river to the vertical cliff of a towering mountain, are other similar buildings for Odd's "den" and for the staff of people who run the lodge. All this melts into the hillside so subtly that it may not be noticed from the small road that passes by.

A wing at "Oddsbu" contains seven rooms for the seven rods, with a covered porch leading to the lounge. There is a coldroom for fish, and the wall is covered with framed photographs of former guests displaying gigantic salmon. The lounge is a large raftered room cozily furnished and ornamented with the heads of moose, elk, and other big game, plus life-size carvings of record salmon taken by Odd and his guests. A tremendous fieldstone fireplace covers one end of the room, except for the doorway leading into the dining area. This has recessed windows with small panes of rippled and leaded glass. One end is occupied by a large bas-relief carving of Vikings at war. The effect is almost medieval.

Meals are served on a heavy oak table, often by candlelight. Following the evening one, anglers retire to the lounge for coffee, smokes, and brandy and usually discuss the fishing until past midnight. Fishing hours are from ten to two and from six to ten. Beats are rotated every half day.

Possibly because of the size of the salmon and the depths and speed of the river, other types of tackle usually are preferred to flies. The Vosso is called a brutal river because of the volume of its water. During the early part of the season (late May and June), when the biggest fish come in, it is almost impossible to get flies down to them. Then, the popular gear consists of strong rods about 7 to 8 feet long with revolving spool reels, monofilament lines of 20 to 30 pounds-test, and prawns, spoons or plugs, the last called "wobblahs" by the gillies. Bait is not allowed. The use of worms is forbidden and viewed with contempt.

Most of the record fish are taken with prawns, shrimplike crustaceans of a little more than finger length. These are embalmed in a dye of blood red, shocking pink, or purple and are impaled on the long pin of a prawn-tackle, which has a rear treble hook and two double ones, plus straight barbs to help hold them into the prawn. Prawn and prawn-tackle are further attached to each other by winding the whole business with red string.

About 3 feet up on the monofilament from the prawn is a three-way swivel. The two opposite rings are connected to the line and its extension to the prawn. The third ring is affixed to a wire onto which lead is bent. The leads usually are bored balls about $3/4$ inch in diameter, weighing about an ounce. One or more are applied (usually two), depending on current speed and river depth.

This rig is cast by reeling the lead nearly to the tip-top, releasing the reel's drag, and flipping the lure over the edge of a current or other spot presumed to be a holding position for salmon. The drag is then reset and the lure is allowed to sink and swing somewhat in the manner of fishing a wet fly. The object is to bounce the lead as deep as possible without catching it or the prawn between rocks or on the moss or grass of the bottom.

I learned the hard way that this requires considerable skill. The angler must sense or feel the rig touching bottom and raise the rod tip to get it off, reeling in a bit from time to time, as necessary. An expert, such as Odd Haraldsen, makes it look easy. A casual flip puts the lure out, and it is kept from snagging and made to swim properly by what looks like a rhythmic up and down rocking of the rod, meanwhile keeping the line from sagging by reeling. When Odd fishes the prawn, it rarely gets into trouble, and he and his guests have hooked most of their giant salmon by the method. In fact, on the Vosso, about 90 percent of the salmon are taken this way. How sporting it is, or how much fun it is, is somewhat debatable.

The second most popular method (excluding fly fishing for the moment) is to use the same or similar tackle with *spoons*. These are the familiar wobblers in elongated oblong shape, selected in weights that will cast well and work near the bottom. They usually are between 4 and 6 inches long and stamped from a silvery metal, although some are gold or other color combinations.

Fishing the spoon is similar to fishing the prawn. Casts are made approximately cross-stream, depending on current speed, and the lure is allowed to sink and then swing on a tight line. If the angler feels or senses it touching bottom, he raises the rod tip to pull it up a little, meanwhile reeling in a bit if necessary. The object is to cover the best parts of the water by letting the spoon work as deep as possible.

When fishing from shore with both of these methods, extending casts are made as far as desirable, each succeeding one a foot or more farther out. Then the angler takes a few steps downstream and repeats them, thus covering the water as thoroughly as desired in much the same manner as you would cover a pool with a wet fly.

One of the most interesting ways of fishing the Vosso, and also used extensively on other Scandinavian rivers, is trolling small *lures,* usually of the slow-sinking type. My gillie announced that we would go out in a rowboat to fish a very wide stretch of thin water, and he attached a very familiar little plug to the same tackle used with the two previous methods. The lad was only sixteen years old, and it was only his second season on the river, but he knew his business pretty well and gave the impression that there wasn't much he didn't know about salmon fishing. He seemed to regard me as a rank novice, which I was, in using these methods.

"Now we will fish the wobblah," he announced.

I glanced at the plug.

"Oh, you mean a plug, not a wobbler," I remarked. "In fact, what you have on there is a Heddon River Runt, which we often use on lighter tackle for a fish we call bass."

The gillie looked at me in a rather condescending manner, seeming reproachful because I had had the effrontery to dispute him.

"No, sir," he said, "that is not a plug. It is a wobblah."

We got into the boat and pushed out to the head of the long, wide, and fairly shallow pool. It didn't look much like a pool, but it spilled into fast water, so salmon could be expected to rest there after their run up the rapids. The plug didn't weigh over half an ounce, and I wondered how it could be used on sturdy tackle suitable for all but the very biggest of oceangoing gamefish.

The gillie rested on his oars. "Let out line," he instructed.

Obediently I tossed out the tiny plug and free-spooled about 50 feet of line from the reel.

"More line," the little gillie ordered.

Finally things seemed to suit him, and he energetically bent to his oars and rowed across the river, with the plug trailing downstream. On reaching the far shore, he whipped the boat around and made for the near shore again, reaching it about 10 feet downstream from his starting point. This was repeated time and time again, each crossing a bit farther down. I looked at the relatively slick water just before it passed over the pool's lip, and I noted that the plug's position would bring it close to the lip on the next crossing.

"If there are salmon here, we'll connect with one next time," I thought. I hoped so, because I was getting bored and was sure the gillie was becoming tired.

I watched the position of the plug with renewed interest. About halfway across the river, there was a swirl where it should be, and I was fast to a large salmon. Setting the hook was unnecessary, because the plug is bountifully equipped with them. The 22-pound fish was no problem on the heavy tackle, and the gillie was far more pleased when he gaffed the salmon than I was.

The description of these three methods is not intended to imply that fishing the Vosso, or the many other rivers whereon they are used, isn't sporting. The angler may encounter a 40- or 50-pound fish, or even bigger, in this fast and deep river at any time, and he should be ready for it. This is big-game hunting, and it isn't sensible to be undergunned. As Odd Haraldsen says, "Fishing with light equipment on the Vosso is bloody nonsense."

In spite of all that, there are many places on the Vosso very suitable to the fly rod and small salmon flies in the 2 to 8 sizes. The two-handed fly rods used there are longer and stronger than my 9-foot graphite, which has taken many salmon in the 25-pound range, and I wanted to see what it could do with a fish of about twice that size. We were there at the end of July, and the big ones are more prevalent in late May or June. I did see a leviathan in that class, but when it rolled on the surface, it showed itself to be a dark and dour fish. I worked on it doggedly, but without result.

Rank, age, experience, or the way one parts one's hair seems to mean absolutely nothing to the precocious gillies on the Vosso. When I insisted on using the fly rod, my young mentor inspected the six boxes in my musette bag containing over four hundred salmon flies dressed by leading experts, and he turned up his nose at all of them. I thought it polite to let him select the proper one, but proposed one that seemed suitable to the conditions that prevailed.

He shook his head disdainfully.

"No," he said firmly, "we must have a brown one."

I rather sheepishly agreed that among this rather imposing collection, there wasn't a single one that could be called brown. We finally agreed on a *Brown Turkey,* which is more or less that. I fished it without result, and when the gillie wasn't looking, I cut it off and sneaked on a *Blue Rat,* which didn't do any better. I decided I wouldn't be caught that way again, however, so when I returned home, I ordered a couple dozen *March Browns!*

While writing about the supergiants among Salmo salar, one could make the logical query of how they get that way. Why are salmon in some rivers so much bigger than those in others? Why does the Vosso reputedly contain the biggest salmon in the world?

Two reasons come to mind.

First, although the Atlantic salmon is one species, the fish indigenous to one river can differ from those of all other rivers enough so that by inspection, their river or origin can be identified. For example, at Black Brook Pool, just below where New Brunswick's Cains River flows into the Miramichi, I was surprised to have guides look at salmon caught below the confluence and say, "This is a Cains River fish" or "This is a Miramichi fish." The physical characteristics of the two types varied enough to tell them apart. Some rivers breed bigger fish, others, smaller ones. Some rivers produce chunky ones, or fish with distinctively shaped heads, while others may breed salmon with different appearances. It is said that an experienced and discerning expert could distinguish the salmon in one river from those in all other rivers in the world.

Second, the longer the salmon live bountifully in the ocean, the bigger they become. In the Vosso, the returning salmon usually have spent between five and seven years at sea, so allowing two years or more for eggs to reach smolt stage in the river, these fish can be ten years old or older. Salmon returning to other rivers may come back after a year or so as a grilse, two years or so as a small salmon, or three years or so as a much larger one; after about three years at sea, salmon can be very big fish. But compare these with Vosso salmon, which can be considerably older. Every year at sea, before the instinct to return to the river predominates, can add on many pounds. For example, studies indicate that grilse, returning after one year at sea, weigh about $4^{1}/_{2}$ pounds on average. The same fish, after two years at sea, could weigh around 7 pounds; after three years, 14 pounds; after four years, 25 pounds; after five years, 42 pounds; and if it should not return until having spent six or seven years at sea, it would be a giant weighing 60 pounds, or possibly more!

The Vosso first was fished with rod and reel in about 1850. If we can call it the river with the biggest fish, we should term the Alta the best sporting salmon river in the world. The two are fished somewhat differently, so let's now have a look at the Alta.

Altafjord, the estuary of the Alta River, is located on the northwest coast of Norway, in the province of Finnmark, precisely on the seventieth parallel of north latitude, which is some 300 miles above the Arctic Circle. The principal occupations of the people of the town of Alta are fishing, slate mining, and forestry. It is also a trading center for the roving bands of Laplanders, who derive their livelihood from the herds of reindeer that they graze across northern Norway and Finland. During World War II, the Germans built an airstrip at Alta, which is currently the commercial airport. Despite its location, only 62 miles south of the North Cape, the climate in summer is surprisingly mild because it is tempered by the warmth of the Gulf Stream. In summer there are twenty-four hours of daylight, and although warm clothing is advisable when fishing, it is not at all uncommon to be comfortable in a woolen shirt during the day.

The Alta River, Norway

Rod and reel fishing began on the Alta in the early 1800s when exploring British gentlemen ventured up the fjords in chartered vessels or in their own yachts and found that many of the rivers emptying into the fjords teemed with salmon. They first put up with accommodations at nearby farms, but after negotiating long-term leases with the landowners, they later built comfortable lodges for themselves and their guests. The landowners welcomed this because the gentlemen were affable and generous, the leases were more profitable and less bother than commercial netting, and the well-staffed lodges offered ample employment.

These Victorian and Edwardian aristocrats protected their rivers with loving care, buying up nets and burning them to keep channels clear and pools unobstructed. They discovered, developed, and promoted the arts of fly fishing in Norway, although it seems obvious that they didn't always use flies. Anglers from other nations followed them, more

recently, Americans and Swedes. High taxes reduced the number of people who could afford fishing rights, and local angling clubs, outfitters, and organizations such as travel agencies and airlines now are in control in many areas.

Of all these rivers, the Alta is probably the most legendary and is still restricted to fly fishing. In the early years, anglers recorded some remarkable catches. For example, the Duke of Roxburghe took thirty-nine salmon in a single night in 1860, and when he first leased it in 1862, he found the salmon so plentiful that he restricted the river to fly fishing, a restriction that carries on to this day. The Duke of Westminster killed thirty-six salmon weighing a total of 792 pounds in a single night in 1906. While these records still stand, there are still plenty of fish to be had.

The Alta is a big river slightly larger than the Restigouche. It has many deep pools and is of a reddish tea color, without silty glacial water. The tem-

The Alta River, Norway

R. VALENTINE ATKINSON

perature of air and water is surprisingly high, with noon air temperatures perhaps as warm as 75 degrees F. and midnight as low as 40 degrees F. The water usually is in the high 50- to 60-degree range in summer.

All fishing is done at night, and from any place a boat can be launched. Regionally designed boats are typically very narrow and usually equipped with powerful outboard engines. Such a boat accommodates only one rod, with two gillies, one of whom acts as a guide while the oarsman brings the boat slowly across the pool, using the harling method described earlier.

Since the river is deep and rapid, and the shores precipitous and rocky, wading or fishing from shore is impractical, and in some places, harling with flies is common. Beats are rotated nightly, and each contains plenty of fish and pools.

The schedule is unusual because experience has shown that salmon take better around midnight,

when the sun is low. Thus, dinner is at about 7:00 P.M., with fishing starting an hour later. Everyone comes ashore for a midnight snack and hot coffee over an open fire. The fishing lasts until 3:00 A.M. Anglers retire at about 4:00 A.M. and get up at noon for a 1:00 breakfast. The afternoon can be used for sea trout fishing or relaxing.

Although mellowing with increased exposure to American ways, gillies have been reputed to be rather dogmatic about tackle and methods. They may recommend rods that are too sturdy because they are anxious for anglers to land their fish. They may insist on flies that are too large, patterns being whatever was successful recently. The popularity of tube flies has necessitated the use of much larger equipment than what I am accustomed to using— generally two-handed rods ranging from 13 feet for a 9-weight line to 15 feet for a 10-weight line.

Discolored water calls for brighter flies, such as those with some white or yellow in them. The gillies may want to trim them down; to avoid this, a few large low-water patterns may come in handy. Traditional classics such as *Thunder and Lightning, Green Highlander, Durham Ranger, Jock Scott, Silver Wilkinson, Silver Gray,* and *Gray Heron* still are occasionally used, but hairwings such as some of the *Rats,* the *Cosseboom, Hairy Mary, Black Sheep,* and adaptations of the classics are more popular. Overall, tube flies predominate; often they are little more than a large hank of black hair, somewhat crudely lashed to a tube, and named for the inspiration of the moment. Many are tied with bunches of goat hair, and some have been refined to the point of being considered patterns.

In a fireside chat with Odd Haraldsen at "Oddsbu," he commented that he had never heard of a salmon having been hooked on a dry fly in Scandinavia, and he seemed incredulous when I told him we had hooked several on dry flies in Iceland. The scarcity of insects in cold countries may explain this, but it would be interesting to hear that it has been done in Norway.

While the Vosso and the Alta are only two of Norway's many famous salmon rivers, their descriptions seem sufficient for the others, including such eminent ones as the Driva, Namsen, Surna, and Jolstra. Others, formerly famous, have declined. For example, the Laerdal used to be the top salmon river in the world, but a power station built on it has damaged its fishery considerably, at least for the present. There are some public rivers in northern Norway, but they usually offer only shoulder-to-shoulder fishing. Most of the others are in private hands, and day beat rentals can be arranged.

Sweden

The salmon rivers of Sweden have suffered largely because so many have been blocked by hydroelectric dams. In fairness, it is interesting to note that the electric power industry is financing the Salmon Research Institute, which studies problems associated with artificial salmon production.

In *The Atlantic Salmon: A Vanishing Species?* Anthony Netboy notes that Swedish salmon hatcheries are among the most efficient and productive in the world. "Salmon are now reared in central and south Sweden and trucked in the autumn or spring in 'fish pullmans' several hundred miles to northern smolt-receiving stations and then planted in the spring in rivers at the foot of the lowermost dams. Here they return one to three years later and an adequate number are stripped of their eggs and milt to start new generations in the hatcheries. The kelts are usually permitted to recuperate and return to the sea. It is estimated that one out of every four salmon now caught in the Baltic Sea is the product of a Swedish hatchery."

This solution, though obviously not the best one, provides power *and* salmon, which surely is better than power *or* salmon, because people will not sacrifice the former for the latter. Sea farming of salmon has, however, impacted and threatened the native fish.

Finland

Northwest of Russia and east of Norway and Sweden are the 130,000 or more square miles of rugged country that is Finland, reputed to offer the greatest Atlantic salmon fishing bargain in the world. Well-traveled salmon fisherman and writer Bill Hunter reports that "salmon are considered a natural resource and are harvested by the most effective means. The Finns fish to gut 'em and eat 'em; however, in recent years, some areas have been restored to fly fishing only." Salmon occur in three Finnish rivers: the Tenojoki, the Naatamojoki, and the Torino. *Joki* means "river," and in conversation is generally dropped from the name, so the Tenojoki is the Teno, or Tana. Incidentally, the world record for salmon on all tackle was established on the Tana River in 1928 by Henrik Henriksen for the 79-pound, 2-ounce fish he landed on the Norway side of the river. This record still stands. The Naatamo is a quantity river with plenty of salmon in the 10-pound class, but only a small proportion of big ones. The Torino produces few fish because of hydroelectric projects. The Tana, which flows along the northernmost tip of the country, dividing Finland and Norway, is the river usually referred to by salmon anglers.

Water becomes ice-free in early May in southern Finland and about a month later in the north. Although salmon fishing is permitted from May 1 through August 30, the best period is generally between June 15 and August 15. The waters, being partly in Finland and partly in Norway, are governed by a Finnish-Norwegian committee that has set up specific regulations covering the Tana. Since these regulations change periodically, anglers anticipating a trip there should do some research.

The swift, rocky Tana has few places adaptable for wading or for casting from shore, and most of the fishing is done by harling. Boats are of the long Norwegian variety, and because of rapid water, the oarsmen do not like to have more than one fisherman in a boat at one time. The Lapp guide works the channels and midstream riffles with two lines out, while the customer uses one or two fly rods. The guide rows back and forth across the current in a series of drops, allowing his lures and the angler's flies to work 50 or 60 feet downstream where he has reason to believe that salmon are lying. When a fish is hooked, the guide hands the busy rod to his sport and reels the others in.

Accommodations in Finland have been very reasonable and still offer one of the world's best buys in salmon fishing. There is a modern, comfortable hotel in the village of Utsjoki, which is located right on the Tana. Flying from place to place within Finland is relatively inexpensive, and low-cost transoceanic excursion rates are available.

Denmark

Denmark, because of its small size and also because of pollution, has no salmon rivers of its own, but it is a leading offender in netting and long-lining the fish stocked or naturally propagated in the rivers of other countries. These depredations, mainly on the high seas, such as in the Davis Straits, so seriously depleted the stocks in the years around 1970 that they were curtailed by international agreement. In spite of this, they still have a dangerously adverse effect on the fishery.

Salmon fattening on the bounty of the sea could be likened to livestock grazing in communal pastures, where the animals are turned out to roam for long periods and then collected and sorted for return to their various owners, who have marked them for quick identification by branding, paint smears, or other methods. There is no doubt about who owns each one, and rustlers or thieves who steal any are dealt with harshly, often having been shot or hanged from the nearest tree.

Many nations having salmon rivers raise salmon in hatcheries, and then release them in the hope that they will return as adults, thus making the expensive investment practical. Some of these fish are marked, and many caught by Danish fishermen (and others) have been identified as having been raised in the rivers of Canada, the United States, Iceland, the British Isles, and other countries. Thus they cannot be compared with other marine species such as herring and cod, which are considered fair oceanic game belonging to whoever captures them.

Regardless of the ethics of the matter, few or no attempts have been made by the Danish government to set up conservation regulations. Salmon of any size are caught, and most of them are sexually immature, indicating they could have had one or more years of added growth before they would have returned to their native rivers—a very wasteful practice, to say the least.

Ideally, in my estimation, the lordly Atlantic salmon should internationally be declared a sport fish, and all commercial fishing on the high seas and along the coasts should be stopped before the species is decimated beyond return. Let the salmon come home to their own rivers and to their rightful owners. Then the proportion that is needed for propagation can be protected, and the surplus used for regulated angling and prudent harvesting. This may tax the "have not nations," such as the Danes, but it would be for the international good. The Danes are kind, intelligent, and beautiful people who should not descend to treating the Atlantic salmon as a cod, a herring, or a fluke, particularly since they have no Atlantic salmon of their own.

Readers who consider going fishing in any of the Scandinavian countries should write to the tourist bureau of the nation in question or, better yet, make arrangements through a reliable tour group. There are now organizations who cater to anglers almost exclusively.

Salmon Flies of Scandinavia

Little need be added to what has been said about favored fly patterns for Scandinavia. The larger hook sizes are little used anymore except by the few anglers wielding the hefty rods that will cast them easily. The fancy classic featherwings popularized by Kelson and Pryce-Tannatt are being employed less and less, except for sentiment, having given way almost completely to their hairwing counterparts and tube-fly adaptations of them. Anglers using fly rods in the 9-foot range can get along nicely with a few hairwing patterns in sizes between 2 and 10 and in color schemes ranging from dark to medium to light. Exactly which patterns is a matter of opinion, but my choice would include *Black Rat, Rusty Rat, Silver Rat, Blue Charm* or *Irish Hairy Mary, Muddler* (the original dressing), and if I should have the same gillie again, the *March Brown.*

Although special patterns are not necessary for Scandinavian fishing, a few historic ones are included here, in addition to the popular *Shrimp.* Following these are several tube-fly patterns, if you are inclined to use them.

Namsen (Norway)

Tag	Oval silver tinsel and yellow floss
Tail	Golden pheasant crest, over which are red hackle fibers and gray mallard
Butt	Black ostrich herl
Body	Seal's fur, in four equal parts, of yellow, fiery claret and dark blue
Ribbing	Oval silver tinsel and fine oval gold thread
Throat	A black hackle
Wing	An inner wing of married strips of yellow, red, and dark blue goose and speckled turkey tail, over which on each side is brown mallard, with barred teal at top of wing over this. Married strips of golden pheasant tail; florican bustard; peacock wing; red, blue, and yellow goose.
Head	Black

Probably the *Namsen,* named for the famous Norwegian salmon river, was first mentioned in *Jones' Guide to Norway and Salmon Fishers' Pocket Companion,* published in London in 1848. He described a fly called the *Major* and added that this fly was known in Norway as the *Namsen.* He gave the dressing as follows: head of black ostrich; tag of silver thread and red silk; tail of golden pheasant crest; and body consisting of sections of pale blue, orange, and wine-red hackle feathers, two snipe feathers, mixed duck and argus pheasant, over which are "two golden threads" (probably golden pheasant crest), with yellow hackle around this.

In preparing this book, I obtained several examples of the *Namsen.* All are different, as sometimes is true on various parts of a long river. The above pattern was sent by Yngvar Kaldal, of Oslo, who considers it the most popular one.

Ola (Norway)

Tag	Oval silver tinsel and golden yellow
Tail	Golden pheasant crest
Butt	Black ostrich herl
Body	In two equal parts: rear half, gray; forward half, black
Ribbing	Wide flat and small oval silver tinsel
Hackle	A black cock's hackle palmered over front half of the body only
Throat	Guinea fibers
Wing	White-tipped turkey slips or blue swan with bronze mallard over
Sides	Barred teal
Cheeks	Jungle cock
Topping	Golden pheasant crest
Head	Black

Veniard calls for a tag of pink floss and the same colors of seal's fur for the body.

Ottesen (Norway)

Tag	Round silver tinsel and scarlet floss (pink is sometimes used)
Tail	Golden pheasant crest
Butt	Black ostrich herl
Body	Flat silver tinsel (some dressings call for white floss)
Ribbing	Scarlet floss
Hackle	A scarlet cock's hackle palmered next to the ribbing (some dressings call for hot orange)
Throat	Barred teal or wigeon
Wing	Two golden pheasant tippets, back to back, over which but not concealing the top and bottom edges are married sections of yellow, red, and blue swan or goose and peacock quill, teal over
Topping	Golden pheasant crest
Cheeks	Jungle cock, of moderate length
Head	Black

As we have seen before, dressings vary in different areas along the rivers. In this case, follow the dressing given, using the alternate materials as a variation.

Peer Gynt (Norway)

Tag	Round silver tinsel and yellow floss
Tail	Golden pheasant crest, over which are a few shorter crimson hackle fibers
Butt	Black ostrich herl
Body	Flat silver tinsel
Ribbing	Oval silver tinsel
Hackle	A crimson hackle palmered forward from second turn of tinsel
Throat	Guinea fibers
Wing	Two strips of brown mottled turkey, with brown mallard over it
Topping	Golden pheasant crest
Cheeks	Jungle cock, about half as long as the wing
Horns	Blue-yellow macaw
Head	Black

This fly was originated in 1963 by John Sand, considered to have been the most famous dresser of

PLATE 122
NORWEGIAN FEATHERWINGS, DRESSED BY BERT STROMBERG

Sheriff

Peer Gynt

Ola

Ottensen

Namsen

trout flies in Norway. This description is from a true reproduction tied by his son, Erling Sand.

Sheriff (Norway)

Tag	Fine oval gold tinsel
Tail	Golden pheasant crest, over which are guinea fibers
Butt	Black ostrich herl
Body	Rear half: flat gold tinsel. Front half: black ostrich herl
Ribbing	Oval gold tinsel
Hackle	A yellow cock's hackle, wound over the herl only
Throat	Guinea fibers
Wing	Two strips of dark turkey tail, with broad strips of brown mallard on each side
Topping	Golden pheasant crest
Cheeks	Jungle cock
Horns	Scarlet macaw
Head	Black

This fly was originated by John Sand, and the sample from which the dressing was taken was again provided by his son, Erling Sand.

Shrimp (Norway)

Tail	The tip of a hot orange hackle, upright
Body	Blood red wool, fairly thick, and tapered
Ribbing	Flat gold tinsel
Hackle	A hot orange hackle leading the tinsel, with two or three large hot orange hackles tied in heavily as a collar at the head of the fly and tied back slightly (there is no wing)
Head	Black

Evidently this fly is a copy of the Swedish *Chilimps*. The *Chilimps* was first tied by Olle Tornblom on April 28, 1942, and its dressing was suggested by Rolf Wilhelmson. The story goes that it was tied with hackle from a shaving brush colored with nail polish, and with thread from a skirt; this later evolved into the above pattern. The fly is intended to imitate a shrimp. Wilhelmson got its name from a child in London who was selling

PLATE 123
TRADITIONAL NORWEGIAN PATTERNS

Namsen #1
dressed by Mustad

Sheriff
dressed by Erling Sand

Namsen #2
dressed by Erling Sand

Namsen #3
dressed by Olaf Olsen

Chilimps (Shrimp)
dressed by Erling Sand

PLATE 124
CONTEMPORARY NORWEGIAN PATTERNS

Flies dressed by Rod Yerger except as noted

Alta Red

Alta Skunk   *Alta March Brown*

Sun Ray Shadow
originated and dressed by Ray Brooks

Alta Ghost   *Bruiser*

Black and Gold

shrimp but who mispronounced the word "chilimps."

The fly is tied in many versions in Scandinavia, one being the *Shrimp Silver* or *Silver Shrimp,* which is identical except that the rear half of the body is silver tinsel without hackling. My pattern is dressed on a #4 hook.

Tube-Fly Patterns for Norway

Sun Ray Shadow

The *Sun Ray Shadow* is one of the earliest, simplest, and most effective of the contemporary tube-fly patterns. It was devised by Ray Brooks and resembles a *Collie Dog*, but does not have a silver body. As tied by its originator, the *Sun Ray Shadow* is dressed on a translucent milky-colored tube with a long wing of black hair and peacock. The example shown is from Stan Bogden's fly box (fished) and tied for him by Brooks.

Alta Ghost

Tag	Fine oval gold tinsel
Body	Black dubbing
Ribbing	Medium oval gold tinsel
Hackle	Heron substitute (Clorox burned goose shoulders)
Under-wing	Black bucktail
Wing	Black goat hair topped with peacock herl
Sides	Jungle cock
Head	Black

Alta Red Fly

Tag	Fine oval gold tinsel
Body	Red dubbing
Ribbing	Medium oval gold tinsel
Hackle	Heron substitute (Clorox burned goose shoulders)
Under-wing	Red bucktail
Wing	Black goat hair
Sides	Jungle cock
Head	Black

Alta March Brown

Tag	Fine oval gold tinsel
Body	Brown dubbing
Ribbing	Medium oval gold tinsel
Throat	Partridge fibers
Under-wing	Brown bucktail
Wing	Black goat hair
Sides	Jungle cock
Head	Brown

Black and Gold

Body	Gold mylar piping, tied down at rear with red thread
Wing	Alternating quarters of black and yellow bucktail
Head	Black

Bruiser

Tag	Fine oval silver tinsel
Body	Black floss
Ribbing	Flat and medium oval silver tinsel
Wing	Alternating quarters of black and blue bucktail
Head	Black

Skunk

Tag	Fine oval silver tinsel
Body	Black floss
Ribbing	Medium oval silver tinsel
Throat	Black hackle
Under-wing	Black bucktail
Wing	Black goat hair topped with white goat hair
Sides	Jungle cock
Head	Red

The above six patterns were sent by professional fly tier Rod Yerger, of Lawrence, Pennsylvania. For the many tube flies he ties, he designed a hook sleeve that he makes from vinyl tubing. These sleeves are tapered over a mandrel, heated, and quenched in order to retain their shape. Yerger writes, "This allows the hook to hold in place during casting, in line for proper fishing, and pivot and pull away after a salmon's take. These are the only sleeves that really work." He adds, "For Norway, eyes of some type, either painted or jungle cock, are considered essential."

The important feature of the goat-hair patterns is the black wing. The shorter bucktail underwing is added to prevent the goat hair from tangling in the hook.

13

Fishing Iceland's Dream Streams

"On the Laxa" courtesy of Bill Young

We who fight the never-ending battle to pre-serve our trout and salmon streams may draw strength by reflecting on those on an island not much larger than the state of Maine where conservation has successfully protected its rivers for about a thousand years.

Imagine your dream stream as you'd like it to be. Clean, cold water you can safely drink. No pollution, no black flies, no artificial obstructions, and efficient fish ladders for natural waterfalls where necessary. Uncrowded fishing under snowcapped mountains where every angler has a mile or so of pools all to himself or to share with a friend.

Imagine your dream stream with every possible fishing situation from crashing waterfalls, sporty fast-water stretches, and wadable shelving riffles against rock-face walls to placid meadow pools. Imagine making the cautious approach on a pool that you'd use for trout, sneaking up on an edge in the flow to accurately present a #8 or #10 hairwing with an 8-foot trout rod, and being rewarded with the smashing strike of a brightly silvered Atlantic salmon of 10 or 20 pounds that takes you so far down into your backing it seems you could be holding a recalcitrant bull on a tether!

Imagine seeing this dream stream alive with salmon. Everywhere you look, you see them rising from resting positions or porpoising in steady parade as they move in from the sea to journey farther and farther upstream. Every river is regulated by the government—your limit may be as many as you can land, or as few as seven fish per day, depending on the rules of that particular river. The prudent restrictions on the number of allowable rods are based on their taking the maximum quantity of salmon without depleting the stocks, this maximum being based on previous rod records.

The fun on your dream stream is more in hooking and handling the fish than in landing them. These are unusually energetic salmon, imbued by heredity with the stamina to combat fast water and to jump high falls. They are beautifully streamlined, with small heads and fat bodies; the crowning challenge on light tackle. Even the most accomplished anglers are lucky to land 50 percent of the fish they hook. When a buster slams the fly, it may hightail downstream where rocks often prevent the angler from following very far. When it is obvious that the fish has won, just snub the reel to break the leader. Tie on another fly while exhaling a hearty "Wow!"

Anglers on Iceland's "dream streams" need plenty of flies, partly because backcasts often break barbs on contact with rocks. "Something with blue in it" is usual, in sizes from 6 to 12, singles, doubles, or even trebles. Patterns without blue also can be useful, however. A red or orange prawn type like Peter Deane's *Red Frances* (also known as the *Black-Eyed Prawn* or *BEP*) often does well. So does the popular *Undertaker*, or a far-out streamer such as one of Joe Hubert's *Sheep* series.

Use as heavy a line as the rod can handle, because casts are often into the wind. A floater is good in thin water; otherwise, use a floater with a sinking tip, or even a sinking line for the rare cases when dour salmon are lying deep in pools—or on some especially cold-water rivers in northwestern Iceland, such as Thorskafjardara, or on the south coast, such as Ranga. Leaders should be as strong as will swim the fly correctly in order to provide greatest possible control over salmon hooked in difficult places, an exception being when working over stale fish, when the finest sensible strength usually proves best.

Retie the fly after every catch. If you neglect to do this, you may lose "the big one," which always seems to strike when you've been careless about a weakened terminal knot or an abraded tippet!

Iceland has more than eighty salmon rivers with significant runs but with varying desirability to anglers. Not all are "dream streams." Some, fed by glaciers, are milky with glacial clays. The others are pure and clean because they come from melting snow masses. During the fishing season, these usually maintain constant level. They roughly can be divided into three types: large, medium, and small. Although some anglers think the large ones lack character, many prefer them to the more confined smaller rivers—the popular Laxá í Adaldal, for example, is a very big river. *Laxa* is the Icelandic word for "salmon river," and the rest of the appellation indicates where the river is. Others may prefer the snow-fed rivers of moderate size, but their ease of access, the quality of accommodations provided, and the cost of the fishing further restrict selection.

Southwestern Iceland

Let's first look at a moderate-size snow-fed stream in southwestern Iceland only an hour's drive from Reykjavik, a favorite I have fished for several years. This "dream stream" is the famous Laxá í Kjós,

Laxá í Adaldal in northern Iceland

ICELAND PHOTO AND PRESS SERVICE, MATS WIBE LUND, JR.

known as the most consistent river because of its steady level in season and the almost constant influx of schools of salmon when angling is allowed between mid-June and mid-September.

Laxá í Kjós has a fishable length of about 12 miles, controlled by a very reliable Icelandic agent who represents the farmers who own it because they own the abutting land. Iceland's conservation-minded government limits the number of rods that can fish this river to ten at one time, and each rod has about a mile of the stream to itself. The river is divided into beats of various lengths, depending on the quality of the fishing in each. For economic reasons, sharing rods is quite common in Iceland—two anglers sharing one rod or three sharing two. This "buddy system" is agreeable to most because twelve hours of fishing per day are allowed: in the south, 7:00 A.M. to 1:00 P.M. and 3:00 P.M. to 9:00

P.M., and in the north, 7:00 A.M. to 1:00 P.M. and 4:00 P.M. to 10:00 P.M.

Laxá í Kjós empties into an arm of the sea just below a highway bridge on the peripheral road along the coast. Just upstream of this bridge is a spectacular rocky waterfall cascading into numerous "steps" or small pools in which salmon rest before jumping the falls. Although not very deep, the water usually is so turbulent that one rarely can see resting fish in these places.

This is exciting sport. A properly cast fly remains in the whitewater of one of the smaller pockets for only an instant or so, but this is enough time for a big salmon to slam it, *if* it wants to. It boils at the fly and takes it with a solid jerk. Then the fun begins! The salmon may try to jump the falls, but the tight line prevents this. It may try to fight it out in one or more of the small pools, or it may streak for the estuary, zigzagging between rocks and racing down the fast current below the bridge, where anglers can't follow. In such spots, many are hooked but few are landed. For such thrills, I'll risk losing a fly anytime!

The solid jerk that a salmon can give a fly has to be felt to be believed. Once, while fishing in this spot, my guide came to speak to me, and I reeled in the line nearly to the leader. During our conversation, I idly flipped the fly into a small, foaming pocket that I had thought too close and too small to bother with. A salmon, obviously very big, hit the fly with such a savage jerk that it broke me off at the fly's knot. The tippet's strength was 12 pounds. I didn't even see the fish because of the whitewater, but no one ever can convince me that salmon don't sometimes strike from anger!

A wide, rock-dotted area just above the falls has many places where salmon can rest. This area can be fished from shore, or by wading near shore. More adventurous anglers wade down farther out, probing each holding position as soon as they can swing a fly into it. They rarely wade far without a hookup. A salmon's first run here may take out line well into the backing, and the fish may swing around boulders. If so, a nimble guide will splash out at full gallop to lift the line free, to the embarrassment of cautious fishermen who won't venture as far. Of course, the guide is an expert at wading and very familiar with the water.

Just above here is another waterfall, with a fish ladder. Fishing is prohibited at the base of the falls because the pool is thick with salmon. They jump in constant procession, many falling back to try again after resting. Near here the lodge is situated, the only one on the river. Its cozy motel-type rooms and excellent food are welcome after a long day astream. After early breakfast, and again after lunch and a short rest, the guides take their anglers to assigned beats. Beats rotate and are changed twice a day, so everyone has his chance at favorite pools.

Above this waterfall, the river becomes narrower and more placid, flowing gently downward through a wide diversity of pools. Some of these are graveled riffles shelving deeply to rock faces. Here you need to sneak up cautiously to work the fast water at the head of the pool first, because salmon often lie just over the lip. Others constantly show in the pool itself, much to the frustration of anglers during the occasional periods when the fish seem of a common mind to strike at nothing.

In mild weather, this sort of pool tempts the use of the dry fly, perhaps a hard-to-sink *Bomber* or a *Wulff*. Although it has been said that salmon won't come to dry flies in northern latitudes, I've seen it happen—right here! Generally speaking, however, relatively few Icelandic salmon are caught on dries. Anglers have had minimal success on Kjós, and there is some dry-fly fishing on the Vatnsdalsá, in the north.

Other pools in this section of the river have varying characteristics offering every possible fishing situation for every taste. A type I delight in is a finely graveled meadow stretch with many bends, seemingly too placid for good holding positions, but here and there immense clods of turf have slipped into the stream to form edges of current. Here you should sneak up, extend the cast dry-fly style, and drop it just above the top of the edge. As it drifts and swings slightly, a big salmon may take it, and this is an easy place to handle it. Get the fish away from the edge and downstream as fast as possible to avoid spooking the others. A good angler may take two fish from such a small spot and possibly three!

Upstream from these placid places, Laxá í Kjós foams through a spectacular canyon area where deep, rocky, crystal-clear pools are sprinkled between fast runs and chutes. This is sporty salmon fishing again. Since the fish often can be seen leisurely finning in large or smaller groups, anglers must take care that the salmon don't see them. As in trout fishing in rocky streams, ledges and boulders can conceal your approach. Measure backcasts against their distance from the rocks, and check your fly often. Despite all precautions, anglers often hear or feel a slight *tick* when a backcast has extended, signaling that the fly has hit a rock and probably has a broken barb.

At the head of the canyon is a baby Niagara about 80 feet high, which is the end of the road for the salmon. The fish mill around in the deep pool below the cataract, some trying a fruitless jump or two, and then drop back to lower pools to select places for spawning. At the falls, it is a precariously steep descent to the river, but once down there, you will usually find fascinating fishing amid the grandeur of one of Iceland's most beautiful rivers. Anglers enjoy fishing the canyon area from the falls to the meadows along the narrow footing between the river and the cliffs and usually emerge with as many salmon as they can carry.

Southwestern Iceland contains more than a score of beautiful salmon rivers that are easy to reach and have excellent accommodations. Beginning in the south, a few others of these are as follows:

The Ranga, 60 miles southeast of Reykjavik, is Iceland's most recently developed river for angling. Fed by cold underground springs, its waters are crystal clear, and good river management has made it one of Iceland's most productive rivers. Its 40 miles provide a variety of conditions in a balanced flow of water. The lower sections of the west and east Ranga are best for salmon, and the uppermost sections are good for brown trout.

The Grimsa, 75 miles north of Reykjavik, is very similar in size, characteristics, and accommodations to Laxá í Kjós, but perhaps with less varied angling situations. With over sixty named pools, the Grimsa is one of Iceland's most prolific rivers. Its bookings are now handled by the farmers' association.

The Thverá and the Kjarrá are two more good rivers, a bit north of the Grimsa. With a total length of approximately 45 miles, these rivers have no barriers to hinder ascending fish.

The Langá, another of Iceland's top rivers, is west of these. The Langá is lake fed, keeping the water level up during dry spells; the lower half of it also benefits from tidal flow. Most pools on the more than 12 miles of fishable water are easily accessible.

The Nordurá in the central southwest (and a little north of the Thverá and Kjarrá), is called "the young man's river" because it is big and rocky and in many places requires considerable walking. During several visits, I enjoyed the widely varying situations and challenges of this diverse river. On one trip, when conditions were far from the best, the trick was to look for rising salmon behind rocks. After seeing two or three rises in the same place, one of us would put a fly there and usually would hook the fish.

On another trip, we rowed across the Nordurá and found a large pool nearby. After climbing around rocky rivers for several days, my boots and my feet were feeling so incompatible that I decided to spend the afternoon at the pool rather than walking farther upstream with the others. Watching a river is a pleasant and profitable prelude to fishing it. I found a comfortable perch on a low shelf of the rock face, where the tiny orchid-colored blossoms of wild thyme mingled with others of yellow and white amid masses of miniature deep green plants clinging to the porous stone. Overhead, patches of cottony white cumulus clouds scudded slowly eastward below the blue. Two small arctic terns, white

Casting in Iceland

with grayish wings and black topknots, cheeped and chirred as they dove toward me in resentment of my intrusion into their remote domain. Finally considering me harmless, they lighted nearby, watching the water for surfacing parr.

My interest turned to the pool. Its entrance was a chute where the current circled counterclockwise—a bad place to work a fly and for resting salmon to lie. Farther down, however, the currents smoothed and widened, fan shaped, as the water thinned into the rocky lip. That seemed to be the place salmon should stop to rest after running up into the pool. It was a very wide area to fish. No salmon showed anywhere.

After fastening a #8 double *Blue Charm* hairwing to the 12-pound tippet, I waded out a prudent distance on the rocky bottom and cast the fly quartering across the thinning tail of the pool. The fly swung beautifully in a very wide arc at just the right speed. When it began to hang, I brought it in, extended the cast a foot or so, and tried again.

Midswing, a salmon showed behind the fly but didn't take. I pondered whether to change the fly or to try the same pattern in a smaller size. Favoring the *Blue Charm* under such conditions, I lengthened the leader by two sections to 8 pounds and tied on the same pattern in the smaller size 10. Without lengthening the cast, I let the fly swing to where the salmon showed. The fish came up again and took solidly.

I quickly coaxed the salmon into the nearer and deeper water. It rushed across the pool, jumped twice, and in about ten minutes it gave up the fight. The rocks along the shoreline were too big for beaching a salmon, but there was a watery cliff between two of them. Leading the salmon into it, I pushed it to safety. My pocket scales weighed it at 10 1/2 pounds.

While resting the pool, I looked among the rocks for a better beaching area. Finding none, I moved several rocks to form a smooth landing ramp, slid the fish into plastic sleeving (knotted at both ends), and laid the package in a corral of rocks made at the edge of the pool. All this had taken only an hour, and there were three more to go before my companions should return.

The pair of terns had been watching all this with considerable interest and seemed quite tame. I

Angus Cameron joined the author in Iceland   LEWIS C. STONE

Looking for the best water

tossed a bit of bread to them, but they ignored it. One suddenly took wing and dove on the pool to pick up a tiny fish, with which it returned, reminding me that fishing has various facets independent of the sport itself.

With the pool now well rested, I waded out once more and laid out the little fly again. In its swing, it passed the spot where the salmon had been hooked, but another fish took it a few feet farther on. It put up a lusty battle, as Icelandic salmon usually do. I worked it smoothly up the makeshift landing ramp, the bottom of which was fine gravel, and put it into the plastic sleeving with the first one.

This tough, transparent sleeving, available in rolls 12 inches wide, offers an excellent way to store and to carry salmon. Enough for the day is light and easy to carry. Cut a piece the desired length and tear it off from the rest. Knot it at one end, slip in one or more fish, and knot the other end. Two packages (if you are that lucky) can be tied together and carried over the shoulder, heads down. It protects cars and clothes, as well as the salmon. It may well be available in the United States, but the mysterious Ice-landic writing on it is very charming, and I always pick up an ample supply in Iceland as a memento of fine times spent there.

I rested the pool again, then laid out the fly a third time. On the second cast, I caught a third salmon. There were two more hours left for fishing.

Why not give the fish a better chance with an even smaller fly and a lighter leader, I thought. I added another tippet of 6 pounds and bent on the smallest *Blue Charm* I had, a size 12. This is so tiny that its hook won't overlap the nail of my little finger! There are those who say that a fly of such small size can't hook and hold a big salmon, but indeed, tiny flies can be as successful as they as satisfying to the angler who chooses to meet the challenge.

The line shot out again. The long leader rolled over nicely, and the *Blue Charm* started its swing. Just before it began to drag, a salmon took it. This fish was about the same size as the others, but it took more time to handle it because of the caution required when using small flies.

Three salmon were hooked on the tiny fly, of which two were beached and one was lost because

A cocked tailer ready for use

the hook pulled out at the last minute. Was this because of the small hook size, or was the hooking so insecure that the same thing would have happened with a much larger fly? Who knows? This was fishing purely for the fun of it!

I relaxed on the rock shelf with my lighted pipe and watched the pair of terns perched nearby. They are very pretty birds, and very lucky to be able to spend their summers fishing in such a place, while I had to rob the piggy bank to be here for only a week!

Angus Cameron, Lew Stone, and our guide, Pall, appeared on the narrow path leading over the rock face. They all looked tired and had no salmon.

Angus plopped down on the low ledge and looked at me inquiringly. "Well, how did you do?"

"Five—about 10 pounds each."

Lew looked incredulous. "We borrowed your tailer, so how could you have landed five salmon among all these rocks?"

I pointed to the landing ramp.

Angus fishing in Iceland

Angus looked at the five salmon, barely afloat in their plastic bags in the rock-circled corral. Then he looked at Lew and pointed to the ramp, where a few silvery scales shone on the gravel.

Angus chuckled. "He not only skunked us good and proper, but *that* is adding insult to injury!"

Pall picked up the salmon and shouldered the other equipment. He laughed contentedly, because guides vie among one another on the number of salmon their sports catch. He turned to Angus.

"You have this pool tomorrow morning," he remarked. "Maybe Joe will let you use his landing ramp."

Northwestern Iceland

Of the four northwestern salmon rivers we will look at here, the farthest, and one of the most beautiful, is the Langá. Cars pause by the bridge to view it and often to watch anglers as their rods bow to the runs of salmon. Near its outlet, it is wide, flat, and rock studded, nd is usually wadable. This area has many holding positions for salmon, which stop to rest here and there after jumping the falls that separate the stream from its estuary. Here is Langá Lodge, where anglers stay amid flowery green fields dotted with cows, sheep, and horses. Upstream, the river bends abruptly and forms a large, pondlike pool at whose head is a turbulent waterfall pouring into a short, rocky chute before it widens into the pond.

Salmon can jump the falls or use its fish ladder; most prefer the former. Red marks on the rocks indicate that anglers must not fish just below the falls but can work their flies in the chute. My wife and I considered this beat our favorite. She was entranced by standing close to the falls to watch salmon leap up, almost at arm's length. I enjoyed the sporty fishing in the chute, and it was here that I lucked into one of the larger salmon taken from the Langá on a fly.

The Langá's salmon are more noted for their quantity and stamina than for size. Their average weight has been a shade under 6 pounds. Although attempts have been made to introduce a strain of much larger fish, this has not yet been successful, and size remains about the same.

There are tricks to fishing this chute, which is turbulent, narrow whitewater rushing between large rocks and over a ledge into the pondlike pool. The fly must land close to the far-side rocks only in cer-

tain places where the currents will take it down into the few unseen holding positions. Correctly done, a salmon will bang it, if one in a taking mood is there. It will rush up the fast water to the falls and jump and fight it out there, or it will elect to run into the pond and down its swifter current on the far side. If no salmon takes the fly, it will swing down over the ledge into the pond and, in retrieval, often will become caught on the moss of rocks on the ledge. This is quite sporty fishing, and we take occasional salmon here, as well as from easier places downstream.

While my wife was watching salmon leaping into the falls, I was concentrating on properly working a #8 *Blue Charm* double in the chute. No taking fish seemed to be there, and on one retrieve cast, the fly appeared to be caught underwater on the ledge. The solution in this situation is to walk down to the pond, just below the ledge, and pull it off.

While doing this, I soon realized that the fly wasn't caught on the ledge, but in the mouth of a salmon that had been nosing up to it. On feeling the steel, the fish raced across the pond, and it was a surprisingly big one.

The fish streaked to the far bank, which was distant enough to take the line far into its backing. The salmon rolled there a bit, and allowed itself to be coaxed in. The problem was to keep it in the quiet water on the left of the pond, rather than to let it get into the fast current on the right. Our guide, who had been with another angler upstream, appeared with him, and cars stopped by the bridge, disgorging a gallery of spectators. Inclined to become nervous when handling a fish before a crowd, I prayed that the hook was secure and nothing would happen to spoil things. Something almost did!

The big salmon made several runs, each a bit shorter, without realizing it could reach safety in the nearby current. The guide stood by with tailer cocked and eventually was able to yank the noose over the tail of the exhausted fish. It weighed 22 pounds on Icelandic scales, which are roughly 10 percent under American ones. (The precise equivalent is 9.1 percent; an Icelandic pound equals 17.5 ounces or 500 grams.) Of course, this fish wasn't very big by the standards of some countries, but both for the Langá and for me, it was notable.

With the salmon safely ashore, I was shocked to note that a blood knot on the leader had begun to

A good catch

From a fly fisherman's point of view, the catch records can be a bit misleading. Rivers catering to anglers visiting Iceland usually are restricted to fly-fishing, particularly during the best part of the season, which normally is from late June through August; however, some of these may permit spinning tackle, with worms or hardware, during off-season weeks. Weekly statistics of the number of salmon caught on a river those weeks near the start and end of the season may look very good, but this may be because they included spinning, whereas the records near the middle of the season may be for fly fishing only.

Of Iceland's more than eighty salmon rivers, the following are statistically the most productive: Nordurá, Thverá and Kjarrá, Laxá á Asum, Rangá, Laxá í Leirársveit, Langá, Selá, Grimsá and Tunguá, Laxá í Adaldal, Ellidaár, Blanda and Svartá and Laxá í Kjós. Catch figures for these rivers vary from year to year; if you are planning a trip, contact the North Atlantic Salmon Fund, the Reykjavik Angling Club, or the Federation of Icelandic River Owners, all of which are located in Reykjavik, for current information.

Some rivers are leased by the Reykjavik Angling Club and others by individuals, clubs, or small groups of people. Permits are sold mostly by private arrangement. Most of these salmon rivers are in the southwest or the north.

Northern Rivers

Anglers seeking large salmon are most likely to find them in the northern rivers. These are a bit farther away, but the air service to these places is very good.

Laxá á Asum is one of the most productive (and also the most expensive) rivers in Iceland. It is a relatively short river with a lake as its sources, so it has a constant water level and a relatively high temperature. From a fly-fishing standpoint, it is superb. Permits mainly are sold on a one-day basis by the owners, who are farmers. A small cabin with several beds is provided, but food has to be brought along and cooked by the anglers. There are summer hotels close by that are frequently used by fishermen.

Laxá í Adaldal, which flows about 50 miles east of Akureyri, is called "the big Laxa," or simply "the Laxa," to differentiate it, as the king of all the Laxas, from all the other rivers in Iceland. Its source is the big lake, Myvatn, which keeps the river at a constant level and relatively warm temperature. Although it is

pull loose and that the tackle couldn't have survived another run. I remembered then that in tying the knot, I had clipped the ends as close as possible. It was the last time I ever did that!

Upstream from these falls and a small but fast gorge, the Langá flows over level gravel until it reaches a canyon area that also produces some superb fishing. In the canyon area, the angler's back often is close to rock faces, making roll casts or Spey casts necessary. The river here is rocky and fast, filled with good holding positions for salmon. Near the mouth of the canyon are several productive pools.

The canyon is the limit of the lower beats. Another outfitter controls the upper beats, which also offer excellent fishing but with less variable situations. Anglers fishing the upper river stay at an excellent lodge close to the water. Above this is a steep gorge with what is reputed to be the longest fish ladder in the world, mostly blasted from solid rock.

30 miles long, falls near the middle stop the salmon and only the lower half is fishable. The river is leased in at least four separate parts and has first-class accommodations along it. It is deep and has a strong current, so some pools are fished from boats. It is excellent for fly fishing and holds the Icelandic record for a salmon caught on a fly: a 36-pounder taken on a #2 *Jock Scott* on July 10, 1942. Although larger and smaller flies can be successful, sizes 6 to 8 are the most popular on the Laxa.

The Midfjardará, with its three tributaries, Vestura, Nupsa, and Austura, lies about 150 miles by road north of Reykjavik. Ten rods are permitted. There are about 130 pools, of which about half are fished regularly. Many of the pools are suitable for fly fishing, but others can be difficult. Some require a lot of walking. Accommodations are excellent and compare with those on the southwestern rivers previously mentioned.

The Vididalsá and its tributary, the Fitja, flow about 20 miles east of the Midfjardará. The Vididalsá permits eight rods on about seventy pools, of which nearly every one offers superb fly fishing. This river also requires a lot of walking. Accommodations are first-class.

Salmon Fishing in Iceland

Salmon fishing in Iceland used to be relatively inexpensive, but it is becoming more costly every year. Why? In addition to growing inflation, the increasing popularity of Iceland's excellent streams among foreigners is largely responsible for driving up the price of the privilege to fish there—often to unrealistic levels. It is natural for the owners of the rivers to want maximum profit; in some respects, it is simply a case of supply and demand.

Flugleidir caters to fishermen and will fly them in comfort direct from several international airports, including New York and Baltimore. The flight to Keflavik Airport in Iceland (about 40 miles from Reykjavik) is spiced by good meals between cocktails and brandy served by accommodating and pleasant flight attendants. An afternoon or night in Reykjavik provides time to recuperate from jetlag and do some sightseeing and shopping. Those fishing the southwestern rivers are picked up by car at their hotel the next morning for the ride to the river. You may get in six hours or so of fishing that same day! No license is required.

Iceland's rivers have produced salmon in abundance since the island was settled in 900 A.D. What accounts for this abundance when the fisheries of so many other countries are suffering? Iceland considers its natural resource of salmon a crop and would no more think of harming it than a farmer would of eating his seed potatoes. All rivers are periodically inspected and limited to a safe number of rods. On most rivers, anglers can catch an unlimited number of salmon and even sell them if they wish; however, fish farming and salmon ranching provide most of the salmon to the trade.

Largely because of Iceland's proud national ethic and a strong cultural honesty, poaching is almost nonexistent there, and the rare poacher is dealt with severely. The rivers, being privately controlled, are carefully regulated and safeguarded, and the government contributes to and supervises stream improvement, the erection and maintenance of fish ladders, and artificial breeding to increase and improve salmon stocks. Pollution of rivers is not tolerated. These facts are merely a quick summary, but other nations could profit by pondering the exemplary manner in which Iceland protects its heritage and its valuable natural resource. Given similar management, how many times more valuable could our North American salmon fishing be?

Iceland is called "the land of fire and ice," and the interior is nearly all composed of lava flows, extinct volcanoes, and glaciers, but the proximity of the Gulf Stream makes summers there very pleasant. The weather is very changeable, however, so no matter how a day starts out, you should always carry a sweater and rain gear. Iceland is an island of stark and everchanging beauty—the kind of beauty that truly enhances the fishing experience.

Salmon Flies of Iceland

In an attempt to discuss the favorite flies of Iceland more factually than my limited years of fishing there permit, I consulted several Icelandic angling authorities for valid data. Angling clubs and premier fly tiers were polled, and collectively they produced a wealth of statistics, as well as interesting new patterns that include variations of the old.

The overwhelming favorite, representing over half of all salmon flies sold in Iceland, is the *Frances*, originated by the famous Peter Deane in England. When this fly was first so dramatically successful in

PLATE 125
SALMON FLIES FOR ICELAND, AS DESIGNATED AND DRESSED BY THE
NORTH ATLANTIC SALMON FUND FLY TIER'S GUILD

Crosfield
dressed by Jon Ingi Agustsson

Laxa Blue
dressed by Jon Ingi Agustsson

Collie Dog
dressed by Jon Ingi Agustsson

Munro Killer
dressed by Bjarni Robert Jonsson

Frances
dressed by Bjarni Robert Jonsson

Cosseboom
dressed by Sigurjon Olafsson

Ally's Shrimp
dressed by Jon Ingi Agustsson

Black Sheep
dressed by Bjarni Robert Jonsson

Night Hawk
dressed by Sigirjon Olafsson

Hairy Mary
dressed by Bjarni Robert Jonsson

Undertaker
dressed by Sigurjon Olafsson

Blue Charm
dressed by Bjarni Robert Jonsson

Iceland during the late 1960s, Icelandic fishermen erroneously used the masculine spelling of the name, Francis, to identify it, and continue to do so; however, the fly was named for Deane's female assistant, Frances, who was tying flies for him at the time the fly was developed. Later, when two black eyes were added, the fly also became known as the *Black-Eyed Prawn* or *BEP.* Although it was not originated in their country, Icelanders regard the *Black-Eyed Prawn* as a true Icelandic pattern, and it is dressed on a standard hook or as a tube fly. The most popular color for fishing Iceland's waters is red, with black being the second favorite.

In general terms, the most popular patterns in Iceland include the *Frances, Black Sheep, Blue Charm,* *Hairy Mary, Collie Dog, Laxa Blue, Dimmbla, Thingeyingur, Munroe Killer, Undertaker, Ally's Shrimp, Krafla, Crosfield,* and *Night Hawk.* Singled out from the preceding list by the Fly Tier's Guild are the *Crosfield, Black Sheep, Krafla, Laxa Blue, Red Frances,* and *Thingeyingur* as being representative of "Iceland premier salmon flies," so chosen "in respect of success, popularity, and uniqueness." Other standard patterns, such as some of the *Doctors,* the *Thunder and Lightning, Sweep, Blue Rat,* and *Black Bear Butt* patterns, are also popular.

The when and why of fly selection, as discussed in chapter 5, holds true in Iceland as everywhere: a dark one for silhouette when salmon see it against low, shaded sun; a medium one when the sun is high

The North Atlantic Salmon Fund Fly Tier's Guild: (from left) Jon Ingi Agustsson, Bjarni Robert Jonsson, and Sigurjon Olafsson

or not shining; and a light or bright one for flash when the sun is behind the salmon. When the sun is bright and low, a bit of flash, such as a silver-bodied pattern, proves good regardless of the location of the fish in relation to the sun. These general rules can overlap a bit, largely because of the wide variety of patterns and the often unpredictable ways of the wily salmon.

Of Iceland's salmon flies, the dark ones, which provide good silhouette, are the *Black Doctor, Night Hawk, Sweep,* and *Thunder and Lightning;* they should do best on dark days or when salmon see the fly against low, shaded sun. The *Thunder and Lightning* is called "the great storm fly," with historic use under such conditions, but the *Black Doctor* should do as well. The *Sweep* and *Night Hawk* are similar to one another, as either featherwings or hairwings, and would also be appropriate. Since modern preference tends toward hairwings, another choice would be the simple *Black Bear* type, with black body, black hackle, and black hair wing, with or without a fluorescent butt of any color and a touch of silver. In

fact, Gudmundur Arnason, a fishing companion and Icelandic angling authority, sent me a fly named *Birna* (female bear) of this same description, with a short but bulky clipped yellow wool tail instead of a butt, saying it is a "killing pattern" in Iceland and asking if I knew its name. My choice in this category would be a fly of this type, without need for anything fancier.

In the medium group, recommended when the sun is high or not shining, are the *Blue Charm, Hairy Mary* (now tied in several different wing colors), and *Black Bear, Green Butt.* This condition is the most common in salmon fishing, which may account for the great international popularity of the first two. If I had to be restricted to only one pattern, it would be the *Blue Charm* dressed as a hairwing of gray squirrel or Irish badger, and I am confident that it would creditably handle nearly all situations. (A. H. E. Wood said the same thing about the *March Brown.*) The *Hairy Mary* and *Irish Hairy Mary* are close substitutes, and the *Blue Rat* is also an efficient go-between. Traditionalists might even choose a *Green Highlander* or *Jock Scott.*

When the sun can reflect flash, the *Night Hawk, Crosfield,* and *Silver* or *Blue Doctor* might prove useful. The *Night Hawk* gives both a dark silhouette and flash, and it might be even more popular when dressed more simply—a silver body with black hackle and a black hair wing, plus whatever embellishments that please the angler. A *Silver* or *Blue Doctor* provides a somewhat lighter silhouette for medium-bright conditions. Those who want something simpler should find the *Crosfield,* with its silver body, blue throat, and gray wing, similarly effective. Note that the original Crosfield was dressed with a yellow head.

While fishing the Sog River with Gudmundur Arnason in July 1979, I asked about his theory for fly selection. His many years of experience make it worth relating, even though it disregards light conditions. Believing that black disturbs salmon the least, he begins with a black fly such as the *Birna.* Then he tries a predominantly blue pattern, such as the *Blue Charm,* then a brown one like the *March Brown.* After these he tries a green fly such as *Roger's Fancy,* and finally a yellow one like the *Grima,* which he thinks disturbs salmon the most. Since he considers yellow the most disturbing, he never starts out with it.

Salmon-Salmon-Ghost of Sage
An army of Scribes will ne'er full capture
with pen and page

GENTLE ON MY MIND

authors Copy
Joseph D. Hubert

PLATE 126
JOE HUBERT'S SHEEP SERIES, DRESSED BY TED GODFREY
Photo from *Salmon—Salmon*

Although opinions vary, early in the season when the water is high, red or dark green flies seem to work best, with blue predominating later in the season. Yellow is also a good choice for high or discolored water. Because of their visibility, red and yellow are both effective "wake-up" colors when salmon are dour and won't look at anything else. Icelandic patterns are often dressed in orange, yellow, blue, black, green, and red—the most popular. The *Frances, General Practitioner,* and *Krafla* are all prawn or shrimp imitations and are useful as wake-up patterns as well as in general situations.

Though such patterns vary widely from what we have become used to thinking of as "standard," they are very valuable in the salmon angler's bag of tricks. They also include Hubert's *Black Sheep* and the *Collie Dog,* both of which suggest elvers, as well as several long bucktail types such as *Gudmundsson's Thingeyingur.* These are usually dressed with black and/or yellow wings on single, double, or treble long-shanked hooks wound with silver tinsel. All are popular in Iceland.

The following patterns are popular with Icelandic anglers:

Birna	
Tail	A tuft of yellow wool, extending only to bend of hook
Body	Black floss or wool, medium
Ribbing	Fine oval silver tinsel
Throat	Black hackle, extending to point of hook
Wing	Black bear hair tips, extending to end of tail
Head	Black

This fly was given to me by Gudmundur Arnason, of Reykjavik, with the comment that it is exceptionally productive. It is simply one of the common *Black Bear* type, with a tufted wool tail or splayed poly tail instead of a fluorescent floss butt. Alternative colors in the tail, both bright and muted, are often used.

Black Sheep	
Tag	Fine oval silver tinsel, or wire
Body	Black wool, not built up
Throat	Medium blue hackle
Wing	Black and yellow bucktail: top one-third yellow; bottom two-thirds black, tapered and 3 inches long
Cheeks	Jungle cock, short
Head	Red

One of the *Sheep* series of flies, this bucktail pattern was originated in 1977 by Joseph P. Hubert, of Duluth, Minnesota, and first was tied by Haraldur Stefansson of Reykjavik, Iceland. Bucktails of this type can be very productive and often are used as "wake-up" flies for dour salmon or to bring fish back that have risen to standard dressings but have refused to take them. Joe Hubert prefers the classics and so called this the *Black Sheep* as he viewed it among the Kelson patterns in his fly box. In fact, Hubert is so committed to the classics that he ended his article revealing his "Band of Sheep" with the words, "May Kelson, Frances, Maxwell and Pryce-Tannatt have mercy on my soul . . ."

The series consists of six patterns that are dressed in a similar manner; in addition to black, the color variations are brown, blue, silver, red, and green. Other variations are quite common, and very useful, in Iceland as well as other places. One calls for black collie dog hair. Another is brown over yellow bucktail. These have bodies of embossed silver tinsel and often the jungle cock is omitted. Presumably they imitate small elvers or eels when they are about 3 inches long

Blue Sapphire (Hairwing)	
Tag	Oval gold tinsel and yellow floss
Tail	Golden pheasant crest veiled with red and blue hackle fibers
Body	Black floss, built up slightly
Ribbing	Fine round or oval gold tinsel
Hackle	Deep blue hackle palmered forward from second turn of tinsel
Throat	Deep blue hackle
Wing	Blue calf tail and European squirrel
Topping	Golden pheasant crest (optional)
Head	Black

This pattern is a hairwing variation of the featherwing pattern given to me by Johann Sigurdsson, an old fishing friend in Iceland. The original featherwing called for an underwing of dark brown turkey and an outerwing of married strips of blue goose, mottled turkey, and bronze mallard. It is a bit fancier than the *Blue Charm,* but no more effective.

Crosfield	
Tag	Fine oval silver tinsel
Tail	Golden pheasant crest
Body	Embossed silver tinsel
Throat	A pale or *Silver Doctor* blue hackle
Wing	Matched sections from a pale gray mallard feather
Head	Yellow (or black)

The above dressing for this popular pattern is considered in Iceland the "true original" and was known as the *Yellow Head.* Icelanders later named the fly the *Crosfield* in honor of its originator, Shet-

PLATE 127
THE CROSFIELD
DRESSED BY GALEN MERCER

ney Crosfield, Ernest Crosfield's brother. The origin of the *Crosfield,* which has often been misunderstood or miscredited, is documented in *Ellidaár: Reykjavik's Angling Treasure,* by Asgeir Ingolfsson. In the book, Shetney Crosfield is described as "the most gifted angler among the British." The author goes on to quote the story of Crosfield finding a gray leg feather from a mallard and remarking it would "probably do for a good flywing." Originally, there were three variations of the fly we now more commonly see dressed with a black head. The first was as above, "with a golden head and blue beard"; the second had darker wings; and the third had a body of silkworm gut. Other patterns developed from the original call for a wing of brown turkey or mallard veiled with strips of barred teal.

Dimmbla

Tag	Oval silver tinsel and deep purple floss
Tail	Squirrel, dyed blue
Butt	Black ostrich herl
Body	Silver tinsel
Ribbing	Oval silver tinsel
Throat	Squirrel, dyed blue
Wing	Black squirrel
Head	Black

The *Dimmbla* was originated by Thordor "Doddi" Petursson, angler, guide, and river warden on the Laxá í Adaldal. Following is another of Doddi's patterns that has been successful in a variety of colors.

Doddi Red

Tag	Oval silver tinsel
Tail	Slips of yellow goose
Body	Red ostrich herl
Wing	Black squirrel
Head	Black

Eva

Body	Rear half: scarlet floss. Front half: black floss
Ribbing	Oval gold tinsel
Throat	Fluorescent green
Wing	Brown squirrel tail with shorter gray squirrel tail over, extending slightly beyond bend of the hook.
Head	Black

This pattern, originated by Johann Thorsteinsson, of Reykjavik, in 1970, seems to be a simplification of the British *Jerram's Fancy,* with a brownish wing instead of a black one.

Fox Fly

Tag	Fine oval silver tinsel and fluorescent yellow-orange floss, lacquered
Tail	Golden pheasant crest
Butt	Black ostrich herl
Body	Black floss (on larger flies, a black hackle is palmered forward from the second turn of tinsel)
Ribbing	Oval silver tinsel
Throat	Black hackle
Wing	Gray fox guard hair
Head	Black

The *Fox Fly* is another of Doddi Petursson's patterns that has been successful on rivers around the world. Writer and angler Art Lee says of it, "The Fox Fly I now believe to be the best all-round dark fly to fish on virtually any salmon river in the world. The Fox has replaced the Black Dose and Black Bear, among others, as my favourite fly for overcast days."

Grima (Yellow)

Tag	Fine oval silver tinsel
Tail	Two yellow hackle tips
Butt	Black ostrich herl
Body	In two equal parts separated by a black ostrich herl butt: rear half, yellow floss; front half, black floss
Ribbing	Fine oval silver tinsel
Throat	Yellow hackle fibers, extending to middle butt
Wing	Brown squirrel tail
Head	Black

This pretty pattern, originated by Kristjan Gislason, of Reykjavik, is reminiscent of a reduced *Jock Scott,* and should do as well. There are two other color schemes for this pattern:

The *Grima (Green)* is the same except that the tail and throat are bright green (*Green Highlander* green) hackle, the rear half of the body is the same green (floss), and the front half is canary yellow. This pattern should do well as a substitute for the *Green Highlander.*

The *Grima (Blue)* is the same except that the tail and throat are dark blue hackle, the rear half of the body is light blue (*Blue Charm* blue), the front half is dark blue (floss), and the ribbing is gold.

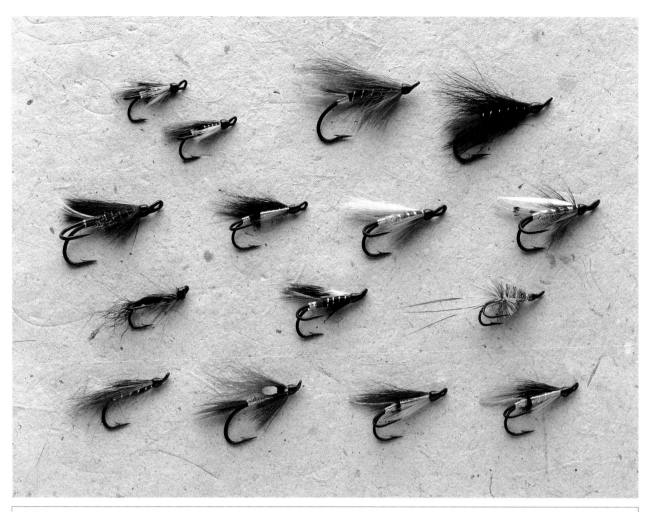

PLATE 128
ICELANDIC SALMON FLY PATTERNS

Gray Hairy Mary
dressed by Rod Yerger

Blue Sapphire
dressed by Bill Wilbur

Skroggur
dressed by Bill Wilbur

Brown Hairy Mary
dressed by Rod Yerger

Stardust
dressed by Galen Mercer

Dimmbla
originated and dressed by
Thordur Petursson

White Wing (hairwing)
dressed by Rod Yerger

White Wing (featherwing)
dressed by Rod Yerger

Tinna
dressed by Bragi Hannesson

Fox Fly
originated and dressed by
Thordur Petursson

Krafla
originated and dressed by
Kristjan Gislason

Eva
dressed by
Johann Thorsteinsson

Stekkur Bla
dressed by Mike Martinek

Laxa Red
originated and dressed by
Thordur Petursson

Laxa Blue
originated and dressed by
Thordur Petursson

PLATE 129
ICELANDIC HAIRWING PATTERNS

Silver Smelt (Variation)
dressed by Mike Martinek

Thingeyingur
originated and dressed by
Geir Birgir Gudmundsson

Grima
originated and dressed by
Kristjan Gislasson

Doddi Red
originated and dressed by
Thordur Petursson

Icy
dressed by Rod Yerger

Veidivon
originated and dressed by
Thordur Petursson

Icy

Tag	Fine oval silver tinsel and fluorescent red floss
Tail	Red goose, long
Body	Flat silver tinsel
Ribbing	Oval silver tinsel
Throat	Yellow hackle
Wing	Black squirrel or bucktail, extending well beyond the bend of the hook
Sides	Jungle cock
Head	Black

Doddi Petursson's *Icy* is one of a number of patterns originated by Icelandic tiers that have been named for the Icy Vodka Company, founded by angler-conservationist Orri Vigfusson. It is the predecessor of the similar and more popular pattern of Petursson's, the *Veidivon*.

Krafla

Tail	Boar bristle (or stripped hackle stems) twice the length of the fly, veiled with white hackle point
Body	Heavily palmered with fairly stiff red or hot orange hackle mixed with white. This hackle is trimmed to a cone shape so that the rear of the lower part nearly touches the hook's barb
Ribbing	Fine oval silver tinsel
Head	Red, with black in front

This version of a shrimp or prawn is by Kristjan Gislasson, of Reykjavik, and is somewhat similar in appearance to Peter Deane's *Frances* or *Black-Eyed Prawn*. The *Krafla (Black)* is the same except for color. Another Icelandic fly dresser does one with a shorter body and brown or gray tail. The rear of the body is yellow and the front is black. Another shrimp pattern is the Raekja, which is a simplified version of the *General Practitioner*.

Laxa Blue

Tag	Fine oval silver tinsel and fluorescent yellow-orange floss, lacquered
Tail	Golden pheasant crest
Body	Light blue floss
Ribbing	Oval silver tinsel
Throat	*Silver Doctor* blue hackle
Wing	Gray squirrel tail dyed *Silver Doctor* blue
Head	Black

The *Laxa Blue* was originated by Thordur "Doddi" Petursson. It has become an international favorite and is named for the Laxá í Adaldal, or Big Laxa, where Doddi worked as river warden. The *Laxa Blue* is now dressed in several other colors, including red.

Silver Smelt

Tag	Dark blue floss
Tail	Light blue hackle fibers
Body	Flat silver tinsel
Wing	White and light blue hair with peacock strands or flashabou
Head	Black or white

Icelandic guide Hilmar Bjornsson passed the *Silver Smelt* on to John Berger, who writes that it is dressed in several variations and is used widely on a number of rivers in Iceland. The *Silver Smelt* is very effective when fished as a streamer and stripped in quickly in the fast water at the head of a pool.

Stekkur Bla

Tail	Soft blue hackle fibers, over which is a smaller bunch of hot orange hackle
Body	Medium silver twist
Throat	A long beard of soft blue hackle and hot orange hackle
Wing	Cobalt blue calf tail or bucktail
Cheeks	Jungle cock

After years of experience fishing the pools that make up the Stekkur beat on the river Nordurá, John Berger, of Jupiter, Florida, combined his experience and desire for variety and beauty in devising the *Stekkur Bla*. He says: "The composition of *Stekkur Bla* was an attempt to capture features that would have a relationship with the place itself. When I discussed the fly with fly tier Michael Martinek, of Stoneham, Massachusetts, he was given the outline of the details and, at the same time, the artistic license to create within the outline. For instance, he came up with the distinct cobalt blue in the wings." Their efforts of 1988 produced one of the most successful flies on the Nordurá.

Skroggur

Tail	Red or hot orange hackle fibers, about as long as the gape of the hook, over and under shank
Body	Black floss or wool, not built up
Ribbing	Fine oval silver tinsel
Throat	Fine black hair, extending to end of tail
Wing	Fine black hair extending to end of tail
Head	Black

This is another of Kristjan Gislasson's patterns, evidently dressed to suggest an elver.

Stardust

Tag	Fine oval tinsel and midnight blue floss, tied slightly longer than normal
Tail	Golden pheasant crest
Body	Black sparkle yarn dubbed on midnight blue floss, picked and teased out after ribbing
Ribbing	Oval silver tinsel
Throat	Dark or midnight blue cock hackle wound and then pulled down, as bright and shiny as can be found
Wing	Black squirrel hair
Head	Black

Originated by Art Lee in the mid-1980s for fishing on overcast days or evenings on the Laxá í Adaldal, the *Stardust* was aptly named for one of the songs that, according to Lee, "I either hum or sing (badly) when I'm fishing a stretch of water, as a sort of nerve calmer in anticipation of a rise."

Thingeyingur

Body	Green wool
Ribbing	Fine oval silver tinsel
Throat	Black squirrel
Wing	Yellow bucktail, long
Head	Black

Originally designed as a streamer fly, the *Thingeyingur* (translated "the people of the thing") named for a district in north-central Iceland, was originated by Geir Birgir Gudmundsson in 1974. It has become firmly established as one of Iceland's prime salmon flies and is now dressed in many variations, including one with an orange wing and a yellow tail.

Tinna

Tail	Black hair
Body	Black wool, not built up
Hackle	Blue hackle
Head	Black

This Icelandic pattern was given to me in Reykjavik by Valur Valsson, to whom I also wish to express thanks for information in this chapter about some of the northern rivers I have not yet fished.

Veidivon

Tag	Oval silver tinsel and red floss
Tail	Fine red hair
Body	Flat silver tinsel
Ribbing	Oval silver tinsel
Throat	Fine yellow hair or hackle
Wing	Black squirrel
Head	Black, extending beyond the bend of the hook

Literally translated as "fishing (or catch) hope," the *Veidivon* is another of Doddi Petursson's original patterns and is an adaptation of his version of the *Icy*. Tiers sometimes vary this pattern by substituting red for yellow in the throat.

White Wing

Tag	Fine oval silver tinsel
Tail	Golden pheasant crest and golden pheasant tippet strands
Body	In four equal sections: yellow, orange, brown, and claret seal's fur (on smaller sizes rabbit dubbing can be used)
Ribbing	Flat silver tinsel and oval silver tinsel
Hackle	Claret
Throat	Blue
Wing	Narrow white goose strips, tied low
Head	Black

The above pattern is the basis for a more popular hairwing version. It differs by eliminating the tippet from the tail, the flat tinsel ribbing, and the body hackle, and using a sparse white goat-hair wing in place of the goose.

Tube Flies

Tube flies, from the very small to the very large, are used extensively in Iceland, particularly in blue combinations, all black, or hot orange. When salmon are hard to hook, many anglers consider the use of the riffling hitch essential. Riffling tube flies are also specially devised for fishing the hitch. The hitch is essentially Lee Wulff's Portland Hitch or Riffled Hitch, described earlier. Orri Vigfusson, head of the North Atlantic Salmon Fund, elaborates on the technique, terming it "hitchcraft" in a book of the same name, and cites the method as his "favorite dimension to fly fishing."

Icelandic Salmon Cookery

Iceland's wonderful people are another of its great natural resources. They are hospitable and hard working, as well as excellent and congenial anglers. They also excel in fish cookery. My favorites of their recipes are baked salmon seasoned with dill seed, and gravlax with its sauce. Here are the recipes.

Baked Salmon with Dill Seed

Skin and bone the fillets of a small salmon and lay them on foil in a baking pan.

Cover the fillets with a mixture of melted butter and oil (I prefer peanut oil).

Season with salt, celery salt, pepper, parsley flakes, and dill seed. Sprinkle on the dill seed lavishly to about half cover the fillets.

Bake for 20 minutes at 350 degrees.

Pour a few ounces of white wine over the fillets when they are about half cooked.

Gravlax

This is not cooked, but the infusion of the flavorings makes it delicious. This recipe is enough for one 8-pound salmon. Fillet it and remove all bones, but not the skin.

4 tablespoons salt (or a lesser amount of coarse salt)
1 generous tablespoon sugar
2 tablespoons white pepper (or about half as much coarsely ground pepper)
4 tablespoons dried dill or about a dozen sprigs of fresh dill
1 teaspoon fennel

Mix the above ingredients and sprinkle them over the fillets to completely coat them. Put one fillet over the other, with a weight on top. Turn the fillets every 8 to 12 hours, and spoon the juice that comes from the fillets over and between them. Store the fish in a cool place for 3 days, turning and basting them periodically.

After 3 days the gravlax is ready. Drain it to remove all liquid. If you want to keep it in the refrigerator for more than a week, cover with oil. If tightly sealed, it can be kept frozen almost indefinitely.

Using a sharp knife, slice the gravlax as thin as possible, on a slant to provide the widest slices, and remove each slice from the skin with the flat side of the knife. Serve with Gravlax Sauce, which is passed in a separate dish. At dinners with Icelanders, gravlax often is the main part of the meal, with several slices served on lettuce to each person. Tomato or asparagus salad makes a good accompaniment, along with cold white wine.

Gravlax Sauce

1 cup mayonnaise
2 tablespoons Dijon mustard
2 tablespoons honey
1 tablespoon marinade from the salmon
1 teaspoon minced dried dill

Mix above ingredients thoroughly and let the blended mixture stand in the refrigerator for an hour or more before serving. The marinade is not essential, and I usually go a bit stronger on the dill. Some recipes call for equal parts of the four ingredients, excluding the marinade. This makes a thinner sauce, which can be avoided by using more mayonnaise. After you try the original recipe, you can vary it to taste using other ingredients such as crushed garlic or substituting olive oil and vinegar (in the standard proportion of about 3 to 1) for the mayonnaise.

14

Fishing North American Waters

"River Men"

CANADIAN SALMON FLIES AND FISHING

Fly fishing for Atlantic salmon in Canada historically has been a sport shared in international friendship by Canadians and Americans, endowing many of us with cherished memories. It seems less important to reminisce further on such excursions, however, than to try to explain why they no longer may be as worthwhile. It is important that the reader understand the trend toward Atlantic salmon disaster in Canada, and what could be done to avert it.

Why is an alarming decline in the fishery happening, and what can be done to restore the "good old days"? One of the most competent people to answer the first part of this question is Dr. Wilfred M. Carter, president of the Atlantic Salmon Federation until 1988 and now president emeritus, in St. Andrews, New Brunswick. In 1979, Dr. Carter wrote:

North American salmon are first exploited by driftnetting off Greenland (approximately 350,000 salmon annually), followed by heavy inshore netting as they move through waters near Newfoundland (approximately 600,000 salmon annually), then in the area off the Maritime Provinces and Quebec, where they face a maze of cod traps, mackerel nets, groundfish gill nets, herring nets and multi-species traps that take an additional 250,000 salmon annually.

Also, in some mainland coastal areas, there are the commercial salmon nets and Indian fisheries in the river estuaries, poachers, and finally, if there are any salmon still alive, anglers who take their modest share.

And that is only the tip of the iceberg. What isn't generally recognized is that our rivers are producing fewer and fewer juvenile salmon to send to the sea each year. The numbers are cut by environmental changes, like erosion, mismanagement, the clear-cutting of forests and water diversion schemes, and acid rainfall as a by-product of industrial pollution. Salmon may also lose part of their food supply because of insect population genocide caused by poisonous chemicals used in forestry and agriculture. The result is that vast natural nursery areas that are needed for feeding and growing are lost, and this reflects directly on the numbers of adult salmon that will return from the sea for harvest.

Also, there is some evidence that the collapse of the capelin fishery due to overfishing could be a contributing factor. Capelin are a major component of the salmon's diet at sea.

Add these three together—overharvesting (both legal and illegal), diminishing natural production of young salmon and collapse of fish food stocks at sea—and it sums up as a crushing impediment to the salmon. It is also an indictment of current management practices in every major Atlantic salmon country, with the possible exception of Iceland.

While it is not incumbent upon an American angler such as myself to stick his nose into the affairs of another nation, anyone has the right to plead the case for the salmon. Among its various facets are the following:

High seas netting should be abolished because it is unethical as well as wasteful. Such nets (and baited longlines), a mile or so in length, can sweep the seas of nearly all of a river's adult salmon and thus ruin the fishery of that river, or of several. I noted earlier that salmon should be considered as belonging to the country of their origin, partly because that country raised them to smolt stage, usually at considerable expense. Although they are then turned out to the communal pasture of the sea, they should be allowed to return to their own rivers, rather than being hijacked in the ocean by fishermen of another country.

Second, high seas netting takes salmon before they have reached their prime. They are swept up in nets regardless of age or size, a very unbusinesslike practice!

Coastal netting should be abolished for the same reasons. Staked nets stretch out from shore in unbelievable numbers, like the teeth of a comb. Salmon follow the coasts to find their rivers, rather than taking the shorter deep-sea route from their feeding grounds to home. Thus they are easy prey for the mazes of coastal nets to be found wherever salmon travel inshore. For example, salmon belonging to the rivers of France and Spain skirt the Irish coast on their way home from feeding grounds off Greenland. So many coastal nets intercept them there that relatively few return. Dr. Carter mentioned similar interception, as it applies to Canada. International attempts to outlaw the netting in these two categories has so far met with some, but very insufficient, success.

Incidental netting also illustrates the gullibility of politicians. In some places, coastal netting has been banned to protect the salmon, but nets in the same places have been allowed for such species as herring, cod, and mackerel. The netters inquired whether they could keep salmon that strayed into their "cod nets," and the politicians said they could if the nets were not intentionally set for salmon. It is very obvious what many of these nets actually were set for.

Many salmon rivers, once privately owned and carefully guarded, have been made public, thus stimulating poaching. Restrictions made in the early 1970s on high seas netting and long-lining allowed many more salmon to return home, thus encouraging anglers for a while. But the nearly unguarded rivers, the increase of salmon, and their rising prices on the market led poaching to develop into a thriving and lucrative business that seriously impacted the entire fishery. The fish stolen by poaching were those that had managed to escape netting and were essential for brood stock as well as valuable for angling.

Poaching developed into widespread, ruthless gangs equipped with walkie-talkies, guards, spies, and everything else necessary for big-scale operations. Salmon thus poached were sold openly, and even advertised by roadside signs. Poaching was encouraged for years by lenient judges who fined the rare poacher who was caught so small a sum that he often was back on the job that same night. In recent years, however, better enforcement, stiff fines, and jail sentences have led to a decline in poaching.

Salmon taken by anglers on the fly are worth many times more to local economies than those taken otherwise and sold commercially. The commercial take, from distant feeding grounds to home spawning streams, has been so severe that too many anglers who would like to travel to Canada no longer do so. Most of them would be willing to spend a few hundred dollars per day to hook a few large salmon, even, perhaps, just one! Yet too many of the fish they hoped to catch are already dead, too many being peddled on the black market for relatively paltry sums by people who had no right to them in the first place.

Miramichi sunset

JACK SWEDBERG

Many of us who hope to see the fishery restored as nearly as possible to the bounty of the 1960s think that the commercial sale of Atlantic salmon should be abolished, with stiff fines for possession of illegal (untagged, for example) fish. This would be an effective deterrent to the currently flourishing black market.

Having thus scanned most of the bad news, let's look at some of the good.

The plucky Atlantic salmon has been in deep trouble before, and concerned groups led by the Atlantic Salmon Federation have effectively dealt with many of its problems. The warning bells are ringing loudly again, and the many friends of the Atlantic salmon are coming to its rescue. Let us hope that whatever cure is decided upon will be permanently effective. In the meantime the Atlantic salmon is helping itself. Its rivers are teeming with more grilse than have been seen in them for many years!

Salmon Rivers of Canada

Fly fishing in some of the more or less typical salmon rivers of Canada has been noted in chapter 1. Here, principal ones are listed in current order of

importance, with brief comments that should apply during the predictable future.

Because regulations and restrictions vary greatly among provinces and rivers, the angler anticipating a trip to Canada should check with experienced friends or local authorities before going there. For example, some rivers require guides, and others do not; some waters are private, and others are public; and on some rivers you can keep salmon, whereas on others you can keep only grilse.

New Brunswick

The famous Main Southwest Miramichi, which is part of this province's tremendous river system, is the highest-yielding salmon river in North America. More Atlantic salmon are taken on New Brunswick's rivers than in any other province. The top salmon rivers in the province are the Main Southwest Miramichi, Restigouche, Northwest

The Miramichi River, New Brunswick

JACK SWEDBERG

Miramichi, Saint John, Little Southwest Miramichi, Nashwaak, Upsalquitch, Sevogle, Renous, and Big Salmon. Spring fishing for black salmon is currently allowed from April 15 to May 15 and takes place primarily on the Miramichi River. Anglers can fish waters provided by outfitters, a list of whom, with pertinent data, can be obtained from the Department of Tourism, in Fredericton, New Brunswick, or from any New Brunswick Tourist Information Center. Fishing licenses are available at any of the many Natural Resources offices in the province.

Nonresident salmon anglers must be accompanied by a licensed guide. Reputable outfitters offer excellent guides for visiting sports and can often make the difference between success or failure.

Quebec

This tremendous and largely remote province offers anglers a wide variety of salmon angling conditions, ranging from the wilderness streams of far-north Ungava Bay to the more accessible and more southerly rivers such as the Matapedia and the Grand Cascapedia.

The most productive rivers are the George, Matapedia, Jupiter (on Anticosti Island), Matane, Natashquan, Moisie, Bonaventure, and St. Jean. (The Restigouche is considered a New Brunswick river.)

Quebec's salmon average larger than those of the other provinces, and large salmon have been outnumbering grilse in the proportion of 3 to 1.

Setting out JACK SWEDBERG

The Margaree River BOB O'SHAUGHNESSY

PLATE 131
THE NIGHT HAWK, DRESSED BY MARK WASLICK

Many rivers provide salmon in the 20- to 30-pound class, or larger.

Outfitters provide excellent fishing on many of Quebec's finest salmon rivers. A list of them, with a "Summary of Sport Fishing Regulations," is available from the Fish and Game Branch, Department of Tourism, Fish and Game, in Quebec, or from any District Wildlife Office.

Nova Scotia

Nova Scotia rivers are open to public fishing, and licenses are very reasonable. Registered guides are not required; however, for those wishing to enhance their chances of success, a list of them, with full fishing information, can be obtained from the Nova Scotia Department of Tourism, in Halifax. Angling licenses can be purchased from all district offices of the Nova Scotia Department of Lands and Forests.

Nova Scotia's principal salmon rivers are the Margaree, St. Mary's, La Have, Medway, Moser, Gold, and Ecum Secum. This province, especially, is a tourist's delight. Anglers should visit the Margaree Salmon Museum in Margaree Center, Cape Breton. Among other things, this little museum houses antique equipment, artifacts of the area, salmon art, displays of prominent tiers, and books. It is also a good spot to obtain information on the area.

Newfoundland and Labrador

More time is spent fishing for Atlantic salmon in these provinces than in any other. All rivers are open to anglers, and roads in many areas are being extended, thus diminishing the necessity to fly to remote camps.

The following ten rivers have produced the most salmon to anglers in these provinces: Humber, St. Genevieve, Gander, Eagle, Pinware, Conne, Exploits, River of Ponds, Grand Codroy, and Portland Creek.

Nonresidents fishing for salmon must be accompanied by a licensed guide except when fishing within a quarter of a mile up- or downstream from any highway crossing of a scheduled salmon river. Licensed guides are required for all types of fishing (with the above exception) in Labrador. Information

All Nova Scotia rivers flowing into the Bay of Fundy have been closed to angling until runs recover.
P. B. R.

PLATE 132
EARLY CANADIAN FEATHERWINGS

Gray Fly
dressed by Dorothy Douglass

Nicholson
dressed by Al Brewster

Ross
dressed by Al Bovyn

Langevin
dressed by Al Bovyn

Carabou
dressed by Rob Solo

Chamberlain
dressed by Ted Kantner

Orange Chamberlain
dressed by Ted Kantner

Lanctot
dressed by John Wildermuth

on outfitters and guides is included in the pamphlet "Fishing in Newfoundland and Labrador," available from the Tourist Services Division, Department of Tourism, in St. Johns, Newfoundland, or any Provincial Tourist Information Center.

Salmon Flies of Canada

With salmon stocks in the northeastern United States declining, American anglers turned to their northern neighbor in pursuit of the King of Fishes, thus combining original patterns from both countries for use on Canadian waters. In spite of a late start, the North Americans did quite well in originating their own patterns in the classic style. Although there are others deserving mention, two patterns stand out as tried-and-true American classics in the British sense: the *Lady Amherst* and the *Night Hawk*. Initially, however, the flies used on Canadian rivers mostly were the best-known British classics, until simplified versions and hairwing adaptations began to more or less take over.

Two American authors writing about the Canadian fishery were Thaddeus Norris (*American Angler's Book,* 1865) and Robert Barnwell Roosevelt (*The Game Fish of the Northern States and British Provinces,* 1884). Both Norris and Roosevelt give credit to Dr. Adamson (*Salmon Fishing in Canada,* 1860), as a resource for flies mentioned in their books, including the *Ross* and the *Langevin,* represented among the flies in this chapter. Roosevelt cites the patterns given by Norris and adds eight others—among these are the *Grey Fly,* the *Nicholson,* the *Chamberlain,* and the *Carabou,* also included in this chapter.

It may have been angling whim that forced these distinctive patterns into obscurity; they are of historic interest, however, and might well be worth the angler's attention.

Not unlike the development of the salmon fly in Great Britain, the return to simplicity in Canadian fly design was gradual—sort of a seesaw between the fancy classics, the simpler featherwings, and the sensible hairwings. There are still those who adhere to the influence of the classic tradition, especially in Newfoundland, the last of the provinces to separate from Great Britain.

In 1970, when I wrote my first book on salmon flies and fishing, I was begrudgingly tempted to title the chapter on North American featherwings "Requiem for the Featherwings" because of their decreasing popularity. At the time, Wally Doak, the Miramichi's oracle on the subject, cited the *Black Fairy, Fiery Brown, Silver Gray, Black Dose, Oriole,* and *Reliable* as his most popular featherwing patterns;

however, their use was dwindling as hairwing patterns gained acceptance. Nowadays, his successor and son, Jerry Doak, acknowledges that there is an old-school appreciation for some of the featherwings, but in general, buckbugs, butterflies, and hairwings account for the bulk of fly sales.

Wallace W. Doak

The modernization of the salmon fly in North America was a transition from feathers to hair that occurred largely because hair was more readily available than fancy feathers. Records of fish taken throughout the provinces do not cite whether hairwing or featherwing was used, so it is of no avail to try to determine the success or failure of hair versus feathers. Conversations with both anglers and proprietors of tackle shops confirm the predominance of the hairwings; even with their declining popularity, however, the featherwing patterns are very important in the history of salmon fishing in North America. Popular British classics that are still in use, whether featherwings or adapted hairwing conversions, include many of the standards mentioned chapter 11. Among them are the *Blue Charm, Dusty Miller, Black Dose,* and *Green Highlander.*

Fly dressers who want to accept challenges should get a particular kick out of some of the prettier patterns such as *Caribou,* the two *Chamberlains, Gray Fly, Griswold Gray, Lanctot, Moisie Grub, Nicholson,* and *Notion.* It is for their interest that these often overlooked patterns have been included.

The melding of the neighboring North American countries of Canada and the United States produced several important contributions to the angling legacy already established by Great Britain. The circle became complete when the standards that were set in North America were adopted by Europeans, particularly in the British Isles. Three of these contributions, devised by Canadians and Americans during the first half of this century, are especially significant: Ira Gruber's distinct new profile for the Miramichi salmon fly, and two notable series of hairwing flies originated for fishing in Canada and now fished worldwide—the *Rats* and the *Cossebooms.*

The Oriole and the Reliable

Ira Gruber became a legend in his own time on the Miramichi River, his favorite, and his flies, with their cigar-shaped bodies and low wings, were strikingly different from other flies of that time. Nowadays, the patterns Gruber favored have more historic interest than practical value, although some, such as the *Oriole* and the *Reliable,* can still be found in fly boxes. Chapter 4 discussed the experimentation of Ira Gruber, experiments that, in part, developed methods for using smaller flies to tempt dour fish. Also mentioned was the fact that Gruber was taught to

---

PLATE 134
W. W. DOAK & SONS

Featherwings dressed by Jerry Doak,
hairwings dressed by Bruce Waugh,
bugs and dry flies dressed by John Lyons

| Buck Bug | Bomber | Green Machine |

| White Wulff | Preacher | Copper Killer |

| Miramichi Cosseboom | Rutledge |

| Logie | Oriole |

| Black Dose | Night Hawk |

---

tie flies by Everett Price, who had an indisputable influence on Gruber, and it is not always clear which of the patterns generally attributed to Gruber were his own, Price's, or combinations of the two. Seventeen of these patterns are shown in Plate 47, as well as the *Oriole* and the *Reliable* in Plate 135. The patterns for the last two flies follow.

Oriole	
Tail	A few fibers of the red body feather of golden pheasant
Body	Black nylon wool
Ribbing	Fine oval silver tinsel, wound on fairly closely
Throat	Brown hackle
Wing	Underwing: several fibers of the brown-red body feather of golden pheasant. Overwing: gray mallard dyed green drake color
Head	Black

This probably is the most famous of the patterns associated with Gruber and still is a standard favorite on the Miramichi.

Reliable	

So named because it was considered a good pattern at any time.

Tail	A few fibers of a red body feather of golden pheasant
Body	Rear third: bright yellow silk floss. Forward two-thirds: black floss
Ribbing	Fine silver oval tinsel
Throat	Black hackle
Wing	Underwing: two matched sections of golden pheasant tippet. Overwing: brown mallard, as a veil, one feather only on each side
Head	Black

PLATE 135
THE ORIOLE AND THE RELIABLE
DRESSED BY IRA GRUBER

The *Rat* and the *Cosseboom* series of hairwing flies are each dressed in many variations and fished around the world.

The Rat Series

According to my late friend Herbert L. Howard, of Mamaronek, New York, the first of the series of *Rat* flies was originated by Roy Angus Thomson in 1911. Howard's version of the story is that he was tying flies for Col. Monell and was experimenting with dressing some with simple wings of hair. Col. Monell brought Thomson to visit Howard, who showed them the skin of a gray fox he had shot, and since Col. Monell considered the outer fur ideal for salmon flies, Howard gave him half a pelt.

That fall, Col. Monell and Thomson went fishing at Monell's guide's lodge and were told that the best fly was a gray or brown one. Thomson tied a fly that was later called the *Gray Rat,* for his initials (R.A.T.)

PLATE 136
THE RAT SERIES, DESCRIBED
AND DRESSED BY HERB HOWARD,
ON PATTERN SHEETS SENT
TO THE AUTHOR

Gray Rat

Tag	Flat gold tinsel (use oval gold tinsel on double hooks)
Tail	Golden pheasant crest
Body	Underfur of gray fox, spun on
Ribbing	Flat gold tinsel
Wing	Gray fox guard hairs
Hackle	Grizzly hackle, tied on as a collar
Cheeks	Jungle cock, short (optional)
Head	Red

The Origin of the Rusty Rat

Most renowned of all the North American hairwings is the *Rusty Rat*, and the story of its origin was first published in October 1949 in *Fortune Magazine's* column "Fortune's Wheel." In an effort to patent his newly successful pattern, American publisher Joseph Pulitzer II wrote to the "Sports Editor" of that magazine saying:

"Having devised a new salmon fly on the Restigouche River this summer, I took it to J. Arseneault, the local fly tier at Atholville, N.B., and had him tie a number for me and others and told him to name it the RUSTY RAT. He informed me that to have this name officially adopted I should write to FORTUNE MAGAZINE. Whether this information is correct I have no means of knowing, but I do recall with great pleasure the fine color feature on salmon flies which you ran in June, 1948.

"For your information this fly is an imitation of an old, worn-out Black Rat Bucktail, on which I took a 41-pounder, and from which the black body had disappeared, leaving the rusty colored dental floss wrapped around the body of the fly. RUSTY RAT proved quite effective and I hereby make formal application to have the name officially adopted.... Meanwhile, I am happy to extend to the editors of FORTUNE the privilege of using it for the next ninety-nine years to their hearts' content."

Arseneault's own version of the story of the *Rusty Rat* parallels Pulitzer's. Sam Day, in his article *A Salute to Three Rats* (*The Atlantic Salmon Journal*, Winter, 1965) quotes "Clovie": "It was in 1949, and the late Joseph Pulitzer had been fishing with one of my large Black Rats. It happened that I had used a rusty floss for the under binding and after he'd taken a salmon or two the fly was pretty well chewed up, the body torn and the rusty tying thread had been cut and came through. But as is often the case, the more disreputable the fly became in appearance the more alluring it must have been to the salmon for Mr. Pulitzer wound up with a 41-pounder.

"He came back to me excited about its performance and enthusiastic about its possibilities. He handed me what remained of the fly and told me he wanted it copied exactly. I got to work and after several tries produced a fly that pleased him, and immediately he named it the *Rusty Rat*."

Further documentation of the origin of the *Rusty Rat* can be found in Pulitzer's diaries that contain detailed fishing logs recorded at Grog Island and Brandy Brook on the Restigouche. The logs tell us that Pulitzer caught his 41-pound salmon on June 24, 1949, and his wife, Liz, took the first salmon, as well as three others, with the new pattern on July 6. The following day the *Rusty Rat* yielded four fish to the Pulitzers, ranging in size from 11 to 22 pounds.

Letters included in the diary also repeat the story of the 41-pound salmon, the 5/0 dilapidated *Black Rat* (or *Rat*), and the subsequent visit to Arseneault, one letter ending with: "I got a good deal of satisfaction out of the success of my last year's invention, the *Rusty Rat* fly. Liz and I together took 76 fish and of those 39 were taken on the *Rusty Rat*. Arseneault, the local fly tier, is selling a good many of them on the Restigouche and on other rivers."

Thus, at last, it is clear to us that the venerable *Rusty Rat* was originated through the collaborative efforts of Joseph Pulitzer II and J. Clovis Arseneault in the summer of 1949.

P. B. R.

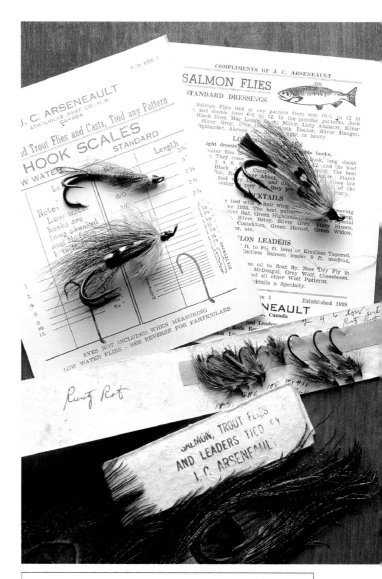

PLATE 137
THE BLACK RAT AND
THE RUSTY RAT, DRESSED BY
J. CLOVIS ARSENEAULT

Black Rat (Rat)   *Rusty Rat*

Black Rat (Rat)

The top left fly shown is Joseph Pulitzer's 5/0 "old worn-out Black Rat" (Rat) that the original *Rusty Rat* was modeled from. This fly was stuck on the wall of Pulitzer's Grog Island camp from 1949 to 1984 when reel-maker Stanley Bogden made arrangements for it to be given to the American Museum of Fly Fishing.

Howard believed Thomson's was the original dressing, although the *Rat* was tied at about the same time and may have been the first one. The *Rat* is the same as the *Gray Rat,* except that the tag is silver and the body is dressed with peacock herl twisted on the tying thread. Gold ribbing is added. This pattern is sometimes referred to as the *Black Rat,* although the *Black Rat* should have a black seal's fur body, ribbed with flat silver tinsel, and a tag of flat silver tinsel.

Perhaps the most popular of the whole series, and indeed one of the most famous flies of all time, is the *Rusty Rat.*

Rusty Rat

Tag	Oval gold tinsel
Tail	Peacock sword or peacock herl
Body	Rear half: yellow-orange floss; forward half: peacock herl. Strands of yellow-orange floss as a veiling from the middle of the body over the rear section
Ribbing	Oval gold tinsel (optional)
Wing	Gray fox guard hairs or mixed black and white hair
Hackle	Grizzly hackle, tied on as a collar
Cheeks	Jungle cock (optional)
Head	Red or black

J. Clovis Arseneault   COURTESY OF DENISE ARSENEAULT ZYVENIUK

When gray fox hair cannot be obtained, several substitutes will do almost as well. In approximate order of preference, these are guard hairs from monkey (commonly known among fly tiers as silver-monkey), from raccoon, mixed black and white monga ringtail, or any other mixture of fairly straight black and white hairs, such as white bucktail with black skunk tail or black bear hair.

Among the many early variations of the *Rat* series, the above have met the tests of time and are fished in waters around the world today. Added to these should be the *Silver Rat,* dressed with a body of flat silver tinsel and oval gold tinsel ribbing. Additional patterns in this ever-increasing series that were developed before 1970 are listed in my earlier book, *Atlantic Salmon Flies and Fishing;* they include the *Brown Rat, Copper Rat, Gold Rat,* and *Red Rat.*

A later adaptation of the series, originated by author and salmon fly dresser Poul Jorgensen, of Roscoe, New York, is the *Blue Rat.* It is the same as the *Rusty Rat* except that medium (*Blue Charm*) blue floss is used instead of yellow floss.

In the fall of 1977, when Poul visited my home, I remarked that the *Rusty Rat* was a very productive fly in Iceland but that flies with "something blue in them" generally were most popular there. Some time later, Poul sent me a dozen of his *Blue Rats,* presumably developed as a result of that conversation. I have used the *Blue Rat* very successfully ever since and consider it one of the best of the series.

Thus, the successful and popular *Rat* series continues to expand and endure. Others include the *Green Rat, Pack Rat, Royal Rat,* and *King Rat.* In my opinion, the most productive ones are the *Rusty, Blue, Silver, Black* (or just *Rat*), and *Gray,* in about that order. As far as wet flies are concerned, under normal conditions one could use these five very successfully in waters all around the Atlantic without requiring any others.

The Cosseboom Series
Another important and successful series of hairwing flies emerged during the first half of this century: the *Cosseboom* series, named for its originator, John C. Cosseboom. The famous *Cosseboom* was first tied in July 1935 aboard the SS *Flueris,* as discussed in chapter 4. Following are the patterns for the *Cosseboom*—the first, as it was originally tied, and the second, a more popular version (sometimes referred as the *Cosseboom Special*), with a yellow collar and red head.

PLATE 138
THE COSSEBOOM AS ORIGINATED ON THE SS FLEURIS
DRESSED BY KEITH FULSHER
Photo of the first *Cosseboom* dressed by John Cosseboom courtesy of Peter G. Walker

Cosseboom (Original)

Tail	A short piece of olive green floss
Body	Olive green floss
Ribbing	Oval silver tinsel
Wing	A bunch of gray squirrel
Throat	Yellow hackle, applied as a beard
Head	Black

Cosseboom (or Cosseboom Special)

Tag	Embossed silver tinsel
Tail	Olive green silk floss, cut off short
Body	Olive green silk floss moderately dressed (Pearsall's shade #82)
Ribbing	Embossed silver tinsel
Wing	A small bunch of gray squirrel tail hairs extending to the end of the tail
Hackle	A lemon yellow hackle tied on as a collar after the wing is applied and slanted backward to merge with the top of the wing
Cheeks	Jungle cock
Head	Black or red

Cosseboom (Streamer or Bucktail)

Tag	Silver tinsel
Tail	A small golden pheasant crest feather
Body	Orange silk floss
Ribbing	Flat silver tinsel
Wing	Extremely small bunches of four items: bronze peacock herl, over which is gray squirrel, over which is green peacock herl, over which is fox squirrel. All four are repeated over this to make eight tiny bunches, one on top of the other
Hackle	A black and white teal feather, wound on as a collar
Cheeks	Very small teal body feathers, one on each side, over which are short jungle cock eyes, if available
Head	Red

Another pattern of historical interest bearing the same name, and presumably also named by or for John Cosseboom, is a streamer fly or bucktail that is said to have originated on the Margaree River about 1922. It contained peacock herl in the wing until it was discovered that the fly worked equally well without it. The fly is dressed on a long-shank hook.

This rather complicated old pattern is included not only because of its historical interest, but also to indicate an early use for streamers and bucktails in salmon fishing—a method that has grown more popular in recent years.

PLATE 140
SALMON FLIES FOR CANADA

Black Bomber
dressed by Mike Crosby

Crosby Special, original
dressed by Mike Crosby

Copper March Brown
dressed by Keith Fulsher

Bastard Dose
dressed by Robert Cavanagh

Preacher
dressed by Bill Wilbur

Orange Blossom Special
dressed by Warren Duncan

Night Hawk
dressed by Warren Duncan

Blue Rat, original
dressed by Poul Jorgensen

Cain's Copper, original
dressed by Mattie Vinceguerra

Pompier, original
dressed by Michel Beaudin

Orange Blossom
dressed by Carmelle Bigaouette

Skinnum
dressed by Vincent Engles

Silver Down-Easter
dressed by Bill Hunter

Royal Rat, original
dressed by Wilhelm Gruber

Jean Special, original
dressed by Jean Michaud

Torrent River Special, original
dressed by Len Rich

Big Intervale Blue, original
dressed by Len Rich

Lightning Bug
dressed by Danny Bird

Abe Munn
dressed by John Atherton

Ross Special
dressed by Eric Baylis

Green Drake
dressed by L. A. La Pointe

The success of the *Cosseboom* patterns led to considerable experimentation, during which many variations were tried. These include the *Black, Orange, Yellow, Red, Peacock,* and *Gold* and are discussed in my book *Atlantic Salmon Flies and Fishing.* On the Miramichi, the fly is dressed with a much darker body and is known as the *Miramichi Cosseboom.* It may well have been Wally Doak who first started using the dark green floss that is now traditional in that area as well as in many commercial dressings.

PLATE 139
COSSEBOOM STREAMER
DRESSED BY BOB WARREN

Miramichi Cosseboom	
Tag	Fine oval gold tinsel
Tail	Green hackle fibers
Body	Dark green wool or floss
Ribbing	Fine oval gold tinsel
Wing	Gray squirrel tail, the white tips of which should be even and approximately one-fourth the length of the wing
Collar	Yellow hackle
Head	Black

Today, the most popular patterns are the *Cosseboom Special,* or *Cosseboom,* as it usually is called; the *Miramichi Cosseboom;* and the *Silver Cosseboom.* The *Silver Cosseboom* is the same as the others, except for a tag, body, and ribbing of silver.

The *Cosseboom Special* is one of the most famous and most popular of all the North American salmon fly patterns. It is dressed as both a standard and a low-water fly and is also very successful for trout. In Norway, sizes 5/0 and 6/0 are popular, and 5/0s often are used on large Canadian rivers.

Creativity, coupled with trial and error, has resulted in the development of newly established patterns, many of which are offshoots of the old. Each region has its local favorites that come in and go out of favor seasonally, and the visiting angler should have fun determining just what these are.

Following is a representative cross section of

both practical and historic North American patterns devised for fishing Canadian waters.

Abe Munn Killer

Tag	Fine oval gold tinsel or gold wire
Tail	Two narrow sections of oak turkey
Body	Buttercup yellow wool
Ribbing	Fine oval gold tinsel
Throat	Brown hackle, veiled (fronted) by oak turkey fibers
Wing	In four sections: two on each side of oak turkey wing
Head	Black

Abe Munn (sometimes incorrectly spelled *Moon* or *Muhn* because that is the way he pronounced it) was a guide in the early days of fly-fishing for salmon in the vicinity of Boistown, New Brunswick. Since he tied this fly about 1925, it seems to be the earliest named North American fly used on the Miramichi River. This dressing and the sample of the fly were provided by Wallace Doak, who copied it from Abe Munn's original pattern.

The fly was popularized in an article in *Fortune* (June 1948) wherein color illustrations of this fly and one called the *Abe Munn Upriver* evidently were transposed, with the latter incorrectly dressed. The *Abe Munn Upriver* is exactly the same as the *Abe Munn Killer* except that it was tied with birch partridge feathers instead of oak turkey. This seems to have been an expedient on Abe's part when he poled his canoe upriver, where he didn't have any oak turkey but where he usually could kill a partridge. The general opinion seems to be that the *Upriver* fly is an unnecessary variation that could be forgotten.

We have noted that one of the Gruber patterns is the *Abe Mohn,* which may have been an attempt to imitate the above pattern from memory.

American Jock Scott

Tag	Fine oval silver tinsel
Tail	Golden pheasant crest
Body	Rear half: medium yellow silk floss. Front half: black silk floss
Ribbing	Fine oval silver tinsel
Throat	Guinea hen fibers, quite short
Wing	White tipped blue mallard, in four sections, two on each side
Head	Black

This is an American simplification, dated about 1930, of the popular British *Jock Scott*. A variation includes a black ostrich herl butt and a wing (in four sections) of bronze mallard side feathers. Color may

be added between the wing sections in red, yellow, and blue. The fancy versions add a topping of a golden pheasant crest feather and include a black hackle throat veiled with guinea hen.

Bastard Dose (Bastard Black Dose)

Tag	Fine oval silver tinsel and yellow-orange or medium yellow silk floss
Tail	Golden pheasant crest
Butt	Black ostrich herl
Body	Rear quarter: light blue seal's fur or wool. Remainder: black seal's fur or wool
Ribbing	Oval silver tinsel
Throat	Claret hackle fibers
Wing	An underwing of a pair of golden pheasant tippets, back to back, over which, in four strips, two on each side, are sections of dark teal not entirely covering the tippets
Topping	Golden pheasant crest
Head	Black

This pattern is as recommended by John Atherton in *The Fly and the Fish.* He says, "In the larger sizes I usually cover the top or back of the wing with strips of bronze mallard."

Big Intervale Blue

Tag	Oval gold tinsel, about five turns
Tail	Golden pheasant crest
Body	Royal or bright blue floss, wrapped heavily for bulk
Ribbing	Oval gold tinsel
Wing	White synthetic or natural polar bear hair
Hackle	Dyed light blue saddle hackle collared to veil the body
Head	Black

Originated in 1987 by Len Rich, author of *Newfoundland Salmon Flies,* the *Big Intervale Blue* has proven particularly successful on the Margaree River in Nova Scotia and on the Gander River (among others) in Newfoundland and Labrador. Having experimented with white-winged patterns for small and clear rivers or streams, Rich wrote: "Water was high on the Margaree after several days of rain, common during late September and early October. Rain and high winds tear leaves from trees and deposit them in small brooks where they eventually wash into the main stream. Orange, yellow, gold and crimson leaves tumble through the pools, caught in the eddies and undercurrents. Somewhere below lie the late run Atlantic salmon, which are expected to discern a fly in this mass of tumbling debris. Perhaps a pattern of cold colours would stand out among the hot colours, I reasoned."

Black Bear, Green Butt

Tag	Oval gold tinsel
Butt	Green fluorescent floss or wool
Body	Black floss or wool
Ribbing	Oval gold tinsel
Throat	Black hackle
Wing	Black bear hair
Head	Black

The butt on this fly can be tied in any other color; however, green is the most popular. Others include the *Black Bear, Red Butt* and the *Black Bear, Orange Butt,* both of which are successful patterns. A variation of this fly, known as the *Conrad,* is also popular in Canada. The only difference between the two seems to be oval silver tinsel.

PLATE 141
SALMON FLIES, ORIGINATED AND
DRESSED BY SHIRLEY WOODS

Roger's Fancy

Black Coltrin

Black Bomber

Tag	Silver wire and yellow floss
Tail	Golden pheasant crest
Body	Black wool
Ribbing	Oval silver tinsel
Throat	Black hackle wound on as a collar
Wing	Black squirrel tail
Topping	Golden pheasant crest
Cheeks	Jungle cock
Head	Black

The *Black Bomber* and the *Brown Bomber,* and presumably the *Silver Bomber,* were originated before 1929 by Joe Aucoin, the well-known fly dresser of Waterford, Nova Scotia. They first were used on the Margaree River and are important all over North America, particularly in Nova Scotia. The British *Black Bomber* is a later fly and probably an adaptation. The *Brown Bomber* has the same tag, tail, ribbing, cheeks, and topping as the *Black Bomber.* It has a butt of black chenille, a body of brown wool, a brown throat, and a wing of fox squirrel tail. The *Silver Bomber* has the same tag and tail as the *Black Bomber.* It has the same topping and cheeks, but they are optional. It has a butt of black chenille, a body of flat silver tinsel, oval silver ribbed, a throat of speckled guinea, and a wing of brown bucktail with a little white bucktail mixed in.

Black Coltrin

Tag	Oval silver tinsel and yellow floss
Tail	Golden pheasant crest
Body	Black seal or black mohair yarn
Ribbing	Silver tinsel
Hackle	Black, tied as a beard
Wing	Black fisher tail, or a substitute such as bear or squirrel. Length not to extend beyond the bend
Cheeks	Jungle cock
Head	Black

Shirley Woods, author of *Angling for Atlantic Salmon,* originated the *Black Coltrin* as his version of a hairwing *Black Dose.* Woods cites this highly effective pattern as his favorite for "high and somewhat murky" water and states that if he were restricted to only one dark fly, this "generic or universal black salmon fly" would be his choice.

Black Dose (Canadian)

Tag	Fine oval silver tinsel and yellow floss
Tail	Golden pheasant crest
Body	Black floss
Ribbing	Oval silver tinsel
Hackle	Black
Throat	Black
Wing	Underwing: golden pheasant tippet in strands. Married strands of red, yellow, and blue swan and golden pheasant tail, outside of which are strips of gray mallard; above this, brown mallard
Sides	Jungle cock
Topping	Golden pheasant crest
Head	Black

This Canadian pattern can usually be distinguished from its more complicated British predecessor by its yellow floss tag and lack of pale blue in the body or butt.

Black Dose Hairwing

Tag	Silver tinsel and palest yellow floss
Tail	Golden pheasant crest, over which is Indian crow (or a few red hackle fibers), half as long (the latter often omitted)
Body	Black floss or wool
Ribbing	Oval silver tinsel
Hackle	A black hackle palmered forward from first turn of tinsel
Wing	Several peacock sword fibers, over which is a small bunch of black or dark brown squirrel tail or black bucktail
Throat	Black hackle, wound on as a collar
Cheeks	Jungle cock
Head	Black

Black Dose (Reduced)

Tag	Oval silver tinsel
Tail	Golden pheasant crest
Body	Black silk floss
Ribbing	Oval silver tinsel
Throat	Black hackle
Wing	Strips of black crow (set to curve upward), extending to the tip of the tail
Cheeks	Jungle cock, very small
Head	Black

This simplified adaptation of the famous *Black Dose* was originated about 1930 by Roy Steenrod, of Liberty, New York, a fishing companion of Theodore Gordon. The pattern was dressed for use on the Little Codroy River in Newfoundland, and was given by Steenrod to Harry A. Darbee, who gave it to me. This is a special dressing on a light-wire (Wilson dry-fly) hook for use as a riffling fly. It is used on most salmon rivers in Maine and Canada and also is tied in regular and low-water dressings.

Black Jack

Tag	Three or four turns of fine round silver wire
Tail	Five or six fibers of a golden pheasant tippet, tied in just below the second black band
Body	Black silk floss, very slim, without taper. (The body occupies not more than two-thirds of the length of the long-shanked hook.)
Ribbing	Very fine oval silver tinsel or silver wire
Hackle	Two black hackles, tied on together as a collar, dressed fairly thickly because this fly has no wing. The longest fibers are no longer than the length of the body
Head	Black

The *Black Jack* is one of the most popular of the low-water patterns in North America and is especially effective on Quebec's Restigouche and Matapedia Rivers.

Blackville (or Blackville Special)

Tag	Fine oval silver tinsel and medium yellow floss
Tail	Golden pheasant crest, slightly longer than the bend of the hook
Butt	Peacock herl
Body	Flat medium embossed silver tinsel
Ribbing	Fine oval silver tinsel
Throat	Bright orange hackle. Forward of this (as a veil) is a very small bunch of guinea hen hackle, applied under the body, as a beard. Both collar and beard barbules are of equal length, extending about two-thirds of the way toward the point of the hook
Wing	Four sections of gray mallard flank feather, two sections on each side, extending nearly to the tip of the tail
Head	Black

This very important fly, used extensively on Canadian rivers, was originated by the famous fly dresser and guide Bert Miner, of Doaktown, New

Brunswick, before 1950. Except for the simplified wing, the fly is very similar to the *Dusty Miller* and was adapted from this old British classic. The *Blackville* and the *Blackville Special* (as it sometimes is called) are the same fly. The *Blackville* has inspired several hairwing descendants, of which the earlier versions are from the bench of Bert Miner. Best known of these is the *Silver Down-Easter,* which has a very similar body and a wing of black squirrel tail hair or black bear hair.

Before 1960, Bert had been tying a fly that is exactly the same as the *Silver Down-Easter* except that it has a wing of natural brown squirrel tail, instead of black. Bert named this version the *Cains River,* and it is popular in that area. It is almost identical to Phil Foster's *Silver Down East,* which became popular about the same time in Maine. Another fly adapted from the original *Blackville* is the *Orange Blossom.*

A fly very similar to Miner's *Blackville,* and unfortunately also called the *Blackville,* is described by John Atherton in *The Fly and the Fish,* as one of his own ten favorites. Evidently it is one of Atherton's several adaptations. It is the same as the above, except that orange floss is used for the tag instead of yellow, the butt is black ostrich herl (or black wool), there is no ribbing; the throat is bright orange with no guinea hen, and the wing is of two sections of wigeon or pintail flank feathers. Both flies originated in Blackville, New Brunswick.

In some of these patterns, the distinctive orange collar is wound on after the wing has been applied. Occasionally, other types of hair, such as polar bear, fitch tail, or brown bucktail, are used. On modern flies, the tag (or butt, when it is not of a feather) is of a fluorescent material. Ira Gruber's *Favorite is* quite similar to the *Blackville.*

Bondatti's Killer	
Tag	Flat silver tinsel
Tail	Golden pheasant crest
Body	Rear half: fluorescent green floss. Front half: orange fluorescent floss
Ribbing	Flat silver tinsel over entire body
Throat	Black hackle
Wing	Gray squirrel tail
Head	Black

Keith Fulsher, incorporating the ideas of his companion, Frank Bondatti, devised *Bondatti's Killer* in 1969 at Bondatti's camp in Doaktown on the Miramichi River. As Keith was tying flies for the next day's fishing, Frank suggested that he devise a new pattern with plenty of fluorescence in it. Combining colors and materials that are particularly successful on the Miramichi, Keith dressed *Bondatti's Killer,* so named after Frank took the first salmon the next day.

Brown Moth	
Tag	Fine oval gold tinsel, or wire and bright orange silk floss, quite sparse
Tail	A few yellow hackle fibers
Butt	Black ostrich herl (black chenille can be used on large sizes)
Body	Medium brown silk floss (not built up)
Ribbing	Fine oval gold tinsel
Throat	Guinea hen fibers
Wing	Four sections, two on each side, of speckled brown hen wing feathers, tied down low on hook (bronze turkey was used for the wing on the original pattern)
Head	Black

This is an old standard pattern, dating about 1929, and is one of the earliest flies used on the Miramichi River. It has been copied, perhaps with slight variations, and given new names, such as the *Brown Mystery* (which calls for a body of orange fluorescent floss), but the above pattern is the original.

Buck Bug	
Tail	Yarn or floss, short (optional)
Butt	Fluorescent green or fluorescent green followed by red (optional)
Body	Deer body hair, clipped: natural, green, or white
Hackle	Brown or orange (colors vary)

The useful, simple, and effective *Buck Bug* is one of the "grass-roots patterns" in fly fishing. Typical of many patterns is the development of new flies from them. These new creations are really little more than adaptations and embellishments of the old. One such pattern that emerged in this way is the *Green Machine.* Father Smith reported to me its astonishing success on the Miramichi in the fall of 1980.

According to Jerry Doak of W. W. Doak and Sons, what we now know as the *Green Machine* initially was a nameless fly tied with brown deer hair that was dyed green, which gave it an olive color. As the fly grew in popularity during the 1970s, it was nicknamed the *Green Gobbler,* and, in 1980, with its success all but legendary, it became known as the *Green Machine.* By this time, the olive green had evolved into a shade of light kelly green that is a blend of insect green and *Green Highlander* green.

Dressed as a *Buck Bug* and in many variations, the *Green Machine* generally has a tag of fluorescent

PLATE 143
SALMON FLIES, ORIGINATED AND DRESSED BY
KEITH FULSHER AND CHARLIE KROM

Orange Reynard
originated and dressed by Keith Fulsher

Gold Fever
originated and dressed by Charlie Krom

Cabin Fever
originated by Keith Fulsher and Charlie Krom, dressed by Krom

Little Red Wing
originated and dressed by Charlie Krom

Silver Tip
originated and dressed by Keith Fulsher

Bondatti's Killer
originated and dressed by Keith Fulsher

Icy Blue
originated and dressed by Charlie Krom

Fulkro
originated by Keith Fulsher and Charlie Krom, dressed by Fulsher

green yarn or floss, a body of clipped deer hair, dyed green, with a brown hackle palmered over the length of the body. Some call it an upstart, some call it a travesty, and some even refuse to fish it. But the fact of the matter is indisputable—it is highly successful.

Cabin Fever	
Tail	Very pale ginger hackle
Body	Mixed cream and red dyed fur
Ribbing	Oval silver tinsel
Throat	Very pale ginger hackle
Wing	Black squirrel tail
Head	Black

Cabin Fever was originated through the joint efforts of Keith Fulsher and Charlie Krom in 1969. Of it Fulsher says: "We wanted a fly with a light colored body that took on a reddish glow. The pattern proved itself that same year when Frank Bondatti used it to take a 23-pound salmon in the Cains River. I hand-tailed the fish for Frank. Art Glowka, an outdoor writer who was fishing with us, wrote an article on the Cains River for the 1972 *Sports Afield Fishing Annual* that featured the catching of that fish with photos and a description of the action. We continue to use the fly successfully."

Cain's Copper

Tag	Fine oval copper tinsel or wire
Tail	Fluorescent red hackle fibers
Butt	Black chenille
Body	Flat copper tinsel
Ribbing	Fine oval copper tinsel or wire
Wing	Gray squirrel tail over orange-dyed hair
Throat	Black, collar style
Head	Black

Having been successful with copper-bodied flies, such as the *Copper Killer,* and flies with a lot of orange in them, Mattie Vinciguerra combined these elements and originated the *Cain's Copper* in 1969.

Caribou

Tag	Fine gold wire; half gold floss followed by black floss
Tail	Golden pheasant crest
Body	Green caribou hair, spun on and clipped short to thin cigar shape, or grass green mohair
Hackle	A gray hackle wound length of body, as ribbing
Throat	A claret hackle wound on as a collar
Wing	Two golden pheasant tippets as long as the body, outside of which are strips of brown turkey, with mallard strips of same length over that, applied in classic style
Cheeks	Narrow strips of blue macaw, nearly as long as the wing
Head	Black

This beautiful old favorite, which was "used extensively with various modifications by the resident fishermen of Fredericton [New Brunswick]" should be rescued from obscurity. It was described in *Fish Hatching and Fish Catching,* by Seth Green and R. Barnwell Roosevelt, in 1879. The head is often finished with black ostrich herl.

Chamberlain

Tag	Fine oval gold tinsel
Body	In two parts: rear third, bright yellow floss; front two-thirds, purple or maroon floss
Ribbing	Oval gold tinsel over entire body
Hackle	A blood red hackle palmered over front part of body only
Throat	Blood red hackle
Wing	Brown mallard or *wild* turkey, upswept in classic style
Head	Black

This handsome pattern was a favorite of angler-author Thaddeus Norris in the 1860s. It was originated on the Nepisiguit River in Canada by his guide, John Chamberlain, and was considered "of great repute." It should not be confused with another *Chamberlain* pattern called the *Orange Chamberlain.*

PLATE 144
THE CHEEKIE SERIES, ORIGINATED AND DRESSED BY ARTHUR ELKINS

As a side adventure and a means of adding something personal to the tying art, Newfoundland's Arthur Elkins created the *Cheekie* series. Rather than adhering to the strict conformity of English tradition as he had been taught, Elkins began by experimenting with overlapping whole feathers to make vertical rather than horizontal color divisions on the wings of his flies. As the series developed, Elkins creatively added several overlapping cheek feathers. His search for suitable multicolored feathers led him to often wasted treasures on unused areas of capes, skins, and wings. The resulting color combinations and patterns are testimony to his success in meeting his own challenge—and his hope that others will be equally inspired.

1   Bittern

Tag	Gold tinsel and yellow floss
Tail	Amherst pheasant crest
Butt	Black ostrich herl
Body	One-third fluorescent green floss; two-thirds brown floss
Ribbing	Oval gold tinsel
Throat	Brown hackle
Wing	Light mottled turkey with a strip of yellow goose over
Cheeks	Jungle cock overlaid witih multicolored reeves pheasant saddle plumage
Head	Black

2   Bulldog

Tag	Silver tinsel and yellow floss
Tail	Amherst pheasant crest
Butt	Red floss
Body	Flat silver
Ribbing	Oval silver
Throat	Blue hackle
Wing	White turkey with a strip of yellow turkey over
Cheeks	Kingfisher overlaid with Amherst pheasant tippets and overlaid with jungle cock
Head	Black

Whiskey Jack

Tag	Gold tinsel and yellow floss
Tail	Golden pheasant crest
Butt	Black ostrich herl
Body	Black floss
Ribbing	Oval gold tinsel
Throat	Black hackle
Wing	Married strips of red and green turkey, pheasant tail and brown turkey; strips of yellow goose over all
Cheeks	Blue jay overlaid with jungle cock
Head	Black

5 *M' Lady Brenda*

Tag	Silver tinsel and yellow floss
Tail	Golden pheasant crest
Butt	Black ostrich herl
Body	Flat silver tinsel
Ribbing	Oval silver tinsel
Hackle	Forward section of body and throat, badger hackle
Wing	Married strips of yellow, red and blue turkey, bustard, green and orange silver pheasant wing and a strip of yellow goose over all
Cheeks	Ring-necked pheasant saddle tips overlaid with jungle cock
Head	Black

6 *Enchanted Prince*

Tag	Gold tinsel and yellow floss
Tail	Amherst pheasant topping
Butt	Red floss
Body	Black floss
Ribbing	Oval gold tinsel
Hackle	Yellow throat hackle
Wing	Married, alternating strips of silver pheasant wing, dyed green, and guinea hen quill, dyed green; yellow goose strips over all
Cheeks	Jungle cock breast feathers, dyed hot orange and nocked to V shape, overlaid with jungle cock eye and overlaid with tip
Head	Black

3 *M' Lady Sandra*

Tag	Gold tinsel and yellow floss
Tail	Golden pheasant crest
Butt	Black herl
Body	Black floss
Ribbing	Oval gold tinsel
Throat	Black hackle
Wing	White turkey overlapped with black turkey and a strip of yellow turkey over all
Cheeks	Small guinea hen feathers with three white dots, closely compacted and overlaid with jungle cock eye
Head	Black

```
1
2   5
 3   6
  4
```

Conrad

In reality, this popular pattern is little more than a *Black Bear, Green Butt*. The fluorescent green butt and tag were added by Charles "Chuck" Conrad, who popularized the pattern in Canada. The *Conrad* is generally tied with oval silver tinsel rather than the gold that is called for in the *Black Bear, Green Butt*.

Copper Killer

Tag	Fine copper wire and pale green fluorescent floss, very small
Tail	Rusty red partridge hackle, small and extending slightly beyond bend of hook
Butt	Bright red floss, quite small
Body	Flat copper tinsel
Ribbing	Round copper wire or very fine oval copper tinsel
Hackle	Bright orange hackle, no longer than the copper part of the body
Wing	Red squirrel tail or Canadian pine, extending no longer than the end of the tail
Head	Red

This fly is an old favorite, especially in the Cains River area of New Brunswick's Miramichi River system. The above dressing was given to me by Bert Miner of Doaktown, New Brunswick, who dressed and fished flies on the river almost since the inception of fly fishing there. He stated that this dressing is the correct one.

Later variations include the use of a tiny bunch of fox squirrel hairs for the tail, presumably because red partridge is not always obtainable. (Bert may have made an error in calling this partridge, because the tail fibers look like the rusty red ones of the ring-necked pheasant.) Sometimes an orange butt is used instead of the green tag and red butt. In modern dressings, the green tag is fluorescent.

Copper March Brown

Tail	Two tiny sections of speckled brown partridge wing, back to back
Body	Round copper wire; oval copper tinsel; or flat copper tinsel ribbed with fine oval copper tinsel
Throat	A darkish brown partridge back feather (a partridge rump feather is used in larger sizes)
Wing	Four sections, two on each side, of strips of hen pheasant wing, tied low on the body (hen pheasant tail strips also are used)
Head	Black

"Great Falls at the Moisie"

The *March Brown* is well known as both a wet fly and a dry fly for trout. This copper-bodied version is popular on North American salmon rivers. John Veniard's *Fly Dressers' Guide* (third edition) lists a British salmon pattern more like the historic wet fly for trout. It has a tag of fine round (or oval) silver tinsel, a tail of a golden pheasant crest feather, and a spun-on body of fur from a hare's face (well picked out), ribbed with silver tinsel. The throat and wing are as above.

Veniard also lists a pair of British "lake flies" that should be good salmon patterns. The *Gold March Brown* is dressed the same as the *Copper March Brown,* except that the body is of gold tinsel. The *Silver March Brown* is the same, except with silver tinsel. Using either partridge or golden pheasant for the tail could be a matter of choice. The original English trout pattern probably dates from between 1840 and 1850. The *Copper March Brown* evidently inspired the American *Copper Killer,* which is better known on North American salmon rivers.

Crosby Special

Tag	Flat silver tinsel
Tail	Golden pheasant crest
Butt	Red wool
Body	In two parts: rear third, fluorescent green floss; the remainder, peacock herl or dark green wool
Ribbing	Oval silver tinsel
Wing	Gray squirrel tail
Hackle	Peach, tied collar-style
Cheeks	Jungle cock
Head	Red

Originated in the late 1970s by Mike Crosby, owner of Mike's Tackle Shop in Halifax, Nova Scotia, this pattern has proven effective in that area as well as other parts of Atlantic Canada.

Dillinger

Tag	Fine oval silver tinsel
Tail	Golden pheasant crest
Butt	Black chenille
Body	Flat silver tinsel
Ribbing	Fine oval silver tinsel
Throat	Medium blue hackle
Wing	Four sections, two on each side, of speckled hen or bronze turkey. The wing is applied close to the body, curving upward
Head	Black

This is one of the early Miramichi River flies, dated about 1930. Since so many flies had been named with the word *killer* at that time, this one was named for a notorious killer and bandit of the period.

Dr. Hale (or Dr. Hill)

Tag	Fine gold wire or oval tinsel
Tail	Golden pheasant crest
Body	Rear quarter: pale yellow silk or wool. Remainder: black silk or wool
Ribbing	Fine oval gold tinsel
Throat	Natural black hackle (blue dun is sometimes used)
Wing	Strips of brown mottled hen turkey tail
Topping	Golden pheasant crest
Cheeks	Jungle cock (the very smallest, tied in very short)
Head	Black

This featherwing was originated in the early 1900s by William Hale, who spent his early youth in Grafton, New Brunswick, on the east bank of the St. John River opposite Woodstock. It was popularized by his second cousin, Robert J. Hale, also of Grafton, who fished the St. John, Miramichi, Upsalquitch, and Restigouche rivers for many years. The black part of the body should be fat. The wings should lie close to the body and should extend only slightly beyond the bend of the hook. Thus, the style of this fly is identical with some of the Ira Gruber patterns, and the dressing bears close resemblance to the several very productive black flies with colored butts, except that this is a featherwing. Although the *Dr. Hale* has influenced several variations, this is the correct original. It sometimes in error is called the *Dr. Hill.*

Hale Special

Tag	Oval silver tinsel and gold floss
Tail	Golden pheasant crest
Body	Rear half: lemon floss. Front half: black floss
Ribbing	Coarse oval silver tinsel
Throat	Black hackle
Wing	Strips of dark brown mottled turkey tail, over which are slips of brown mallard
Topping	Golden pheasant crest
Cheeks	Jungle cock
Head	Black

This fly is evidently one of the variations of the *Dr. Hale.*

Evil Weevils

Arthur Elkins, creator of the *Evil Weevils,* devised this series of bug patterns in an effort to create "a spun hair classic." He writes: "As more and more birds were listed as endangered species, the decline in the supply of materials for featherwings hit us older tiers right where it hurts a tier the most. I watched with revulsion the onset of hairwing substitutes for my English featherwings. Likewise, the development of

PLATE 145
THE EVIL WEEVIL SERIES, ORIGINATED AND DRESSED BY ARTHUR ELKINS

Birch Bark Weevil   *Starigan Weevil*   *Pine Cone Weevil*

Pinchgut Weevil   *Codroy Caddis Weevil*   *Serpentine Weevil*

spun hair bug tying and crude looking match-the-hatch floating and weighted flies, sometimes including synthetics, was a form of blasphemous sacrilege of the old ideals.

"I resisted the new tying styles as long as I could, but my instinct to keep on tying was too strong, and reluctantly I made the change. My first hair flies looked drab because I was used to the bright colors of featherwings. I wanted my hair flies to have more eye appeal to bolster my tier's pride. To date, I've experimented with different body shapes for hair flies and the inclusion of decorative patterns in the body structure of my spun hair bugs. That seemed to give me the same tying satisfaction as featherwing classics had given me in the past."

Of varied colors with striking spots outlined in black, the Evil Weevils are constructed of clipped deer hair with tails of squirrel tail and hackles of grizzly saddle hackle, all dyed to match the dominating color. The heads are three-sectioned: the front and rear of the same dyed deer hair and the center to coordinate with the body. The casings are Krystal flash, and the feelers are made of synthethic paintbrush hairs, with the ends melted.

Fraser Special

Tag	Light yellow floss
Tail	Light yellow wool extending to bend of hook
Body	In three equal sections of wool: rear, light yellow; middle, dark green; front, black. Not built up
Ribbing	Embossed silver tinsel
Wing	A very few each of yellow, red, and green hairs, over which is gray squirrel tail hair, all extending to end of tail. The gray squirrel is at least three times as much as the colored hairs combined
Throat	Black hackle, wound on as a collar after the wing is applied. The hackle extends only halfway to the point of the hook
Cheeks	Jungle cock
Head	Black

This was the favorite pattern of T. B. "Happy" Fraser, a past president of the Atlantic Salmon Federation. The dressing is from an original sent to me by Fraser to correct *Atlantic Salmon Flies and Fishing.*

Fulkro

Tag	Oval silver tinsel and fluorescent orange floss
Tail	Several short strands of red-dyed calf tail
Body	Black wool
Ribbing	Oval silver tinsel
Throat	Brown hackle
Wing	Red squirrel tail
Head	Black

This variation of the *Squirrel Tail* was originated by Keith Fulsher and Charlie Krom (coauthors of *Hair-wing Atlantic Salmon Flies*) in Doaktown, New Brunswick, in the fall of 1967. They report that after several days of slow fishing in low water, they finally stirred some interest with a simple squirrel tail pattern. That evening they modified the pattern to the above dressing, and they proceeded to hook twenty-three salmon with it during the remainder of the week. Coincidence? They don't believe so!

Goblin

Tag	Flat silver tinsel
Tail	Golden pheasant crest
Body	There is no body material. The ribbing is put on as usual and is lacquered
Ribbing	Flat silver tinsel
Throat	Iridescent blue-green peacock breast feather fibers, fairly short
Wing	Black bucktail, over which are a very few peacock breast fibers about half the length of the bucktail
Topping	Golden pheasant crest
Cheeks	Jungle cock, very small and short
Head	Red

This fly originated in Newfoundland before 1910. There are several patterns in this series, all having no body material other than the ribbing on a bare black hook. Various Scottish, English, and Irish tiers did bodies this way, usually lacquering the hooks in various colors.

Gold Fever

Tag	Flat gold tinsel and yellow floss
Tail	Black hackle fibers
Butt	Black wool
Body	Embossed gold tinsel
Ribbing	Oval gold tinsel
Throat	Guinea hen
Wing	Gray squirrel tail over yellow-dyed gray squirrel tail
Head	Black

The *Gold Fever* was originated by Charlie Krom about 1974. He writes: "Like most patterns, they are born of imagination, frustration, desperation, something different, or pure scientific analysis. All to be proven or disproven by a finny adversary who can make or break us as fly tiers. As I think back over the years when this pattern was developed, I believe the inspiration came from the vapors of a bottle of Glenfiddich—desperate times called for desperate measures. Rivers were low, salmon uncooperative—something new and unseen by man or fish had to be designed."

Gold Turkey

Tail	Honey dun hackle fibers
Butt	Fluorescent orange floss
Body	Flat gold tinsel
Ribbing	Gold wire
Throat	Honey dun hackle fibers optionally applied as a collar or bunched under the hook
Wing	Canadian pine squirrel tail, over which are sections of gold barred wild turkey tail feather, both of same length
Head	Black

This simple pattern was originated in 1957 by Donald F. Leyden, of Brookfield Center, Connecticut, as a dark-water fly to go with his *Silver Turkey,* a clear-water one dressed earlier. This one's secret of success is the wing of *wild turkey tail* sections, which have at the feather's tip a wide jet black band with an iridescent gold band in the middle of it. This iridescent band is of major importance. The underwing of Canadian pine squirrel tail hairs makes it easier to apply the feather sections in roofed fashion.

PLATE 146
THE GOLD AND SILVER TURKEY
ORIGINATED AND DRESSED BY
DON LEYDEN

The growing abundance of wild turkeys, particularly in our northeastern states, which have open seasons on them, should make these valuable iridescent feathers easily obtainable.

Green Drake	
Tag	Oval gold tinsel and yellow silk floss
Tail	Golden pheasant crest, over which are a very few shorter golden pheasant tippet fibers
Butt	Peacock herl, very small
Body	Pale honey yellow silk floss
Ribbing	Flat gold tinsel, followed by a black thread
Hackle	A honey-colored hackle palmered from second turn of tinsel
Throat	Partridge hackle
Wing	Four strips, two on each side, of gray mallard flank feather, dyed olive green. The strips meet at the top, flaring out slightly below
Head	Black

This mayfly imitation in simpler form is well known as a trout pattern. It is dressed with many variations, depending on the region where it is tied. These include an adaptation by Ira Gruber that was popular on the Miramichi. This is the pattern of the La Pointes, who were famous salmon fly dressers in the Matapedia area. The fly has been an old-time favorite in Canada, but its use has not been observed in recent years, perhaps because other patterns such as the green *Cosseboom* are preferred. Charles Phair, in his famous *Atlantic Salmon Fishing,* says that the *Green Drake* and the *Abe Munn Killer* were considered the two best flies (about 1935) on the Miramichi, and that the former also is good on the Matapedia, Restigouche, and St. John Rivers.

Gray Fly	
Tag	Fine silver wire and deep orange or salmon-colored floss
Tail	Gray mallard and golden pheasant tail fibers, mixed, tilted slightly upward, extending to end of topping
Body	Gray mohair
Ribbing	Flat or oval silver tinsel
Hackle	Gray hackle wound on from tail
Throat	Carmine hackle
Wing	Two wide strips of brown turkey tail fibers, covered by strips of brown mallard extending to end of tail
Shoulders	On each side, near top and bottom of wing, a strip of a very few fibers of blue macaw tail extending as long as the bend of the hook
Cheeks	Each a golden pheasant tippet, covering the front part of the wing and extending half the length of the body
Topping	Golden pheasant crest curving to end of tail
Head	Black

This handsome pattern was described in the writings of Seth Green and R. Barnwell Roosevelt in 1879. It is of interest more to collectors than to anglers and may be the progenitor of the popular *Nepisiguit Gray.*

Griswold Gray

This is very similar to the *Silver Doctor* and the *Silver Gray* and would substitute for either. It is the same as the *Silver Doctor,* except that the body is of embossed silver tinsel, there is no blue at the throat (only wigeon), the cheeks have double jungle cock (the inside one a bit longer than the outside one), and there are a topping and blue and yellow macaw horns. The wing is complicated and nearly identical to the other two.

FISH FACTS AND FANCIES

BY
F. GRAY GRISWOLD

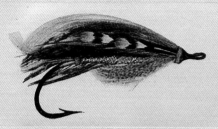

"GRISWOLD GRAY"

CHARLES SCRIBNER'S SONS
NEW YORK · LONDON
MCMXXVI

PLATE 147
THE GRISWOLD GRAY
DRESSED BY BILL WILBUR

This pattern is a variation preferred by Frank Gray Griswold, author of *Fishing Facts and Fancies* (1926), and was often used by him on Canadian rivers such as the Grand Cascapedia. Between 1920 and 1930, Griswold wrote at least seven books on angling, some of which were privately published.

Grizzly King	
Tag	Silver tinsel
Tail	A section of a red ibis, red swan, or goose feather, or a few red hackle fibers
Body	Green silk floss
Ribbing	Oval silver tinsel
Wing	Mixed brown and white bucktail, or gray squirrel
Hackle	A grizzly hackle, wound on collar-style
Head	Black

This is a popular salmon pattern, especially in the Restigouche area of Canada. It should not be confused with the trout wet-fly pattern of the same name, which usually is dressed with a tail of red or scarlet hackle fibers, a green floss or dubbing body, gold ribbing and tag, a grizzly hackle throat, and a wing of gray mallard.

Half Stone	
Tag	Fine oval silver tinsel
Tail	Golden pheasant crest (or a few strands of some speckled feather, such as wood duck)
Body	Rear third: yellow seal's fur, dressed thin. Remainder: black seal's fur, dressed thin
Ribbing	Fine oval gold tinsel
Throat	Black or dark furnace hackle, thin and short
Wing	Speckled hairs from the base of a fox squirrel tail, dressed very thin and short
Head	Black

This low-water pattern is taken from *The Fly and the Fish,* by John Atherton, in which he says it is his own adaptation. It evidently was one of his favorites. It seems to bear little or no resemblance to the British (Devonshire) *Half-stone,* which is discussed in several variations in angling classics, including the works of Halford, Taverner, and Veniard. The British fly was tied to represent a hatching nymph. In this low-water pattern, a light-wire hook is used and the dressing is very sparse, occupying only the forward half of the hook shank. John Atherton, who lived in Shaftsbury, Vermont, was an outstanding artist, particularly of angling subjects, as well as an accomplished angler and fly dresser. A significant portion of his collection is now at the American Museum of Fly Fishing in Manchester, Vermont.

Icy Blue	
Tag	Flat silver tinsel and fluorescent blue floss
Tail	Golden pheasant crest
Body	Flat silver tinsel
Ribbing	Oval silver tinsel
Throat	Blue hackle
Wing	Gray squirrel tail, dyed blue, over white hair
Head	Black

The *Icy Blue* was designed by Charlie Krom at a sportsmen's show in 1976. A gentleman observing Charlie tie commented that the fly he was creating should do well in Iceland. Charlie gave him the fly, and the gentleman proved himself correct. Charlie writes: "Several weeks later, I received a phone call from this gentleman, telling me of the great sport he had while the fly lasted and asking whether I would tie him several dozen in different sizes and please give it a name, all in one breath. Thus *Icy Blue* came to be."

John Special (or Jean Special)

Tail	A few yellow goose fibers, over which is golden pheasant crest
Body	Flat silver tinsel, dressed slender
Wing	Goat hairs applied no longer than two-thirds of body length. Over them are strips of yellow goose wing feathers, about half as long as the body and prominently raised
Throat	Dark mink tail hair
Head	Medium green caribou hair, spun on and clipped short, *Muddler*-style

This pattern was originated by Jean Michaud, of Montreal, about 1950. It often is called the *Green Muddler,* but its highly cocked wings give it a very different appearance. It is dressed in several versions on different sizes of hooks, depending on water conditions. In addition to the standard version, it is used as a low-water fly and does well when riffled.

Patterns with a lot of yellow in them are very popular in Canada, including the *Lanctot, Langevin, Lanctoboom, Mickey Finn,* and *Colonel Bates.* It has been noted that they are particularly effective in discolored water and as "wake-up" patterns.

Lady Amherst

Tag	Fine oval silver tinsel and golden-yellow floss
Tail	Golden pheasant crest and strands of teal
Butt	Black ostrich herl
Body	Flat silver tinsel
Ribbing	Oval silver tinsel
Hackle	A badger hackle, from the second turn of tinsel
Throat	Teal, the longest fibers extending nearly to the barb of the hook
Wing	Two long jungle cock feathers cocked upward about 30 degrees, extending to bend of hook. Over these on each side are two pairs of Lady Amherst pheasant tippets, the first applied to show only the tips of the jungle cock. The tip of the second feather should meet the second black bar on the first feather
Sides	Jungle cock
Cheeks	Blue chatterer or kingfisher
Topping	Golden pheasant crest
Horns	Blue and yellow macaw
Head	Black

This famous Canadian pattern is dressed in classic style. It was originated about 1925 by George D. B. Bonbright, president of the Seaboard Airline Railway, and was extensively used by him on Canadian rivers, especially the Grand Cascapedia. Charles Phair, author of *Atlantic Salmon Fishing,* says that he commercialized the pattern under the name *Bonbright No. 2* to distinguish it from the earlier pattern he had named for Bonbright, called the *No. 1.* The fly was so popular on the Grand Cascapedia that at one time it was the only one guides wanted anglers to use, normally in sizes as large as 5/0 for that big river. The change of name to the present one was to avoid confusion and to highlight the Amherst pheasant feathers that dominate the wing. The pattern is beautiful and unusual, and is evidently excellent for big or discolored rivers.

Lanctot

Tag	Fine gold wire or oval tinsel and canary yellow floss
Tail	Red duck or swan feather
Butt	Black ostrich herl
Body	In two parts: rear third, canary floss; front two-thirds, black floss. Between the two parts, the body is butted with black ostrich herl, and the rear part is veiled above and below with bright yellow toucan (or substitute) feathers extending to the rear butt
Ribbing	Fine oval gold tinsel on each section
Hackle	Black hackle, over black floss only
Throat	Guinea hen body feather
Wing	Four canary yellow (saddle or neck) hackles extending to end of tail
Cheeks	Jungle cock
Topping	Two golden pheasant crest feathers
Horns	Blue and yellow macaw
Head	Black ostrich herl

Although named for and by Charles Lanctot, an ardent angler and attorney general of the Province of Quebec during the late 1920s, the *Lanctot* salmon fly was most probably originated about 1930 by Ivers Adams, a founding member and longtime president of The Moisie Salmon Club. According to Edward Week's 1971 chronicle *The Moisie Salmon Club,* Adams had tied a fly that was "conspicuous for its tawny feather" and requested that it be copied by Forrest of London. Lanctot complied with Adams's request and had the fly tied in a variety of sizes—and named it for himself.

Years later, Lanctot is reported to have commented to his friend and angling companion L. Alexander Taschereau, a former premier of Quebec, "Fame is a fleeting thing. You, my good friend, are known everywhere as the prime minister of Quebec, but fifty years from now, you will be forgotten, while I shall be remembered for this!" To emphasize his point, Lanctot gave his leader a tug and set out to fish *his* fly.

PLATE 148
THE SILVER SATAN AND THE LADY ATHERTON
ORIGINATED AND DRESSED BY CHARLIE DeFEO

Silver Satan

Tag	Fine oval silver tinsel and radiant orange floss
Tail	Golden pheasant crest
Butt	About two turns of very bronze peacock herl
Body	Rear two-thirds: flat silver tinsel. Front third: black floss
Ribbing	Oval silver tinsel over all
Wing	A few golden pheasant tippet fibers, over which is a small bunch of gray squirrel tail hair
Cheeks	Jungle cock, very small and short
Hackle	About two turns of Plymouth Rock hackle applied as a collar
Head	Red

Bearing a resemblance to the *Silver Rat* and to the hair-wing version of the *Blackville*, the *Silver Satan* was originated by Charles DeFeo, of New York City. When he sent me the fly shown in this plate, Charlie wrote: "This fly has been used or fished on every river in Canada, Labrador, Matane, St. Jean, and by Al McLane on the George River. He said for a whole week he had not been able to get a salmon to take. He tried everything. Then he spotted this fly in his box. He put it on and got action at once. My big fish were all taken on it, on the Matane and the St. Jean. One day on the Cains I lost six big fish in a row, and then landed a 22, a 28 and a 34 pound salmon in a row. Now I am just happy to be on any salmon river. Fish or no fish."

Lady Atherton

Tag	Oval silver tinsel and fluorescent orange floss
Tail	Golden pheasant crest (optional)
Body	Black wool or dubbed black bear underbody fur
Ribbing	Oval silver tinsel
Throat	Natural black hackle
Wing	Two long and coarse black bear hairs (as "feelers"), half again as long as the hook with black bear hair, short and on top of horns
Cheeks	Jungle cock, very small
Head	Black

The *Lady Atherton* was originated by Charlie DeFeo and cited by him (with the *Silver Satan*) as one of his two favorites. He wrote to me: "The *Lady Atherton* was named for Mrs. John Atherton. I gave the fly to Maxine [Mrs. Atherton] to try on one of her salmon trips. She sent the fly to me that winter and said she took and released thirty-six salmon on it. She puts all of her fish back. She is a truly great angler and has fished all over the world."

In the simplified versions of the fly, the tail is golden pheasant and/or red duck wing fibers, and the body butt and veilings are eliminated. The throat sometimes is of mallard fibers, and the wing is yellow goose strips or less destructible yellow calf tail.

Langevin

Tag	Fine gold tinsel or wire and yellow floss
Tail	Two narrow strips from yellow goose wing feathers, curving upward, of normal length
Body	Yellow floss, dressed gradually fuller toward head
Ribbing	Black thread
Hackle	Yellow hackle starting midway on body and wound more fully at head to provide a throat
Wing	Two wide strips from yellow goose wing feathers, extending to tip of tail
Head	Black ostrich herl

In the village of Port Rouge on the Jacques-Cartier River there is a pool called the Langevin, named for a minister in the Ottawa government who was a resident of Quebec city. This fly was named for him also.

The *Langevin* was described in Thaddeus Norris's *The American Angler's Book* in 1865 and by Robert Barnwell Roosevelt and Seth Green in *Fish Hatching and Fish Catching* in 1879. Later, Roosevelt published the description again in his own book *The Game Fish of the Northern States and British Provinces*, and it is included in more recent angling references, such as J. Edson Leonard's *Flies*, first published in 1950 and since reissued. Popularly known as "the yellow fly," the *Langevin* is very similar to the *Yellow May* or *Yellow Miller* found in Mary Orvis Marbury's 1892 book *Favorite Flies*.

Little Red Wing

Tag	Flat silver tinsel and fluorescent red floss
Tail	Golden pheasant crest
Butt	Black ostrich herl
Body	Flat silver tinsel
Ribbing	Oval silver tinsel
Throat	Black hackle
Wing	Black squirrel tail over bright-red-dyed hair
Head	Black

Originated by Charlie Krom in 1973, this fly is sometimes varied using strands of fluorescent red floss in the underwing. Krom writes of the *Little Red Wing:* "This pattern was developed from colors I like in salmon flies. I felt the red tip (tag) wasn't noticeable enough, and adding a strand of red floss under the wing gave it just the right balance. Whether fished on light or dark days, this pattern over the years has proven to be deadly."

Lightning Bug

Tag	Fine oval gold tinsel
Tail	Red fluorescent nylon wool, cut off short
Body	Rear third: green fluorescent nylon wool. Forward two-thirds: peacock herl
Ribbing	Fine oval gold tinsel, on forward part only
Wing	Black bear hair or black squirrel tail hair, sparse, short, and close to the body
Throat	Black hackle, sparse and short
Head	Black

This is a simple green-butt pattern with a red tail added, especially popular near the mouth of the Cains River, on New Brunswick's Miramichi River. The green fluorescent nylon wool, which represents the fluorescent rear section of a lightning bug, provides a translucent and very "buggy" appearance.

Moisie Grub

Tag	Fine flat gold tinsel, very small
Tail	Golden pheasant crest
Body	In two equal sections: rear half, cream-yellow mohair or spun fur; front half, black mohair or spun fur (or peacock herl). About two turns of a black hackle are made between the two sections
Hackle	At throat only, several turns of long fibered guinea fowl feather, a bit wider than the black hackle, and tied backward only slightly
Head	Red

This grub pattern was found in the original cabins of The Moisie Salmon Club and was created by Henry P. Wells, originator of the *Parmacheene Belle* trout fly, about 1887. He considered it a "change-of-pace" fly from the *Jock Scott*.

My old friend and angling companion John L. Baxter, Sr., of Brunswick, Maine, gave me several examples of another grub or shrimp pattern used on the Restigouche and other Canadian rivers. Neither of us know its name, and it isn't to be found (so far) in the literature, although it is quite similar to a few of the British grubs. Here is the dressing:

Tail	A reddish golden pheasant body feather wound on as a collar and tied back to an angle of about 45 degrees, nearly twice as wide as the gape of the hook
Body	Embossed silver tinsel. Midway on the body are upper and lower veilings of red feathers, which would be Indian crow, if available, but which are the tips of red hackles extending beyond the tail. Just forward of these are two or three turns of a badger hackle about as wide as the gape of the hook
Wing	Two jungle cock feathers extending to bend of hook, angled about 45 degrees
Throat	Badger hackle, a bit wider than the middle one
Head	Black

PLATE 149
GRUB PATTERNS

Grub
dressed by Mark Waslick

Canadian Grub   *Scottish Grub*
dressed by Robert Hibbitts

Grub   *Grub*
(John Shields & Co.)   (John Shields & Co.)

Moisie Grub
dressed by Robert Hibbitts

Nicholson

Tag	Fine flat gold tinsel
Tail	Brown mallard mixed with golden pheasant tippet
Body	Blood red seal's fur, slightly picked out
Ribbing	Fine oval gold tinsel
Hackle	One blue and one blood red hackle palmered the length of the body, with an extra turn or two at the throat
Wing	Strips of brown mallard set well above the body, extending to end of tail
Head	Black

This has been a popular Canadian pattern since the 1950s. In *Favorite Flies,* Mary Orvis Marbury says, "The Nicholson, sometimes called the *Blue and Brown,* has for many years been popular for salmon as well as for large trout." It is named for an old salmon fisher of St. John, New Brunswick. Nicholson dressed it in various colors of body and hackle according to the state of the water, brighter for the high water of early season, duller later in the year. For all versions, the wing was brown mallard, set at a sharp angle above the body, and the head was black ostrich herl. The above dressing is the original version, as set down by Thaddeus Norris, with whom it was a special favorite.

Night Hawk

Tag	Oval silver tinsel and yellow silk floss
Tail	Golden pheasant crest, over which is kingfisher, half as long as the crest feather
Butt	Red wool
Body	Flat silver tinsel
Ribbing	Oval silver tinsel
Wing	Two sections of black turkey feather, extending to the tip of the tail
Throat	Black hackle
Shoulders	Jungle cock
Cheeks	Kingfisher
Topping	Golden pheasant crest
Head	Red

This is one of the more valuable old Canadian patterns dating from the 1880s. Reliable authority indicates that it was originated by the noted architect Stanford White when he was fishing the Restigouche from Dean Sage's Camp Harmony in the 1890s or perhaps earlier. The hairwing version, more popular today, is as above except that it has no tag, cheeks, or topping. The jungle cock eyes are short, and the wing is of black hair, such as dyed squirrel. The *Night Hawk* is often tied as a hairwing by simply substituting black hair for the black feather.

Nepisiguit Gray

Tag	Fine oval silver tinsel, or silver wire and bright yellow floss
Tail	Golden pheasant crest
Butt	Two or three turns of peacock herl or black wool
Body	Medium gray wool, not built up
Ribbing	Fine oval silver tinsel
Throat	Barred-rock hackle feather
Wing	In four sections, two on each side, of bronze mallard
Head	Black

This is an old-time pattern, first tied near Pabineau Falls, on New Brunswick's Nepisiguit River, during or before the 1880s. It was a prime favorite of Dean Sage, who fished the Restigouche as early as 1875 and who, in 1879, built his own camp, Camp Harmony, at the junction of the Upsalquitch and Restigouche, sharing ownership with his friend Charles Lawrence, of Brooklyn, New York.

Sage's dressing is as above except that he preferred muskrat fur for the body. In the larger sizes (used then more than now), the wing was more ornate: an inner wing of oak turkey over which were married strips of blue, red, and yellow swan, with an outer wing of bronzed mallard. The ornate pattern also called for jungle cock eyes and a topping of golden pheasant crest. In the simplified modern version, brown bucktail (or something similar) replaces the bronze mallard. The *Gray Rat* should do as well. No authentic information is available as to when, where, or by whom the *Nepisiguit Gray* was originated, this evidently being lost in antiquity.

Notion

Tail	Golden pheasant crest below a few shorter fibers of blue macaw
Body	Flat gold tinsel
Hackle	Ginger hackle palmered from midway of body, with extra turns at the head
Wing	Two wide golden pheasant tippets, outside of which are strips of teal and married or laid on strips of yellow swan, brown mottled turkey tail, and gray swan, these occupying, and as long as, the middle third of the wing
Shoulders	Tips of woodcock feathers, half as long as the body
Cheeks	Blue kingfisher
Head	Black

The pattern illustrated in Mary Orvis Marbury's *Favorite Flies* also shows strips of four or so joined fibers of blue macaw applied as horns. In her book, she says: "The Notion was first made and named by John Shields, the veteran (c. 1880–1900) fly-maker of Brookline, Massachusetts. It was intended for landlocked salmon, but we hear of it as also successful for salmon, trout and black bass. Dressed on large hooks it is very beautiful, the gilt and golden brown harmonizing perfectly; it can also be adapted to a small hook. It is a fly that many anglers 'take a notion to,' and value it for the good it does as well as for its beauty."

Orange Blossom

Tag	Oval silver tinsel and orange (or yellow) floss
Tail	Golden pheasant crest over which is Indian crow (or substitute), half as long
Butt	Black ostrich herl
Body	Embossed silver tinsel. (An alternate dressing calls for the rear half of the body to be dressed with embossed silver tinsel and the front half with bright yellow floss or seal's fur.)
Hackle	Yellow hackle (only on front half in alternate dressing)
Ribbing	Oval silver tinsel, wound over the hackle (if it is used)
Wing	Pale brown bucktail
Throat	Bright orange hackle, applied as a collar
Head	Black

This is the authentic dressing from Carmelle Bigaouette, whose shop was next to the Restigouche Hotel in Matapedia, Quebec. A variation of this pattern that is often successful is the *Orange Blossom Special,* as follows.

Orange Blossom Special

Tag	Silver tinsel and gold floss
Tail	Golden pheasant crest, over which is red hackle and barred teal
Butt	Black ostrich herl
Body	Embossed silver tinsel
Ribbing	Oval silver tinsel
Wing	Natural white hair
Throat	Bright orange hackle, applied as a collar
Head	Black

Orange Chamberlain

Tag	Fine flat gold (or silver) tinsel and black floss (sometimes omitted)
Tail	Golden pheasant crest, quite long
Body	Orange mohair, picked out
Ribbing	Flat gold (or silver) tinsel
Hackle	Orange hackle following ribbing
Throat	Yellow hackle applied as a collar
Wing	Brown mallard and shelldrake (or golden pheasant tail) strips, mixed
Head	Black, with black ostrich herl

PLATE 150
THE NOTION, DRESSED BY JOHN OLSCHEWSKY

This version of the *Chamberlain* is another Green and Roosevelt pattern dated about 1879. The attractive flies of these two angler authors seem to have become forgotten, but a few are resurrected in this book. This one should do well in high or discolored water or as a "wake-up" fly. It is reminiscent of the popular bucktail called the *Warden's Worry.* (See *Streamer Fly Tying and Fishing,* 1995.)

Pompier (or Fireman)	
Tag	Fine oval gold tinsel
Tail	Golden pheasant rump feather fibers
Body	Black chenille or wool, fine
Ribbing	Gold tinsel
Wing	Yellow bucktail under a few hairs of yellow polar bear
Throat	Green Highlander green hackle, applied as a collar
Cheeks	Jungle cock
Head	Fireman red

This popular and successful Gaspe pattern was originated in 1979–1980 by Michel Beaudin, whose job as a fireman during the winter inspired its name. Beaudin, who guides and fishes during the season, reports that most of his fish are caught on this pattern.

Preacher	
Tag	Fluorescent orange floss
Tail	Golden pheasant crest
Butt	Fluorescent red floss
Body	Black wool
Ribbing	Oval silver tinsel
Wing	Black skunk hair (or substitute)
Throat	Black hackle, applied as a collar
Head	Black

This old Restigouche pattern is tied in several variations that incorporate portions of other successful and primarily black flies. For this reason, it is often confused with flies such as the *Undertaker,* which has a tag of both red and green fluorescent floss, a body of peacock herl, and gold tinsel.

Price's Dose

Tag	Fine oval silver tinsel and bright yellow floss
Body	Black wool, fairly slim
Ribbing	Fine oval silver tinsel
Wing	A few golden pheasant tippet fibers, over which are a few red hackle fibers. Veiling these on both sides and meeting at the top are sections of gray mallard flank feather. The wing is set low, nymph-style
Throat	Black hackle
Cheeks	Jungle cock, extending to end of body
Head	Black

This dressing is taken from an original pattern by Everett Price, a member of a prominent angling family that lived in Lower Blackville, New Brunswick. The original was dressed on a #10 double hook and was retired after catching many salmon. Evidently Price made some of his double hooks by using two singles, cutting off the eye of one, honing them to match, and binding them together. This fly is somewhat similar to a reduced *Black Dose* or a *Reliable.* It is fairly typical of the popular and productive featherwings in the Miramichi area.

Professor

Tag	Flat gold tinsel
Tail	Golden pheasant crest
Butt	Black ostrich herl
Body	Yellow silk floss
Ribbing	Oval gold tinsel
Throat	Brown hackle
Wing	Four narrow strips of gray mallard breast feather, applied as two pairs, tied low against the hook
Cheeks	Jungle cock
Head	Black

This early American salmon fly is an adaptation of a trout pattern. A tail of two thin sections of swan or goose feather, dyed red, is often used instead of the golden pheasant crest.

Orange Reynard (Reynard Series)

Tag	Oval silver tinsel and fluorescent orange floss
Tail	Guinea hen fibers
Body	Silver tinsel
Ribbing	Oval gold tinsel
Wing	Red fox guard hair, taken from the center of the back of the fox. Hair should have a dark base, cream-colored center, and fiery brown tips.
Throat	Orange hackle, applied as a collar
Head	Black

Originated by Keith Fulsher in 1982, the *Reynard* series consists of five patterns: blue, black, orange, green, and yellow. In explaining the dressings, Fulsher writes: "All patterns have guinea hen fibers for the tail and wings of red fox guard hair, taken from the center of the back and having a dark base, cream colored center and fiery brown tips. Each pattern has a hackle color and fluorescent tip color to match its name. The *Orange* and *Blue Reynards* have oval silver tags and silver bodies with an oval gold rib; the *Green* and *Yellow Reynards* are the reverse, with oval gold tags and gold bodies with an oval silver rib. The *Black Reynard* has a silver tag and rib, a *lacquered* black floss tip, and a black wool body. These patterns were designed around the wing material. Red fox hair has been little used for winging salmon flies, yet the hair as described for these patterns makes an excellent wing—good color and easy to use. The *Blue Reynard* has been very good in Iceland, and others have been successful in New Brunswick and Newfoundland."

Roger's Fancy

Tag	Fine oval silver tinsel and yellow fluorescent floss
Tail	A few peacock sword fibers, not to extend beyond the wing
Body	Kelly green seal or mohair
Ribbing	Oval silver tinsel
Throat	Green Highlander green over bright yellow hackle fibers
Wing	Gray fox hair
Cheeks	Jungle cock
Head	Black

This internationally popular pattern was originated about 1970 by Shirley E. Woods, of Ottawa, Canada, author of *Angling for Atlantic Salmon.* It was named for a friend, Maj. Gen. Roger Rowley, and was developed for use on the Ste. Anne River, where patterns with green predominating are preferred. Woods commented in his book, "I consider the Ste. Anne an especially brilliant star in the galaxy of Gaspe salmon rivers."

Ross Special

Tag	Silver oval tinsel
Tail	Golden pheasant crest
Body	Red wool, dressed fairly full
Ribbing	Silver oval tinsel
Throat	Yellow hackle
Wing	Red squirrel tail
Cheeks	Jungle cock
Head	Black

This fly was illustrated in a June 1948 *Fortune* article, "Atlantic Salmon." It is a popular pattern on Canadian rivers, especially the Margaree. It is rather similar to the *Red Abbey* and the *Abbey* British trout fly and seems to be an adaptation.

Ross

Tag	Black silk
Tail	Green parrot
Body	Cinnamon floss
Ribbing	Gold twist
Hackle	Red over rear of body; black over front of body, with extra turns at throat
Wing	Mallard
Topping	A few peacock herl fibers
Head	Black

Published by Green and Roosevelt in 1879, the *Ross* may be the ancestor of the previous pattern, the *Ross Special*.

Rutledge Fly (or Cains River Special)

Tag	Fine oval silver tinsel
Tail	Light green fluorescent floss
Body	In two equal parts dressed rather full: rear half, light green fluorescent floss; front half, peacock herl
Throat	Peacock sword and black hackle
Wing	Fine black hair
Head	Black

This pattern was given to me in 1968 by Wallace Doak, proprietor of a prominent tackle shop in Doaktown, New Brunswick. Wally Doak always wanted new patterns to attract his customers, and this probably was one of them, because it seems to be an adaptation of the valuable *Lightning Bug*. These fluorescent-butt patterns are great salmon attractors, so this one merits publication as well.

Silver Down-Easter

Tag	Fine oval silver tinsel
Tail	Golden pheasant crest
Butt	Black ostrich herl
Body	Medium flat silver tinsel
Ribbing	Fine oval silver tinsel
Throat	Bright orange hackle
Wing	Black squirrel tail
Head	Black

The *Silver Down-Easter* is an important and popular pattern on Maine and Canadian salmon rivers. It is attributed to Bert Miner, of Doaktown, New Brunswick, and is one of several variations described earlier under the *Blackville*. In addition to these are the *Down East Special* and the *Silver Down East,* which were originated in Maine.

Silver Tip

Tag	Oval yellow tinsel
Tail	Red wool, cut short and flat
Body	Several fine strands of oval yellow tinsel, wrapped on as a unit (oval gold tinsel can be substituted)
Wing	Silver-tipped grizzly bear hair
Throat	Yellow hackle, applied as a collar
Head	Black, with a red ring at the base

A good choice for bright, sunny days, the above pattern is from Keith Fulsher, who originally tied it as a trout fly and later adapted it to a salmon fly. It should not be confused with another fly of the same name that is popular in Newfoundland. That fly is tied with a long, flat silver tinsel tag; a body of black floss; ribbing of wide, flat silver tinsel; and a wing of black moose hair.

Silver Turkey

Tail	A few dark dun hackle fibers
Butt	Fluorescent red floss
Body	Flat silver tinsel
Ribbing	Silver wire
Throat	Dark dun hackle fibers, optionally applied as a collar or bunched under the hook
Wing	A small bunch of black fitch tail hairs, over which are sections of wild turkey body feather, both of same length
Head	Black

This simple pattern was originated in 1955 by Donald F. Leyden, of Brookfield Center, Connecticut, to go with his *Gold Turkey*. The development of the *Silver Turkey* and the *Gold Turkey* was influenced by Charlie DeFeo and Preston Jennings, both friends of Leyden's and innovative tiers who worked to create iridescence and translucence in the many patterns they originated. The deep metallic sheen of a wild turkey body feather gives a similar effect to more complicated combinations, and the single feather is simpler to use. I, along with many others, prefer these now easily obtainable feathers to other blackish ones, such as crow, for all patterns that call for such.

The hair underwing helps the feather overwing to set properly in roofed fashion. The *Silver Turkey* is a clear-water fly while its counterpart, the *Gold Turkey,* is better in high or discolored water. Both have slim bodies and should be dressed fairly sparsely.

Skinnum

Tag	Fine flat silver tinsel
Tail	Blue dun cock hackle fibers
Body	Peacock quill
Throat	Blue dun cock hackle fibers, rather long
Wing	Strips of woodcock wing feathers
Head	Black

This pattern, tied in the classic trout wet-fly style, was a favorite of Percy E. Nobbs, first president of the Atlantic Salmon Association, and has been used very successfully by many other prominent anglers. Thus it is well worth remembering.

Spate Fly

Tag	Oval gold tinsel
Tail	Golden pheasant crest
Body	Dark brown seal's fur or polar bear fur, spun on and slightly picked out
Ribbing	Medium-size oval gold tinsel
Throat	Black hackle, the longest fibers reaching nearly to the point of the hook
Wing	Brown bucktail
Shoulders	Fairly wide strips of barred wood duck, set on both sides of the bucktail and two-thirds as long
Head	Red

This attractive and unusual fly was originated in 1946 by Harry A. Darbee, of Livingston Manor, New York. Originally it was dressed on the Margaree River, Cape Breton, Nova Scotia. It is dressed in sizes to suit water conditions and is used when rivers are in spate—that is, high and discolored—and has accounted for many large fish under such conditions.

The Taylor Specials

Arthur Taylor's Taylor Special

Tag	Oval silver tinsel
Body	Rear half: fluorescent green floss. Front half: dark green floss
Ribbing	Oval gold tinsel
Wing	Gray squirrel tail, dyed bright green
Throat	Yellow hackle, applied as a collar
Head	Black

Bill Taylor's Taylor Special

Tag	Fine oval silver tinsel
Body	Rear half: fluorescent green floss with a veil of the same material. Front half: peacock herl
Ribbing	Fine oval silver tinsel, front half only
Wing	Gray squirrel tail, dyed fluorescent green
Throat	Bright yellow hackle, applied as a collar
Head	Black

PLATE 151
THE TAYLOR SPECIALS

dressed by Arthur Taylor
dressed by Bill Taylor

This popular and successful pattern was originally created by Maine artist Arthur Taylor on the Miramichi River in 1986. Arthur shared his success on the river that year by giving Bill Taylor of the Atlantic Salmon Federation one of his "little green flies," which Bill subsequently modified as above. Although both would be modest about it, each of the Taylor men for whom these flies are aptly named holds a special place in the salmon world, and the *Taylor Specials* have represented them well from the river of their origin throughout Nova Scotia, the Gaspe, Newfoundland and Labrador.

Teagle Bee

Tail	Two sections of red swan feather, as long as the wing
Body	In four parts, alternating black and yellow chenille, quite thick
Wing	Black bear hair
Collar	Brown, quite long and full
Head	Black

As discussed in chapter 8, this pattern is from a fly formerly owned by Walter C. Teagle, who popularized it fishing the Restigouche during the 1930s.

PLATE 152
SALMON FLIES, DRESSED BY ALEX ROGAN

Professor

Teagle Bee

Grizzly King

PLATE 153
THE UNDERTAKER, DRESSED BY WARREN DUNCAN

Tobique Special

Tag	Fine oval silver tinsel
Tail	Fibers of a golden pheasant tippet, long enough to show two black strands
Body	Rear half: medium yellow wool. Front half: black wool
Ribbing	Fine oval silver tinsel, over entire body
Wing	Pine squirrel tail hair
Collar	Buttercup yellow hackle
Head	Black

This is merely an adaptation of one of the prolific "yellow butt, black body" hairwing designs. It is included here because it is popular by name in the Tobique Valley of Canada's Tobique River.

Torrent River Special

Tag	Oval silver tinsel
Body	Fluorescent white floss
Ribbing	Oval silver tinsel
Throat	Single turn of webby furnace or badger hackle, applied as a collar
Wing	White calf tail
Head	White, with clear or white lacquer

While attempting to create an effective wet version of the *White Wulff,* Len Rich originated this fly in the mid to late 1970s. Rather than call it the "Wet White Wulff," it was named for the Torrent River, where it was christened in the 1980s. Earlier versions had a golden pheasant tail and a wool body. The fluorescent white floss, which turns pale blue when wet, was later substituted for the wool, and the tag and ribbing were added for "flash." Rich will often begin by floating a dry *White Wulff* over a slow-moving pool and then change to his wet version, the *Torrent River Special.*

Undertaker	
Tag	Fine flat gold tinsel, fluorescent green floss, and fluorescent red floss
Body	Peacock herl
Ribbing	Oval gold tinsel
Throat	Black hackle
Wing	Black bear hair
Cheeks	Jungle cock (optional)
Head	Black

Warren Duncan, owner of Dunc's Fly Shop in St. John, New Brunswick, is responsible for popularizing this pattern but does not claim origin to it. Duncan developed the *Undertaker* in 1979 by adapting a discarded fly a friend had picked up (after surreptitiously observing its success!) on the banks of the Nashwaak. Unable to locate a similar dressing in his fly-tying references, Duncan worked on a pattern. Out of respect for his favorite *Rat* series of flies, he incorporated peacock herl and gold tinsel in the already black fly. Soon the *Undertaker* found its way into fly catalogs and later around the world, where it has been successful on many rivers.

SALMON FLIES AND FISHING IN NEW ENGLAND

*B*efore New England's colonists dammed and polluted their rivers, every suitable coastal stream from the Canadian border to Connecticut's Housatonic proliferated with Atlantic salmon to the extent that they were considered more or less a nuisance and commonly were used as fertilizer. Annual runs in Maine during the eighteenth century were estimated to be as large as five hundred thousand, with commercial catches sometimes in excess of 100 tons. By 1947, the last year directed commercial fishing was allowed in Maine, only four hundred salmon were gleaned from Maine's waters by commercial fishermen.

In New England, the longest river is the Connecticut, which originates in the Connecticut lakes near Canada, borders New Hampshire and Vermont, and flows through Massachusetts and Connecticut to empty into salt water in Long Island Sound. Once salmon in abundance traveled upstream for more than 400 miles, leaping high waterfalls to spawn in the headwaters of the river and its many tributaries.

By 1800, however, all this was changed by the profusion of factories and the many dams that were built for power needs. The first of these was the

On the river, Maine 1941

Upper Locks and Canal Company Dam near South Hadley Falls in Massachusetts. Built in 1797, this dam closed off the upper 300 miles of the river and effectively blocked upstream passage. We only can imagine, in the first few years after this blockage, the thousands of bright mature salmon futilely jammed below the dam and unable to proceed to their destinations.

These dams, along with overnetting and wanton pollution, caused the salmon to vanish completely. In 1815, when a single stray fish was netted near the mouth of the river, its appearance was so unusual that the fishermen could not identify it!

Shortly after this, attempts were made to reintroduce salmon into the Connecticut, but lack of adequate fish passage facilities, continued pollution, and lack of understanding of the biology prevented success. Seines and gill nets near the mouth of the Connecticut effectively blocked the return of the salmon so that no permanent stocks could be established, and the reintroduction ceased. Factories and municipalities dumped their wastes into the river, turning it into a malodorous sewer.

It was not until 1967 that a cooperative state and federal program was initiated, with the primary purpose of bringing back fishable runs of Atlantic salmon and enhancing the shad population—a project much more complicated than it might seem. The implementation of this program within a reasonable time span made it necessary to accomplish several difficult projects concurrently. These efforts were enhanced by the Clean Water Act of 1974. Among other things, the act required that the rivers be made clean, or nearly so, once more. This necessitated the building of sewage disposal plants by towns and cities. It also required factories to dispose of their wastes somewhere other than in the river, a requirement that should have been mandatory in the first place, because rivers are public properties no group or individual has the right to defile.

Second, since most of the dams provided electric power, ways had to be found to get the salmon

Ai Ballou on the Sheepscot River   COURTESY OF MAINE FISH AND
GAME DEPARTMENT

start the new stock with eggs taken from another river's genetic strain and to raise them to smolt stage in Connecticut River water so that they would be imprinted by tht river and believe they were Connecticut River salmon. It was hoped that this would impel the mature salmon to return to their river of imprint.

In the early 1980s the results of the program were encouraging, if not spectacular. During the first twenty years, almost fifteen hundred salmon returned to the Connecticut, and by 1984, the first Atlantic salmon in two hundred years found its way to the White River in Vermont. The goal of the seventies has become a dream for the nineties—to restore and maintain a spawning population of wild Atlantic salmon in New England waters.

While at sea, the salmon mingle with fish from other nations in waters off Greenland. There they feed, mature, and survive together until it is time to migrate homeward. Rather than make a beeline across the ocean to their birth river, they take a coastal route through the zones of other countries. The dangers encountered on this journey threaten any progress made in the restoration program, as well as the very existence of the species. Again, the ultimate predator is man.

Fortunately, the plight of the salmon traveling from its oceanic melting pot became a matter of concern to North Atlantic governments and groups with salmon interests. In 1983, a need for collaboration among nations was realized, and with stronger support from the private sector, the North Atlantic Salmon Conservation Organization (NASCO) was founded. It is the mandate of this organization to research the complexities of the species and to protect it with strict international regulations. It is hoped that the combined efforts of involved member nations will ensure the return of adequate healthy stocks to their native rivers.

The Connecticut River is noted for its abundant supply of American shad, often called "the poor man's salmon" but an excellent sport fish, particularly when taken with fly rod and fly. A popular place to do this is at the big pool below the low and easily passable Enfield Dam, only a few minutes' drive from my home. Because of careful conservation and restoration efforts, anglers in the future may be in for surprises there: Instead of hooking shad of

over or around them. Five Connecticut River dams were targeted by the restoration program for fish passage facilities. In 1955, a lift facility was installed at the Holyoke Dam and, for the next thirty years, local power companies, concerned businesses, and involved federal agencies managed to complete several fishways to accommodate adult salmon returning to spawn.

Third, young salmon planted in a river have to be imprinted by that river in order to find their way back after a period of time in the ocean. We can't merely dump the little fish in the water, from where they will travel thousands of miles to the west coast of Greenland, and expect them, a year or more later, to successfully return.

The precarious but necessary alternative was to

6 pounds or so, they may catch leaping Atlantic salmon of several times that weight!

In the state of Maine, attempts to restore runs of Atlantic salmon started about twenty years earlier. Maine's Atlantic Sea Run Salmon Commission was organized in 1948 to restore a resource that, by then, was sadly diminished. The former abundance of salmon in Maine's streams, and what happened to them, parallels the fate of the Connecticut and other New England rivers. To put this into proper perspective, let's look at the situation at the famous Bangor Salmon Pool on Maine's most important salmon river, the Penobscot. This pool, at the head of tidewater, lies in a densely populated area between the cities of Bangor and Brewer. Fish stories of pioneer times tell us that salmon were so thick in this pool that they interfered with paddling canoes. However exaggerated this may be, we do know that the salmon were bountiful.

In 1890, however, only 148 salmon, averaging 17 pounds, were reported taken; in 1927, 112 fish, averaging 11 pounds; in 1935, 57 salmon, averaging

The old Bangor Pool on the Penobscot River

Fishing the Penobscot
BOB O'SHAUGHNESSY

*Leon Thomas and his
rod shop in Bangor, Maine*

10 pounds; in 1945, 42 salmon, averaging 9 pounds; and, in 1952, 38 fish, averaging only 8 1/2 pounds. There were so few salmon in the river that the Penobscot Club closed later in the 1950s and did not reopen until 1975 when the run started to improve. Counts of fish caught gradually increased, and in 1980, 392 salmon were recorded in the club's book. Since then, however, there has been another decline, and now, even with the practice of catch and release, the number of Atlantic salmon returning to the Penobscot is alarmingly low.

The Bangor Dam breached in 1977 and has since been removed. The better holding water is now upriver. I have a nostalgic feeling about the old Bangor Pool, however. It was there I caught my first

Atlantic salmon, before World War II, when I went to Bangor to buy a fly rod from Leon Thomas at the old Thomas Rod Company, which was started by Leon's famous father, Fred. Leon took me to the old clubhouse, a small and dingy building beside the pool, handed me a Thomas split-bamboo rod too long and heavy by modern standards, and we shoved off in a canoelike rowboat to anchor above a prominent edge of current near the middle of the swift and rocky pool.

Leon was an expert guide, explaining to this neophyte just where to put the fly, how to let it swing in the current, how to gradually extend casts, and what to do in case a fish should strike. Eventually one did, with a strong pull and a lusty run that took the line far into its backing. The bright, silvery fish made several spectacular jumps while Leon brought the boat to beach, where the fish eventually was landed. It was a cock of about 11 pounds, and it hooked me on salmon fishing for life!

Historically, Atlantic salmon are moving into Maine rivers by the middle of May, and by Memorial Day fish should be in many of the popular pools. Some rivers are too high, too fast, or too cold early in the season, so advance inquiries are recommended. By the end of June, the waters of some rivers are too warm for good fishing, but action picks up again in the fall. Between June and September, dry flies do better than wets. Fishing is both by wading alongshore and from boats. Anglers alongshore must wait their turns during peak periods to fish over the good holding positions, but they do this with good sportsmanship and humor. Visitors shouldn't expect quick success. It may take several days to connect with a salmon, if at all!

The Maine salmon fishing season runs from April 1 to September 15 on inland waters and is extended to October 15 in tidal areas. Later changes may be made in these dates, depending on the abundance of salmon. Nearly all the rivers or pools are restricted to fly fishing only, and the future may bring changed regulations on hook sizes and types. Presently, inland waters require an Atlantic salmon stamp as well as a fishing license.

Although the Penobscot is the biggest of Maine's salmon rivers, there are seven others that have not lost all of their original genetic integrity, and strong efforts are being made to sustain them. In Maine, beginning with the Penobscot, all rivers flowing into the Bay of Fundy are considered "Down East" of one another and are described as such. Elsewhere, however, this terminology can be confusing, so, assuming that I will be forgiven by my Down East neighbors, I will describe Maine's rivers as they appear on the map.

A bit to the southwest of the Penobscot is the Sheepscot, best fished in tidewater south of Alna and the Headtide Dam. To the east is the Union, with a considerably larger run. To the northeast of the

The Sheepscot River, Maine

JACK SWEDBERG

The Narraguagus River

Union is the popular Narraguagus, one of the best salmon streams in the state.

The Narraguagus offers as many as twelve productive pools, the most famous being the Cable in the town of Cherryfield. The best of these can become very crowded during peak season, but the anglers cooperatively regulate themselves into well-spaced progression as the line of four or so fishermen works its way down the pool. Though you may have to wait an hour or so before fishing, this arrangement gives everyone a chance to work all the lies in a relatively short period of time.

Other downstream pools, such as Gull Rock, the Maples, Dynamo, Pump House, and Railroad Bridge, are popular and often productive in May and early June. After that, some of the upstream ones, such as Little Falls, Deblois Bridge, and Schoodic, usually offer interesting fishing. Where any of these pools are so crowded that anglers must wait to fish, the time passes quickly and often productively in conversations with local anglers, most of whom are affable and cooperative.

Next northeastward is the Pleasant River, a stream that fits its name but so far has produced few salmon. Beyond it is the famous Machias, which has the largest self-sustaining Atlantic salmon runs in the state, as well as many of the finest pools. All dams were removed in 1973 to give fish unimpeded access to the entire river, thus distributing them along its length. In spring, fishing is best in the tidal areas at Mony Island and the Point Pool near Whitneyville, Machias Gorge, and Munson's Pitch. Hereabouts in the late 1800s a man with a dip net could take about sixty salmon in a day. Machias Gorge, in the town of Machias, forms a turbulent barrier of ledges and rocks that is impossible for most of the salmon to overcome except during low water, so successful fishing depends a great deal upon water level. After early June, the upriver pools, such as Great Falls, Holmes Falls, and Wigwam Falls, provide the best chances for action.

The East Machias flows about 5 miles east of the town of Machias and runs through the towns of Jacksonville and East Machias. Berry, Mill, and Hydro Pools offer small runs of salmon in the tidal areas between these two places. This river and the Dennys offer excellent canoe trips between Pokey Dam on Crawford Lake and the eastern shore of

The early hope and vision of the restoration program were not realized, however, and numbers of returning salmon were so depleted that in September 1995, the U.S. Fish and Wildlife Service and the National Marine Fisheries Service announced that the remaining populations of wild Atlantic salmon in Maine's seven Down East rivers (Dennys, Machias, East Machias, Narraguagus, Pleasant, Ducktrap, and Sheepscot) were designated "threatened" under the Endangered Species Act. This proposed listing, strongly supported by the Atlantic Salmon Federation and its Maine Council and the New England Salmon Association, provides protection for the salmon on a catch and release basis. It is hoped that this decision will enable the success of Maine's Atlantic salmon restoration program.

P. B. R.

Clyde   JACK SWEDBERG

Hadley Lake northwest of Jacksonville, an area that includes Great Meadow Riffles, Munson Rips, Wigwam Riffles, and Crooked and Sawmill Pitches. Salmon fishing also is often good near the Maine Central Railroad bridge in Jacksonville and in the Mill Pool in East Machias.

The most northeasterly salmon river in Maine is the Dennys, which enters tidewater at Dennysville, 30 miles east of Machias. Fish come upriver about mid-May and can provide good sport for a month or so, after which rising water temperatures decrease success. The local sportsmen have cleared one bank of the river for over half a mile to allow ample room for casting. Those who know the river prefer Ledge Pool, Community Pool, Dam Pool, the Rips, the Gut, Charlie's Rips, and Fisher's Stump. Farther upstream, as the season progresses, salmon can be found at the Trestle, Dodge Pool, and the Narrows. Beyond the Dennys is the St. Croix, which borders Canada.

As of the 1980s, Maine was the only state having self-sustaining runs of Atlantic salmon in its rivers. Since that time, it has had its peaks and valleys. If there is to be any hope for the future of New England rivers, the restoration program is critical. The sport value to anglers and the income provided by them should far outweigh the costs and efforts of bringing the beautiful King of Fishes back to the rivers wherein it was once so abundant.

Salmon Flies of New England

Since salmon fishing in Maine has been in the doldrums for some time, and elsewhere in the northeast for even longer, there are few purely New England salmon fly patterns. An exception to this is a group of patterns created by the productive tiers from the Penobscot region of Maine. New England, and Maine in particular, is famous for the development of streamer and bucktail patterns used for landlocked salmon and occasionally for Atlantic salmon. For the most part, Americans have enjoyed their salmon fishing in Canada, and many of the popular patterns used there were developed by them—some from New England and others from different parts of the country.

So, how should these well-established patterns be divided, since they are international in scope? It may be helpful to include in this section the ones

The author and Bruce Bates on the Rangeley Lakes in 1946

developed specifically for fishing Maine's rivers, remembering that these flies also are valuable elsewhere. Many of the flies listed for Canada and the British Isles also would be appropriate for use in New England. Most good patterns are productive all around the Atlantic, even though each area has its favorites.

Much of the development of the hairwing salmon fly took place in New England during the first half of this century. Resourceful and practical individuals used materials readily at hand to tie their flies. The simple flies that emerged were known by type rather than pattern and were often named for the hair and materials they were tied with, such as the *Black Bear* and the *Squirrel Tail*. The basic idea is a plain body of wool, ribbing, a tail or butt of floss, and a wing of hair. Butts used on these flies evolved from the colorful tags of the British classics. Attribution of origin was not an issue, but catching salmon was, and these successful early flies are the basis for countless contemporary patterns.

The *Black Bear*, dressed with the hair of the eastern black bear, was originated in Maine in the 1920s by Harry Smith, of Cherryfield, where anglers often stay while fishing the Narraguagus. Another of this type, called the *Black Spider,* which had a wing of black squirrel and an orange butt, was originated by Ira Gruber in 1935.

An enterprising individual by the name of Charles "Chuck" Conrad embellished these simple patterns by adding a tinsel tag and green fluorescent butt, creating what is now known as the *Conrad,* or *Black Bear, Green Butt,* and thus popularizing the now-familiar butt patterns. These patterns, as well as the innumerable others that were inspired by them, are effective and popular all around the Atlantic.

Black Bear Fly	
Tail	Two thin sections of a black feather
Body	Black wool
Throat	Black bear hair
Wing	Black bear hair
Head	Black

It is from this rudimentary pattern that many patterns have evolved, including the *Conrad,* or *Black Bear, Green Butt.* Tails are unnecessary; if used, they

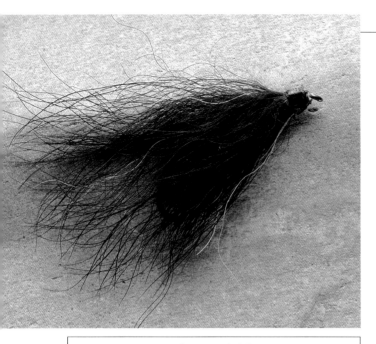

PLATE 154
THE BLACK BEAR, ORIGINATED AND
DRESSED BY HARRY SMITH

are usually a few wisps of hackle such as red or yellow. Wing material can be varied, with squirrel tail, woodchuck, or any other appropriate hair. Bodies usually are heavily dressed in a cigar shape, more often of floss than of wool. Butts are most popular in light green, yellow, red, and burnt orange. Although one color seems about as productive as another, my preference is for a small butt of light green fluorescent floss. Many say that if they could have only one fly, this would be it.

Clarkent

Tag	Fine gold wire and yellow floss
Tail	Golden pheasant crest, over which are two or three fibers of an orange feather half as long as the crest
Butt	Black ostrich herl
Body	In three equal parts of black floss, black seal's fur, and crimson seal's fur
Ribbing	Oval gold tinsel
Hackle	Black hackle from the rear third of the body
Throat	Black hackle of moderate fullness and length
Wing	A pair of Amherst pheasant tippets, outside of which is a pair of golden pheasant tippets extending to the first black bar of the Amherst pheasant so that the outer bar of the golden pheasant covers the first inner bar of the Amherst pheasant. Over these on each side is a medium black hackle set midway of the tippets and slightly longer than them
Shoulders	Jungle cock, extending to first inner bar of the golden pheasant
Cheeks	Orange toucan or orange feather tip
Horns	Blue and red macaw
Topping	Golden pheasant crest
Head	Black

This attractive classic-type pattern was originated in 1979 by Frank Clark and Robert W. Ent, of Bangor, Maine, in a successful attempt to design a new and different salmon fly reminiscent of the Kelson era. It is included here not only because of its beauty, but also because it has been proficient in hooking Atlantic salmon in the Bangor-Veazie area of Maine's Penobscot River.

Pinkent

Tag	Oval silver tinsel
Body	In two sections: rear section, pink flourescent wool; forward section, bronze peacock
Wing	Gray squirrel
Collar	Yellow and orange hackle
Head	Black

Bob Ent originated the *Pinkent* for fishing the Penobscot River. Originally the rear section of the body was dressed with a blend of three or four furs, giving it a shell pink color. Later, when the pattern was tied in production, the furs were replaced with the more efficient pink fluorescent wool.

Colburn Special

Tag	Fine oval silver tinsel, very short
Tail	Black monga tail over green monga tail, short and thin
Body	Light green fluorescent silk, built up to cigar shape, and butted in the middle with a narrow band of black ostrich herl
Wing	Black monga hair over green monga hair, fairly sparse and reaching about to tag only
Throat	A sparse turn or two of a bright yellow hackle, applied as a collar, and reaching about to body butt only
Head	Black

Related to this pattern is the *Colburn* series of flies, whose bodies are of the same design, with colors varying according to name. These include the *Claret Colburn,* the *Blue Colburn,* the *Yellow Colburn,* and the *Orange Colburn.*

This purely Maine pattern was originated in the mid-1960s by the late Walter O. Colburn, of Bangor, Maine. It has been used successfully on the Matane and Upsalquitch Rivers in Canada and on the Narraguagus River in Maine. Many salmon have been taken on this fly on the Penobscot River, especially in the famous Bangor Pool. The dressing is by prominent angler Frank T. Clark, of Bangor.

band, Wallace, for many years and fished with them often on the Rangeley Lakes. During World War II, Carrie devised a streamer fly for me and named it the *Captain Bates*.

Over the years, both the fly and I were promoted to the rank of colonel, and in 1969, Jimmy Younger, of Dumfries, Scotland, winner of the British Fly Dressers Guild award, originated a salmon fly of the same name using a similar color scheme.

Following are the patterns for both the streamer fly and the salmon fly.

Colonel Bates Streamer Fly	
Tail	A small section of red duck or swan wing feather
Body	Medium flat silver tinsel
Throat	A small bunch of dark brown saddle hackle fibers
Wing	Two yellow saddle hackle feathers with a slightly shorter white saddle hackle feather on each side
Shoulders	Gray mallard or teal feathers, nearly half as long as the wing
Cheeks	Jungle cock
Head	Red, with black band

The red head, distinguished by a black band, was Carrie Stevens's signature on her streamer flies. On some patterns she reversed these colors, and on patriotic patterns, such as the *General MacArthur*, she finished the head with red, white and blue. The red band on the black head of the *Colonel Bates* salmon fly honors Carrie Stevens as the originator of its predecessor.

Colonel Bates Salmon Fly	
Tag	Fine oval silver tinsel and pale yellow silk floss
Tail	Golden pheasant crest, over which are two small strips of red goose and kingfisher, both half as long as the crest
Butt	Scarlet wool
Body	Flat silver tinsel
Ribbing	Oval silver tinsel
Throat	Natural red game (brown) hackle, followed by natural guinea fowl hackle
Wing	Four golden yellow saddle hackles, with a white saddle hackle on each side half as long as the yellow. Over this on each side is a fairly wide strip of a yellow swan wing feather as long as the wing, with thin strips of red swan wing feather married to it, top and bottom. Over this is a wide strip of barred Mandarin duck to level with the butt (both feathers on each side)
Topping	Two golden pheasant crest feathers
Shoulders	Jungle cock, of moderate length
Cheeks	Kingfisher, over the jungle cock, and shorter
Head	Black, with red center band

PLATE 155
FLIES DRESSED
BY BOB ENT

Claret Colburn   Pink Ent

Clarkent

Colburn Special   Yellow Colburn

Colonel Bates

Reminiscent of the early days in Maine, the *Colonel Bates* salmon fly shares my New England roots, for its predecessor, the *Colonel Bates* streamer fly, was originated by Upper Dam's legendary tier, Carrie Gertrude Stevens. Both she and the streamer flies she developed are revered by fly tiers, fishermen, and collectors. I was fortunate to know her and her hus-

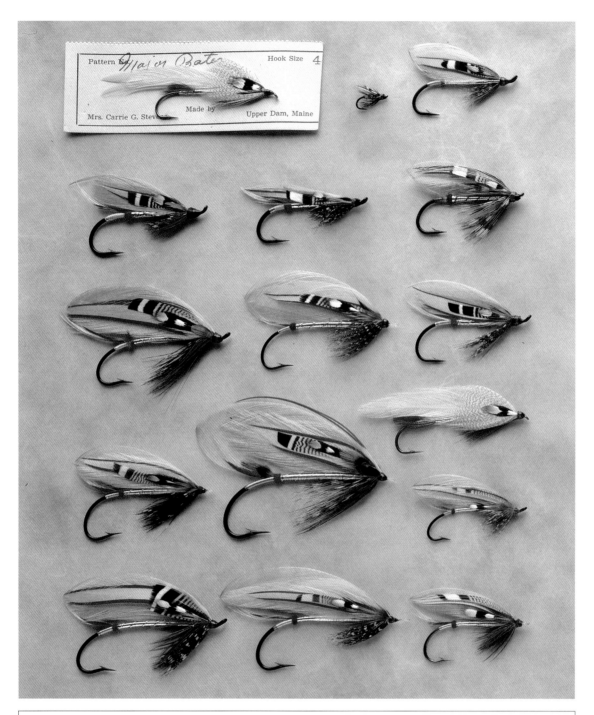

PLATE 156
THE COLONEL BATES, PAST AND PRESENT

dressed by Carrie Stevens	dressed by Megan Boyd	dressed by Ted Kantner
dressed by Bob Ent	dressed by Charlie DeFeo	dressed by Alex Simpson
dressed by Judy Lehmberg	dressed by Wayne Luallen	dressed by William Byrnes
		dressed by Michael Martinek
dressed by Greg Hunt	dressed by Paul Schmookler	dressed by Tom Juracek
dressed by Marvin Nolte	dressed by Michael Radencich	dressed by John Olschewsky

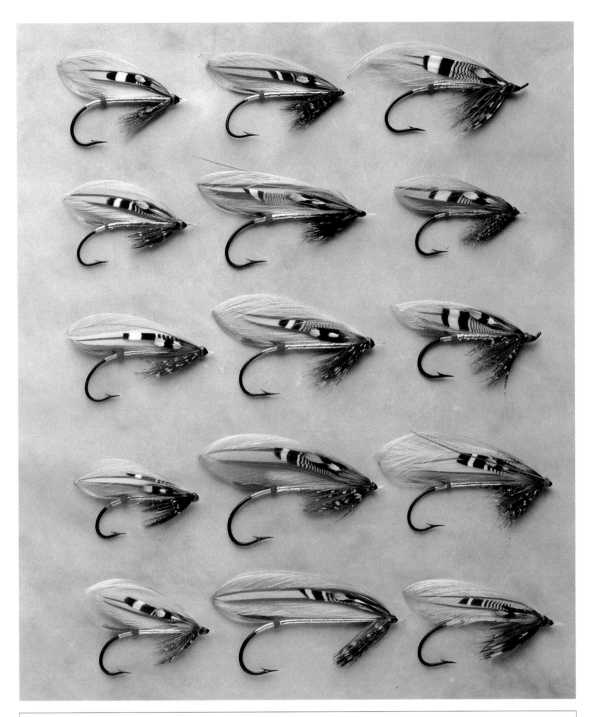

PLATE 157
THE COLONEL BATES, PAST AND PRESENT

dressed by Ron Alcott	dressed by Mark Waslick	dressed by Jimmy Younger
dressed by Dorothy Douglass	dressed by Bob Veverka	dressed by John Wiildermuth
dressed by Eugene Sunday	dressed by Bob Warren	dressed by Belarmino Martinez
dressed by Peter Caluori	dressed by John Walker	dressed by Steve Gobin
dressed by Pam Richards	dressed by Charles Chute	dressed by Mike McCoy

PLATE 158
THE MICKEY FINN SPANS
THE DECADES

dressed by Bill Wilbur

originated and dressed by John Alden Knight

Mickey Finn

Body	Medium flat silver tinsel
Ribbing	Narrow oval silver tinsel
Wing	A very small bunch of yellow bucktail, over which is a very small bunch of red bucktail, with a bunch of yellow bucktail equal in size to the first two bunches over this. (In dressing this fly correctly, it is important to note that the lower yellow band and the red band are of the same size, but that the upper yellow band is about twice the size of the lower one.)
Head	Black

This pattern was unnamed and unknown until popularized by the late John Alden Knight, of Williamsport, Pennsylvania, in 1932. Originally known as the *Red and Yellow Bucktail,* and later called the *Assassin,* its bright colors were presumed to give the impression of small pond dwellers such as sunfish. After sharing considerable success with the fly, noted writer Gregory Clark rechristened it the *Mickey Finn.* The popularity and use of this pattern have endured for over half a century. Today in salmon fishing, such a bright fly ordinarily is used only under adverse conditions, such as high or discolored water, or in an attempt to interest reluctant salmon by showing them something different.

Certainly, a bright fly such as this is valuable in the salmon angler's "bag of tricks." We can dress it in salmon style with the traditional shorter wing,

embellish it with a brightly colored throat and jungle cock eyes—or even modernize it as a tube fly for fishing other waters. Like the *Black Bear* type, it is easy to dress, and so it is recommended to fly dressers with little experience who want to hook salmon on flies they have tied themselves.

The Chief

Tag	Narrow flat silver tinsel
Tail	A section of red duck or goose wing feather
Body	Red silk. (The original version, as dressed by Chief Needahbeh and shown in Plate 159, has a red hackle "throat" one-third of the way forward on the body. A similar effect could be obtained by palmering a red hackle, but it was not done in this case. The purpose of the "throat" evidently was to give greater action to the fly.)
Ribbing	Narrow flat silver tinsel
Throat	Red saddle hackle tied on as a collar after the wing has been applied. It is dressed rather full
Wing	A red saddle hackle on each side of two yellow saddle hackles
Cheeks	Jungle cock, rather short

This is another bright streamer fly that is from the Rangeley area of Maine and is popular for fall salmon fishing. It was originated by Chief Needahbeh, also known as Chief Roland Nelson, a Native American Penobscot and proprietor of Needahbeh's Shack, a tackle shop at Moosehead Lake in Greenville, Maine. The Chief also dressed this fly, originally intended for trout and land-locked salmon, without a tail or secondary throat, and with orange hackles in the wing instead of red.

Mitchell

Tag	Oval silver tinsel and golden yellow floss
Tail	Golden pheasant crest, over which is blue chatterer (or kingfisher) half as long
Butt	Black ostrich herl
Body	Golden yellow floss, forward of which is a second butt of bright red ostrich herl, with the remainder of the body black floss. The black floss occupies about four-fifths of the body
Ribbing	Fine oval silver tinsel, over black floss only
Throat	Yellow hackle, forward of which is black hackle
Wing	Two sections of black crow, swan, goose, or duck wing feathers
Topping	Golden pheasant crest
Cheeks	Jungle cock, fairly long, veiled by blue chatterer (or kingfisher)
Head	Black, with rear band of bright red lacquer

This fly was originated by Archibald Mitchell, of Norwich, Connecticut, in 1887. There is a variation

North America's greatest experts on Atlantic salmon angling. Before moving to Canada, Father Smith had parishes in both Massachusetts and Maine and fished New England waters. He says: "On a day when no fish were being taken, I took four on this fly. It is rather bizarre, but it is killing in cold-water pools, also effective in slow water if movement is imparted. It is a proven killer also in the fall. The pattern was given to several anglers, who did well with it. They went to Wally Doak for more, and now it is a standard pattern with him as well as with L. L. Bean, Stoddard's of Boston, and other tackle stores."

A fly called the *White Miller,* often used on the Miramichi, is very similar except that it does not have fluorescent body material and has a red hackle tail and white hackle throat.

PLATE 159
THE CHIEF

originated and dressed by Chief Needahbah
dressed by Warren Duncan
dressed by Randy Giffen

with a silver body that is very similar to the *Night Hawk.* In *Favorite Flies,* Mitchell says: "I conceived the idea that a very dark fly would be a success on the Penobscot River [Maine] for salmon, and tied a few of them for the first time during the winter of 1887–1888. It is my own invention and was not copied from any other fly." In Mitchell's original pattern there is no gold floss at the rear of the body, the red butt [evidently floss] being immediately forward of the tail. The *Mitchell* is a favorite fly in Newfoundland and other areas. It is dressed with many slight variations, usually in 6s and 8s.

The Priest (or Church of England Fly)	
Tag	Oval silver tinsel
Tail	Light blue dun hackle fibers
Body	White fluorescent wool (has a decided purplish hue when in the water)
Ribbing	Oval silver tinsel
Throat	Light blue dun hackle
Wing	White calf's tail
Head	White or black

This fly was originated by the Reverend Elmer J. Smith, of Prince William, New Brunswick, one of

PLATE 160
SALMON FLIES, DRESSED BY THE
REVEREND ELMER J. SMITH

The Priest (original)
The Mitchell

Silver Down East and Down East Special

Tag	Flat silver tinsel
Tail	Golden pheasant crest
Butt	Black ostrich herl
Body	Flat silver tinsel
Ribbing	Oval silver tinsel
Wing	Fitch tail or red squirrel tail
Throat	Bright orange hackle, applied as a collar

Phil Foster, of Farmington, Maine, writes that he originally devised this fly during the early sixties with a body of gray chenille or wool, and named it the *Down East Special,* for the area of its origin in Maine referred to as "Down East." Thinking a brighter version might do well, he changed the body of the fly to tinsel and named that fly the *Silver Down East.* He states that the success of the fly carried it to other rivers in the province of New Brunswick, where it was modified to have a black wing and no tail or butt. It is very similar to the *Silver Down-Easter,* a Canadian pattern credited to Bert Miner.

Squirrel Tail

Tail	Red hackle fibers or red hair, fairly short
Body	Black floss or wool, slightly built up to cigar shape
Ribbing	Fine silver tinsel
Throat	Black or brown hackle
Wing	Canadian red squirrel (not fox squirrel)
Head	Black

This is a type, rather than a pattern, because it is tied in so many variations for Maine and Canadian rivers. Clipped floss or yarn in red or other colors often is used for the tail. This gave way to the tailless fly with a floss or wool butt that finally became fluorescent. Butts are popular in red, yellow, orange, or green, depending more on whim than reason, and they may occupy as much as half the body. Hooks, in size and type, suit the desires of the tier, and can be bronzed and offset.

Patterns of the Penobscot

Although a small fishery by international standards, the Penobscot River is steeped in tradition and is the home of a prolific and enthusiastic group of fly-tying fishermen. Fishing there is either by boats or by rotation from the riverbank. Angling presently takes place from the Veazie Dam to Bangor, and much of it is centered around several clubs. Active both in conservation and in camaraderie, these include the Eddington Salmon Club, the Penobscot Salmon Club, the Northern Penobscot Club, the Veazie Salmon Club, and the Penobscot Conservation Association. The oldest of these is the Penobscot Salmon Club, established in 1923.

On April 1, 1912, after catching two salmon at the famous Bangor Pool, Karl Anderson thought that sending President Taft one of the salmon would bring honor and respect to the city and the species. Thus an annual tradition of presenting the first bright salmon caught on the Penobscot to the president of the United States was established, with a lapse between the Eisenhower and Reagan administrations. The angler who caught the first salmon of the season would personally present it to the incumbent president at the White House. Currently, however, the Penobscot is a catch and release river, and the tradition of the Presidential Salmon has been discontinued until the salmon runs improve.

Several of the flies in the following section have successfully taken Presidential Salmon. In two subsequent years, Claude Westfall and his son took the Presidential Salmon, both on flies originated by Westfall: the *C. Z. Special* and the *Wringer,* named for the Wringer Pool on the Penobscot. In May 1988, Charlie Carron took the Presidential Salmon on his *Penoby Joe.*

Salmon flies for the Penobscot are generally hairwings, and large flies, from 1/0 to 3/0, are commonly used. It may be that there are now more flies originated for the region than there are fish to tempt with them; however, with the efforts of organizations such as the Penobscot River Coalition, this situation may improve in time.

Gayland Hachey, owner of Hachey's Rod and Fly Shop in Veazie, reports that the following flies originated by the tiers of the Penobscot have been successful for that river as well as others.

Anniversary Fly

Tag	Oval silver tinsel and red fluorescent wool
Tail	Golden pheasant crest
Butt	Black ostrich herl
Body	Black floss
Ribbing	Flat silver tinsel
Hackle	Hot orange
Wing	Red squirrel tail
Head	Black

The *Anniversary Fly* was originated in 1978 by Jean R. Guerin to commemorate the tenth anniversary of the Veazie Salmon Club.

Bastard Thunder and Lightning

Tag	Three turns of medium oval gold tinsel, tied in just at the bend, and red floss
Butt	Black ostrich herl
Body	Black floss, not built up
Ribbing	Four turns of medium oval gold tinsel
Wing	Brown under yellow under red or pale red bucktail, tied in layers, very sparse. End of wing no longer than the bend of the hook. Reverse the red and the yellow bucktail for variation
Head	Black

Roger D'Errico of Brewer, Maine, originated *Roger's Bastard Thunder and Lightning* in 1977. Halfway through constructing his version of the classic pattern, D'Errico realized he had not tied in a tail and did not have the correct feathers for the body hackle and throat, but he completed the fly with materials at hand. Unimpressed with the finished fly, he put it aside until a slow day when he had nothing to lose—and then proceeded to land two salmon on the Bangor Pool. This accidentally simplified pattern has since been very successful.

Copper Slider

Hook	Double, low-water
Thread	Yellow
Body	Flat copper tinsel, lacquered and leaving adequate space for the collar and spun deer-hair head
Wing	Natural red squirrel tail, extending just beyond the bend of the hook. This is followed by bucktail dyed yellow, enveloping the hook and slightly longer than the underwing
Head	Deer body hair dyed yellow, clipped to form the collar and head

Designed by Bill Drexler in 1985, the *Copper Slider* is reminiscent of the *Copper Killer,* with its copper body, and the *Muddler,* with its clipped deer-hair head. Drexler reports that it is better under rainy conditions, and that with it he caught seven salmon in seven days, all weighing between 15 and 20 pounds.

C.Z. Special

Tag	Flat silver tinsel and fluorescent green floss
Tail	Fluorescent green over black hackle fibers
Butt	Black ostrich herl
Body	Rear half: black floss. Front half: peacock herl
Ribbing	Fine oval silver tinsel, over black floss only
Wing	Four peacock sword feathers over fluorescent-green-dyed squirrel tail
Throat	Fluorescent green hackle, applied as a collar
Head	Black

The fly that bears his initials was originated by Claude Z. Westfall, of Orono, Maine. It is a popular pattern on the Penobscot, where Westfall fishes his own patterns exclusively.

Dickson Bear

Tag	Oval silver tinsel and fluorescent green floss
Tail	Fluorescent green floss, doubled
Butt	Black ostrich herl (optional)
Body	Black floss
Ribbing	Oval silver tinsel
Throat	Hackle dyed insect green or fluorescent green
Wing	Black bear over several insect green hackle fibers
Head	Black

Designed by Ron Newcomb as an improvement of the *Black Bear, Green Butt,* the *Dickson Bear* (or *Dickson Bear Hair*) was first used on the Penobscot's Dickson Pool, for which it is named. On its first evening out it took two salmon, and it has continued to work well under low-light conditions throughout the season. While fishing with Ron Newcomb in 1981, I was delighted to land a Penobscot salmon with a *Dickson Bear.*

PLATE 162
PENOBSCOT PATTERNS

Ruhlin's Riot
dressed by Richard Ruhlin

Copper Slider
dressed by Bill Drexler

Penoby Joe
dressed by Charlie Caron

Sidewinder
dressed by Gayland Hachey

Foxfire
dressed by Claude Westfall

Turk's Red Butt
dressed by Donald Clough

Eddington Fly
dressed by Dave Worcester

Thunderhead
dressed by Ron Newcomb

Wringer
dressed by Claude Westfall

PLATE 163
PENOBSCOT PATTERNS

Anniversary Fly
dressed by Jean.Guerin

Ghost
dressed by Gayland Hachey

C. Z. Special
dressed by Claude Westfall

Verdict
dressed by Gerry Clapp

Dragon
dressed by Fran Stuart

Dickson Bear
dressed by Ron Newcomb

Mi Fli
dressed by Gayland Hachey

Newcomb's Rock
dressed by Ron Newcomb

Bastard Thunder and Lightning
dressed by Roger D'Errico

"Two Guides"

Dragon

Tag	Silver wire
Under-body	Flat silver tinsel
Overbody	Fluorescent green floss
Ribbing	Black ostrich herl, counterwrapped with fine silver wire
Collar	Webby black saddle hackle

Fran Stuart, an avid Penobscot angler, first tied the *Dragon* on the bank of that river in a tent by lantern light. The following day, she landed a bright 12-pound salmon with it. It is one of a series dressed in fluorescent color combinations, among them red or orange with gold tinsel and yellow with silver tinsel.

Eddington Fly

Tag	Fine oval gold tinsel and yellow floss
Tail	Golden pheasant crest
Butt	Yellow ostrich herl
Body	Black floss
Ribbing	Medium oval gold tinsel
Wing	Raccoon guard hair (or gray fox) with half the fur removed
Throat	Yellow hackle
Head	Black

The *Eddington Fly* is the collaborative effort of a fly-tying class at the Eddington Club taught by Bob Ent. Named by Ent for the club, the pattern can be credited to Bob Boucher and Dave Worcester, who both attended the class the evening the fly was designed. To stimulate interest for the class, Bob brought in a fur collar that had markings he thought would work well to wing a fly; the result is the *Eddington Fly.*

Foxfire

Tag	Flat silver tinsel and fire orange floss
Tail	Fluorescent orange over black hackle fibers
Butt	Black ostrich herl
Body	Black floss
Ribbing	Fine oval silver tinsel
Wing	Four peacock sword feathers over squirrel, dyed black
Throat	Fluorescent orange hackle, applied as a collar
Head	Black

The *Foxfire* was originated by Claude Z. Westfall, of Orono, Maine.

Ghost

Tag	Flat gold tinsel and fluorescent red floss
Tail	Fluorescent pink hackle fibers
Butt	Fluorescent pink ostrich herl
Body	Peacock herl
Ribbing	Oval gold tinsel
Wing	Squirrel tail, dyed black
Throat	Fluorescent pink hackle, applied as a collar

Gayland Hachey, owner of Hachey's Rod and Fly Shop in Veazie, Maine, originated the *Ghost* in 1988.

Mi Fli

Tag	Flat silver tinsel
Tail	Golden pheasant crest
Butt	Fluorescent orange floss
Body	Black wool
Ribbing	Oval silver tinsel
Wing	Four peacock herl over black squirrel tail
Hackle	Hot orange and black hackle, mixed and applied as a collar
Head	Black

Mi Fli is another of Gayland Hachey's original patterns. It was devised by him in the 1970s, when one could still fish above the dam on the Penobscot.

Newcomb's Rock

Tag	Silver tinsel
Tail	Fluorescent red hackle tip or floss, doubled
Body	Rear half: fluorescent green wool, tapered. Front half: peacock herl
Ribbing	Fine oval silver tinsel
Wing	Dyed black squirrel or bear hair
Topping	Two strands of green crystal hair
Hackle	Black, collar-style
Head	Black

Originated in the late 1980s by Ron Newcomb, *Newcomb's Rock* can account for six salmon caught on opening day on the Penobscot. The fly has also been successful on the Matapedia River in Quebec.

Penoby Joe

Body	Robin's egg blue floss. The first quarter is separated by a butt of peacock herl
Ribbing	Oval silver tinsel
Throat	Sparse bunch of black hair, applied as a beard and extending almost to the butt
Wing	Small bunch of grass green hair extending to the barb of the hook
Head	Black

On May 1, 1988, the Presidential Salmon was caught on this fly by its originator, Charlie Caron. He writes that the fly has been successful in sizes from 6 to 2/0 from the West Coast to the East Coast. Charlie prefers it in a low-water style and finds it a good early fly on its native river in sizes 1/0 and 2/0.

Ruhlin's Riot

Tag	Flat silver tinsel
Tail	Red hackle fibers
Body	Fluorescent green wool, in cigar shape
Wing	Yellow bucktail, fine
Head	Black

Originated in 1963 by Senator Dick Ruhlin from Brewer, Maine, the *Riot* fly was first dressed with a wing of fine yellow bucktail; in 1968, yellow mohair was substituted for the bucktail. *Ruhlin's Riot* is also tied with a wing of gray squirrel and is then sometimes referred to as the *Guagus Riot*.

Sidewinder

Tag	Flat gold tinsel and fluorescent yellow floss
Tail	Fluorescent orange hackle over golden pheasant crest
Butt	Fluorescent yellow ostrich herl
Body	Peacock herl
Ribbing	Oval gold tinsel
Wing	Fluorescent yellow calf tail
Hackle	Fluorescent yellow hackle, applied as a collar
Cheeks	Fluorescent orange hackle tips
Head	Black

The *Sidewinder* was originated by Gayland Hachey and Gary Dinkins.

Thunderhead

Tag	Oval silver tinsel and fluorescent green floss
Tail	Fluorescent orange floss, doubled
Butt	Black ostrich herl
Body	Black floss
Ribbing	Oval silver tinsel
Hackle	Bright orange palmered from second turn of ribbing. End hackle with two or three turns and pull down
Wing	Squirrel, dyed black
Topping	Four barbules of peacock sword over a few strands of bright yellow calf tail
Head	Black

The *Thunderhead,* designed by Ron Newcomb, was inspired by the classic *Thunder and Lightning.* It was originated and successfully tested on the Penobscot in the spring of 1988. Newcomb suggests an undercoat of white correction fluid to enhance the brightness of the fluorescent tag.

Turk's Red Butt

Tag	Oval gold tinsel and fluorescent red yarn
Tail	Golden pheasant crest
Body	Peacock herl
Ribbing	Oval gold tinsel
Throat	A bunch of crinkly black bear hair, short and sparse
Wing	Black bear hair, very sparse

The pattern for *Turk's Red Butt* is by "Turk" Tarini and originally dressed for him by Bob Ent. Although he had just one hand, Turk was an accomplished angler, and his fly has been successful in Maine and Canada.

Verdict	
Tag	Flat gold tinsel and fluorescent rose yarn
Tail	Golden pheasant crest
Body	Black floss
Ribbing	Flat gold tinsel
Wing	Black dyed squirrel tail, as shiny as possible
Throat	Hot orange hackle, applied as a collar

Aptly named, the *Verdict* was originated by Jerry Clapp, a retired Maine state police officer, in the early 1980s.

Wringer	
Tag	Flat silver tinsel and golden yellow floss
Tail	Golden pheasant crest
Butt	Black ostrich herl
Body	Black floss
Ribbing	Fine oval silver tinsel
Throat	Kingfisher blue hackle fibers
Wing	Squirrel tail hair dyed red under squirrel tail hair dyed yellow, in equal amounts to reach bend of hook
Head	Black

This popular Penobscot river pattern, named for Wringer Pool on that river, was originated in the late 1970s by Claude Z. Westfall, of Orono, Maine.

Very similar to the hairwing version of the *Thunder and Lightning,* it is a good general pattern that should be effective on all rivers.

Featherwing patterns are rarely seen on Maine rivers today, but there still are a few sentimentalists who cling to classics such as the *Durham Ranger, Jock Scott,* and *Silver Wilkinson.* Anglers prefer the patterns in which they have confidence, and many of us think that fancy ones do greater honor to the Silver Leaper and that they are more fun to use.

When Maine rivers warm up a bit and subside to less than moderate flow, the dry fly becomes popular because it can interest more fish and certainly offers more fun. Popular patterns include bivisibles (such as *Pink Lady*), the *Bomber, Irresistible, Macintosh,* and the famous *Wulff* series. No matter where I go around the Atlantic, five flies of two types seem as useful as all the others put together: a black and a white *Bomber* and a black, a white, and a gray *Wulff.* Don't be afraid to use large sizes such as 2s and 4s, but go smaller when rivers thin down and warm up or when salmon are uninterested in the bigger bits of fluff.

Let's emphasize again that the patterns in this section are primarily those designed by New Englanders for fishing their rivers. A number of other productive patterns devised by anglers from the northeastern United States are included in the Canadian section of this chapter.

JOSEPH D. BATES, JR.
1903–1988

Epilogue

*T*he appreciation of Atlantic salmon fishing and its flies is augmented by understanding not only the remarkable life cycle of the species but also the currently precarious existence of the salmon itself. Predators such as birds and seals account for some of the losses, but this is nature's way, and the loss is small in comparison with the damage done by the greatest predator of all, which is man. Without regard for tomorrow, man has unwittingly dammed and polluted the rivers essential for the survival of the salmon. Many now fear that depredations of Atlantic salmon stocks could cause Salmo salar to become extinct. Such an extreme view is somewhat softened by the dedication of growing groups of conservationists committed to the restoration of the Atlantic salmon population to its former strength. Individuals interested in joining the battle (and it is just that) to save our salmon will find the names and addresses of several worthy organizations in need of support in the back of this book.

In addition to the multinational problems caused by both dams and pollution, the alarming decline of Atlantic salmon stocks has been, and still is, largely due to the avarice of relatively small groups of people who think more of their own temporary profits than of the welfare of the most purposeful, most beautiful, and most valuable fish that nature has provided. We are nearing the zero hour for these self-serving groups to be controlled by strictly enforced regulations; regulations which would be extremely beneficial to the many at slight discomfort to the few. It is high time for politicians to put aside thoughts of temporary personal gain and pay profound attention to the long-term benefits that a restored Atlantic salmon population would mean for all nations bordering the Atlantic Ocean.

On the open ranges of the sea, salmon tend to congregate in vast schools wherever food is abundant. Commercial fishing boats equipped with electronic devices easily locate these concentrations and snare them—nets of nearly transparent nylon mesh tied together form traps up to eighteen miles long. Consider that sentence. Not meters, not yards, but miles! In addition, long-lines of awesome lengths, equipped with hundreds of baited hooks, are drifted through hungry schools. Such tactics can wipe out, or nearly so, all the salmon (to say nothing of the dangers to other species such as whales). Drift-netting and long-lining have become excessive in recent decades, made possible by sophisticated locating devices, improved equipment such as larger ships and lighter nets, and the discoveries of great concentrations of salmon in places such as the Davis Strait off southwestern Greenland and areas north of the Faroe Islands. Of the million or more Atlantic salmon taken annually on the high seas, nearly half are of North American origin.

Atlantic salmon aren't similar to other fish considered free for the taking on the high seas or along coastal areas. Atlantic salmon are born in the fresh water of rivers, where they are protected and often raised artificially at great expense. Although it is nature's way that they grow to adulthood in the ocean, they should be allowed freedom here to return to their natal rivers without harassment. When they reach their rivers of origin, the nation that owns that river should be free to jurisdict a limited harvest of the excess crop and allow a generous number to proceed upstream for spawning or for regulated angling. This is only fair to the nations that produced them and to their regional economies.

Now, let's deal with more localized situations. While the residents along the rivers have primary interest, there are some who abuse it. Abuse can come from excessive netting in the estuaries, a situation authorities should be able to control. Abuse can also come from poachers, a situation that has existed on salmon rivers everywhere ever since people learned how to fish. A man who needs a salmon or two to feed his family may have an excuse, but those who ruthlessly net, snag, or otherwise unlawfully take salmon in quantity have no excuse. They are simply robbers and should be dealt with as such.

In these days of walkie-talkies and cellular phones, poachers often operate in groups, and apprehending them is difficult. In local situations where everybody knows everybody else, law enforcement officers, because of insufficient numbers or intimidation, usually can't cope or don't wish to. There was a time when rustlers who were caught stealing cattle were lucky to be shot because the alternative was to die in the noose of a rope hung from the nearest tree. We need to find an effective way of dealing with the thieves.

The Atlantic salmon face many problems which, I believe, can be solved with cooperation and common sense. Don't penalize the anglers who by and large are conservationists who want to see the salmon thrive and who are willing to go to great trouble and expense to make this possible.

A decade or two ago I feared that the Atlantic salmon was a vanishing species, but now I believe man's greed can be controlled with conservation measures and practices such as catch and release—the beautiful leaper again will prosper and be restored.

Why have I changed my mind? We who are interested in the welfare of the salmon have risen to arms. We are angry that tremendous quantities of salmon are being pulled aboard boards and thrown into holds as if they were common bottom fish, to be sold as such. We particularly resent countries having no salmon of their own and making no contributions to their welfare, scooping up dangerously large quantities of fish raised to adolescence by other nations.

Purposeful organizations such as the Atlantic Salmon Federation and the North Atlantic Salmon Fund are growing and becoming so powerful that they no longer can be ignored. Depredations on the high seas are being reduced, and there is now a total ban on this type of fishing. The New England Salmon Association, now based in Massachusetts, is an organization dedicated to the restoration and management of wild Atlantic salmon back to their native New England rivers; NESA also educates young people through its Grants and Internship Fund. Every large salmon river and tributary in North America have clubs and associations working regionally. For example, the Connecticut River has its Connecticut River Salmon Association and its Farmington River (a tributary) Watershed Association, and Canada's Miramichi River has its Miramichi Salmon Association. These groups work to keep their rivers clean, regulated, and safe for the salmon in them.

We have made a strong start to renew and protect our Atlantic salmon fisheries. Even at this near-zero-hour, we are seeing promising results. If we cooperate—and that is essential—future generations (and, hopefully, ours) will see a flourishing North Atlantic salmon fishery and will enjoy greater sport in hooking Salmo salar, our respected and cherished leaper, on rod and line and with the beautiful salmon flies described in this book.

"Evening Star"

Fly Dressers Represented

Jón Ingi Agústsson
Charles Akroyd
Ron Alcott
J. Clovis Arseneault
John Atherton
Dan Bailey
Joseph D. Bates, Jr.
Eric Baylis
Michel Beaudin
Fran Betters
Howard Biffer
Carmelle Bigaouette
Ralph Billingsley
Danny Bird
Larry Borders
Al Bovyn
Megan Boyd
Al Brewster
Ray Brooks
Besse Brown
Geoffrey Bucknall
Lou Butterfield
William Byrnes
Peter Calouri
Charles Caron
Robert Cavanagh
Charles Chute
Gerry Clapp
Howard Clifford, Jr.
Donald Clough
Mike Crosby
Roger D'Errico
Harry Darbee
Peter Deane
Charles DeFeo
Jerry Doak

Wallace Doak
Dorothy Douglass
Bill Drexler
Esmond Drury
Warren Duncan
Arthur Elkins
Vincent Engles
Robert Ent
Philip Foster
T. B. Fraser
Keith Fulsher
Don Gapen
Paul Gillespie
Kristjan Gislasson
Sydney Glasso
Steve Gobin
Ted Godfrey
Theodore Gordon
Francois Gourdreau
Elizabeth Greig
Ira Gruber
Wilhelm Gruber
Geir Birgir
  Gudmundsson
Jean Guerin
Gayland Hachey
Bragi Hannesson
Ellis Hatch
Edward Hewitt
Robert Hibbetts
Herb Howard
Greg Hunt
Bill Hunter
Maurice Ingalls
Bob Jacklin
Preston Jennings

Bjarni Róbert
  Jónsson
Poul Jorgensen
Tom Juracek
Ted Kanter
Charles Krom
John Alden Knight
Paul LaBlanc
George M. L.
  LaBranche
L. A. LaPointe
Yann LeFevre
Judy Lehnberg
Don Leyden
Jan Londal
Wayne Luallen
Dave Lucca
John Lyons
Maxwell MacPherson
P. D. Malloch
Michael Martinek
Belarmino Martinez
Michael McCoy
Galen Mercer
Jean Michaud
Chief Needahbah
  (Roland Nelson)
Ron Newcomb
Ted Niemeyer
Marvin Nolte
Sigurjón Olafsson
John Olschewsky
Olaf Olsen
Thordur Petursson
Paul Phinney
T. E. Pryce-Tannatt

Michael D. Radencich
Len Rich
Pamela Bates Richards
Alex Rogan
Richard Ruhlin
Earling Sand
Paul Schmookler
Helen Shaw
Alex Simpson
Elmer James Smith
Harry Smith
Rob Solo
Carrie Stevens
Bert Stromberg
Fran Stuart
Eugene Sunday
Arthur Taylor
Bill Taylor
Johann Thorsteinsson
Bob Veverka
Mattie Vinceguerra
John Walker
Bob Warren
Mark Waslick
Jedde Waterman
Bruce Waugh
Claude Westfall
Bill Wilbur
Harry Wilcox
John Wildermuth
William Wilsey
Shirley Woods
Dave Worcester
Lee Wulff
Rod Yerger
Jimmy Younger

Atlantic salmon anglers might find it rewarding to join one or more of these very worthy organizations.

The American Museum of Fly Fishing
P.O. Box 42, Seminary Avenue
Manchester, VT 05254

The Atlantic Salmon Federation
P.O. Box 807
Calais, ME 04619-9975

The Miramichi Salmon Association, Inc.
Boistown, New Brunswick
E0H 1AO Canada

The New England Salmon Association
33 Bedford Street, Suite 19B
Lexington, MA 02173

The North Atlantic Salmon Fund
Skipholti 35
105 Reykjavik, Iceland

Bibliography

*A*nglers who absorb the lore and methods of Atlantic salmon fishing succeed when they apply book knowledge to stream challenges. Fly dressers want not only practical patterns, but often enjoy reproducing classics. Collectors use books to identify the flies in their possession. A sensibly selected library on Atlantic salmon flies and fishing provides not only enjoyment and instruction but can become a valuable investment as many volumes appreciate in value over the years, often exceeding investments of other kinds.

Of the hundreds of volumes that have been published on Atlantic salmon fishing only a relative few are of value to the modern angler and fly dresser. Many of the leading ones have been included here and could be the basis for an expanding collection. Many cherished volumes are not included here because of their rarity and cost.

Publication dates are given here. Recent books still in print can be located in catalogs distributed annually by angling mail-order houses. For others, you may need to contact sellers of out-of-print and rare fishing books.

Atherton, John. *The Fly and the Fish.* New York: MacMillan, 1951.

Bates, Joseph D., Jr. *Atlantic Salmon Flies and Fishing.* Mechanicsburg, PA: Stackpole Books, 1970. Reissued 1995.

Bates, Joseph D., Jr. *Streamer Fly Tying and Fishing.* Mechanicsburg, PA: Stackpole Books, 1966. Reissued 1995.

Bates, Joseph D., Jr. *The Atlantic Salmon Treasury.* St. Andrew's, Canada: The Atlantic Salmon Association, 1975. Privately printed in an edition of 1,000.

Betters, Fran. *Fran Betters' Fly Fishing–Fly Tying and Pattern Guide.* Wilmington, NY: Adirondack Sports Publication, 1986.

Blacker, William. *Blacker's Art of Fly Making.* London: 1855.

Chaytor, A. H. *Letters to a Salmon Fisher's Sons.* London: 1910.

Deane, Peter. *Peter Deane's Guide to Fly-Tying.* Hackensack, NJ: Steoger Publishing Co., 1993.

Ephemera (pseud. Edward Fitzgibbon). *The Book of the Salmon.* London: Longman, Brown, Green and Longmans, 1850.

Frodin, Mikael. *Classic Salmon Flies: History & Patterns.* New York: Bonanza Books, 1991.

Fulsher, Keith, and Charles Krom. *Hair-Wing Atlantic Salmon Flies.* North Conway, NH: Fly Tyer, Inc., 1981.

Francis, Francis. *A Book on Angling.* London: Longmans, Green & Co., 1867. And other editions.

Hale, Captain J. H. *How to Tie Salmon Flies.* London: Sampson, Low, Marston, 1892. And other editions.

Hardy, John James. *Salmon Fishing.* London: G. Newnes, 1907.

Hewitt, Edward R. *A Trout and Salmon Fisherman for 75 Years.* New York: Scribner's, 1948.

Hewitt, Edward R. *Secrets of the Salmon.* New York: Charles Scribner's Sons, 1925.

Hill, Frederick. *Salmon Fishing.* London: Chapman & Hall, 1948.

Hodgson, W. Earl. *Salmon Fishing.* London: A. & C. Black, 1906.

Hubert, Joseph P. *Salmon—Salmon.* Privately printed in an edition of 100 copies, 1979.

Jorgensen, Poul. *Salmon Flies.* Mechanicsburg, PA: Stackpole Books, 1978.

Kelson, George M., *The Salmon Fly.* London: 1895. And other editions.

Kreh, Lefty, and Mark Sosin. *Practical Fishing Knots.* New York: Lyons and Burford, 1991.

LaBranche, George M. L. *The Salmon and the Dry Fly.* Boston: Houghton Mifflin Co., 1924. Reprinted with *The Dry Fly and Fast Water.* New York and London: Charles Scribner's Sons, 1951.

McDonald, John. *The Origins of Angling.* New York: 1963.

Netboy, Anthony. *The Atlantic Salmon—A Vanishing Species?* Boston: Houghton Mifflin Co., 1968.

Norris, Thaddeus. *American Angler's Book.* Philadelphia: 1864. And other editions.

Oglesby, Arthur. *Salmon.* London: MacDonald & Co., Ltd., 1971.

Oglesby, Arthur, and John Buckland. *A Guide to Salmon Flies.* Ramsbury, Marlborough, and Wiltshire, England: The Crowood Press, 1990.

Phair, Charles. *Atlantic Salmon Fishing.* New York: 1937.

Pryce-Tannatt, T. E. *How to Dress Salmon Flies.* London: A. & C. Black, 1914. And other editions.

Roosevelt, Robert B. *The Game Fish of the North.* New York: 1884. And other editions.

Schmookler, Paul M. *The Salmon Flies of Major John Popkin Traherne (1826–1901).* Millis, MA: The Complete Sportsman, 1993.

Scott, John. *Fine & Far Off.* London: Seeley Service & Co., 1952.

Stewart, Dick, and Farrow Allen. *Flies for Atlantic Salmon.* Intervale, NH: Northland Press, Inc., 1991.

Stout, Andrew, and Silvio Calabi (editors). *A Hard Look at Some Tough Issues, New England Atlantic Salmon Management Conference.* Newburyport, MA: New England Salmon Association, 1994.

Taverner, Eric. *Fly Tying for Salmon.* London: Seeley Service & Co., 1942.

Taverner, Eric. *Salmon Fishing.* London: Seeley Service & Co., Ltd., 1348.

Vigfusson, Orri. *Hitchcraft.* Reykjavik, Iceland: The North Atlantic Salmon Fund, 1994.

Waddington, Richard. *Salmon Fishing—A New Philosophy.* New York: Charles Scribner's Sons, 1948. Printed in Great Britain.

Wade, Henry. *Halcyon.* London: Bell and Daldy, 1861.

Weeks, Edward. *The Moisie Salmon Club: A Chronicle by Edward Weeks.* Barre, MA: Barre Publishers, 1971.

Wulff, Lee. *The Atlantic Salmon.* New York: A. S. Barnes & Co., 1958.

Wulff, Lee. *Lee Wulff on Flies.* Mechanicsburg, PA: Stackpole Books, 1980.

Index

Index of Flies

Page numbers in italics indicate fly patterns. Page numbers after plates indicate plate locations.

General Index

Entries and page numbers in italics
refer to illustrations.